AT THE LIMITS OF THE SECULAR

At the Limits of the Secular

Reflections on Faith and Public Life

Edited by

William A. Barbieri Jr.

WILLIAM B. EERDMANS PUBLISHING COMPANY
GRAND RAPIDS, MICHIGAN / CAMBRIDGE, U.K.

Published 2014 by

Wm. B. Eerdmans Publishing Co.

2140 Oak Industrial Drive N.E., Grand Rapids, Michigan 49505 /
P.O. Box 163, Cambridge CB3 9PU U.K.

Printed in the United States of America

20 19 18 17 16 15 14   7 6 5 4 3 2 1

Library of Congress Cataloging-in-Publication Data

At the limits of the secular: reflections on faith and public life /
edited by William A. Barbieri, Jr.

pages   cm

Includes bibliographical references and index.

ISBN 978-0-8028-6877-0 (pbk.: alk. paper)

1. Christianity and politics — Catholic Church.

2. Christianity and politics — United States. 3. Catholic Church —
United States. 4. Taylor, Charles, 1931- Secular age.

I. Barbieri, William A., Jr., editor of compilation.

BX1793.A24   2014

261 — dc23

2014003479

www.eerdmans.com

Contents

CONTENTS

Contents

CHARITY

IV. Religion in a Post-Secular World

COMMUNITY

HUMANISM

PLURALISM

Foreword

This very illuminating collection carries further a discussion which has already begun in many places in and alongside the Catholic Church. This concerns how our Church can be in and speak to our present age, which in the Western context can perhaps be described as "secular."

Being in and speaking to any age is no simple matter for our Church. We have to hold in balanced tension two stances towards our world, the two kinds of catholicity which Robert Schreiter articulates in his essay: one concerned with reading the signs of the times and reaching out to our world in solidarity and communication — with particular concern for the poor and deprived in all dimensions; the other more focused inward and concerned with maintaining the full integrity of the deposit of the faith.

In a sense the context of Vatican II might seem to have pushed us too one-sidedly into the first stance. In this it was reacting to the anti-modernism of the nineteenth- and early twentieth-century Church, which with Pius X reached close to absurd lengths. The inward gaze was becoming myopic and all-controlling. One of the strengths of the theologians who prepared the ground for Vatican II was that they criticized this cramped "anti-modernism" through a deep recovery of Patristic sources. They showed in fact that "anti-modernism" was in the grip of certain narrow assumptions of the post-Reformation European world.

But they also showed that the best way to speak to one's own era, and to read the signs of the times, is to be deeply rooted in the whole tradition of the Church, through many epochs and civilizations. This doesn't make the task easy. Indeed, those great theologians may turn out to be a hard act to follow. In fact, certain tendencies in the contemporary world may render our task even harder. For instance, Vincent Miller explores in depth a trend to fragmented, narrowly defined, and often mutually hostile identities which is encouraged by the present shape of the electronic public sphere. This does not create a propitious environment for a sacramental union, uniting people of very different cultures, who feel bound to each other and want to know each other more.

These divisive forces are all the stronger in that there is already a tendency in the Church to divide into factions, each of which arises from a one-sided and over-simple identification with one of the stances of Catholicity identified by Schreiter. This polarization has not been helped by the magisterium, and seems to be worsening rather than abating.

In the face of this, the different chapters in this collection offer paths out of the resulting impasse, and hints as to how we can live in the secular world creatively and without self-stultification. There are illuminating discussions of the public sphere and dialogue (chapters one and two) and of the religious/secular distinction and post-secularity (chapters four and five, as well as the essays in Part IV). There are reminders of how we need to get out of a narrow North Atlantic perspective (chapter two). There are paths out of a narrow sense of confinement in the immanent frame in Part III, in particular a new understanding of the role of embodied agency.

This is a marvelously rich and suggestive book, which has helped to jar me out of the ruts I had fallen into. I am sure it will do the same for many others.

CHARLES TAYLOR

Acknowledgments

The Secularity Project out of which this book emerges is the brainchild of George F. McLean, the distinguished emeritus professor of philosophy at the Catholic University of America. It was he who, perceiving the deep significance of Charles Taylor's monumental study *A Secular Age* for the efforts of the Catholic Church to chart its way forward in our current times, conceived of the value of coordinating a group of scholars to investigate the implications of emerging understandings of secularity for the role of religion in public life. He then called this undertaking to life under the auspices of the organization he directs, the Council for Research in Values and Philosophy, and inaugurated it with a major public event in November 2009, that brought together Charles Taylor and Francis Cardinal George, then-president of the United States Conference of Catholic Bishops, for a discussion of "Faith in a Secular Age." Professor McLean's accompaniment in word, deed, and spirit was instrumental to the revolving seminar that subsequently unfolded over the next twenty months in Washington and Chicago as the participants in the Secularity Project labored to forge common understandings and articulate a cohesive vision. It can only be hoped that the volume our group has produced contributes in some appreciable measure to the visionary program he has outlined and continues to pursue.

The deliberations of the Secularity Project benefited immensely from the generosity and insight of a number of eminent colleagues who accepted invitations to meet with us. First among these is Charles Taylor, whose gracious participation in our initial workshop was instrumental in establishing the group's intellectual framework, and whose continued moral support helped sustain our efforts. José Casanova also served as a valued interlocutor at several sessions, and his critical acumen and sociological sensibility provided welcome ballast in our discussions. Stimulating presentations and other important contributions to the group were made by Fred Dallmayr and Hent de Vries; and Regina Schwartz and David Power enlivened our sessions with their challenging interventions and astute commentary. Although they were not in the end represented in the essays constituting this volume, Chad Pecknold and Paul Weithman were active members of the Project whose probing questions and historical knowledge had a significant impact on its outcome. Other colleagues who contributed to our workshops include Adriaan Peperzak, Matthew Ashley, Scott Paeth, Ilia Delio, John Haughey, Jack Haught, Carolyn Chau, Manuel Reus, and Teodor Baba.

A special debt of gratitude is due to Daniel McClain, who assisted in all aspects of the Secularity Project, from its conceptualization and framing to the staging and documentation of all the meetings. His scholarly and logistical support was integral to the whole enterprise.

At the Project's home base in Washington, D.C., in the Center for the Study of Culture and Values at the Catholic University of America, Hu Yeping provided all necessary support and shepherded the group's work through each of its phases with customary care and aplomb, while Jack Hogan helped formulate the research objectives for the project. Frank Rieger ably delivered the index. At the Center for World Catholicism and Intercultural Theology at DePaul University, Francis Salinel assisted in the staging of our group's meeting in Chicago. The hospitality of the Missionary Oblates of Mary Immaculate also provided a leaven to the camaraderie of our group at our Washington meetings.

All those associated with this volume are fortunate to have found in Jon Pott, editor-in-chief at Eerdmans, a patron who shares their sense of the timeliness and importance of the research presented here, and in Eerdmans a press that is marvelously responsive, easy to work with, and expansive in its mission.

The Secularity Project would not have been able to carry out its work without the funding provided by the Raskob Foundation for Catholic Activities, and we are very grateful for their support. The views expressed in the essays — and their flaws — remain those of the authors themselves, however.

The contributors to this volume displayed an admirable commitment to the goals of the Secularity Project, and lavished considerable time and energy on the discussions and writing our undertaking demanded; moreover, they constituted a congenial and intellectually stimulating fellowship. As editor I extend my deep thanks to them, along with my hope that as a collective we grew at least a bit in wisdom in our attempt to plumb the prospects for religion in the swirling currents of secularity and post-secularity.

WILLIAM A. BARBIERI JR.

Introduction

WILLIAM A. BARBIERI JR.

In the United States today we are confronted with a bewildering array of indices regarding the state of religion and its place within the modern world. Contrasting portraits of American society can place emphasis on the high percentages of citizens who affirm ties to organized religions and profess belief in God; or the significant numbers of people who change religious identifications or mix and match their doctrinal beliefs and practices as they see fit; or the continually fracturing and pluralizing landscape of denominations, new religious movements, "spiritual but not religious" persons, and "nones" (those with no religious affiliation); or the increasingly secular, materialist assumptions of most Americans. Scholars disagree over whether it is the United States or Europe that constitutes an exception to broad trends of secularization and religious practice; whether a global "resurgence" of religion is underway or whether the worldwide strength of religions has continued unabated; and whether religions stand as the greatest threat to global peace or present the greatest hope for successful conflict resolution and reconciliation. Surveys tracking the behavior of religiously affiliated "values voters" are countered by studies showing that political partisanship trumps religious identities in electoral results. Some religionists and skeptics agree in arguing that religions hold too much sway over politics and should be banned from public roles, while others contend that faith communities have been unfairly excluded or muzzled and have much to offer in the political realm.

In this welter of divergent indicators it is difficult enough reliably to identify large-scale present-day developments, trends, continuities, and shifts in the dynamics of religious belief, practice, and influence. It is all the

1

more challenging to attempt to penetrate to an understanding of deeper and longer-term mechanisms, causes, and historical processes at work in the unfolding of religious traditions. And most daunting of all must seem attempts to project emerging tendencies, forecast future formations, and formulate accounts of how best to meet them. Yet such a look ahead is the task undertaken in this volume.

Scholars of religion are fortunate to have been beneficiaries of a particularly powerful recent analysis of the deep workings of religion and modernity in the shape of Charles Taylor's 2007 book *A Secular Age,* and it is from this landmark study that the present volume takes its initial bearings. In his much acclaimed work, Taylor undertakes a dual task: to trace how the Christian cultures of the modernizing West moved from an epistemic landscape in which belief in God was literally unquestionable to one in which it has become optional, and even problematic; and to provide a portrait of the regnant "conditions of belief" marking the contemporary state of secularity in North Atlantic societies. The results of his treatment are a powerful and complex narrative (the "Reform Master Narrative") of how diverse historical and theological developments produced a new modern "imaginary" hospitable to a stance of exclusive humanism; and an insightful and nuanced set of meditations on the pressures toward closure and the countervailing prospects for openness of the "immanent frame" linked to that stance in our secular age. While Taylor's ground-breaking attempt to characterize both the provenance and the current contours of the secular episteme is admittedly provisional and incomplete, it provides a singularly promising perspective from which to gauge the contemporary challenges facing religious communities in general and Taylor's own Catholic Church in particular.

It was with this objective in view that the Council for Research in Values and Philosophy organized a public event entitled "Faith in a Secular Age" in November 2009 featuring an exchange of views between Charles Taylor and Francis Cardinal George, then-president of the U.S. Conference of Catholic Bishops.[1] That event was conjoined with the launch of a multidisciplinary research project taking Taylor's contribution as a catalyst for a sustained investigation of the implications of ongoing patterns and fissures in the deep dynamics of secularity for the role of faith communi-

1. A video of this encounter may be accessed at http://video.cua.edu/CONFERENCES/Year4Priest/faith.cfm.

ties in public life.[2] The team that took up this task, comprising Catholic scholars of theology, philosophy, politics, sociology, and religious studies, established a seminar that met periodically over the next two years, presenting and refining theses, airing disagreements, and forging a complex set of interlocking reflections on the nexus of faith and public life under evolving conditions of secularity and "post-secularity." Those reflections make up the present volume.

The remainder of this introduction, first, presents some of the central themes in Charles Taylor's portrait of secularity that have set the stage for our inquiry. I then offer a consideration of the conception of "public" informing our work, and describe the "heuristic" methodology used to organize the work of the contributors. The subsequent section provides an overview of the individual chapters, followed by a concluding discussion of some of the chief agreements and divisions emerging from the work of our group.

1. Themes in *A Secular Age*

So probing is Charles Taylor's magnum opus in its interpretations and reflections, so attentive is it to the complexities and messiness of intellectual history, and so patient is it in its pursuit of insights into the modern spiritual condition that it would be fruitless to attempt to reproduce the richness of its narrative, analysis, and arguments in a short summary. And yet it is necessary to characterize the broad thrust of his work in order to indicate how it has served as the launching pad for our effort. Taylor himself casts his book as a story explaining how it came to pass that it was "virtually impossible not to believe in God in, say, 1500 in our Western society, while in 2000 many of us find this not only easy, but even inescapable."[3] His book is therefore an inquiry into the origins and drivers of the titanic change in the "conditions of belief" — in "the whole background framework in which one believes or refuses to believe in God"[4] — that has

---

2. A second research project was initiated at the same time examining the future of the *humanum* in a secular age. For the results of their inquiry, which included a dialogue with Jürgen Habermas, see John Haughey, ed., *Addressing Transhumanism's Aspirations* (Washington, D.C.: Council for Research in Values and Philosophy, forthcoming).

3. Charles Taylor, *A Secular Age* (Cambridge, Mass.: Harvard University Press, 2007), p. 25.

4. Taylor, *A Secular Age*, p. 13.

resulted in our current "secular age." In his account, this shift is set in motion by what he calls, with deceptive simplicity, the *opening of a question* — the possibility of unbelief — that had been foreclosed in an era of naïve religious faith, and it culminates in the cultural hegemony of "exclusive humanism," a stance of human self-sufficiency that brooks no final goals beyond human flourishing. Within the overall arc of this story, Taylor discusses numerous contributing developments: the upsetting of a cultural equilibrium between forces of structure and anti-structure through a rigorous late medieval and early modern project of "Reform" — a drive to make society conform to gospel standards; the emergence of a new, "buffered" sense of self that is capable of detachment from the cosmos and hence sees itself as invulnerable and autonomous; the gradual "disenchantment" of a world naïvely perceived as populated by God and spirits, accompanied by the "disembedding" of modern people from their former contexts of a sacred cosmos operating under a regime of higher time, and a social womb marked by collective ritual and identity; the crystallization in the eighteenth century of a "modern social imaginary" envisioning moral order in terms of a collection of sovereign individuals interacting in a secular public sphere and engaging in commercial relations for mutual benefit; and the ironic transformation of the order of nature, painstakingly distinguished by Christian thinkers from the supernatural order, into the basis for the "immanent frame" within which scientific materialism, instrumental rationality, and a sense of self-sufficiency govern human agency. The outcome of this series of concatenating changes is a modern situation in which the human pursuit of "fullness," of moral and spiritual aspiration, tends by default to focus not on God but on exclusively human or natural sources. The resulting condition of secularity does not entail that religion disappears: indeed, Taylor details how diverse religious, "spiritual but not religious," and more generally humanist options have proliferated profusely in recent years. But even believers now live in a world deeply marked by the optionality, and even the problematization, of faith.

At a thematic level, *A Secular Age* can be read as an account of the steamrolling of the modern spiritual landscape. The dominant metaphor in the book is of flattening: thus, the forces of "Reform" and "discipline" squeeze out the carnivalesque elements of the religions that had balanced them out and given them their fulsomeness since the Axial Age; then, a variegated social landscape is homogenized and compressed as a modernist social imaginary initially confined to elites spreads irresistibly to the masses; next, within the resulting immanent frame, "clock time" crowds out the sense of salvation history embodied in the registers of "higher time," and "closed world structures" emerge that systematically root out vertical perspectives of human transcendence while reinforcing the horizontal motifs of naturalism; soon, a "subtraction story" about the detrimental effects of belief pares down our accounts of self, agency, time, and society; and finally, a "therapeutic turn" in spiritual practice flattens out our moral experience. Against the backdrop provided by Taylor's story, a twofold question arises. How resilient will religious traditions prove to be in the face of such bulldozing forces? And what can believers construct on the leveled terrain of modernity?

When it comes to his survey of our present spiritual situation, there is a Tolstoyan quality to Taylor's book — quite apart from its heft. Like Tolstoy in his *Confession,* Taylor provides a probing — and poignant — analysis of the different responses he sees around him to the question of transcendence. Just as Tolstoy considered the "ways out" of the human quandary constituted by ignorance, Epicureanism, strength, and weakness before describing his return to faith, Taylor meditates on atheists, seekers, existentialists, and doubting believers before giving us his own heartfelt defense of belief.

A particularly salient feature of the picture of our current condition that Taylor gives us is that secular humanists and modern Christians are equally products of the same historical process of immanentization. They are, he says, "brothers under the skin." The encounter between faith and humanism, it follows for Taylor, should be carried out in a spirit of humility dedicated not to vanquishing the other, but to striving to see "who can respond most profoundly and convincingly to what are ultimately commonly felt dilemmas."[5] Taylor also insists on the importance of appreciating the positive aspects of modern modes of spiritual searching, emphasizing the values of personalism, commitment, and authenticity that they embody. It is his optimistic hope that the modes of devotion and practice associated with such seekers will form a symbiosis, rather than a destructive tension, with the more traditionalist forms of religion that remain on offer.

Today's encounter of varying timbres of religiosity and secular searches for fullness takes place in what Taylor calls a post-Durkheimian scenario in which religious allegiances, despite their highly individualist character, still tend to accrue not to societies or polities so much as to other collectivities — for example, churches. What does this mean for how religiously

5. Taylor, *A Secular Age,* p. 675.

supported social action should work? What follows with respect to how religious groups should intervene in public debate and public policy? How do divergent experiences of modernization, on the one hand, and various forms of globalization on the other shape the prospects for belief and what Paul Tillich termed the "theonomous" shaping of common life? In what ways might a religious approach redeem and find meaning in the secular?

2. Public Life

As rich and complicated as Taylor's analysis is, its focus is ultimately on epistemic matters rather than on a detailed consideration of the social and political dimensions of secularity. And while he has elsewhere weighed in on some of the questions surrounding the notion of public reason debated by John Rawls, Jürgen Habermas, and others,[6] a broad field of exploration remains regarding the implications of Taylor's work on the "conditions of belief" for the role of faith with respect to public life. Carrying out some of this exploratory work is the central task taken up by this book.

What do we mean by public life? It is worth devoting a bit of attention to delineating our field of concern, especially since "public" is a term with a history that is bound up in complex ways with the career of the secular. This is nowhere more so the case than with the phrase "public sphere," which has come, through the work of Habermas and his interlocutors, to denote a particular space for untrammeled civic debate essential to modern, liberal democratic orders.[7] In this volume we employ "public life" to refer to a broader arena of human interaction, a domain expansive and capacious enough to encompass related notions such as "public square" and "public realm." The term combines the sense of place suggested by these terms with a reference to certain sorts of actors: to begin with, the amorphous collectivity we refer to as "*the* public"; but also those plural bodies known as "publics," and indeed the smaller, oppositionally defined entities variously called "counterpublics"[8] or "subpublics."[9] Since these are

6. See the discussion in Eduardo Mendieta and Jonathan VanAntwerpen, eds., *The Power of Religion in the Public Sphere* (New York: Columbia University Press, 2011).

7. Jürgen Habermas, *The Structural Transformation of the Public Sphere: An Inquiry into a Category of Bourgeois Society,* trans. Thomas Burger (Cambridge, Mass.: MIT Press, 1989); Craig Calhoun, ed., *Habermas and the Public Sphere* (Cambridge, Mass.: MIT Press, 1992).

8. Michael Warner, *Publics and Counterpublics* (London: Zone, 2005).

9. Martin E. Marty, "The *the* Public and the Public's Publics," in *The Power of Religious*

not exhaustive identities but rather roles taken on by persons in particular contexts, we can speak of public life as a mode of being, one marked by certain general features.

One feature of public life is that it is a circumscribed set of relationships. Public affairs are those involving a midrange of interlocutors: dealings with people encountered not as family members or intimates, but neither as aliens or utter strangers. In this manner "public" points to a realm of encounter and engagement characterized by a *limited* degree of plurality, otherness, or alterity. Occasional talk of a global public notwithstanding, to speak of public life usually implies that there is some larger world beyond those with whom we deal publicly — other societies or political communities, constituting their own publics and immersed in their distinct projects — even as there is a set of more immediate relations that do not rise to the status of public. The point at which we begin to consider relations public is a function of a second feature: the deeply embedded dichotomy between public and private.[10] It is a persistent feature of discourse about publicity that accounts of what it consists in are built around contrasts with realms, relations, and figures characterized as private: as domestic, economic, personal, interior. This structuring endures despite the decisive intervention of feminist critics who have pointed out the role of this binary in the marginalization and disadvantaging of women in societies in which "public" spaces and activities are strongly correlated with male prerogatives.[11]

The term "public" is, third, to be distinguished from additional related concepts. Thus the public — *publicus* — is historically distinct from *populus* — the people. It is also not to be conflated with politics per se: neither in that term's most expansive sense, as relating to all questions of power, a sense that outstrips the public; nor in its much narrower sense of the affairs of state and governance, a scope that the public readily exceeds.

The precise manner in which the notion of "public" meshes with or diverges from related concepts such as "private" or "political" is, of course,

---

Publics: Staking Claims in American Society, ed. William H. Swatos Jr. and James K. Wellman Jr.(London: Praeger, 1999), pp. 1-18.

10. For an attempt to expose some common mistaken assumptions about the public-private dichotomy, see Raymond Geuss, *Public Goods, Private Goods* (Princeton, N.J.: Princeton University Press, 2003).

11. See, for example, Jean Bethke Elshtain, *Public Man, Private Woman* (Princeton, N.J.: Princeton University Press, 1981), and Catherine MacKinnon, *Toward a Feminist Theory of the State* (Cambridge, Mass.: Harvard University Press, 1989).

historically contingent — as a comparison of Roman and modern conceptions of the public or sociological debates about the privatization of religion amply show. Hence, a further feature worth noting is that the meaning of "public" is a moving target, responsive to the shape of political institutions of the day, large-scale economic forces, the evolving character of communications media, philosophical and theological developments, and other changing cultural factors.[12]

Public life, in short, takes place in evolving social locations — configurations of persons and spaces — marked by human relations at once familiar and formal, in ways structured by discursive embranglements with concepts such as "private" and "political." Within this broad arena of public life, we can next identify a series of distinctive moments characterizing, in a formal sense, the interactions that take place there. These elements, taken together as a kind of theory of publicity, reflect the manner in which the idea of public life manifests a sort of agential structure, an ethical orientation attuned to the prospects for collective action.

A first moment in the constitution of public life consists in the existential relation of *having common interests:* a stake in what transpires to affect the fortunes of a group. It is in this sense that we speak of *"res publica"* or of the "public interest" — a term that can point either to patterns of aggregated interest or to the common good of a community. An additional moment involves an element of *problematization* through which a matter of common interest comes to be perceived as an "issue." It is to this process that John Dewey pointed in his famous definition of a public as a collectivity that takes on through its representatives the task of regulating those "conjoint actions of individuals and groups" that, for good or ill, seriously affect all of its members.[13]

Two further characteristic elements of public life are related to the human function of vision or perspective. First, in a basic sense, to be public is to be *visible,* capable of being seen by others — especially non-intimates. Thus we say that someone does something "in public," or "in the public eye." This is an aspect of publicity in which advancing technologies and

12. Alastair Hannay, *On the Public* (London: Routledge, 2005); José Casanova points out that the public-private binary, deriving as it does from the ancient *oikos-polis* distinction, does not mesh neatly with the division of modern society into family, state, and civil society (*Public Religions in the Modern World* [Chicago: University of Chicago Press, 1994], p. 42).

13. John Dewey, *The Public and Its Problems* (Chicago: Swallow, 1927), p. 35. Dewey staked out his position in response to the critique of populism mounted by Walter Lippmann in *The Phantom Public* (New York: Macmillan, 1927).

shifting forms of media exert a constant pressure, as practices of surveillance and our digital interconnections render our words, images, and activities increasingly accessible to strangers and extend the reach of public spaces into virtual realms.

Building on the idea of visibility is, further, the practice of focused seeing, of *attention,* for which we strive when we "publicize" an event or "publish" a text or "go public" with an allegation. To be present in public life is to be not just visible but subject to scrutiny, to purposive viewing. The purpose referred to here is properly ordered to the demands and aspirations of common life. We might insist, therefore, that activities carried out in the public trust be transparent and open to review and criticism: indeed, the German term for publicness, *Öffentlichkeit,* is rooted etymologically in the idea of openness. But of course, the attention that comes with publicity is not always benevolent, and can readily become exploitive, abusive, or even hostile. To be visible is also to be vulnerable.[14]

Alongside these modes of seeing, publicness can be linked to characteristic stances or postures. Inasmuch as public life is ordered to a purpose of coexistence with non-intimates under conditions of plurality, an attitude of *civility* — a blend of self-control, manners, distance, acknowledgment, and tolerance — comes to be called for in dealings with others.[15] And as the scope of public concerns expands within complex, large-scale modern societies, an accompanying standpoint of *generality* emerges, building on a recognition of the publicness of language (as attested to by Wittgenstein) and the public dimensions of taste (as reflected in Kant's account of the *sensus communis*), enabling members of a public to envision ties ("public relations") to anonymous others ("the general public") who share their interests and with whom they are involved in a common enterprise.[16] Under the right conditions, a stance of solidarity and commitment to the corpo-

14. Paul Virilio makes this point sharply in his *War and Cinema: The Logistics of Perception* (London: Verso, 1997).

15. Benet Davetian, in *Civility: A Cultural History* (Toronto: University of Toronto Press, 2009), identifies *tact* (as distinct from *politeness*) and *poise* as particularly important elements of public demeanor (p. 172). See also Taylor's nuanced and somewhat critical treatment of civility and its relation to piety in *A Secular Age,* pp. 99-112; and Norbert Elias's classic *The Civilizing Process,* rev. ed. (Oxford: Blackwell, 2000).

16. Benedict Anderson's discussion in *Imagined Communities* (London: Verso, 1983) of the role of novels and newspapers in altering apprehensions of time and contributing to the imagining of modern national communities is instructive here (pp. 22-36), as is Michael Warner's analysis in *Publics and Counterpublics* of the significance of reflexivity, discourse, and temporality in the acts of imaginative projection through which publics arise (pp. 90ff).

rate good — public virtue, as Montesquieu called it, or public-spiritedness — can emerge, but this is more a normative than a descriptive feature of publicness, which can also readily be taken over by fractiousness, avarice, and self-interest.

These stances in turn inform the central forms of communication that are at the heart of public life. A foundational pursuit associated with publicness is the acquisition and dissemination of *information,* for a deep base of dependable knowledge is a sine qua non for the effective prosecution of collective responses to shared problems. This function unites the broad range of media sources in modern societies with the various organs that contribute to scientific research, and one of its hallmarks is a striving for objectivity of a sort that might enhance the reliability of the "public opinion" in which it issues. Public opinion is further purified through two additional elements of public life. First, *conversation* — exchanges of views, debates, *disputationes,* dialogues — is a critical component of public discourse because the introduction of novel perspectives is a constant spur to insight and the mutual refinement of understanding. Such interchanges nourish a second moment of *critique* or critical reflection, a discipline of challenging and testing initial conclusions. If the apotheosis of these processes, the "public sphere" of unconstrained discussion limned by Habermas in his history of liberal bourgeois society and reconstructed in his account of communicative action, remains an elusive ideal in a world marred by the pervasive influence of propaganda and money, it still points us to the indispensable role of argument in the overall project of agency embodied in public life.[17]

And in the overall orientation of public life toward practical reason, we come to a last significant moment of communication in the form of *deliberation:* a give-and-take about how collectively to proceed. At this point, agreement must be negotiated out of dissensus and then converted into "public policy," a plan of rules, measures, and aspirations crafted to serve the public good. As this description suggests, the elements of communication described here as part of the formal structure of publicness bear an affinity to the theory and practice of democracy — although they are also seen as normative in nondemocratic regimes.[18] Beyond these tasks

17. See David Tracy's discussion of these matters in his chapter below; and Michael Walzer, *Thick and Thin: Moral Argument at Home and Abroad* (Notre Dame, Ind.: University of Notre Dame Press, 2006).

18. As Taylor notes, "The public sphere is a central feature of modern society. So much

of communication, finally, lies the field of *action* in which publics, through their agents, attempt to carry out the measures they have devised.

From this admittedly somewhat stylized account of elements of the arc of doing that structures publicness — from perceiving shared interests and rendering persons visible and processes open, to attitudes of solicitude and recognition, to seeking and refining knowledge and applying it to collective plans — we see clearly the derivation of public life from the exigencies of communal agency, within the context of complexifying social conditions. And even where these elements become distorted through the workings of power and self-aggrandizement — in the forms of surveillance, or discrimination, or misinformation, or economic exploitation — they continue to furnish an internal normative logic of publicness.

How, then, do these features of public life interact with religion? Certainly, the public place and face of religion is in question today. One sometimes hears it asserted either that religion has been essentially privatized in modern societies — a sweeping empirical claim of dubious merit; or that it should be — a normative proposition that is certainly debatable. Various Western countries profess to embody a separation between church and state or a principle of *laïcité* in their political organization. There can be no question that through processes of secularization of property and power, the historic religions in the West have ceded much of their influence in economic and political affairs. Nonetheless, however, religious communities continue to bear significant impact on public life, and moreover remain constituted as public entities themselves, in multifaceted ways.[19] Indeed, there is a deep, mutually constitutive role here that has played out historically in ways that are central to the rise of modernity. Four cases, dealing respectively with "the public sphere," "public reason," "public theology," and "public religion," help illustrate the contemporary complexity of relations between religion and publicness.

The first two cases highlight oppositional relations between religion and the public. First, the emergence in the eighteenth century of the public sphere (in the narrow sense) as a staple of modern society brought with

---

so, that even where it is in fact suppressed or manipulated it has to be faked" (*A Secular Age,* p. 185).

19. On how "public" and "church" can mutually inform one another see Kristen Deede Johnson, " 'Public' Re-Imagined: A Reconsideration of Church, State, and Civil Society," in *A World for All? Global Civil Society in Political Theory and Trinitarian Theology,* ed. William F. Storrar, Peter J. Casarella, and Paul Louis Metzger (Grand Rapids: Eerdmans, 2011), pp. 135-53.

it a tension with religious outlooks. Charles Taylor describes this tension as rooted in an emerging outlook of exclusive humanism that understood the public sphere as constituted apart from, and hence independent of, any higher temporal order predicated on "something which transcends contemporary common action." The public sphere established itself as a realm of discourse that was "radically secular" in its assumptions about "the way human society inhabits time."[20] The result, in Taylor's telling, is the dominance, in modern democratic as well as authoritarian societies, of a zone of culture and a way of imagining collective agency from which traditional religious assumptions have been displaced.

This situation helped make possible a second development, in which a conception of "public reason" has arisen to contest the appropriateness of making religiously grounded claims in public debate, at least within democratic states. The conception of public reason, as articulated by Rawls, Habermas, and others, is embedded in the sense that rational deliberations within a constitutional order must be founded on premises that are neutral or shared by all participants, and hence cannot invoke the authority of private convictions of faith. The intent of this principle is not to exclude what Rawls calls "citizens of faith"[21] from public discourse; however, it does entail that any views that persons operating from a religious framework wish to assert regarding public order be translatable into the impartial idiom of secular reason. As Taylor points out, the idea of public reason relies on the assumption — misplaced, in his view — that there is an "epistemic break" between secular reason and religious thought.[22] It was this set of arguments surrounding public reason, as well as the practices associated with it, that Richard John Neuhaus assailed in his illustrious attack on "secular humanism" and the "naked public square."[23]

Two further cases display more integrative accounts of the relation between religion and public life. The first concerns the emergence of the contemporary notion of "public theology." The term itself is, of course, a testament to the prevalence of the notion that religion has become a private affair. In attempting to counter this perception, however, expositors of the term argue that there has always been a robust public dimension to

20. Taylor, *A Secular Age,* p. 192.
21. John Rawls, *The Law of Peoples, with "The Idea of Public Reason Revisited"* (Cambridge, Mass.: Harvard University Press, 1999), p. 149. Michele Dillon remarks on the oddity of this characterization in her chapter in this volume.
22. In Mendieta and VanAntwerpen, eds., *The Power of Religion,* p. 49.
23. Richard John Neuhaus, *The Naked Public Square* (Grand Rapids: Eerdmans, 1984).

theology. "All theology is public discourse," as David Tracy influentially put the thesis in his *The Analogical Imagination,* before going on to illuminate the ways in which theologians, in their work of reflecting on the implications of religious faith, necessarily (if at times implicitly) address three "publics": the church, the academy, and society at large.[24] As Tracy shows, the theologian's task of interpreting the lessons of religious "classics" fits well into the broad parameters of public life as a mode of collective agency; what theology adds, on his account, is a concern not just with information, knowledge, or meaning, but with truth. Properly understood, public theology stands not for attempts to revive theocratic models of governance or to unite the beliefs of a religiously diverse society into a single theological system, but rather for the effort "to express theological commitments in a reflective and sustained way, while addressing fellow citizens as citizens."[25]

This task arises in a context marked sociologically by the perdurance of "public religion." This last term generally denotes the manifold ways in which religious communities, although no longer established as state churches, continue to exert influence in public affairs and transgress the boundaries envisioned for them in the design of modern liberal societies. José Casanova details, for example, how contemporary public religions manage to assume public roles, to exercise political influence, to mobilize ethical challenges to various differentiated sectors of society, and ultimately to prompt renegotiations of the public-private distinction itself.[26] He concludes that a global process of "deprivatization" of religion is afoot. Another practice that casts religious life into a public form is the institution of civil religion described most influentially by Robert Bellah, in which symbols and motifs extracted from traditional religions are incorporated into official, national creeds and rituals in the interest of promoting civic solidarity. Together these models evince the multiplicity of ways in which religious impulses contribute to the agential arc of public life.

In the composite picture assembled here, we see components of modern public life that have departed from or differentiated themselves from religion through various modes of secularization, as well as components that continue to coexist with or even rely on religious traditions. Beneath these relations, it is evident that the shape of public life as we know it

---

24. David Tracy, *The Analogical Imagination* (New York: Crossroad, 1981), pp. 3-46.

25. Jeffrey Stout, *Democracy and Tradition* (Princeton, N.J.: Princeton University Press, 2004), p. 113.

26. Casanova, *Public Religions,* pp. 40-66.

has emerged through a history that is inseparable from the fortunes of religion. At the same time, religious communities — as churches, denominations, cults, sects, and other bodies — bear the indelible imprint of the emergence of modern forms of publicness. In short, as Casanova puts it, "religion itself is intrinsically connected with the modern historical differentiation of public and private."[27]

From this picture emerge a number of questions that are central to the conception of this book. If Taylor is correct in his portrayal of the "radically secular" underpinnings of the modern public sphere, does the potential exist for reshaping this important component of the "modern social imaginary" to make it more open to faith? At the same time, to what extent should religious perspectives engage and appropriate the secular features of modern public life rather than straining against them? How might the epistemic claims and the conception of rationality informing the idea of public reason be expanded to incorporate the insights of "faith seeking understanding"? What theologies and practices can religions plausibly offer in order to enrich public life and contribute to its characteristic activities and goals, and how might receptivity to those contributions be cultivated? How are changing modes of public visibility and media interaction likely to alter religious life, and how should religions respond?

It is these questions that have set the agenda for our study of faith, secularity, and public life. These are topics that for the most part lurk at the fringes of *A Secular Age,* but that might be profitably reflected on in light of Taylor's powerful portrait of our contemporary situation. As a resource for our work, his analysis is joined by numerous additional questionings of religion and secularity that seem to have cropped up as part of the *Zeitgeist:* an abundance of sociological criticisms of the "secularization thesis"; the emergence of religion as a central theme among philosophers and cultural theorists; the increasing tolerance for various types of religious involvement in the public sphere in secularist democracies such as the United States; and, more and more, intellectual challenges to the very conception of the secular mounted by thinkers as diverse as neo-Augustinian and Radical Orthodox theologians and social theorists such as Talal Asad and William Connolly. In bringing the respective disciplinary legacies and perspectives of our participating theologians, scholars of religion, philosophers, ethicists, sociologists, and political theorists to bear on these materials, our group has sought to make a contribution to

27. Casanova, *Public Religions,* p. 40.

Catholic — and catholic — thought on the public ramifications of shifts in what Taylor calls the "conditions of belief."

3. Heuristics

To structure our speculative survey of faith in public life under shifting conditions of secularity, our group adopted a framework of heuristic terms loosely adapting the idea of "keywords" first popularized by Raymond Williams in his vocabulary of culture and society, and finding more proximate precursors in volumes on the study of religion edited by Mark C. Taylor and David Morgan. In Williams's approach, he developed essays constituting inquiries into terms that impressed themselves on his awareness both through their centrality in the field of discourse in which he was working, and through the complexity of the often instructively divergent meanings they took on. A further feature of these terms was the close relationship between their usage and their signifieds: the nuances of the words tend to be bound up with the shape of the problems they attempt to encompass.[28] As Morgan puts it, "Key words are words that do important cultural work."[29] They are conceptual tools that play a significant role in defining a field of inquiry. As the critical inquiry into the study of religion organized by Mark Taylor showed, keywords readily yield an "incomplete web of open and flexible terms" that provides "something like a map for exploring the territory" of the given subject.[30]

Our team similarly organized our work around a collection of terms, but rather than using them as the basis for a lexicon in the style of Williams, we appropriated them in a more heuristic fashion as a sort of internal architecture for a connected series of reflections on the emerging field of relations among religion, publicness, and secularity. We began our project with a list of words suggested by an audit of issues intriguingly broached, but not truly plumbed, in the discussions of secularity surrounding *A Secular Age* and its reception.[31] Our objective was thus to produce a study of

28. Raymond Williams, *Keywords: A Vocabulary of Culture and Society,* revised ed. (New York: Oxford University Press, 1983).

29. David Morgan, ed., *Key Words in Religion, Media, and Culture* (London: Routledge, 2008), p. xi.

30. Mark C. Taylor, ed., *Critical Terms for Religious Studies* (Chicago: University of Chicago Press, 1998), p. 17.

31. The web-based discussion on the Social Science Research Council's site *The Imma-*

the "leading edge" of concerns produced by new recognitions and insights regarding the situation of (especially Christian) faith communities in the modern West. Each contributor was assigned a word to use as a heuristic in drafting and presenting his or her reflections on our collective theme: these reflections were then refined in light of our ensuing discussions. The resulting mosaic makes no claim to be comprehensive or exhaustive of any particular term. The approach has, however, produced points of contact and criss-crossings of ideas, and these are noted in the texts.

The heuristics we incorporated are:

Agency: How does "the secular" condition the perception and character of human freedom and autonomy? And what forms of social agency — and especially self-determination — emerge from the secularization of the public sphere?

Catholicity: How is the church's self-understanding in its relation to the world shaped by the processes of secularization marking the current age? What models of communion and authority accord with our globalizing situation?

Charity: What place is there for the Law of Love in a secular, or post-secular, society?

Community: Modern conceptions of church and state — and distinctions between public and private, and *Gemeinschaft* and *Gesellschaft* — have emerged in large part through the dialectic of secularization. How are they evolving; how can, or should, they be reformed?

Culture: How does secularity, or post-secularity, inform the complex dialectic of religion and culture in modern societies? What are the implications of the uneven globalization of secularity for intercultural relations?

Humanism: Taylor links secularity to the rise of "exclusive humanism" and refers as well to the excesses of "religious anti-humanism." But what of the prospects for a non-exclusive or even religious humanism (if that is not an oxymoron) today?

Imagination: Taylor's work on social imaginaries usefully contextualizes the way in which the emergence of Western modernity is rooted in historically particular ways of envisioning society, hu-

---

nent Frame (http://blogs.ssrc.org/tif/) has been especially helpful here.

man relations, and the cosmos. What new vistas — even utopias — are opened up as possibilities for a post-secular ethos?

Pluralism: The dynamics of pluralization have produced a world of competing religious and non-religious visions and forms of life. How might political institutions and practices best cope with the intellectual and existential challenges posed by this diversity?

Post-Secularity: What commonalities exist among the discourses in various fields that have appropriated the term "post-secular"? Does "post-secular" imply an end to the secular, or a modification of it? Are we entering an era of post-secularity?

Public: In what different ways does religion impinge on, and contribute to, the public realm in modern societies? To what extent does religion help constitute publics? What is the appropriate public face of religion in liberal democratic orders? How does religion relate to public conceptions of reason?

Religion: What limitations attach to general conceptions of "religion" or "religions"? To what degree is the religious-secular distinction valid or constructive? In what ways have religions been constructed through nonreligious dimensions of modern society such as capitalism and nation-state politics?

Tradition: What are the implications of the present dynamics of secularity for the characteristic functions of religious traditions? What challenges are posed for religious traditions by emergent cultural, political, economic, and technological trends?

4. The Essays

The contributions to this volume fall into four sections. The first of these, on "Religion and the Public," brings together interlocking reflections on how religion both infuses and is shaped by publicness. In the book's lead essay on the keyword "public," David Tracy, whose work on the public dimensions of theology has been seminal, provides a masterful résumé of the plurality of ways in which religious faith has a role to play in public life. His chapter weaves together a theory of the public through reflections on three types of public interaction: publicness in the form of rational inquiry, characterized by dialectic and argument; publicness in the form of dialogue with "classics," marked by interpretation and conversation; and publicness in the form of engagement of "realities beyond the limits of reason," encountered in mystical and prophetic "movements of excess." In his development of these themes, Tracy is at pains to show that the conditions of secular modernity harbor a tendency to truncate and narrow the forms of reason at work in public life, precisely when a broadening of reason is called for. As he shows, religion has the potential to serve as a leaven for publicness in numerous ways. "The public realm," he concludes, "needs the aid of realities beyond public reason."

In the second chapter, Peter Casarella takes issue with both Taylor's analysis of secularity and Tracy's account of publicness, arguing that they show significant limitations when confronted with the realities of Latin America. Casarella, writing on the keyword "culture," embarks on the ambitious enterprise of bringing North American perspectives into dialogue with Latin American perspectives in the interest of developing an intercultural basis for a new approach to public theology. The trajectory of his argument takes him from a discussion of contrasts in Northern and Southern conceptions of "public," through a disquisition on links between beauty and justice in liberation theology, to an examination of divergent theological views of the links between personhood and public reason — with the figure of Simone Weil wandering in and out of the text. The prospect for intercultural dialogue with which he leaves us is at once agonistic and hopeful.

Robert Schreiter, too, addresses the impact of a world of cultural diversity and ongoing globalization on the public character of Catholicism. The concept that serves as his keyword, "catholicity," continues to serve as the focal point for discourses within the church about its role in a changing, post-secular world. After recounting the central role this concept has played in historical articulations of the church's identity, Schreiter demonstrates how the contemporary "public" constituted by the church is riven by two competing contemporary interpretations of catholicity: one emphasizing engagement with the wider world (solidarity, dialogue, inculturation), and the other holding up the contemplation of beauty, the truth of revelation, and liturgical life as an antidote to a world sunk in crisis. In order to overcome the conflict between these two accounts of catholicity and the divergent approaches to public life that they underwrite, Schreiter sets about showing how they can be combined in various respects, including the respective critiques they offer of globalization and their complementary commitments to communion. The dynamism these contending approaches lend to the discourse of catholicity, he contends, generates a variety of strategies for acting publicly within post-secular society.

Introduction

The second section of this volume, "Post-Secularity? Critical Reflections," contains a trio of essays that attempt to describe and come to terms with the shifting perceptions of secularity and religion that have given rise to speculations in numerous quarters about the "post-secular." In the first of these, William Cavanaugh delves into the historical construction of his keyword, "religion," highlighting recent research revealing how religion is not a stable, transcultural reality but rather an invented institution. The religious-secular distinction, he maintains, is a creature of modern Western political orders, propagated in a manner that tended to serve the interests of the emergent nation-state. In supporting this thesis, he tours some attempts to define religion and set it apart from the secular, revealing flaws in "substantivist" and "functionalist" approaches before endorsing a "constructivist" alternative. In his ensuing genealogical study of the emergence of the religious-secular distinction in modern Europe, Cavanaugh is careful to identify points at which his narrative, with its focus on power relations and the structural exigencies of states, departs from yet complements Taylor's account of shifts in the social imaginary. Cavanaugh's chief concern is to reveal how the contingency of the religious-secular distinction has been masked along with its potential to legitimate certain forms of lethal violence, and his treatment culminates with a note of caution regarding idolatrous "migrations of the holy" into state and market.

William Barbieri next grapples with the task of sorting out the diversity of attempts to name our present condition that revolve around the keyword "post-secularity." Is post-secularity simply a stage within a broader unfolding of secularity, or is it something new? In approaching this issue, Barbieri draws on the typology of secularities developed by Taylor in *A Secular Age,* relating them to assorted accounts of post-secularity advanced in turn by public intellectuals, sociologists, theologians, philosophers, political theorists, and genealogists. Following an investigation of linkages and conflicts among the different post-secularities he has canvassed, Barbieri argues that post-secularity is best thought of not as a monolithic historical shift, but rather as a renovation or renegotiation of the secular, a corrective designed to open it up to the impulses of religious inspiration and insight. Post-secularity is, in short, a project, part and parcel of the program of agency that makes up public life, and as such it is served by strategies contributing to the refiguring of the secular social imaginary.

In the following chapter Vincent Miller seeks to gauge the challenges posed by a rapidly changing cultural context to religions as they move into the twenty-first century. Taking "tradition" as his keyword, he re-

19

flects on the difficulties involved in maintaining both the continuity and critical openness to change necessary to a healthy church under conditions of post-secularity. He begins his essay with a rich meditation on post-secularity, the emergence of the modern public sphere, and the strategies religions have developed to adapt to modernity. Religious critiques focused on coping with secularity and the order of nations, he argues however — Taylor's included — fail to speak to a new climate profoundly shaped by globalization and burgeoning information technologies. These powerful forces are solidifying a "cultural ecology" characterized by widespread processes of deterritorialization, fragmentation, and deregulation. These processes in turn threaten to unmoor, splinter, and disperse religious communities. Only by properly recognizing the contours of this dire situation, Miller maintains, can we formulate a strategic response that might help the church retain its living traditions and its character as an actor in the world.

The third section of the book, "In and Beyond a Secular Age: Theological Anthropology," encompasses essays that work broadly in a theological idiom while probing the limits of secularity as a description of our condition. Anthony Godzieba initiates this task, presenting a philosophical and theological account of the keyword "imagination" that aims to augment Taylor's study in two respects: by filling in some of the workings behind Taylor's rather broadly sketched notion of "social imaginaries," and by limning those imaginative capacities that enable us to "transfigure" the boundaries of exclusive humanism and the immanent frame of modernity. Godzieba anchors his argument in a phenomenological theory of imagination and embodiment which, he asserts, points us to those attributes of the human makeup that enable us to overcome the limits to human experience attached to both the "buffered selves" Taylor associates with secularity and the commodification of culture characteristic of modern societies. In his account, "thinking otherwise" and "thinking by means of the body" become maxims for a theological aesthetics that focuses on the sacramental imagination as the source for transcendence of our secular condition.

Philosophical and theological themes similarly converge in Philip J. Rossi's consideration of the keyword "agency"; however, in his account it is not phenomenology but Kantian thought that serves as a source of illumination. This chapter focuses on questions emanating from Taylor's study regarding the character and role of human freedom, the shape of plausible faith commitments, and the public relevance of faith under conditions of secularity. Rossi's response begins with a reading of Kant's modern conception of autonomy that places it in continuity with older conceptions of agency and highlights its embeddedness in social existence and its dependence on mutual recognition and respect. Recasting autonomy in social terms, he argues, opens the way to articulating how agency can be rooted in a formative context of faith rather than encountering faith as a countervailing, heteronomous principle. This step contributes in turn to a renewed understanding of how autonomous agency, formed in faith, can function publicly by engaging pressing issues in the secular sociopolitical order in the form of an "enacted hospitality." By presenting autonomy in this light, Rossi challenges narratives of modern secularity that associate it with individualism and emancipation from a divine order.

In her contribution, organized around the keyword "charity," Mary Doak explores the public significance of those dimensions of theological anthropology surrounding Christian understandings of love. While her discussion encompasses a range of Protestant and Catholic Christian sources, she takes as her focus the mature account of Trinitarian and Eucharistic love found in Pope Benedict XVI's encyclicals. In illuminating Benedict's understanding of the social, political, and economic significance of love, she traces a distinct pattern of development in his views and carefully draws out his considered teaching regarding the relation of love and justice. She then considers the practical implications of his doctrine of Christian love for the public role of the church, emphasizing the importance of solidarity with the dispossessed and resistance to the hegemony of consumerist forces. In balancing a respect for diversity with a set of powerful insights about personhood and sociality, she proposes, the vision espoused by recent Catholic teaching offers a valuable corrective to the anthropological assumptions and accompanying politics of secular modernity.

In the final section of this book, "Religion in a Post-Secular World," the contributors explore practical aspects of the role of religion in the emerging "post-secular" public landscape, drawing in social scientific perspectives and examining specific cases of religion in action. In the initial chapter, Michele Dillon provides a stimulating reflection on the keyword "community" that challenges several widely held views about the current religious context. At the heart of her essay is a reconceptualization of community that aims to take account of the social-structural changes and shifting conceptions of selfhood accompanying modern society; based on this model, she then argues that, contrary to oft-heard narratives of decline, participation in community life remains resilient and robust. In like fashion, she goes on to make the case that the ongoing pluralization of religious attitudes and practices in American society, far from producing atomization and anomie, continues to coincide with a drive for unity and community among diversity. The view of community and religion she espouses leads her both to contest Taylor's account of contemporary society as "post-Durkheimian" and to criticize Habermas's newfound post-secular tolerance for religious actors on the grounds that it relies on terms that ultimately disqualify much that is of value in religion. For her part, Dillon suggests intriguingly that "the partial unhooking of religion and spirituality from institutional traditions may, in fact, be helpful toward more fully realizing the pluralism that inheres in democracy."

Continuing this reflection on a proper role for religion in political life, Slavica Jakelić, in a discussion of the keyword "humanism," explores the potentials for cooperation between faith-based and nonreligious outlooks and actors. In doing so, she probes the limits of the orientation of "exclusive humanism" that is so central to Taylor's analysis of secular modernity. After working through a critique of how the "secular humanism" of Edward Said and the "theological humanism" of William Schweiker have responded to some of the excesses of Enlightenment enthusiasm regarding the human prospect, Jakelić proceeds to argue that religious and secular humanisms need not be thought of as mutually exclusive and can, in fact, enrich one another if properly "chastened" and refined. Noting that this relation can best be demonstrated with respect to actual practical collaborations, she develops her thesis through a discussion of the example of religious and secular comradeship in the Solidarity movement in Poland. The resulting portrait provides a hopeful vision for how secularity can coexist with and even contribute to a constructive religious politics.

The closing chapter by J. Paul Martin develops a concern with the keyword "pluralism" into an argument that new "rules of the road" are needed to normalize the role of religion in international affairs in a post-secular climate. The essay delivers a nuanced diagnosis of ongoing shifts in relations between states and religious communities, both globally and within states, on the basis of which Martin argues that a secularist-separationist stance can no longer be viewed as appropriate to the emerging post-secular order. Rather, new standards must be set for engaging religions in public affairs, including a revised conception of public reason. Martin asserts, *contra* Rawls and Habermas but with Taylor, that religions should be treated on the same footing as other civil society actors for most public purposes. In order to illustrate what is at stake in this matter, he analyzes the recent case of international responses to communal violence in Nigeria. He concludes that the task of developing "rules for the road" could profit significantly

From: Eerdmans Publishing Company
2140 Oak Industrial Dr NE
Grand Rapids MI 49505
Telephone: (616) 459-4591

Ship Via CUST PICKUP

To: **COMMONWEAL**
PAUL BAUMANN
475 RIVERSIDE DR-RM 405
NEW YORK NY 10115

INVOICE # 91593   **PO #** 6877 0762

CARTON CONTENTS

QTY	ISBN	TITLE
1	9780802807625	Visions of Amen

TOTAL TITLES 1   **TOTAL UNITS** 1

Carton #: 100000105   Carton 1 on Invoice 91593

from consulting both the experience of the United Nations regime dealing with human rights and religion and the wisdom regarding the public potentials for faith accumulated in the Catholic Church's documentary record and practical achievements.

5. Findings

It remains in this introduction to provide an overview of the results of our collective reflections on faith, secularity, and public life. What were our principal areas of agreement? With reference to which issues did we persistently disagree? How did our work respond to and build on Taylor's compelling characterization of the rise of a secular age?

As our project took shape, we quickly encountered divisions among members of our research team. An initial point of difference concerned the respective merits of focusing on secularity or post-secularity as the primary subject of analysis. Some shared Taylor's skepticism about the utility of the term "post-secular," judging that our "secular age" is deeply entrenched and that the issues of greatest concern to the public face of religion today are deeply bound up with the "immanent frame" and "exclusive humanism" he describes as constitutive of the modern secular imaginary. Others saw more promise in the possibilities inherent in the varying constructions of the "post-secular" that have cropped up in recent years.

A separate set of alignments emerged around conflicting attitudes regarding the value of secular institutions and outlooks from a religious standpoint. From one perspective, the key challenge of our secular condition involves adopting a stance of affirmation and openness to the prospects for mutual learning and cooperation in the encounter of faith and secularity. The opposing view counsels alertness and resistance to the dangers of untruth, erosion, and co-optation with which secular forces confront religion. These starting points readily become bound up with contending historical narratives, analyses of current problems, and prescriptions for how best to move ahead.[32]

These two sets of differences, rooted as they are in the differing prem-

---

32. Although we were not able to include it in this volume, the work of C. C. Pecknold on this issue, especially regarding the temporal sense of the term "secular" both in Augustine and in current debates, played an important role in our discussions. See his "On Augustine's Use of the *Saeculum*" (unpublished manuscript).

ises and assessments of our participants in both empirical and theological matters, were not resolved by our deliberations, even if they were tempered somewhat. As a result they remain reflected in the organization and content of the essays. Underlying these areas of difference, however, a couple of deeper areas of accord took shape over the course of the project and established its overall tenor.

One of these areas concerns the imbrication of secularity with contemporary large-scale social forces. Our group held in common a concern with the manner in which broad economic, political, and sociological developments can not only exert an impact on religious life, but in fact *inform* the entire category of religion. This concern arises in the historically minded attempts by Cavanaugh and Godzieba to augment or problematize Taylor's narrative about the rise of modernity, as well as in the several essays (Casarella, Schreiter, Miller, Martin) that engage the theme of globalization in an attempt to plot out likely unfoldings of the dialectic of secularity in the near future. With respect to the present moment, assessments diverge as to the most influential and potentially pernicious "secular" force acting to shape religious community: where some emphasize the power of commercialism and the commodification of experience (Godzieba, Doak, Rossi), others direct attention to the violent prerogatives of the nation-state (Cavanaugh) or the Promethean influence of information technology (Miller, Tracy). These disparate views were founded, though, on a common recognition that dominant political, economic, and social paradigms set the terms within which religions establish their public forms — in ways that can run the risk of fostering idolatry, as Cavanaugh and Doak point out. By analyzing these connections, including the landscape of cross-cutting publics and "counterpublics" they produce, our contributors extend the sociological reflections of *A Secular Age* on relations between society and church, and open up new vistas of investigation into the nexus of religious pluralization and democratization.

At a deeper level, the essays making up this volume evince a shared interest in identifying what might be called breaches in the immanent frame — openings in or limitations to the secular circumscription of the conditions of belief that Taylor describes. Our authors have gone about this task in a number of different ways. Some (Dillon, Jakelić) set out to provide enriched accounts of what it means, in both theory and practice, to function as religious and secular at once. Cavanaugh, meanwhile, in addition to problematizing the term "secular" by exposing its genealogical link to certain political structures, has taken the tack of calling into question the very notion of the modern "optionality" of religion around which Taylor builds his case. The idea of the limits of the secular permeates the debates about post-secularity addressed by several of our chapters, and issues in Barbieri's speculation regarding the formation of new mutations in the secular social imaginary. A number of essays (Tracy, Casarella, Dillon, Martin) reflect the broadly shared sense in our group that the notion of "public reason" sometimes used to rule faith-based considerations out of bounds requires significant revision and broadening if it is to be intellectually responsible and credible in its approach to religion — all the more so under conditions in which the divide between public and private continues to be eroded and renegotiated.[33] This theme is extended, by Tracy and others, to the more sweeping critique that modern conceptions of reason have tended to be drawn too narrowly and need to take greater account of religious, aesthetic, and embodied forms of rationality associated with contemplation, sacramentality, and mysticism. One further strand of our discussions questioned the premises regarding transcendence and immanence built into Taylor's portrayal of secularity, suggesting that a much different and less constraining perspective on the secular can attend alternative constructions of transcendence.[34] As distinct as the tangents explored by our contributors might have been, they were united by a core concern with how, to cite a phrase with which Taylor initially confronted our group, belief might be made more believable. They share, too, a recognition that ongoing perceptions and shifts with respect to the conditions of belief are ultimately linked to the prospects for developing a salutary basis for the integration of faith in public life in our diverse modern world.

The purpose of all these explorations is a public one, in the agential sense outlined above. For on each of these unifying themes — the critical role of social developments in the construction of religion, and the probing of limits to the secular — what is being addressed are not simply forces, or occurrences, or circumstances, but rather *endeavors.* Whether religion becomes reformed and reconfigured in ways that continue to foreclose what Taylor calls fullness, or becomes infused with new possibilities for shaping our common life is, finally, at least partly in our hands, and as a result the fate of faith can lay claim to a vital place on the public agenda.

33. The expertise of Paul Weithman — a member of our research team whose work could not be included here — was of particular value on the topic of public reason.

34. Here, the work of another interlocutor for our group — Fred Dallmayr — played a central role. See his "A Secular Age? Reflections on Taylor and Panikkar," *International Journal for the Philosophy of Religion* 71 (2012): 189-204.

PART I

Religion and the Public

1. Religion in the Public Realm:
Three Forms of Publicness

DAVID TRACY

A defining characteristic of a public realm in modern pluralistic, democratic, secular societies is that the notion of publicness is defined by some
understanding of reason. It may be useful, I suggest, to reopen the discussion on religion in the public realm by focusing on three distinct notions
of public reason, that is, publicness, from the ancient Greeks until today:
hence, Publicness One, Two, and Three.

1. Publicness One as Rational Inquiry: Dialectic and Argument

A truly public discussion must be free inquiry not simply because freedom is a basic value, indeed a human right, but because inquiry precisely
as inquiry demands such freedom. For example, any model of theology
— whether the classical model *fides quaerens intellectum* or any contemporary model — demands inquiry and therefore freedom for that inquiry
to function.

The central question that this first reflection will address, therefore,
is what is inquiry?

On the simplest level, to engage in inquiry is to provide reasons for
one's assertions. To provide reasons is to render one's claims shareable,
public. To provide reasons is to be willing to engage in argument. Argument is the most obvious but not the sole form of all disciplined inquiry.
To engage in argument is to make claims and to give the evidence, warrants, and backings for those claims. Argument is not exhausted by the
purely deductive procedures of the traditional syllogism or by too narrow

29

understandings of either logic or evidence. The classical scholastic theologians knew this well; the later neo-scholastics, far more concerned with certainty than with understanding and inquiry, did not. To be reasonable does include the need to be logical. To be logical is not to contradict oneself and to be consistent. To argue is also to be as coherent as the subject matter allows. Sometimes — especially on issues of religion — the coherence will be a "rough coherence" or what William James in *The Varieties of Religious Experience* nicely called "on the whole" coherence. Indeed, James, both facetiously and seriously, named his position on religious issues "on the wholism." Less imaginatively than James, I have regarded both the evidence for and the desired coherence of strictly religious (as well as aesthetic and ethical) claims of publicness as claims to "relative adequacy" in harmony with Bernard Lonergan's excellent description of true judgment as a virtual, not absolute, unconditioned. In judgments of coherence, the relevant questions and evidence have been addressed to the relevant community of inquiry. Then one has reached a virtually, never absolute, judgment (usually in religious questions a judgment of relative adequacy). Further, more sophisticated questions and further relevant evidence may occur later. Then one should rationally change one's earlier judgment. For the present, however, one has the rational right to claim to have reached a reasonable, that is, public judgment (either as knowledge or as reasonable belief).

To argue is also to be satisfied, as Aristotle and Thomas Aquinas insist, with the kind of evidence appropriate to the subject matter under discussion. To argue is to engage — to defend and correct one's assertions to the larger community of inquiry — by providing the appropriate evidence, warrants, or backings relevant to the concrete subject matter under discussion. Entailed by this commitment to public argument is the willingness to render explicit the criteria appropriate to the particular subject matter under discussion. Those criteria will prove to be — in any case where the question is other than one of pure coherence — criteria of relative adequacy, relative to the appropriate subject matter and relative to the evidence presently available on this subject matter. Such judgmental relative adequacy is in no way equivalent to modern relativism — a desperate position largely determined by a double bind: too narrow a notion of rationality (for example, idealism, positivism, scientism) curiously joined to too weak a notion of the self-correcting power of reason itself. Reason when allowed to function normally can be trusted to reach judgments that are virtually unconditioned, that is, judgments of relative adequacy. As Aristotle, "the master of argument," rightly insisted, arguments must always be proper to the subject matter under discussion (for example, poetics, rhetoric, metaphysics, logic, ethics, politics, and so on).

For example, to attempt to make a political judgment as an adequate argument on metaphysics or theology (or vice versa) is to commit a category mistake. Political (more accurately with Aristotle ethical-political) arguments are always valid once one has established a metaphysical or theological claim — not in place of that claim.

If there is a community of inquiry, there is a public realm where argument is not merely allowed but demanded of all participants. This means, as well, that truth is likely to lead to some consensus — a reasonable consensus of the community of inquiry cognizant of and guided by the criteria and evidence of the particular subject matter under discussion. In that sense, a community of inquiry must be democratic, even radically egalitarian, that is, public, in the most fundamental sense: the sense that no one is accorded privileged status in an argument, all are equal, all are bound to produce and yield to evidence, warrants, backings. The emerging consensus must be a consensus responsible to the best evidence. That remains the epistemological-ethical heart of any serious notion of inquiry and the first notion of publicness.

Inevitably, as in all inquiry, errors will be made. The self-correcting process of inquiry, however, can and should be trusted to spot and correct those errors as arguments are articulated. All serious inquiry yields its results to the appropriate community of inquiry. Any secular silencing of argued religious public claims — as when religious concerns are, in principle, silenced and ruled inappropriate to the public realm — is a position clearly unreasonable in principle. When that happens, the societal public realm properly instituted by a communally endorsed secularity (democratic, pluralistic, and egalitarian) yields to an ideology of secularism (for example, *laïcité* in 1905 France).

Many religiously originated positions, even before secular modernity, were argued in the wider public realm, for example, Marsilius of Padua. This became even clearer in modernity where the Catholic social justice traditions since Pope Leo XIII employed a Thomist notion of reason to argue for such ideas as "the common good," "solidarity," a "just wage," human "rights" and "goods," "religious tolerance," and "pluralism" for modern secular democratic societies. It is not difficult to find many Catholic ethical and political philosophers and theologians (for example, John Courtney Murray and Jacques Maritain) defending their positions with purely philosophical arguments. To be sure, their philosophies usually originate in some cognitive implications of Catholic theology, for example, analogical theological understandings of the relationship of grace and nature; charity and justice for society; the relational notion of the person (a first theological, then philosophically relational concept distinct from the modern liberal individual); and other social relationships to both church and state. Personalism did not originate, as frequently claimed in histories of modern philosophy, in a modern historical and sociological "personalism." The notion of the individual person as intrinsically related reality *(pros-opon; per-sona)* originated among the Cappadocians as a new philosophical category needed to help understand inner Trinitarian relations and was then applied analogously to humans as *imago Dei,* as grounded in the relational Trinity and thereby relational themselves — hence personalism as distinct from liberal individualism.

In most modern secular democracies the "separation" of church and state, as Charles Taylor has persuasively argued, should welcome this first form of publicness for considering religion in the public realm: reasoned, argued, evidential arguments on social justice. Except possibly in the historically complex case of France (the law of 1905), modern secular church-state separation (as the Second Vatican Council argued) aids all publicly reasoned positions on public issues on justice by religious bodies and religious thinkers. To refuse to endorse such religiously reasoned public contributions to the public realm is, ironically, to betray reason and publicness.

2. Publicness Two: Dialogue with Classics

The first responsibility of inquiry and publicness, therefore, is the responsibility to give reasons, to provide arguments. Argument has traditionally been and remains a primary candidate for inquiry. And yet there is an often unacknowledged (by many liberal theorists) second candidate for publicness as well — one related to, yet distinct from, argument. That candidate is the phenomenon of dialogue or conversation with all classic expressions (whether text, event, symbol, story, image, music; whether in art, ethics, or religion). More exactly, conversation or dialogue is a phenomenon that in a general epistemological sense is scarcely distinguishable from argument. This is so insofar as there is no genuine conversation unless the general criteria for inquiry are also observed: criteria of intelligibility (coherence), truth (warrants/evidence), right (mean what you say you mean), and equality of every person and every other — for example, a text (reading is also a dialogue) — in a conversation-dialogue. These general reasonable criteria are roughly identical to those Jürgen Habermas developed for communication, although Habermas himself is too narrowly focused on argument alone unlike, say, Hans-Georg Gadamer, who defends, correctly in my judgment, dialogue-conversation over argument as the primary form of rational inquiry. Gadamer is to Habermas as Plato is to Aristotle. The public realm is a realm of civilized conversation before it is a realm of argument.

The difficulties of a genuinely public realm in our contemporary secular, democratic societies precede the difficulties of religion in the public realm. Without a more expansive notion of reason than the modern scientistic and merely technical rationality in the public open space of the political realm, the encroaching techno-economic realm, so powerful in societies and globally, will confine argument to efficient means and reject the traditional political arguments over ends or goals as either impossible (because of the pluralism of goods in modern society) or irrelevant (since only technical arguments on efficient means are, on that reading, rational arguments). All else is merely personal preference. Hence, the exclusion of any public discussion of justice for the marginal and poor in a late capitalist increasingly global society with massive global suffering of whole peoples and regions. It is not merely that religion has been excluded from the public realm; increasingly so has a notion of reason more encompassing than either scientist or techno-economic (solely technical) arguments on means, not ends. The religions, which along with the arts provide powerful visions of the Good for society, are denied entry to the public realm unless they argue in Publicness One terms (as they rightly do on social justice issues) or on purely technical reason terms. Even Habermas — who persuasively analyzes the danger that the techno-economic realm (and therefore solely technical reason) is gradually conquering and colonizing the political realm where we all meet — restricts argument to Publicness One terms. But even Habermas believes that only rights, not goods, can be rationally argued. The question recurs: is there a second form of publicness that can allow reasonable discussion of goods? The American founders assumed that a genuinely public discussion of political ends and values would endure (as occurred in the extraordinary public political discussions of *The Federalist Papers*). The founders did not foresee a situation where the public realm of political debate and dialogue might be swamped by the techno-economic realm.

The serious intellectual difficulties of the often allied positions of a scientistic (not scientific) model of rationality and a techno-economic realm smothering all public, reasoned, political-ethical discussion of shared values in a pluralistic, democratic secular society like our own endangers any public realm at all. Sometimes it seems that Max Weber's pessimistic metaphor of the "iron cage" is even more accurate than Habermas's "colonization" metaphor or Charles Taylor's far more optimistic reading of secularity (as distinct, of course, from secularism). There is enough social evidence to suggest that we had best pay attention to Taylor's brilliant new narrative of strong affirmation of the ordinary in a secular world as well as to the more pessimistic readings of Weber and Foucault. At times it does seem that religion has been so privatized that it is merely another consumer-item for personal preference. The public realm is in danger of becoming commercialized (or colonized?) by the juggernaut of the techno-economic and technological powers of late capitalism crushing every alternative reality — religion, art, ethics, and eventually reason itself.

Religion, as a public contribution to the public realm, has been admirably defended by some religious thinkers but abandoned by others whose lives of Christian witness seem relatively unconcerned with the need to think through how the religions can play both a role of witness (a surely admirable role — we always need such witnesses as Amish or cloistered orders) as well as a role of showing how religion can prove to be public-reasoned. That public-reasoned entry of religion into the public realm can happen either through argument (Publicness One) or through dialogue with the great classics, especially the religious classics for visions of the Good, including the good life of an individual and a society. The great religious classics (texts, events, persons, rituals, symbols) even if one is not a believer have much to suggest for reflection by any serious thinker in the public realm. No one has to become a Buddhist to learn from the Buddhist's unique ability to think and feel equal partner to and even participant in "all sentient beings." The Buddhist and Taoist traditions are as insightful on ecological issues as the prophetic traditions (Judaism, Christianity, Islam) are on social justice issues. On the former, Buddhist and Taoist traditions seem to me to provide even richer resources for rethinking our relationships with the Earth than the prophetic traditions. On the latter, George Orwell was right to say boldly to his fellow secular thinkers that our secular societies have lived ethically-politically on the interest of the Judeo-Christian traditions of justice and love. Now we are starting to spend not the interest but the capital. Without learning new skills to dialogue with all the classics of all the traditions (starting with our own Catholic Christian tradition) we may well see Weber's nightmare vision becoming more and more plausible: religion will be privatized with no claim to public truth; art will be marginalized with no claim to disclosing some truth about our condition; science will be interpreted only scientistically; the techno-economic realm, with its global reach, will continue its brilliant successes via technical reason. Then all particular, age-old traditions and all their public resources for reflecting on the Good in their classics will be more and more leveled by contemporary global technology (for example, the new information technologies) and large-capitalist economies.

On that nightmare scenario (not a completely implausible one) any genuinely public realm will become a vague reminder of what once was an open space for any reasonable argument or dialogical account by thoughtful persons discussing the visions of the Good in the classics of religion and art. Reason itself would then become so technicized that it could join a privatized religion and a marginalized art. I hope — indeed I pray — that this possible scenario will not become reality. But the seeds are there. Perhaps religion — in its public performances — can not only enrich a public discussion of ends (for example, a good society attendant to the common good and the human dignity and rights of each person) but, ironically perhaps, help the public realm itself resist a continuing techno-economic colonization. Neither optimism nor pessimism is fully warranted here. Both outlooks, plausible as they sometimes seem, are based on partial social and historical evidence as well as the author's temperament and life history. For the Christian, however, hope (along with faith and love) is a supernatural, not natural, virtue. Hope is pure gift-grace. We live in hope and surely can find better public ways to communicate the uniqueness and necessity of that hope to any optimist and pessimist willing to listen.

It is interesting to observe Jürgen Habermas's intellectual journey. Originally his theory of communication did not consider either art or religion to be candidates for truth-bearers in the public realm. In the last ten years, Habermas, with characteristic intellectual honesty, changed his mind: he now acknowledges that both art and religion are truth-bearing candidates for the discussion of justice issues in the public realm. Habermas still holds to what I am here calling Publicness One (reasoned argument) as the only way for religion and art to be truth-carriers as distinct from motivational resources in the public realm. This is as unfortunate as it is unnecessary. But Habermas is hardly alone here. Indeed, until fairly recently, Catholic social theorists (for example, John Courtney Murray) were reluctant to employ their explicitly religious (for example, biblical-prophetic) resources as resources for the secular, as distinct from the ecclesial, realm. Such intellectual reluctance to think out how the classics of religion and art can claim publicness and truth by their very disclosive, truth-bearing power *(aletheia),* distinct from and prior to truth-as-correspondence arrived at through dialogue or argument or scientific method, is equally unfortunate.

Hence the importance of a second form of reasoned publicness. There are forms of conversation that are so distinctive in the kind of truth they attain (namely, a disclosure or manifestation — *aletheia*) that they demand reflection: a public conversation with the classics as candidates for entry to the public realm.

A classic is a phenomenon whose very excess and permanence of meaning resists definitive interpretation. The classics of art, reason, and religion are phenomena whose truth value is dependent on their disclosive and transformative possibilities for their interpreters. This means that the concrete classics of art, reason, and religion are likely to manifest disclosive and transformative meaning and truth in a manner that is not reducible to an argument. Truth as disclosure-transformation is the primal hermeneutical understanding of truth (Heidegger, Gadamer, Ricoeur) available in principle to all who will risk entering into genuine conversation with the classics and their disclosive-transformative visions of the Good. This is especially appropriate for the principal mode of inquiry engaged in by theologians as critical interpreters of the classic texts, symbols, doctrines, narratives, events, and the like of a particular religious tradition. On the hermeneutical model, conversation-dialogue becomes, first, the entry by the interpreter into the to-and-fro movement of the questions and responses of the classic other. The interpreter, of course, enters with some preunderstanding of those questions and maintains her critical alertness throughout the conversation, for example, in acknowledging the aspect of a classic vision of the Good that needs serious criticism. Nonetheless, the interpreter is willing to risk that preunderstanding by noting the claim to attention by the classic as genuinely other. That claim to attention may range across a whole spectrum, from a tentative resonance to a shock of recognition. A shock of recognition is an aesthetic category analogous to the grace of faith as a recognition of revelation. The primary experience of any genuine classic is one of a reality that is first acknowledged as important and true in the experience of conversation with the classic. All reasonable persons (not only believers) can, in principle, become part of the wider conversation with a religious classic. All genuine classics of all traditions are candidates for a disclosure of some truth in the public realm. All the great theologians and philosophers (for example, Augustine, Anselm, Aquinas, Simone Weil, Edith Stein) seek understanding. When they achieve it — including when they employ critical reason to purify the vision disclosed by the classic (as when Augustine de-literalized Christian apocalyptic) — they enrich their faith. Of course, in this delicate enterprise of theological critical inquiry, errors will occur (as they did for Augustine, Anselm, Aquinas). The larger community of theological inquiry, however, can be trusted to spot the errors eventually — just as the community of the public realm can spot which religious classics can help the issue of ends, values, and the good (for example, Buddhism and Taoism on ecological issues; Judaism, Christianity, and Islam on justice issues).

It is important to note that this modern hermeneutical understanding of inquiry as conversation with the classics as a public event fit for entry into the discussions of the public realm on goods and values does not involve either a purely autonomous text or a purely passive recipient-interpreter. The key to a conversation with any classic is neither the text nor the interpreter but the to-and-fro movement between them. The central moment of truth for this conversation with the classics of art, reason, and religion is the moment of disclosure-transformation that can occur when the interpreter risks addressing (and thereby entering into genuine conversation with) the claim to attention of the classic (for example, Chalcedon). As conversation, this interaction is genuine inquiry and will also likely yield critical reflection.

If we are really engaged with a classic (and not a mere period piece) this means that the interpretation-as-conversation will necessarily be a different interpretation from that of its original author or its original audience. It is the effect of the classic that remains public, not the origin. The origin of the classic is, however, also of interest for the public realm. Every classic is highly particular in origin and expression but public in effect. The classic achieves its publicness not by rejecting its particularity but by moving so deeply into that particularity (of historical and personal context, of family, of personal temperament) that it paradoxically achieves a public — even, in the greatest classics, a universal — status through its very particularity (for example, Dante, Joyce, Proust, Virginia Woolf).

The classics of any culture have always functioned culturally as phenomena in the public realm of some particular culture through their disclosive and transformative shareable possibilities. Those possibilities come to us through the more elusive, but no less real, form of inquiry as conversation with classic texts, persons, symbols, rituals, and the like rather than through the more usual form of argument. For example, among other things saints teach us that, in the old Italian proverb, a good heart crosses all borders. Saints, mystics, prophets, sages can cross into the public realm and provide new resources for our common search for values. Classics usually appeal first to the imagination, not to argument or to preference. But once the possibilities of the disclosive vision in the classic are acknowledged as possibilities, they come to us as candidates for some new consensus on possibility itself for the entire community of inquiry — candidates that now function with the public impact of a truth as disclosure, not truth as the result of an explicit conclusion of argument.

Since the disclosures of the classics of art and religion come to us as inquirers, they do not come to passive recipients interested only in reconstructing their origins (although that can be a valuable moment in the inquiry). Rather, the classics appear with a claim to truth, a claim to our attention. We inquirers are now those willing to enter into conversation with the largely particular and genuinely public classics in the public realm. As conversation partners, we must remain open to a needed retrieval of their classic disclosures. As conversation partners, we must remain equally open to any necessary critique or suspicion of any errors as well as any systemic distortions also possibly present in the classics and in the history of their effects. Every great work of civilization, as Walter Benjamin justly observed, is also a work of barbarism. There is no innocent tradition, classic, or reading. Every great classic, every classic tradition, needs both retrieval and critique-suspicion. Every classic needs continuing conversation by the community constituted by its history of effects as well as conversation by any intrigued inquirer outside the community of faith or art.

As an example of a Christian classic yielding public effects, consider the phenomenon of the 1950s named by someone "Atheists for Reinhold Niebuhr." Strange as it may seem, many agnostic and atheist political thinkers of that period — Arthur Schlesinger Jr., Morton White, et al. — found Reinhold Niebuhr's Christian realism far more politically realistic than John Dewey's, even though none of them shared Niebuhr's explicitly Christian faith and theology. They read Niebuhr's interpretations of Christian classical doctrines (for example, original sin) and his interpretations of Augustine's *City of God* to portray-disclose the ambiguities, tragedy, and hope in history. On the full spectrum of responses to the Christian (more exactly here Augustinian) classics in human being and human history, Niebuhr, as an explicitly Christian believer and thinker, possessed a shock of recognition (faith) of the classics' truth, and while the Atheists for Niebuhr possessed no such "shock of recognition" in the Christian classics, they did sense through Niebuhr's reading a more true and disclosive portrait of human history and society: no shock of recognition, but quite enough response to the Augustinian classic to disclose a human public possibility.

The community of inquiry as interpretation of the classics is also responsible for rendering explicit its criteria of relative adequacy for discerning good, bad, better (more adequate) readings of the classics. Any personal response to the disclosive power of the classic is by definition highly personal. But once that understanding is expressed, it becomes a public concern — subject to the rules for publicness of the entire community of inquiry and interpretation. It is unlikely, as noted above, that the same response to the classics of any particular religious tradition will be found among both participants in (believers in) that tradition and others interpreting that tradition from "outside." But if the religious classics of any particular tradition are genuine classics, then they also provide public, disclosive possibilities available to all as appeals to imagined possibilities (for example, Utopian possibilities in eschatological classics).

Any classic text in any tradition bears a certain permanence and excess of meaning that resists definitive, once-and-for-all interpretation. That is the paradox of the classic, that however particular in origin and expression, it is public in effect. That is why classics are excellent candidates for discussion of ends and values for any inquirer in the public realm. On this reading, therefore, religious thinkers should not confine themselves only to rational argument for their positions to become resources in the public realm. They should also present their classical (especially biblical) resources as plausible candidates for public acceptance of their truth-value along the wide spectrum of response — from shock of recognition on one end of the spectrum to tentative possibility on the other. Great social theological thinkers and activists like Dorothy Day, Martin Luther King, Jr., and Dietrich Bonhoeffer, or any liberation or political theologian instinctively know how to discern which classics (especially mystical and prophetic ones) bear truth for all sensitive, attentive, reasonable, and responsible human beings.

The actual reception of any classic vexes, provokes, and elicits a claim to serious attention that is difficult to evade. It is just this claim to serious attention that provokes anyone's preunderstanding into a dual acknowledgment. First, we come to acknowledge how contingently, historically formed, each of our preunderstandings in fact is. As we will analyze in the following section on Publicness Three, we may even allow that our pre-understanding often needs some disturbance from a genuinely prophetic voice for genuine inquiry and action to occur. Second, we acknowledge the vexation or provocation elicited by the claim to attention of this text, event, symbol, ritual, et al. That provocation is public and, if actualized in dialogue with the classic, a possible bearer of disclosive truth.

Therefore, there is always some interaction between a classic text or event or symbol on the one hand and the interpreter on the other. Then the significant question becomes, what model can help explain this public interaction? Here Hans-Georg Gadamer made his major innovation on inquiry as conversation and conversation as a particular kind of game. Think of any game: the whole point of the game is not the attitude of the players. That self-conscious attitude is what one has to get over in order to play the game. Hermeneutics, after all, develops out of phenomenology. Gadamer is trying to describe the phenomenon of the game. Fundamental to that phenomenon is the back-and-forth movement of the game itself, sometimes to the point that we are "in the zone." The worst thing that can happen in the game are self-conscious players. They literally cannot let go to enter the interaction, the back-and-forth movement, of the game. They are like a self-conscious actor who destroys the play (unless it happens to be a Brecht play, in which case the self-consciousness is supposed to occur as part of that kind of dramatic game).

The analogy of the game is Gadamer's first innovation for understanding inquiry as conversation. His second innovation comes from his reading of Plato. Plato's dialogues suggest that there is a peculiar kind of public game that occurs with inquiry as conversation or dialogue. In the back-and-forth movement of the conversation, you allow the logic of questioning to take over. You will go anywhere the question leads you. In this way, you allow the claim to attention of the other, whether that other is an actual person whom you are speaking with, or a text that you are reading, or a historical event like the Second Vatican Council. At the same time, you will enter into conversation with that text or event in as critically sharp a manner as possible if genuine inquiry is to occur in the reasoned, that is, here dialogical, public realm.

What I have presented thus far, therefore, is the basic Plato-Gadamer model of inquiry as dialogue or conversation with classics. One must also consider three criticisms of Gadamer's model since all three criticisms are also relevant for public inquiry. To begin with the less difficult one: it is the criticism of many critics of Gadamer, but Paul Ricoeur develops it most persuasively. Ricoeur is, after all, also a hermeneutic theorist. He holds that the model of conversation that Gadamer develops is basically correct but does not take sufficient account of necessary interruptions in many conversations, especially in the public realm. In conversation, one often finds the need to interrupt the conversational inquiry to allow explanations, theories, and methods in order to develop, to challenge, or to change one's original understanding. Indeed, this is exactly what first happened when Aristotle interrupted the Western Platonic dialogical conversations and insisted on argument in the Aristotelian form.

Aristotle also wrote conversational dialogues. We do not happen to have them save in fragments. What we do have are Aristotle's treatise-like collections of arguments, some of which Aristotle probably did write himself, others of which are probably student lecture notes. The first interruptions of conversation even within Plato's dialogues are arguments. Dialogue with classics (Publicness Two) often but not always needs the relative interruptions of arguments or explanatory theories in order to be understood. There are, of course, many arguments in Plato. In Aristotle, by contrast, one finds a discussion of what kinds of arguments you need if you are going to ask a particular question of a particular subject matter.

In the contemporary period, to converse well one must also become familiar with explanatory theories and methods that inform arguments across all the disciplines: in social science, anthropology, literary theory, philosophy, theology, or any discipline. Any serious contemporary inquiry into modern society, for example, has to understand at least the basic explanatory theories of Durkheim, Weber, and Marx and their successors. These theories inform the basic kinds of arguments that necessarily impinge on one's attempt to understand any particular social phenomenon. That is what makes public inquiry so complex today. Contemporary theories and explanatory models are more difficult but qualitatively not different from the original Aristotelian interruption via modes of argument employed by the classic scholastics. Ricoeur's model of hermeneutics also insists that interpretation is fundamentally a conversation trying to develop understanding, but he rightly further insists that sometimes a conversation needs interruptions, whether they are arguments, theories, or explanations.

The second criticism of Gadamer also does not devastate the model of interpretation of classics as public dialogue and conversation, although it does challenge it even more strongly than the first. This criticism is based, to use Ricoeur's now familiar phrase, on the "hermeneutics of suspicion" model. Gadamer is very much a classical European humanist just as Hans Urs von Balthasar is a classical Christian humanist. Both have great trust in the Western tradition as having within itself all the necessary resources for any problems with the tradition that may emerge through public conversation and argument. The difficulty, however, is that conversation and mere traditional arguments, explanations, and theories work well when the only problem is conscious error. But what if one begins to suspect (and this is where the phrase "hermeneutics of suspicion" comes from) that the problem we face in a particular conversation with a classic is not just conscious errors but unconscious and systemically functioning illusions? Then one finds another problem for any public realm. One needs some new kind of argument — one today called critical theory. Critical theory is a form of theory developed to spot and, if possible, heal or at least help undo not conscious error but unconscious, systemic illusion. That is why the model of classical psychoanalytical theory was so crucial for the early Frankfurt School or for almost any form of ideology critique. Ideology, in the hard sense, is not a conscious error. Anyone who agrees (as I do) that sexism, racism, classism, antisemitism, homophobia, and the like are more likely to be unconscious systemically functioning distortions than they are likely to be conscious errors needs to imply a hermeneutics of suspicion just as a theological anthropology needs not only the nature-grace paradigm but also the sin-grace paradigm. Sin as disorientation of the self curved in on itself (as a nation also can be) is the ultimate systemic distortion. The public realm should welcome all critical theories to help assure that the public realm remains genuinely public, not just a cockpit for the clash of powerful egos and exclusivist groups.

The third correction is what might be called the ever greater insistence (since Gadamer's original formulation of hermeneutics) on otherness and difference in inquiry. Of course, the original Platonic and Gadamerian model of inquiry as conversation is, in its own way, quite insistent on otherness. Nevertheless, a stronger affirmation of otherness and difference is especially important to acknowledge for a public realm in our secular, democratic, pluralistic society. Publicness Two, unlike Publicness One, cannot be content merely with a common reasonable consensus on shared values. Publicness Two also includes ways to allow differences in particular cultures to play a public role. To ignore this second form of publicness (as many otherwise admirable religious thinkers do) is impoverishing to the public realm. Why should religious thinkers ignore — as public resources

— the richest aspects of one's tradition (for example, the eschatological narratives, the prophets, the saints, the mystics)? Learning to discern — interpret — these resources and to render them available to the public realm is a much needed public task.

The very first step in conversations, as we saw above, is to allow the serious claim to attention of the other, whether that other is a person, a text, an event, a symbol, or a ritual. One must allow that genuine otherness to impinge on one; otherwise, the interaction is a noninteraction. Without that attention to the conversational other, one never learns anything because one already knows all one thinks one has to know, and, therefore, one is never in genuine interaction with another. Indeed, there is no other. Hermeneutics is, in fact, based on a notion of otherness, though Gadamer does not speak of it as such. In contemporary thought (especially that called post-modern), however, it becomes necessary to puzzle more than hermeneutics does about the radicality of the otherness of every other.

Each of these three corrections of interpretation as conversation, including conversations with the classics in the public realm, is important in itself and related to the other two. Conversations with the classics in the public realm are difficult, complex — and necessary. All the more reason to defend anew two principal claims of this chapter: first, public inquiry is constituted not only by argument but also by the broader and more flexible model for public inquiry, conversation with classics; second, we are all interpreting all the time in order to understand at all and thus inquire — hence we should consider, therefore, the model of public inquiry in the public realm as not only argument but conversation. Public inquiry as conversation with the classics, properly construed, aids any public community of inquiry in a realm where all are in principle equal, all are to be listened to, and all are expected to respond in conversations respecting each different other. Public inquiry — both Publicness One as argument and Publicness Two as conversation with the classics — could prove a modest but real gain for how religious classics might function in the public realm.

3. Publicness Three: Resources beyond the Limits of Reason

Unlike the first two forms of publicness with their appeals of either dialectical-argumentative reason (Publicness One) or dialogical-hermeneutical reason or the interpretation of classics (Publicness Two), there is the important fact of the public value of realities beyond the limits to reason (for example, the Incomprehensible, revelation-faith, the Inexpressible). The third form of publicness is grounded in a paradox: the public realm needs the aid of realities beyond public reason. This need is twofold. First, to assure that the political realm (related, as above, to the techno-economic realm and to the cultural realm) does not close into a totality system where all social reality, in effect, is constituted by the political. The separation of church and state is designed to assure that the churches do not control the political realm and that the state does not control the realm of the religions. In principle, the society served by the public realm is composed of three realms: the techno-economic; the political; and the cultural, including art, religion, and popular culture. In a well-functioning society, no one realm overwhelms the other two. One of the principal functions of the public realm is to assure, as much as reasonably and legally possible, that each realm performs its proper task. Publicness One and Two, as noted above, are designed to defend reason and to resist the serious encroachments of the contemporary powerful and pervasive techno-economic realm.

The cultural realm of society is as endangered as the political realm by the invasion of the techno-economic realm and a resultant colonization of the realm of culture. Even in religion, the consumerization of religion (especially in the burgeoning mega-churches) can be strong: religion as another consumer item for the possessive individual. Indeed, Robert Bellah and others are surely correct; possessive individualism is the major problem of our society. The narrative of the decline of the noble ideals of individual human rights to possessive individuals is a saddening one. If religion becomes merely another consumer item for the radically autonomous individual, religion betrays two central aspects of its nature: the notion of the intensely relational, communal self; and the demand of obligations to and responsibility for others (the unchosen neighbor, not merely the close friend), especially the poor, the downtrodden, the marginalized (the Christian preferential option for the poor).

The cultural realm is also endangered if everything, in effect, is read as political. In principle, the public realm is at home in both the political and the cultural realms. As my earlier argument suggests, the classics of the different great traditions — as particular and different — provide new cultural and religious resources for the public realm.

In my judgment, Johann Baptist Metz and Gustavo Gutiérrez are correct in their criticisms of Karl Rahner and Hans Urs von Balthasar and all other wisdom traditions not, of course, for what they do so well (for example, Rahner's transcendental theology and Balthasar's theological aesthetics) but for what they do not do: work out the political (theologically the prophetic-mystical) dimension of their theology. Rahner accepted this "political" criticism from Metz; indeed one of Rahner's last articles is a defense of Gustavo Gutiérrez. Metz continues to acknowledge his great debt to Rahner. No theologian need choose between the prophetic (ethical-political) and the meditative-mystical-metaphysical-aesthetic. Both are necessary for understanding Christianity in its fullness. Both can also aid the public discussion of value issues in the public realm. The "option for the poor" is a valuable idea not only for the church, but for the whole public realm wherein the society must decide culturally, politically, and economically on its responsibility to the poorest members of its own society as well as its responsibility to the poor and oppressed throughout the world. Justice transformed by the "impossible" ideal of Love as well as love-compassion transformed by the relentless demands of justice are both shareable, public ideals worthy of the serious attention in the public realm of every democratic, pluralistic, secular society.

To return to the contours of the paradox of Publicness Three: one should defend the value of encouraging public discussion of realities beyond the limits of reason (and therefore Publicness One and Two) because these beyond-the-limits-of-reason realities include movements of excess (mystical wisdom as distinct from ordinary knowledge) and movements of excessive, disruptive ethical-political demands (prophetic, eschatological, excessive, interruptive demands). Such mystical-prophetic resources can be employed, even in secular terms, by thinkers like Walter Benjamin in his brilliant and disturbing "Theses on History."

As Kant argued: to recognize the limits of reason is one of the greatest achievements of reason. In our own post-Kantian and post-modern period, philosophical and theological attempts to name and employ a reality beyond the limits of reason (for example, Derrida's "Justice to Come" and "Democracy to Come") have returned to demand attention by all thoughtful parties as paradoxical (Publicness Three) realities.

The issue of the limits of reason has been a central one in Western thought: from Plato's "the Good beyond Being" that happens but is not achieved by reason to the present. For example, in the fourth century there were debates on this issue in all three intellectual communities — pagan (Plotinus), Christian (the Cappadocians and Augustine), and Jewish (the rabbis articulating what became the Babylonian Talmud). These debates were on the limits of dialectic and dialogue, that is, public reason as developed in argumentative form by the Greeks. The Jews and the Christians, of course, held that "revelation" as pure gift was God's own self-manifestation (Exod. 3:14), beyond anything reason could achieve. Revelation, moreover, possessed implications for the public and political realms — as Augustine argued in *The City of God.* Any thinker who has faith-trust in God's revelation believes that a new way, both personal and public, has been given to us as pure gift. Moreover, as reasoners we are capable of achieving "analogous, imperfect, partial but real understanding" of revelation. To consider such revelation relevant only to the individual is to refuse to realize that the religious individual with deep personal faith is a relational individual, a person related to all other persons, to all society, to the community of believers, the church, to nature and to the cosmos, and above all to the Incomprehensible God who is Love.

Faith is also a new knowledge: not just new cognitive beliefs but also a new foundation for knowledge — a foundation of radical trust *(fides fiducialis)* leading to every new, indeed unending (Nyssa's *epektasis*), knowledge climaxing in mystical union with God. Mystical knowledge is beyond the usual limit of reason. As knowledge, mystical knowledge (which is not so rare among believers as often thought) should also enter the public realm directly: neither as a result of rational argument (Publicness One) nor only as a cultural-religious classic (Publicness Two). Rather, mystical-prophetic knowledge — as excess, as interruption, as (contra Kant) knowledge beyond the limits of modern rationality — is more and more, sometimes under the accurate rubric of post-modern thought, entering the public arena. In Augustine's *City of God,* in Catholic social thought, in Niebuhrian Christian realism, in political and liberation theologies, in the explicit use of biblical-theological reason, in Pope Benedict XVI's *Caritas in veritate:* all these are examples of mystical-prophetic knowledge operative in the public realm. Even Max Weber (unlike Durkheim) defended the occasional need for prophets in the public realm of every society.

Similar attempts of trying to name the reality (the Real beyond the limit of reason) can also be observed in some central philosophical debates of our day, starting with the late Heidegger's effort to find a new mode of "meditative" thinking. Those new forms of thinking beyond the limits of reason (whether philosophically meditative or straightforwardly theological) deserve consideration as a third and paradoxical form of publicness beyond the limits of the reason functioning dialectically-argumentatively in Publicness One or hermeneutically in Publicness Two.

In phenomenology and hermeneutics, there are several new modes of thinking that are post-dialectical and post-hermeneutical, especially Heidegger's search for a meditative thinking; Levinas's arguments with the dialogical thinking of Buber; Derrida's critique of Gadamer in their famous non-dialogue on dialogue (1981) as well as Derrida's later work on a new way of thinking appropriate to the category of the Impossible; Marion's "new phenomenology" of the gift and *caritas;* and if I may presume to mention it, my own attempts to develop a "new" hermeneutic (parallel to the "new" phenomenology) that is deliberately more fragmenting (or, I prefer, frag-eventing, that is, interruptive and excessive, prophetic-mystical) than traditionally dialogical or dialectical. These contemporary options are not anti-dialogical or anti-reason, but they do claim to manifest a knowledge and thinking present-absent reality of the Incomprehensible, the Impossible, the Ineffable in our midst as manifested suggestively in these new forms of philosophy and as disclosed decisively in the self-manifesting revelation of God.

Certain contemporary continental philosophers debate the limits of dialectical and dialogical reason. These new claims bear a striking resemblance, as briefly mentioned above, to recent historical analyses of the move away from dialectical argument and dialogue to contemplative thought in late antiquity by the neo-Platonists, the rabbis of the Babylonian Talmud, and the Nicene largely neo-Platonist Christian theologians. This late antique debate is analyzed in the book entitled *The End of Dialogue in Antiquity,* edited by Professor Simon Goldhill from a valuable conference at Oxford a few years ago on the dialogue form in antiquity.[1] The family resemblances between the fourth century and contemporary "post-modern" debates are striking.

Some major phenomenological and hermeneutical thinkers argue for modes of thinking beyond the limits of modern analytical philosophy (Publicness One) or even Gadamerian dialogue with classics (Publicness Two): new modes of thinking to describe and assess either works of art (Heidegger) or the radically other in ethics (Levinas), different events of religious awe-filled manifestation (Otto) or enlightenment (Plotinus, the Buddha). Dialectics and dialogue sometimes end their effectiveness — even in the public realm, not because of some interfering power but for a very different, very positive philosophical reason: namely, dialectic and

---

1. Simon Goldhill, ed., *The End of Dialogue in Antiquity* (Cambridge: Cambridge University Press, 2008).

dialogue can reach their natural limits. Thereby they may provide an opportunity for attempting some new mode of thinking (and therefore publicness) based on a new experience of the Real beyond the limits of reason.

Reason may disclose its limits — and beyond its limits — what Heidegger named "The Impassable," what Derrida called "The Impossible," and what Levinas, in his reading of Descartes's *Third Meditation,* called "The Infinite." For Descartes, unlike in Kant, as finite beings we cannot reach the Infinite through reason; nonetheless, we possess the concept of the Infinite. That concept must, therefore, be given to us by the Infinite itself, namely, God. (Contrast Kant here on God not as given but as a limit-concept, thought but not known or experienced.) The need to think and speak beyond the Kantian limits of reason — even before any claim to a revelatory or enlightening event of art, ethics, or religion — is also an intrinsically philosophical need, as Hegel argued against Kant: we could not even name a limit as limit unless we were already in some manner beyond it.

Dialectic and dialogue are constituted by reason in its discursive functions. They are temporal; dialogues literally "take time." The interlocutors in good dialogue or in a serious, sustained argument can be so taken up by the logic of the question itself that they find themselves caught up in the to-and-fro movement of questioning. Dialogue partners are being played by the questioning more than they are playing. Like athletes, they sometimes find themselves "in the zone." When argumentative dialectic or dialogue (like discursive reason, like ordinary time) reaches its natural limit, one experiences and understands one's limit as one's inescapable finitude and one's ineluctable historicity. At that point — as in Plato and Plotinus, in Gregory of Nyssa and Augustine, in the medievals, in Cusa and Descartes, and in certain contemporary philosophers — the thinker may also receptively attend to and await a possible experience of what within reasonable dialogue and its fidelity to rational conditions of possibility seemed Impossible. Then the Impossible becomes possible. The Impossible as new possibility becomes a new candidate for open discussion in the public realm.

If a rich experience of some event (of art, of religion, of the ethical other) does happen, then the claim for a new mode of thinking is reasonable: take, for example, the late Heidegger's meditative thinking on great works of art and the increasing influence of Taoist modes of meditative thinking on his work, or Kierkegaard's recovery of the category the "Impossible" as a positive, not negative, category in his critique of Kant. As

Plotinus insisted in his quiet, meditative, yet also rigorously dialectical and dialogical mode of reasoning, a thinker gradually rises in the journey to return to one's true home by rigorous moral and intellectual purifications, including dialectical and dialogical reasoning. By careful intellectual work, including dialectical arguments and dialogue, the thinker moves ever upward to a final achieved moment in the realm of the Intelligible. On one's own, however, one can go no further. One has to learn to wait attentively. In Plotinus's moving image, the thinker now rests and waits as if on a shore, waiting for the tide to come in. Of course, the tide may not rise during one's time there. But if the tide does come in, it will lift one to glimpse what reason cannot reach on its own, the transcendent Incomprehensible, Infinite experience of one's true home and origin, the ultimate reality — the One and the Good.

The experience of what different thinkers label apophatically the Impassable, the Impossible, the Incomprehensible, the Ineffable, or the Infinite may happen "suddenly" as the experience of the Beautiful happens in Plato's *Symposium*. This disclosure beyond dialogue may happen more quietly and gradually as in the experience of the Good beyond Being which, Plato asserts, is prepared for but not achieved by the whole intellectual-moral journey of the divided line in *The Republic*. There one moves upward from opinion and belief to mathematics, to elenchic argument and dialectical reason to the point where the Good beyond Being may or may not happen to be glimpsed. On my reading, the experience of the Good beyond Being for Plato is an experience beyond the range of discursive reason even at its dialogical and dialectical Platonic best. At the same time, the Good beyond Being is deeply relevant (as Publicness Three) to a crucial discussion of the Good and goods in any genuine public realm. The very text *(The Republic)* where Plato describes the movement of reason past opinion and belief via Socratic elenchic and increasingly complex Platonic dialectical arguments to the place where a possible manifestation of *The Good beyond Being* may happen is the very same text where Plato describes the goods and the good of order needed for a good *polis*.

We can personally achieve dialogue and dialectic by rational performance. An experience of the Good beyond Being, however, is impossible as a rational achievement. Reason prepares for it but the event does or does not happen on its own, not as our rational achievement. If it does happen, we may say, with Heidegger, *"es gibt,"* "it gives." If the event does not happen one can only say, with Blanchot and the early Levinas, *il y a:* that is, the Real is not giving, not generous, not overflowing (as *es gibt* suggests and the "Good beyond Being" insists). The Real then is simply there *(il y a)*. In either sense, it is given: either as a gift *(es gibt)* or simply there *(il y a)*.

Eschatological motives are used by Derrida to argue for the need in the public realm of politics for an impossible eschatological not teleological Justice to Come. In a similar fashion the use of the Christian naming of God as Love and ourselves as empowered and commanded to love the other — especially by love working-through-justice — has been employed by some new phenomenologists (for example, Jean-Luc Marion, Jean-Louis Chrétien). These strictly philosophical thoughts provide new "Publicness Three" resources for the public realm and suggest how philosophical theology (on the Impossible made possible in revelation) may also function in the public realm.

4. Conclusion

"Without vision the people perish." Publicness Three united with Publicness One and Two can greatly help the battered public realm of our society by making available the rich resources of the Christian (and, of course, other) religious traditions. Once joined to theologies sensitive to their own public responsibilities, such philosophies of publicness can play a vital — that is, public not sectarian role — in the shared public realm. Catholic Christianity is a church, not a sect. Catholic theology's natural affinities for the role of philosophy and reason, its communal self-understanding concretized in its central ideas of the person, not the individual; such central concepts as the common good, solidarity, subsidiarity; its recent turn to the mystical-prophetic privileged status of the poor and oppressed; its ever new rethinking of the intrinsic relationship of love and justice: all these Catholic particular resources should play a strong role in the public realm of our society through either the argumentative reason of Publicness One, the hermeneutical reason of Publicness Two, or the contemplative-meditative and prophetic reason of Publicness Three.

2. Public Reason and Intercultural Dialogue

PETER CASARELLA

1. The Post-Secular Problematic and Intercultural Dialogue

Various accounts of a possible eclipse of our secular age converge in the so-called post-secular problematic.[1] This term encompasses Jürgen Habermas's writings on "the post-secular society," Peter Berger's claims for a global revival of religious discourse aimed at "desecularization," a spate of recent literature on religion and international relations,[2] and diverse renewed attempts by theologians to rebut the hegemony of secular reason's immanent frame in matters pertaining to ultimate transcendence and social engagement. Within this broad but fertile matrix there is considerable room for dialogue and debate. For example, there are differences in the aforementioned cluster as to whether post-secularity still places a burden on adherents to religious discourses to translate their truth-claims into a less particularistic mode of expression. Some see the decline of secular hegemony as an opportunity to revive Jacques Maritain's provocation, re-

---

1. I thus agree with this thesis as developed in William Barbieri's "Introduction" to this volume regarding the competing claims to determine the meaning of "post-secularism."

2. See, for example, Scott M. Thomas, *The Global Resurgence of Religion and the Transformation of International Relations: The Struggle for the Soul of the Twenty-First Century* (New York: Palgrave Macmillan, 2005).

This chapter includes material from but also develops further what I have already published in "Dar Razón de Nuestra Esperanza: Teología Pública y El Desafío Actual del Diálogo Intercultural," in *Dar Razón de Nuestra Esperanza. El anuncio del Evangelio en una sociedad plural,* ed. Cecilia Inés Avenatti de Palumbo and Jorge Scampini, O.P. (Buenos Aires: Agape Libros, 2012), pp. 203-20.

cently invoked by David L. Schindler, that metaphysics will one day bury its undertakers. Others prefer pragmatically oriented retrievals of religious rhetoric that, like secularism itself, eschew metaphysics and anything but the most thinly conceived normative claims.

With the new dialogue we must also confront the present reality of globalization. Robert Schreiter argues in his chapter in this volume that economic globalization and secularization are not good dance partners. Where they work in tandem, the results do not always advance necessarily toward a secular global utopia but tend instead to manifest new syncretisms. New and old instances of global religiosity are continually surprising those who wish to reduce religion to its social constituents. Schreiter's contribution in this volume highlights the complex interaction between globalization, perduring secularism, post-secularity, and multiple idioms of catholicity. Citing the sociologist Saskia Sassen's term from a different context, Schreiter says that the current proliferation of catholicities is attended by an "unbundling" of Catholic identity. The fragmentation of the Catholic system of belief is not only a Euro-American problematic. Young people across the globe are bombarded with multiple forms of secularization, globalization, and efforts at religious formation inspired by competing presuppositions regarding culture, faith, and social location. Sociologically, there exists no fixed port of entry into the Catholic form of life. One can celebrate the removal of virtually all fixed parameters in global Catholicism, but not without wondering about the basic anthropological presuppositions of the faith in diverse cultures, including the question regarding the very nature of the human person.

Charles Taylor for his part sets the framework for a Christian theology performed in the public space of a secularized globe. It is worth considering the close proximity between this trend and the new theological encounters with the notion of "global civil society," an idea advanced with some caution by John Keane that has found currency among agents advocating social change by working within nongovernmental organizations.[3] Keane makes a modest argument for global ethical norms to create "spaces of hope" that still fall short of a global government.[4] In response Kimberly Hutchings registers serious disagreement with Keane: "The argument that

3. See, for example, the diverse essays collected in Will Storrar, Peter J. Casarella, and Paul L. Metzger, eds., *A World for All? Global Civil Society in Political Theory and Trinitarian Theology* (Grand Rapids: Eerdmans, 2010).
4. John Keane, "A World for All? Thoughts on Global Civil Society," in Storrar et al., eds., *A World for All?* pp. 17-39.

'global civil society' can act as a panacea for the 'international' depends upon conceptual and ontological distinctions that do not hold."[5] While drawing on and critiquing transnational feminist activism, Hutchings prefers a civil politics of mutual recognition, translation, and negotiation to the more coercive and universalist construct of a global civil society. Here, too, the mere hope for global norms immediately confronts secular misgivings regarding a project construed with such a universal scope.

Unlike his frequent interlocutor Jürgen Habermas, Charles Taylor does not demand a retranslation of religious beliefs from the ground up as a condition for religious believers to participate in the project of "publicness." On the other hand, Taylor's contribution to the post-secular problematic is more post-Hegelian and genealogical than metaphysical and pre-modern. His monumental book *A Secular Age* relativizes the importance of a widely disseminated narration of the development of the secular West as that narrative has been developed and handed on by followers of Max Weber and Karl Marx. These theorists were convinced that Christianity would eventually dissipate as a cultural force as modernity made its inevitable advances.[6] Today more than ever one can question whether the forces of secularization are as dominant in North America and Europe as was claimed in the secularization paradigm of Weber and Marx. A new narration of the story of religion and secularization was desperately needed. Secularization, as Charles Taylor has shown, introduces self-assertion as a "ratchet effect" that prevents a return to the pre-secular past, but it hardly levels the playing field within the complex field of possibilities for belief and unbelief.[7]

Taylor's re-narration, however, is strangely silent with regard to the dialogue between North America and South America. The grand narratives regarding the genesis of our secular age focus almost exclusively on Europe and North America.[8] Although Taylor's theses on post-secularism have not

---

5. Kimberly Hutchings, "Can Global Civil Society Civilize the International? Some Reflections," in Storrar et al., eds., *A World for All,* p. 41.

6. Cf. Alan Wolfe, "Faith and Modernity," *The New York Times,* December 26, 2010, BR18, accessed on September 10, 2011. For a more comprehensive presentation of this topic, see the essay by Slavica Jakelić in this volume.

7. On the term "ratchet effect," see Taylor's "Comparison, History, Truth," in *Myth and Philosophy,* ed. Frank Reynolds and David Tracy (Albany: State University of New York Press, 1990), p. 52. At an address at the Divinity School at the University of Chicago in February 2009, Taylor also pressed this point with regard to his multilayered interpretation of modernity in *A Secular Age.*

8. The contributions to a conference on secularization held in Rio de Janeiro in 2011 attempted to redress this deficit: *Secularização: Novos Desafios,* ed. Maria Clara Bingemer

gone unnoticed in Latin America, the urgent problem of fostering a dialogue between religious thinkers in North America and those in Latin America has not been marked by a post-secular frame.[9] This is not helpful given the generally Spanish-speaking character of global Christianity today, nor especially given the current demographics of Roman Catholicism.[10] Taylor does mention David Martin's work on the Protestantization of Latin America, and he shows concern for subtle differences that differentiate the path to modernity in the United States from the Catholic baroque order of the European West. Taylor is convinced that the authoritarian imposition of puritanical morality cannot pull back the levers of the ratchet effect in any part of the Catholic world. On this point there is no need for subtlety, for to this extent secularization surely applies equally to the North and the South of American Catholicism. But Taylor also sees the alleged impotency of liberation theology as an entrée for an unlikely return through neo-Protestantism to something like the sensibilities of Catholic Europe after the Protestant Reformation:

> Certain attempts at Reform in Latin America, post-Vatican II and in its spirit, like those around "liberation theology" seem to have repeated the old pattern of "clerical dechristianization," depreciating and banning popular cults, and alienating many of the faithful, some of whom — ironically — have turned to Protestant churches in the region, who have a greater place for the miraculous and the festive than the progressive "liberators" had.[11]

---

and Paulo Fernando Carneiro de Andrade (Rio de Janeiro: Editora de PUC-Rio, 2012). In this volume Paulo Fernando Carneiro de Andrade looks at the relationship between religion and politics, Maria Clara Bingemer highlights the importance of autobiographical narratives that witness to faith, William T. Cavanaugh looks at the various idolatries regarding the violent nature of religion that are perpetuated in a secular culture, and I take on the question of spiritual genealogy in the light of the perduring need for intercultural dialogue.

9. Cf. Pablo Lazo Briones, *El sentido hermenéutico del pensamiento ético-político de Charles Taylor* (Ediciones Coyoacán, 2007); and Pablo Lazo Briones, "Cosmovisión tzeltal Frente a las demandas de la actual secularización en Mexico," in *Pueblos indígenas, Estados y derechos humanos,* ed. Xabier Etxeberria Mauleón, Manuel Ramiro Muñoz, and Juan Pablo Vázquez (Mexico City: Universidad Iberoamericana de México, 2012), pp. 207-20. I wager that Taylor's work on intercultural thought resonates more deeply with Latin American concerns than his *A Secular Age,* but this hypothesis is open to debate.

10. On the latter issue John L. Allen Jr.'s *The Future Church: How Ten Trends Are Revolutionizing the Catholic Church* (New York: Doubleday, 2009) still remains a handy resource.

11. Charles Taylor, *A Secular Age* (Cambridge, Mass.: Harvard University Press, 2007), p. 503.

Taylor sees profound irony here because he envisions the rejection of the promise of modernization within liberationist thought as wholly unrelated to the Pentecostal revival. The symbolic potential for Latin America in this analysis is limited by dual outcomes of Europe's struggle with modernity in the sixteenth and seventeenth centuries: "Reformation" or "dechristianization." This duality, if left unexamined, remains precisely the problem that Latin Americans, Latino/as, and other global participants in the North-South dialogue are aiming to overcome when we propose a dialogue about the lived reality of intercultural difference. By leaving the debate here, Taylor surfaces an end point that really should be seen as a possibility for the creation of new and more elucidating discourse.

There are, of course, other ways of thinking about Latin American religiosity in the face of secularization. The theology of liberation is surely no longer as powerful as it was in the 1970s and 1980s, but its impact in the present hardly needs to be interpreted solely through the narrow lens of Taylor. There are interpretations of liberation thought born of experiences in the United States that provide a rival version of the story of modernization. For example, Roberto Goizueta's thesis that the key to the theology of liberation is "praxis as encountered by God's Word" would complicate Taylor's revisionism quite a bit.[12] Most problematic for Taylor is the new sociology of religion developing in Latin America itself. The highly detailed treatment of the new forms of religiosity in Latin America in Cristián Parker's *Otra Lógica en América Latina* yields an even more troubling conclusion for Taylor:

> We can affirm that the processes of capitalist urbanization in Latin America, because of its underdeveloped and dependent character, does not lead automatically to a process of secularization that dissolves all religious sentiment on the level of the mentality of the people *(en las clases populares).*[13]

Parker is not agreeing with Taylor on the virtual substitution of liberationist Christianity with Pentecostalism, but he is also not at all ignoring the effect of secularization. Parker sees a ratchet effect somewhat simi-

---

12. See Roberto Goizueta, "Gustavo Gutiérrez," in *The Blackwell Companion to Political Theology,* ed. Peter Scott and William T. Cavanaugh (Oxford: Blackwell, 2007), pp. 288-301, here at 298.

13. Cristián Parker, *Otra Lógica en América Latina: Religión Popular y Modernización Capitalista* (Mexico City: Fondo de Cultura Económica, 1993), p. 142, translation my own.

lar to Taylor's within Latin American society, which he characterizes as a "change of mentality" that allows for new forms of creativity, including a revitalization of popular Catholicism among the victims of urbanization's injustices. He differs sharply from Taylor in seeing secularization as only a relative phenomenon — because its effect needs to be considered in the light of a simultaneous possibility of renewal whose very fount is the call for liberation that Taylor seems to dismiss out of hand.[14]

While Latin America stands at the borders of the work of Habermas and Taylor, the issue of publicness raised by Habermas and Taylor is hardly unknown to theologians in Latin America. In fact, there is a growing literature in Latin America that invokes public theology as such. In Brazil, for example, public theology is a way of talking about the sometimes difficult relationship between church and state on the question of public support for research on religion and theology in the state-supported academy. Rudolf von Sinner, a Swiss Lutheran émigré to Brazil, concludes that there is a tradition of reflection that is both critical and self-critical in Brazil and that understands itself as a public theology in the academic context.[15] In making this claim, von Sinner traces the lineage of this Brazilian form of public theology back to an essay on Reinhold Niebuhr written in 1974 by Martin Marty, Professor of the History of Christianity at the Divinity School of the University of Chicago.[16] Carlos Mendoza Álvarez develops in the context of Mexican Catholicism a proposal for a public theology that constructs public spaces for discourse. He utilizes the pragmatist thought of Helmut Peukert. In his view, public space appears to be "like the unceasing task of the social condition of the human being, of his or her intersubjectivity, of his or her wager for a sustainable future for humanity."[17] Building on a post-modern retranslation of Christian eschatology, Álvarez avoids utopian constructs that cannot be realized within history. He is attempting to unmask the ultimate experience of women and men who offer their lives for others. An even more intercultural proposal for a Latin American

14. Another rival version would be the liberationist ethics of Enrique Dussel, which for limitations of space I cannot develop here.

15. Rudolf von Sinner, "Teologia pública no Brasil," in *Teología pública. Reflexoes sobre uma área de conhecimiento e sua cidadania acadêmica,* ed. Afonso Maria Ligorio Soares and João Décio Passos (São Paolo: Paulinas, 2011), p. 274.

16. Von Sinner, "Teologica pública," p. 265.

17. Carlos Mendoza Álvarez, "Introducción," in *El papel de los cristianos en la construcción del espacio público,* ed. Carlos Mendoza Álvarez (Ciudad de México: Universidad Iberoamericana, 2011), p. 10.

public theology is that of María Clara Bingemer from Rio de Janeiro, who integrates the witness of Euroamerican women writers from the twentieth century (including Etty Hillesum and Dorothy Day) into her liberationist synthesis.[18] Unlike von Sinner she does not take the academic context as the primary site for going public. She argues that Christian faith from its origins has been very much a faith of living witnesses and not just texts *(uma fé de testemunhas, e não tanto de textos)*.[19] She looks to women who stood in solidarity with the marginalized through journalism, spiritual writing, new modes of contemplation, and advocacy for justice. She draws, for example, on the life and writings of Simone Weil:

> I believe that the way in which Weil understands the intellectual voca-
> tion is a public one, since it is elaborated and pronounced in the public
> square. Yet it is also an ecclesial one in the sense that, even while it does
> not place itself in the ecclesiastical space, it questions and challenges the
> church's *modus operandi* when exercising theological thinking.[20]

Both Brazilians, von Sinner and Bingemer, succeed in bringing an intellectual and ecclesial vocation into the public square. Bingemer's contribution,
in particular, comes from prioritizing the narration of an experience lived
through solidarity with the poor. The public sphere is entered by means
other than a publicly recognized institutional or political office. In sum,
North Americans like Taylor can rightfully defend a certain form of public
theology as having a universal appeal, but they cannot do so without acknowledging its roots in and dependence on the experience of being Christian in North America in the 1970s. When public theology travels south
of the border, it can retain the title but the new, migrated way of thinking
takes on an identity of its own.[21] Without this intercultural reflection, the

18. Maria Clara Bingemer, *O Mistério e o mundo. Paixão por Deus em tempos de De-
scrença* (Rio de Janeiro: Editora Rocco, 2013).

19. Maria Clara Bingemer, "Secularizaçao e Experiência de Deus," in Bingemer and
Carneiro de Andrade, eds., *Secularização*, p. 127.

20. Maria Clara Bingemer, "Theology as an Intellectual Vocation: Some Thoughts
on the Theo-logical Vision of Simone Weil," *International Journal for Public Theology* 6
(2012): 37-55, here at 55. See also Maria Clara Bingemer, "Francesco di Assisi e Simone
Weil: Umanesimo Cristiano e Mistica della Povertà," in *Per un Nuovo Umanesimo: Francesco
d'Assisi e Simone Weil*, ed. Massimiliano Marianelli (Rome: Città Nuova, 2012), pp. 39-63.

21. The difference between Catholic and Protestant approaches to civil society is addressed, albeit inadequately, in Max Stackhouse, "Civil Society, Religion, and the Ethical
Shape of Polity," in Storrar et al., eds., *World for All?* pp. 59-74. Stackhouse takes the dom-

dominant modes of public theology in North America become de-racinated from their own multiethnic religious roots and from their sibling relationships by the juggernaut rivalries with publics in the Global South.[22]

Taylor's failing on the question of theological dialogue between North and South America parallels the problems I have already identified with the very notion of public theology. In particular, I have argued that David Tracy's three forms of publicness have to be approached with caution in considering the exigencies of an authentic dialogue between North and South.[23] Tracy's typology takes seriously the way in which liberating reason interrupts the linear continuity of modern, secular progress as well as those modern theological forms that fail to unmask the ideological foundations of secular progress. But this insight is buried within the third form of reason and can easily be submerged to the open interplay of the three forms. There are many cultural assumptions within Tracy's taxonomy that are not spelled out and need to be made explicit in terms of the problems that are likely to arise in intercultural dialogue today.

In the remaining sections of this essay, I consider three such problems. The first concerns the very notion of publicness as that term is employed by Tracy and others. I question whether publicness as that term is used in Western Europe and North America carries the same meaning in Latin America and among Latino/as. Second, I return to the issue of public reason and liberation in order to show that there is a certain neglect of the public role of beauty in Tracy's proposal regarding public reason. Third, I develop some critical questions regarding the concept of person in public theology and show how the recent work not only of Tracy but also of David Schindler and Roberto Goizueta helps to move beyond the current impasse.

---

inant Protestant approach to be "federal-covenantal" and the dominant Catholic one to be either "organic" or a "hierarchical-subsidiary model" (p. 72). Much more nuance could be added to both sides of this equation. He does rightly note the need to seek to promote the complementarity of the two approaches, a question that is implicitly taken up in the last section of David Tracy, "Public Theology, Hope, and the Mass Media — Can the Muses Still Inspire?" in *Religion and the Powers of the Common Life*, vol. 1 of *God and Globalization*, ed. Max L. Stackhouse with Peter J. Paris (Harrisburg, Pa.: Trinity Press International, 2000), pp. 231-54.

22. Benjamín Valentín's *Mapping Public Theology: Beyond Culture, Identity, and Difference* (Harrisburg, Pa.: Trinity Press International, 2002) is a notable and praiseworthy exception.

23. My critique of Tracy is developed at greater length in my essay "Dar Razón de Nuestra Esperanza" (see above). Here I simply repeat the major lines of critique so that I can develop on a more positive basis the elements of a new approach to public theology.

2. "Publicness" — Lost in Translation?

The master narrative that seems to govern the discourse about secularization and the post-secular problematic marks distinct publics or defends the idea of publicness. Wittgenstein's argument against the possibility of a private language is a helpful way to think about this issue. Each articulation of a public or a general category of publicness carries its own presuppositions. No one public can encompass all publics. Many publics are de facto private. One can argue against publicness as such for the sake of keeping theological language in a cultural and political vacuum. But that is not the point here. David Tracy's articulation of a public reason is founded on the presupposition that it has multiple, overlapping forms. Before analyzing Tracy's approach to publicness, we might consider the genesis of his own path to becoming a public theologian.

Recently, Stephen H. Webb, a former student of Tracy from the University of Chicago Divinity School, praised Tracy profusely as "our Erasmus."[24] Webb's portrait is generous and accurate even though Webb now takes issue with the main lines of the liberal theology that he inherited from Tracy. The celebrated professor emeritus whose photo once adorned the *New York Times Magazine* does seem like a close cousin of Renaissance humanism's famed defender of a *philosophia Christi,* the polymath who wrote *In Praise of Folly.* But Webb's Tracyesque analogy loses sight of a much more homegrown source for Tracy's path to public theology, namely, Tracy's own Irish American Catholicism. If, as Charles Taylor avers, the strict separation between public and private spheres is a distinguishing feature of our modern, secular age, then the Irish Catholic milieu in which David Tracy first received his twin vocations to the priesthood and a scholarly life is surely an exceptional case. All three publics (church, academy, and society) about which Tracy wrote so eloquently in the 1970s and 1980s were already co-implicated in the European immigrant Catholicism of the New York City of the post–World War II era.[25] The passage from this milieu

24. Stephen H. Webb, "David Tracy, Our Erasmus," *First Things,* April 22, 2009, online edition, accessed on December 15, 2012, at http://www.firstthings.com/onthesquare/2009/04/david-tracy-our-erasmus.

25. Andrew Greeley is an Irish American priest and sociologist whose work is often praised by Tracy. Clearly, the ethnic, national, and political preconditions of the genesis of liberal Catholic theology in the United States in the late twentieth century have escaped the notice of both its defenders and critics. This is not the case in Latin America. Emilce Fabiana Cuda Dunbar performs a retrieval of the Irish American narrative in the twentieth century

to the neo-Erasmian world of the University of Chicago is not so much an "unbundling" in the sense invoked by Schreiter as a reconfiguring of three pre-existing publics into an entirely new synthesis.

Tracy was born in Yonkers, New York, in 1939, the same year in which Francis Spellman was appointed as archbishop of New York.[26] Spellman, a military chaplain and an outspoken anticommunist, displayed extraordinary confidence in his ability to exercise influence in Rome and in U.S. politics. Indeed, he was an advisor to Franklin Delano Roosevelt. Spellman in this era was a public face for the alliance between Irish Catholic labor politics and the Democratic Party. But Spellman seems more likely — and here my judgment is conjectural — to be the foil to the path in the Church that David Tracy followed. As a young priest in New York City, he came in contact with Dorothy Day, founder of the Catholic Worker newspaper and houses of hospitality in New York City and elsewhere. Cardinal Spellman incited a dispute in the summer of 1949 with the much admired Eleanor Roosevelt over her opposition to federal funding for parochial schools, and Dorothy (as she was known to most) took on the eminent cardinal by taking exception, in a highly respectful manner, to his anti-labor position in the 1949 Gravediggers' strike. Moreover, Irish Catholic Democratic politicians from Al Smith (three-time governor of New York and presidential candidate in 1928) to President John F. Kennedy testify to the presence of a preconciliar public Catholicism and to its agonistic, often protean character.

Msgr. Florence Cohalan was among those who exercised the role of public intellectual to Irish Americans in New York.[27] Cohalan's father was Daniel Cohalan, a judge of the Supreme Court of New York, an outspoken advocate for Irish Nationalism, a kingpin of Tammany Hall, and a fierce opponent of Woodrow Wilson's proposal for a new League of Nations on account of Wilson's failure to grant the Irish self-determination at the Peace Conference of 1919. He served as historian for the archdiocese and

---

as an exercise in public theology in her *Catolicismo y democracia en Estados Unidos 1792-1945* (Buenos Aires: Agape, 2012). Her critical appraisal of North American social justice Catholicism represents an attractive concord between church and state for certain of the more empowered sectors of Latin American society.

26. On Spellman's public Catholicism, I rely on Patrick W. Carey, *Catholics in America: A History* (Westport, Conn.: Praeger, 2004), pp. 224-25, and Florence D. Cohalan, *A Popular History of the Archdiocese of New York* (Yonkers, N.Y.: United States Catholic Historical Society, 1983), pp. 265-330.

27. I want to thank Joseph Komonchak for bringing the figure of Florence Cohalan to my attention and noting his influence among the seminarians of this generation.

was a member of the Irish Catholic Historical Society. Msgr. Cohalan mentored David Tracy and other noted Catholic scholars (for example, Joseph Komonchak, Bernard McGinn) through St. Joseph's Seminary in Dunwoodie. He wrote an "admirable" popular history of the Archdiocese of New York that one unimpressed reviewer nevertheless claimed "relies on anti-Catholicism as a general explanation for all non-Catholic criticism of his central characters."[28] Cohalan admired John Henry Cardinal Newman — and especially his critique of liberalism — and produced with his seminarians a collection of essays on Newman on the occasion of the centenary of his conversion to Catholicism.[29] He also contributed book reviews to the *Catholic Historical Review* on European topics ranging from the Oxford movement to G. K. Chesterton. If Tracy is our Erasmus, then we might consider Msgr. Cohalan as the Newman to this generation of aspiring Catholic scholars. His attitude was not progressive, but his model of Catholic learning would have facilitated considerably Tracy's later appropriation of Lonergan's theological method and Reinhold Niebuhr's Christian realism.

How does this admittedly crude sketch of mid-twentieth-century ethnic Catholicism relate to Tracy's mature public theology? The milieu was conservative religiously and politically. In the U.S. Catholic Church of the Cold War period, for example, followers of the anticommunist Joseph McCarthy outnumbered the Catholic anti-McCarthyites.[30] But the New Yorkers were also prepared to accept reform. (Spellman defended John Courtney Murray at the Second Vatican Council.) The election of a Democratic Catholic president, the Second Vatican Council, and the upheaval of the 1960s accelerated the pace of change dramatically. But it was not just a shift from right to left. Other dynamics changed too. Anti-Catholicism was a fact of life for Irish Catholics in New York and reinforced communal identity in parishes and an already long history of public witnessing

---

28. Rev. Msgr. Florence Cohalan, *A Popular History of the Archdiocese of New York* (Yonkers, N.Y.: United States Catholic Historical Society, 1983). The work was commissioned by Terence Cardinal Cooke and was never intended to replace more scholarly studies. An admiring review was written by Francis X. Curran in *The Catholic Historical Review* 71, no. 1 (January 1985): 105. The criticism cited above comes from Peter W. Williams's review in *Church History: Studies in Christianity and Culture* 53, no. 3 (September 1984): 424.

29. Florence Cohalan, *Newman: Commemorative Essays* (New York: Paulist, 1946). For the comment on the present-day relevance of Newman's critique of liberalism, see Cohalan's review of a 1967 edition by Martin Svaglic of the *Apologia Pro Vita Sua* in *Catholic Historical Review* 56, no. 3 (October 1970): 582-83.

30. Carey, *Catholics in America*, p. 109.

and social action. The three publics of Church, academy, and society were never entirely separate domains for this rapidly assimilating and decidedly urban community of faith.

In 1981 Tracy wrote expansively:

The now beleaguered non-neo-conservatives in every tradition may find that something like an analogical imagination is at work among us all. The need — my need and theirs — is to find better ways in the future of articulating that imagination and that strategy in both theory and in practice. Otherwise, the alternatives left to us seem bleak. Perhaps we should simply announce, with La Pasionara [sic] at the end of the Spanish Civil War, "They took the cities, but we had better songs. It is a consoling thought." And we do have better songs. But consolation is not necessarily what theology has to offer. It is time for the genuine pluralism among theologians to affirm itself again as a conversing, arguing, conflictual pluralism grounded in a common commitment to publicness. It is time to join in authentic conversation on the differences, the similarities-in-difference, the hidden and often repressed negativities in the communal task. It is time to forget the '70s and the consolations of our former songs and to try again to take the cities.[31]

Here he attempts to "break through from the swamp of privateness" that plagues both the left and the right. In many ways, he is positioning himself as a worldly, progressive thinker without abandoning a distinct form of public and intellectual discourse that he knew from his early years as a New York Irish Catholic. The post–World War II Catholicism of Tracy presented itself as highly "bundled" *and* resolutely public even though there was already ample evidence since the previous century of secular incursions.[32] Tracy has elsewhere signaled that he understands the project of retrieving a critical social theory for theology under the banner of "the Muses."[33] For Tracy the latter term signifies all the symbolic resources ma-

31. David Tracy, "Defending the Public Character of Theology," *The Christian Century*, 1 April 1981, p. 356.

32. Jay P. Dolan states that the Irish in nineteenth-century New York City never heard the social gospel but were already experiencing a church Sunday Mass attendance at only between 46 and 66 percent (of the Catholic population). See Jay P. Dolan, "Immigrants in the City: New York's Irish and German Catholics," *Church History* 41 (1972): 354-68, here at 364-66.

33. Tracy, "Public Theology, Hope, and the Mass Media," p. 233.

terially embedded in a society. In his own biography the first Muses available to him were the ones that animated the lives of Irish Catholic families in the environs of New York in acts of defiance, charity, and public witness. Thus, the retrieval of the ardently pro-communist voice emanating from the Spanish Civil War (La Pasionaria) here has a twofold meaning. To the neo-conservative Catholics like his former parishioner William F. Buckley, he is displaying his firm alliance with progressives inside and outside the Church and claiming that they may still hold conversation with classic texts and persons, adhering to a tradition of popular wisdom on the ground that eludes the "culturalists." To his fellow travelers on the left, he is asking for a reprieve from mindless social action that has no cultural grounding (and thereby laying the groundwork for a more traditional traditionalism than the new voices on the right had been able to conceive).

This is the — comparatively speaking — "private" background to Tracy's own development as a public theologian. The later developments are better known to his readers. Already in his masterpiece of 1981, *The Analogical Imagination: Christian Theology and the Culture of Pluralism,* he laid out the intellectual foundations of its basic terms.[34] Six years later he expanded his concept of dialogue in *Plurality and Ambiguity: Hermeneutics, Religion, Hope* in terms of the latest developments in philosophy of language and hermeneutical theory.[35] Finally, in 1990 his *Dialogue with the Other: The Inter-Religious Dialogue* worked out further implications in terms of global religious differences.[36] In 1992 and then again in 2000, he contributed essays to multi-author volumes indicating his high regard for Habermas's elaboration of a critical social theory that lays out the conditions for understanding the publicness of theology today.[37] His treatment in this volume of the three forms of publicness is by far his most fully developed contribution to date.

The question about the intercultural dimension of Tracy's notion of publicness begins with the translation of the term itself. In the earlier works

---

34. David Tracy, *The Analogical Imagination: Christian Theology and the Culture of Pluralism* (New York: Crossroad, 1981), pp. 1-31.

35. David Tracy, *Plurality and Ambiguity: Hermeneutics, Religion, Hope* (San Francisco: Harper & Row, 1987).

36. David Tracy, *Dialogue with the Other: The Inter-Religious Dialogue* (Leuven: Peeters, 1990; Grand Rapids: Eerdmans, 1991).

37. David Tracy, "Theology, Critical Social Theory, and the Public Realm," in *Habermas, Modernity, and Public Theology,* ed. Don S. Browning and Francis Schussler Fiorenza (New York: Crossroad, 1992), pp. 19-42, and Tracy, "Public Theology, Hope, and the Mass Media," pp. 231-54.

(from *Analogical Imagination* to *Dialogue with the Other*), it was clear that Tracy was working through the hermeneutical differences between prophetic discourses and discourses of manifestation and disclosure in order to show how a Christian theologian could analyze, appropriate, and offer a critique of both secular reason and U.S. civil religion. These attempts highlighted pluralism as a hermeneutical exigency and as an outcome for theological reflection. Tracy's essay on the three forms of publicness in this volume moves beyond both the phenomenon of argument in the public square (dialectic and its partners) and the academic study of texts and prophetic witnesses. In the third form post-modern retrievals of love as justice are fused with the liberating interruptiveness of the cry of the poor. But this is where the category of publicness begins to display potentially problematic internal inconsistencies.

To illustrate that "publicness" may not function as a universal category, one need only consider the word itself.[38] In speaking of public reason, Tracy is using resources like (to cite just representative examples): American Puritanism (which is multi-layered), Abraham Lincoln (who is notoriously difficult to pin down in the religious terms that are used today), Reinhold Niebuhr (who spawned disciples of many persuasions), John Courtney Murray (whose legacy is broad but conflicted), John Rawls (whose openness to religion is questionable), and Jürgen Habermas (whose determination of the very notion of publicness most closely resembles Tracy's own even though Tracy considers it by itself deficient).[39] "Publicness," like any transparent philosophical concept, is a product of translation and is subject to interpretation when translated. In speaking to a group of theologians in Buenos Aires about Tracy's three forms, I was faced with the challenge of finding an acceptable translation of "publicness." I consulted the principal Spanish translation of Habermas's book on the subject for help and discovered that *Öffentlichkeit* was rendered as *"opinión pública."*[40] This is extremely interesting because it shows that the Spanish transla-

---

38. I am not claiming here that the adherents to public theology necessarily claim universality for the term. I am only trying to confirm and extend the analysis that others have already undertaken about its historical conditioning in order to assess its usefulness for the dialogue between North and South.

39. These qualifications regarding the perduring need for analogical participation are important and are specified in the two articles cited in n. 37 above.

40. In Spanish the critical seventh chapter of Habermas's book on publicness is entitled *"Historia y crítica de la opinión pública.* This appears in Jürgen Habermas, *La transformación estructural de la vida pública* (Mexico City: Editorial Gustavo Gili, 1986).

tor inadvertently brought into play the relationship between publicness and popular representation. Habermas, for example, relies heavily on the French concept of *publicité*, which is sharply demarcated from "publicity," *"publicidad,"* and all instrumentalizations of public reason for the purpose of political or economic utilitarianism. The real issue here seems to be the concept of *el pueblo,* which has no direct equivalent in other languages from what I can tell. In Habermas's book on publicness, *Öffenlichkeit,* and *publicité* have nothing to do with popular opinion in either the sense of public relations or populism.[41] *El pueblo* can refer to a geographically fixed place like a small town or village. *"Mi pueblo"* typically is used with endearment to refer to the fixed place on the globe that spawned familial, cultural, and religious traditions (what Tracy calls "the Muses") that formed one's original identity before interculturality made its appearance in one's life and self-consciousness. But *el pueblo* can also refer to a social group. The biblical phrase *el pueblo de Dios* (literally, "people of God") thus resonates in Spanish in ways that are lost in an English translation. As a consequence, the term *opinión pública* refers to the representation of a concept, idea, or symbol *en el pueblo* and with that carries meaning topographically as well as demographically. There is an incarnational heuristic involved in the very elaboration of the concept of publicness once one travels south of the border. That movement of thought is inaudible without the active employment of translation and interculturality as dynamic forms of reason. Two viewpoints are necessary in order to carry out the dialogue. The result is a polycentric as opposed to a monocultural use of reason.

What is the theological import of this linguistically based cultural analysis? The Latin American understanding of public reason is more autochthonous.[42] Tracy's three forms are not disjoined from history, for they embody the very principle of using complex historical and sociological analyses to typify forms as they develop over time in different contexts. At the same time, all of his types hover strangely above the enculturated

41. The paradoxical question of defining the "people" and articulating the democratic foundations for populism have a long and controverted history in the field of Latin American politics and need further elaboration than I am able to offer here. See, for example, the nuanced presentation in Paulina Ochoa Espejo, "Paradoxes of Popular Sovereignty: A View from Spanish America," *The Journal of Politics* 74, no. 4 (2012): 1053-65.

42. It would be interesting to consider in this regard the "autochthonous Church" of Bishop Samuel Ruíz and the experiences of lay leaders in Chiapas in this regard. Pablo Lazo Briones of the Universidad Iberoamericana has already undertaken a study of this region in the terms used by Taylor in *A Secular Age.* See his "Cosmovisión tzeltal."

forms of lived religion that might claim rootedness in a specific place. I am not claiming here a post-modern turn to the land as an alternative to public reason. The question of universality and the debate about the universal claims of reason remain just as vital for *el pueblo de Dios* as they do for public theology. In fact, the universality is not vanquished by claiming its place in a specific people. On the contrary, the universality becomes more translucent through the locating of public reason in a people who make a claim to belong to a particular place.[43]

3. Beauty *and* Justice as Forms of Public Theology

Tracy's second form of public reason emphasizes the hermeneutic engagement with the classics, and the third form looks at resources beyond the limits of reason. This typology could have the unintended effect of bifurcating the beholding of the beauty of the form from the search for social justice. Similarly, my colleague William T. Cavanaugh, whose essay on "The Invention of the Religious-Secular Distinction" appears in this volume, also questions whether Tracy needs to add a fourth form of public reason based on the lived experiences of believing communities that are working for justice. Cavanaugh questions the matter-of-fact way in which Taylor presents "optionality" as a secular condition from which we may no longer have the option of de-mythologizing. In that regard, Tracy's three-forms schema also seems to occlude or render ambiguous religious efforts as promoting modern progress whose roots lie in forms of belief and action that have little or nothing to do with secular optionality.

For this reason I would like to consider the contribution to the discussion of public reason in a secular age of a Latino theologian whose work deals with the interplay between beauty and justice.[44] The late Cuban American thinker Alejandro García-Rivera starts neither from eternal beauty nor from the social history of empirical communities. He wrote about holiness *in medias res* — in the little stories in which the poor proclaimed the beauty and holiness of the saints. These stories include the witness articulated in the form of a semiotics of culture of St. Juan Mar-

43. Implicit in this statement is the issue of the place of the biblical-theological category of Israel in a Christian public theology. A recent engagement with this issue is J. Kameron Carter, *Race: A Theological Account* (Oxford: Oxford University Press, 2008).

44. Other Latino/a theologians have dealt with this same theme, including Roberto Goizueta, Michelle González Maldonado, Cecilia González Andrieu, and myself.

tin de Porres, Nuestra Señora de Guadalupe, and Caridad de Cobre (who floats — he writes — at the middle of the cosmos).[45]

He too draws on the Muses and narrates the true witness of a newborn named Estefanía. She was a two-month-old child of a Puerto Rican couple. She died of AIDS in a shabby housing project. García-Rivera was called as the pastor to perform a burial in a barren lot overrun with weeds. The father of Estefanía was also buried in this lot. Alejandro recognized a pauper's grave and a seed in the faith of these people for what was to become the St. Martin de Porres Lutheran Church in Allentown, Pennsylvania. Alejandro then tells the story of how this experience called him back to his Catholic roots and enabled him to recognize the Church as beautiful and holy.

From an unmarked gravesite to a church with a mark, that is, a name, I saw in this experience God calling me back to my Roman Catholic roots. Eventually, I did return and am now a Roman Catholic lay professor of theology at the Jesuit School of Theology at Berkeley. I have written several books including one on St. Martin as well as several on the theology of the beautiful, such as *The Community of the Beautiful* and *A Wounded Innocence.* I wrote these books out of this experience. I had learned something profound about the reality of the church: it has marks. More important, these marks are often unrecognized by academic theology, but are seen quite easily by the poor. There is one special mark, however, that by its very visibility truly defines the church. It is *kalokagathia,* the union of the beautiful and the holy. *Kalokagathia* is a Greek word for which we have no modern counterpart. It is a word that grasps an intrinsic connection between the good *(agathos)* and the beautiful *(kallos).* I see that mark in that statue of St. Martin de Porres. As such, *kalokagathia,* as represented by this simple statue, calls to question what the world has come to know as either beautiful or holy. It also recovers one of the lost marks of the church. . . . The church has marks. I saw this as I stood in front of the unmarked gravesite of little Estefanía. I sensed then that God would not leave that place unmarked. In the ecumenical miracle of a St. Martin de Porres Lutheran Church, I saw that a very special mark of the church transcends the sins of the human church. It is the innocence of those who stand at an unmarked

45. See Alejandro García-Rivera, "Wisdom, Beauty, and the Cosmos in Hispanic Spirituality and Theology," in *Cuerpo de Cristo: The Hispanic Presence in the U.S. Catholic Church,* ed. Peter Casarella and Raúl Gómez, S.D.S. (New York: Crossroad, 1998), pp. 106-33.

gravesite yet hope for things unseen. Such hopes then become marks, marks that have filled the church with music, color, tapestries, statues, paintings, dance, drama, and a thousand other forms since its beginning. It is the mark of a wounded innocence. It is the mark of *kalokagathia*. It is a mark of the church.[46]

There is a universal dimension to the story of Estefanía and the marks of the Church that she brought to life. In his theology García-Rivera recovers the doctrine of the communion of the saints by exploring the convergence of two truths that have become separated in our contemporary discourse and experience. First, he develops a theory that explains how beauty and goodness are perceived in the wounded innocence of the poor of Jesus Christ. Second, he articulates a theology of cultural difference rooted in a semiotic understanding of faith and culture. Cultural difference is exalted by virtue of the perception of beauty and goodness in the concrete lives of the faithful. Likewise, beauty and goodness are neither descending nor ascending. Those transcendentals of being come to light as refracted through difference in both nature and culture. In Tracy's terms, all three forms of publicness come together.

What kind of theory of aesthetic perception does García-Rivera defend? His fullest statement is found in *The Community of the Beautiful.*[47] The book begins with Hopkins's poem "Pied Beauty," which is transformed into a theory of praise for the cosmic community of signs in both nature and culture. Working through and beyond the theological aesthetics of Hans Urs von Balthasar, García-Rivera embraces the analogical difference between creator and creature. Through C. S. Peirce and Duns Scotus, he embraces the formal distinction as a lens for grasping the semiotic community of difference in created reality as a created good.

His theology of cultural difference builds on this semiotically construed ontological realism. The key insight in *The Community of the Beautiful,* which is buttressed by Josiah Royce's extension of pragmatism into the social domain, concerns the continuity between the experience of St. Juan Diego and the call at Medellín in 1968 and by contemporary Latino/a theologians to recognize the preferential option for the poor. Popular

46. Alejandro García-Rivera, "The Church Is Beautiful and Holy," in *The Many Marks of the Church,* ed. William Madges and Michael J. Daley (New London, Conn.: Twenty-Third, 2006), pp. 71-73.

47. Alejandro García-Rivera, *The Community of the Beautiful: A Theological Aesthetics* (Collegeville, Minn.: Liturgical, 1999).

Catholicism, theological aesthetics, and solidarity with the poor all stem from a single, unified vision of faith grounded in the concrete perception of beauty and goodness. An aesthetic imagination makes judgments about reality based on the perception of beauty and goodness. Drawing on the Magnificat of Mary, as well as the liturgical canticle of the three youth in the furnace (Dan. 3:57-88, 56, from the Sunday morning prayer of Week I of the Liturgy of the Hours), he suggests that an enculturated "lifting up of the lowly" will establish an aesthetic mode of interpretation that is not only doxological but also redemptive and liberating. I conclude with his own words on the redemptive power of a new aesthetics: "Redemption, in light of God's ordaining power, is less a state of mere existence or an invisible inner reality than an ordained existence, a common reality in the midst of marvelous differences, a community where the invisible becomes visible by the power of a bold and daring spiritual imagination which makes manifest communities of Truth, Goodness, and above all, the Beautiful."[48]

García-Rivera constructed his work as an exercise in the anagogical imagination in order to draw a contrast with the work of David Tracy on the analogical imagination. He never espoused the idea of a public theology, but his vision of redemption is cosmic, personal, and social. My own sense is that the contrast he makes between anagogy and analogy might be drawn too sharply. At the same time, there is a convergence of beauty and justice in García-Rivera's work that calls into question the typology of Tracy. The contrast between García-Rivera and Tracy lies in popular wisdom about beauty and justice that Latino/a Catholicism foregrounds.[49] This foregrounding brings into view the kind of intercultural dialogue that needs to take place in the United States in order for there to be a more effective dialogue between North and South.

4. Personhood and Public Reason

Public theology has been silent on the question of the concept of the person. Tracy's three forms of publicness provide a taxonomy that presupposed a variety of approaches to the constitution of the human person. In the form

48. García-Rivera, *The Community of the Beautiful*, p. 195.
49. This wisdom is also the fruit of worship and popular piety. For more details, see the closely linked chapters on "Worship and Devotion" and "Public Catholicism" in Timothy Matovina, *Latino Catholicism: Transformation in America's Largest Church* (Princeton, N.J.: Princeton University Press, 2012), pp. 162-218.

of a taxonomy (even if generic specification can be a productive mode of thought), this delineation of types does not and is not intended to admit of an easy synthesis. Accounts of the human person that are merely taxonomic betray presuppositions about cultural fragmentation that Tracy himself has been the first to subject to critical analysis. His theory of analogy is at least implicitly anagogical, as we have just seen. Taylor, for his part, famously addressed the question of selfhood in his magnificent tome *Sources of the Self* prior to writing *A Secular Age*.[50] Taylor's views on selfhood spawned a lively discussion of conceptualities regarding personhood that extend beyond the domain of public theology. But the lineage of public theology that began with Martin Marty's essay on Reinhold Niebuhr has not advanced the question of personhood significantly beyond the perspective of Niebuhr's *Moral Man and Immoral Society*. That influential text contains provocations of lasting value but cannot be said to ground the task of public theology in a concept of the human person that addresses either the post-secular problematic or the new intercultural demands of a North-South dialogue. Niebuhr's text trades on a dialectical expression of creaturely personhood that is metaphysically unbalanced and utterly impractical from the standpoint of Hispanic forms of identity rooted in popular religion, as described sociologically by Cristián Parker and theologically by García-Rivera.

New avenues of inquiry are thus needed in order to ground the discussion of public reason in such a way as to promote more adequately the dialogue between North and South. For this reason I have chosen three representative points of entry. These are hardly exhaustive but together are intended to shed new light on the post-secular problematic vis-à-vis intercultural dialogue. David Tracy has been focused on the problem of the person since his earliest publications, especially in *The Blessed Rage for Order* and *The Analogical Imagination*. These works, taken as a whole, laid out a mystical-political view of personhood that de-privatized in a decidedly non-secular fashion the hegemonic, secularizing views of personhood that constrained the free participation of believers in the project of a public reason. In this sense, the taxonomy of selfhood set forth in his contribution to this volume is complemented by the more synthetic and participatory mystical-political vision.[51] His most recent work on the topic proves de-

50. Charles Taylor, *Sources of the Self: The Making of Modern Identity* (Cambridge: Cambridge University Press, 1989).

51. Many of his students could be mentioned in this regard. But the work of Alexander Eduardo Nava, *The Mystical-Prophetic Thought of Simone Weil and Gustavo Gutiérrez* (Al-

cisively that he has developed profound and synthetic insights into the kind of concept of person that is needed for public theology today. As a result, the three starting points under review will be David Tracy's newest retrieval of the development of a person as *prosopon,* David L. Schindler's treatment of the Marian *fiat* as a starting point for Catholic engagement in the world, and the anthropology of *nosotros* (literally, "us") developed in several works by Roberto Goizueta Jr.

Prosopon: *David Tracy's Masked Anthropology of Love and Justice*

In his book *The Presentation of Everyday Life* (1959), the sociologist Erving Goffman maintained that the self is a person who adopts a mask depending on the setting in which he is found. The mask or part can be changed, and there is also a self who is hiding backstage that can shed public personae altogether. In his recent writings on person as *prosopon,* Tracy too highlights the metaphor of a mask, but precisely in order to counter the quintessentially modern idea, exemplified here by Goffman's influential thesis, that the masks that we wear in distinct social settings are not inherent or permanent aspects of personhood. Tracy foregrounds person as *prosopon,* originally signifying "face" or "mask" in classical Greek drama, in order to articulate a relational ontology of personhood that is profoundly sensitive to suffering and the tragic dimension of life.

This novel re-appropriation of *prosopon* can be traced in three steps. The first concerns a rereading of the trajectory of Greek thought from the pagan tragedians to the Cappadocian theologians of the fourth century and then back to the tragedians.[52] The second concerns the medieval heritage.[53] The third concerns the relevance of these patristic and medieval retrievals for contemporary life and thought.[54]

---

bany: State University of New York Press, 2002), is particularly noteworthy in the light of our discussion of the urgency of intercultural dialogue.

52. David Tracy, "Mask, Faces, Persons: The Relational and Embodied Self," unpublished manuscript provided by the author.

53. David Tracy, "Trinitarian Theology and Spirituality: Retrieving William of St. Thierry for Contemporary Theology," in *Rethinking Trinitarian Theology: Disputed Questions and Contemporary Issues in Trinitarian Theology,* ed. Giulio Maspero and Robert J. Wozniak (London and New York: T&T Clark, 2012), pp. 387-420.

54. Here I draw on David Tracy, "Simone Weil: le masque et la personne," in *Simone Weil,* ed. Emmanuel Gabellieri and François L'Yvonnet (Paris: Les Cahiers de l'Herne, 2014), p. 301-6.

The tragedians played with the metaphor of *prosopon* to show, so says Friedrich Nietzsche, that the person is the face behind the mask. The Greek term originally signified a face peering through a mask at another face. This direct embodied encounter at the level of a meeting of two distinct gazes remains essential in unveiling the concept of interpersonal dialogue. The temptation to hide your self behind the mask becomes less potent when your eyes meet those of another. Cappadocian theology immediately had to amend this notion for fear that the concept of a Trinitarian person would be only a mask for true personhood. In the Christian tradition this way of thinking was branded as the heresy of Sabellianism or Modalism. In the Cappadocians the relational term *prosopon* was joined to the non-relational term *hypostasis* in order to create a new concept of personhood that displayed the basic and irreducible relationality of the divine communion without falling into incipient Modalism. The affirmation of the Trinity as three *hypostaseis* (persons) in one *ousia* (being) did not diverge from the interpersonal relationality expressed originally by the Greek concept of *prosopon.* Tracy then offers a slight corrective to the Cappadocian concept of person not by swerving back toward Modalism but by reminding contemporary theologians that the Greek tragedians did a better job than the still-too-Platonic Greek theologians in seeing how the self is an embodied center of personal agency subject to chance and still capable of free self-determination.[55] What Tracy terms "the tragic self" of the Greeks is inscribed into a sometimes fatalistically construed body politic capable of responding with disgust and compassion to the deep flaws in others, in the social body, and above all in one's own psyche.

Tracy is no stranger to medieval Trinitarian thought, and his recently published essay on the scholastic thinker William of St. Thierry could easily have been extended into a broader consideration of historical and systematic concerns. In this essay, being as communion translates into a theology of mystical union. The Trinitarian context is equally significant. In sum, William stands at a crossroad when the affective mysticism privileged by St. Bernard of Clairvaux will be surpassed by the intellectualism of thirteenth-century scholasticism. William did not choose a middle path; he argued, rationally and with a rigor and acumen that influenced thirteenth-century doctors, for a position whereby by the gift of faith and the gift of love both broaden the scope of reason itself. He proposed in a

55. Limitations of space do not permit here a consideration of Tracy's reading of Augustine, but the presence of Augustine and Augustinian themes cannot be underestimated.

rather daring way that "the soul, by the grace of the *unitas Spiritus* (unity of the Spirit), experiences its participation in the loving union of the Trinity's own inner self."[56] This invitation by God to the inner life of the Trinity as an inner life of love makes possible a view of affectivity previously consigned to mysticism of a more anti-intellectualist bent. Today's post-secular defenders of public reason are likely still to have difficulty with either Trinitarian mysticism as a dogmatic construct or mystical union as a practice of belief unsupported by background arguments. William's brilliance, which is also his limitation in this field, is that he focuses on the rational underpinnings of practices designed for medieval monasteries while articulating in carefully reasoned ways a more universal spiritual path to follow out of an inward desire for the Good. For the believer the unfathomable Good looks and tastes like the ultimate reality of Trinitarian love. Others standing on the outside of Christian faith could still be impressed with that path of intellect and desire, for the pursuit is not only attractive as an intramural task. It also shares deep affinities with spiritual practices in other traditions.

How can medieval love mysticism and the suffering self of the Greek fathers of the fourth century be articulated in the public realm today? As with Bingemer, Tracy claims that the clue to marking this transition lies in the far too easily neglected testimony of Simone Weil. She is the perfect mode of access to both ancient Greek tragedy and Christian mysticism because she read deeply in both traditions and created a new and modern synthesis out of them. She desires the Good excessively, and her passionate but rigorous writing (her brother was a mathematical genius who towered above virtually all others of that class in the twentieth century) about that desire managed to be both accessible and erudite. Tracy links Weil to the ancient *prosopon* by dint of a philosophical distinction highlighted by Hans-Georg Gadamer: "a mask is not *Vorstellung,* i.e., an image standing in for some other absent reality through the image-mask. Ancient mask is not *Vorstellung* but *Darstellung,* i.e. a rendering present of a reality through the very image-mask."[57] Weil died tragically in England at the age of thirty-four by limiting her physical nourishment to what French citizens under the Vichy regime were receiving, and this in spite of a doctor's orders to attend to her tuberculosis. Her love for others marked her thought and life as excessively oriented toward an objective vision of the Good of humanity. Recognizing and enacting self-limitation for the sake of that pursuit was no mere cos-

---

56. Tracy, "Trinitarian Theology," p. 405.
57. Tracy, "Simone Weil," p. 302.

tume that she wore. It was represented in what she read, what she wrote, and no less in acts of solidarity with the most vulnerable persons in society.

What is the value of these manifold reflections on persons as self-representing masks for a better understanding of the theological anthropology of the public reasoner? These hermeneutical retrievals methodologically exemplify the second form of public reason while drawing heavily on the mutual broadening of reason and faith in the first form. The retrievals from the ancient, patristic, medieval, and modern settings point to a relational self radically attuned to the tragic sense of life but also attracted in an excessive way to the Good. Tracy is therefore arguing for a new grasp of how authentic personhood is always already engaged in a search for a love that does justice (Publicness Three). Trinitarian theology and philosophical mysticism both contribute equally to this vision. The Good toward which human existence is attracted is not attained through a private self or through the discarding of one's multiple and malleable social selves for the sake of pursuing a private project behind the stage on which social and natural suffering is taking place. Tracy's epitaph for this self is a line from Sophocles's *Antigone* that was much prized by Simone Weil: "I was not born for hate but for love." Such a statement is a necessity in explicating the basic requirement for understanding the personhood of public reason.

Fiat: *David Schindler's Marian Metaphysics of Beauty and Freedom*

Tracy has developed a view of the person oriented toward divine love and justice. Simone Weil articulated that orientation in terms of a philosophy of the human desire for the Good that might fit with Habermas's requirement that philosophy must re-express "what it learns from religion in a discourse that is independent of revealed truth."[58] In other words, Weil takes us to the limit of the friendly and non-hostile neo-Kantian secularization advocated by Habermas.[59] Tracy is not a neo-Kantian, for his third form of public reason is designed to stretch this project to its utter limits, to its point of excess. But maybe that modern project of secularization will not withstand the pressure of being driven to its limits. Maybe that project is not capa-

---

58. Jürgen Habermas, *Time of Transitions,* ed. Ciaran Cronin and Max Pensky (Malden, Mass.: Polity, 2009), p. 164, as cited in Matthew T. Eggemeier, "A Post-Secular Modernity? Jürgen Habermas, Joseph Ratzinger, and Johann-Baptist Metz on Religion, Reason, and Politics," *The Heythrop Journal* 68 (2001): 3.

59. Eggemeier, "A Post-Secular Modernity?" p. 3.

ble of being stretched to the point marked by a hunger for the Eucharist and a willingness to accept radical sacrifice such as is made evident in the testimony of Weil. In that case, a more radical form of critique of modern secularization is not only possible but necessary.

A well-known criticism of Habermas on this point was made by then-Cardinal Joseph Ratzinger. These two have dialogued about their differences in such a fashion that the dialogue itself represents a model for public reason in action. In the words of one recent commentator:

> Ratzinger has expressed broad agreement with Habermas's suggestion that in a post-secular society believers and non-believers should enter into a mutually critical dialogue. This agreement about the importance of a renewed dialogue between faith and reason gives way, however, to two very different accounts of reason and approaches to the legitimation crisis in contemporary democracy. Where Habermas has advocated for a postmetaphysical approach to reason and procedural account of democracy, Ratzinger insists that it is necessary to retrieve a metaphysical understanding of reason and an approach to politics in which the state receives knowledge of what is good from outside of itself — specifically from the moral resources of the Christian tradition. Finally, where Habermas expresses support for the Kantian project of translation, Ratzinger proposes a form of translation that invites non-believers to act "as if God exists" and accept the Christian moral tradition as authoritative.[60]

The approach of Ratzinger foregrounds the question of metaphysics. He is not rejecting modern secular reason altogether but rather insisting that its positivistic and instrumental usages require a broadening that only Christian revelation can provide.

In North America the most vigorous and compelling advocate of this view of Ratzinger is David L. Schindler, one of the editors of the English-language *Communio: International Catholic Review.* I turn now to Schindler's view on the kind of human personhood necessary for public reason, focusing on the connection Schindler has drawn between the response of the Virgin Mary to the message of an angel and the need to develop a non-modern, non-Kantian ontology of human freedom.[61] The broad contours

---

60. Eggemeier, "A Post-Secular Modernity?" p. 4.

61. This analysis is based principally on David L. Schindler, "Civil Community Inside the Liberal State: Truth, Freedom, and Human Dignity," *Josephinum Journal of Theology* 16,

of Schindler's ontology are thus captured by these words of Pope John Paul II:

> Mary is totally dependent on God and completely directed towards him, and at the side of her Son, she is the most perfect image of freedom and of the liberation of humanity and of the universe.[62]

Three strands of Schindler's thinking about public reason come together here: the Mariology of Hans Urs von Balthasar, the Christocentric humanism of *Gaudium et spes,* #22 ("Only in the mystery of the Word made flesh does the mystery of the human person become clear"), and an existential Thomism that reconfigures the priority of substance into a priority of relation.[63] The Virgin Mary is the perfect form of creatureliness. Her words "Let it be done to me [according to thy Word]" symbolically express the purest form of creaturely existence. Her acceptance of the task presented by the angel who posed the question coheres perfectly with the response. As the perfect exemplum of creatureliness and creaturely freedom, she is most suited to be God-bearer. Her witness on the plane of the purely creaturely and pure creaturehood refracts beautifully the light on human existence that emanates solely from the Word and Deed of the Incarnate One. Stratford Caldecott shows how Schindler moves from *theotokos* to a metaphysics of freedom while at the same time endorsing von Balthasar's claims on the self-enrichment of the Triune God.[64]

Crucial to Schindler's gift-ontology is the fact that created being, too, has a triadic structure because it participates in this Trinitarian form; it is "from," "in," and "for" (or "toward") — with receptivity fundamental to its nature as gift. The "constitutive relation from and toward God *(Esse)* establishes in the creature . . . an intrinsic relation also from and toward all that participates in *Esse*" in and through Jesus Christ. Mary, as pure creature divinized by grace, manifests this receptivity, which in God may

---

no. 2 (2009): 232-87. See also David L. Schindler, *Heart of the World, Center of the Church: Communio Ecclesiology, Liberalism, and Liberation* (Grand Rapids: Eerdmans, 1996).

62. John Paul II, *Redemptoris Mater,* 37, quoting from the Congregation for the Doctrine of the Faith, *Instruction on Christian Freedom and Liberation,* 97.

63. For an overview of Schindler's thought, one may consult the essays in *Being Holy in the World: Theology and Culture in the Thought of David L. Schindler,* ed. Nicholas J. Healy Jr. and D. C. Schindler (Grand Rapids: Eerdmans, 2011).

64. Stratford Caldecott, "The Marian Dimension of Existence," in Healy and Schindler, eds., *Being Holy in the World,* pp. 281-94.

be called divine maternity or spiritual motherhood. Her active role in the annunciation — the activity by which, cooperating with grace, she exercises her human freedom to the full in accepting the divine will — therefore has its deepest root in God himself. It is an aspect of the divine image and likeness in her, not a falling away from likeness.[65]

The *fiat* embodies the fullest potential of human liberation — personal and social — because it is the inscription of the divine will and destiny for all being into the common, faithful language of a poor Jewish woman. She is in no way divine or even a representative of the Romantic symbolical language of Goethe's "eternal feminine." She expresses the primordial "letting-be" of human creatureliness. She is a creature of God who liberates human freedom for a higher destiny by instantiating a grace-filled potential for receptive activity in the world. The reasoning exhibits a logical form, one imbued with an aesthetic dimension. In the high Middle Ages a similar form of Marian existence was captured by the scriptural epithet: "Tota pulchra es, amica mea (You are entirely beautiful, my beloved)."[66]

What does the metaphysical reconstruction of the Marian *fiat* teach us about public reason? Schindler's point of departure is the hidden agenda of the modern nation-state to promote liberal freedom as an ideological system without any implications for metaphysics or radical creatureliness. His critique extends to formal processes of liberal justice as well as to those Catholic defenders of political liberalism such as John Courtney Murray who consider the liberal procedures of justice in the liberal regime to be articles of peace rather than articles of faith.

Hence the paradox peculiar to the liberal-juridical state in the matter of truth: such a state protects the virtually unlimited freedom and right (which are limited politically only by the demands of public order) of each citizen equally to seek his own truth and argue publicly on its behalf. This unlimited freedom, however, is mediated covertly to society via an instrumentalism that *eo ipso* does violence to the truth and goodness of things in their defenseless givenness, as well as to the arguments made in terms of truth and goodness so understood.[67]

65. Caldecott, "The Marian Dimension of Existence," pp. 289-90.

66. For a full-fledged theological aesthetics on this theme, see Nicholas of Cusa, *Sermo* 243, in Nicolai de Cusa, *Opera Omnia,* Sermones IV (1455-63), ed. Walter Andreas Euler et al. (Hamburg: Meiner Verlag, 2002), pp. 254-63. See also the elucidating commentary in Ann W. Astell, *Eating Beauty: The Eucharist and the Spiritual Arts of the Middle Ages* (Ithaca, N.Y.: Cornell University Press, 2006), pp. 1-26.

67. Schindler, "Civil Community," p. 267.

By neutralizing the question of whether things have their givenness from outside of the natural order of things, Schindler claims that procedural liberalism silently and violently wrests away the excessive dependence of creaturely being on its source of being. Schindler uses a variety of metaphors to convey the sense of his critique (proceduralism; instrumentalism; technological, "liberal-juridical" state; sacramental vs. positivistic churches, etc.), all of which bear an analogy to the mechanistic nature of modern science. Liberal procedures functionalize the relationship between creature and Creator so as to observe the utterly novel epiphany of beauty that allowed a Jewish girl to manifest perfectly free obedience to Yahweh and give flesh to the living Son of God. In the liberal juridical state there is an unacknowledged bias against the construal of the relationship between creature and Creator as one of communion. That prejudice ultimately blocks authentic social solidarity.

Schindler challenges post-secularists to ask whether their accounts of public reason have unveiled all of the hidden assumptions of secularism. He is by no means dismissing the modern project of asserting with the Second Vatican Council the *justa autonomia* (rightful autonomy) of earthly affairs.[68] The creature does not merge into the Creator, and creaturely freedom thus upholds its capacity for free self-determination and radical engagement in social affairs. The Marian creature is just as fully open to the world and committed to solidarity with the downtrodden as Weil's objectively passionate and tragically vulnerable self. Schindler is calling for a new, fully modern, and fully post-secular self that accords with the notion of being given out of an act of Trinitarian love:

> The most basic task of a public reason consistent with an ontology of being as gift from God is to recover the roots of public reason itself in an understanding of *being as given,* in all the depth and breadth of what is implied in this *givenness.* It is to seek to recuperate as far as possible in this manner the original and most basic meaning of all being, including public institutions in their being as constructed by man, inside the givenness of all being as gift.[69]

Schindler thus ends his critique with the hope that some form of public reason can be developed that reconstructs the givenness of things in terms of their sacramental, non-instrumental, non-technological, non-

---

68. *Gaudium et spes* (Pastoral Constitution on the Church in the Modern World), #33.
69. *Gaudium et spes,* #52.

pragmatic luminosity. This is both a hope and an urgent task, but not one that his own rich efforts at a theological aesthetics are capable of fully articulating. In the midst of the post-secular problematic, David L. Schindler remains nonetheless a new kind of Delphic oracle, one whose incisive wisdom regarding the givenness of self *and* society should not be ignored.

Nosotros: *Roberto Goizueta's Transmodern Aesthetics of Liberation*

David Tracy takes a trope from fourth-century theology and retrieves it such that it reverberates in a contemporary key. The public struggle of Simone Weil is, depending on how one enters into her witness, classical, modern, and perhaps even post-secular. She forged a blending of mysticism and politics that is uniquely her own and also, I believe, representative of Tracy's own contribution to the selfhood of public reason. David Schindler's Marian metaphysics sharpens the divide between pre-modern synthesis and modern (and post-modern) fragmentation. That represents a deliberate provocation for those post-secularists still beholden to what Michael Sandel calls "deontological liberalism."[70] Schindler's proposal is contemporary precisely in the sense of raising questions about modern, secular selfhood and the liberal notions of justice that some would consider settled and beyond question. We turn now to a third concept of personhood that differs from the first two in at least two respects. First, the third form of public personhood has its genesis in an intercultural dialogue, one that is lived each day by Latino/a Catholics in the United States. Second, this third form of personhood circumvents secularism without being either modern or unmodern. It disrupts and unveils new ways of thinking about persons in society by situating itself within what the Latin American philosopher Enrique Dussel calls "transmodernity."[71] This category leaves open the possibility that the usual demarcations of culture (pre-modern, modern, post-modern, secular, post-secular, etc.) have been centered on conflicts that are overly Euroamerican and not necessarily focused on what lies generally at the border of Euroamerican thinking, namely, the reality of Latin American and Latino/a thought.

Roberto Goizueta follows Alejandro García-Rivera in adumbrating a

70. Michael Sandel, *Liberalism and the Limits of Justice* (London: Cambridge University Press, 1982).

71. Enrique Dussel, "Transmodernity and Interculturality: An Interpretation from the Perspective of Philosophy of Liberation," accessed online at http://enriquedussel.com/txt/Transmodernity%20and%20Interculturality.pdf, on February 28, 2012.

new synthesis of beauty and justice, but there are distinctive accents to Goizueta's account that address the question of public reason and post-secularity more directly than is the case in García-Rivera's account.[72] Whereas García-Rivera foregrounds little stories like the testimony of Martín de Porres or Estefanía, Goizueta develops a philosophy of action that delineates the aesthetic, practical, and poetic dimension of Hispanic popular Catholicism. Goizueta highlights "domestic life" as a new category for theological reflection. The daily rhythms of existence in a family are forms of *praxis* and *poesis* that should empower rather than subjugate women and need to be seen as part of the idiom of a new theological narrative of emancipation. This reflection is just one example of how certain forms of liberationist thought have followed Marx's overturning of theory and contemplation to the exclusion of art and creativity. The production of art, of devotions, and of spiritual realities enfleshed in the cultural patterns and beliefs of living communities is ignored when all of life is subsumed under the category of *praxis*.[73] Goizueta's theology remains true to the creative presence within Latino/a Catholicism of expressions of faith such as the celebration of La Virgen de Guadalupe, and is thus a new theo-poetics as much as a transmodern form of emancipatory *praxis*.

Goizueta foregrounds a theology of accompaniment of the poor, an item mentioned in Tracy's third form of public reason but not at all readily transparent in Schindler's account. On this point Goizueta's philosophy of liberation emerges directly out of his dialogue for more than twenty years with the theology of Enrique Dussel.[74] Two elements of Goizueta's theology of social solidarity need to be highlighted. First, the prime locus of intercultural interaction and therefore formation of selfhood takes place at the border.[75] The border should be neither the site where fences are

72. I am using the term "follows" in the sense of a formal parallel born out of mutual conversation and criticism. As collaborators in the Academy of Catholic Hispanic Theologians in the United States, it is very difficult and ultimately pointless to isolate the lines of influence between these two theologians. Their work proceeded *en conjunto* with one another and with others.

73. Roberto S. Goizueta, *Caminemos con Jesús: Toward a Hispanic/Latino Theology of Accompaniment* (Maryknoll, N.Y.: Orbis, 1995), p. 130. The theo-poetic and liturgical category of *fiesta* has been developed by Goizueta here but also by other thinkers like Eduardo Fernández, S.J., and Francisco Taborda.

74. See, for example, Roberto S. Goizueta, *Liberation, Method, and Dialogue: Enrique Dussel and North American Theological Discourse* (Atlanta: Scholars, 1987).

75. Roberto S. Goizueta, *Christ Our Companion: Toward a Theological Aesthetics of Liberation* (Maryknoll, N.Y.: Orbis, 2009), pp. 136-37.

built to restrict free mobility and the expansion of selfhood nor a utopian place of romanticized, socially dislocated communion. It is the birthplace of a new *mestizo* identity that requires a painful struggle of liberation and intercultural interaction in order to take shape and be empowered. Second, drawing on Gustavo Gutiérrez's reading of Bartolomé de las Casas, we can say that the poor of Jesus Christ put forward their own daily lives as bread for the world.[76] Las Casas recognized the unjust Eucharistic logic of the conquistadores. In the colonial system, one could not offer the bread of life without seeing that the Indians whose work and livelihood were being exploited by the Spaniards were in fact being consumed as "ill-gotten" bread for the world. "Las Casas thus implicitly recognizes," writes Goizueta, "that the only authentic act of worship (aesthetic praxis) is one whose material, or economic mediation (the bread) is itself the product (poiesis) of ethical-political and economic relationships in which human lives are valued as ends in themselves rather than as mere instruments of production."[77] The beautiful symbolic disclosure of the liturgy and the painful struggle for social justice are intertwined in this reflection in a provocative but significant matrix.

Goizueta's specific proposal regarding the concept of the human person is that of *Nosotros.* The first-person plural pronoun in Spanish, this linguistic marker simultaneously connotes community, identity, agency, and being formed within the crucified body of Christ. Goizueta confronts the individualistic tendencies of U.S. culture by proposing the narratives of popular Catholicism as the new habits of the heart.[78] By foregrounding an emancipatory vision of domestic theo-poetics, Goizueta breaks down the usual dichotomy between private and public. One could extend this reflection in another direction. Where is the witness of the millions of Latinas and Latinos who work daily in the homes and gardens of others, while remaining under the radar of public documentation and so-called publicness? Does our category of publicness dignify these undocumented products of economic activity?

Christocentric anthropology is also a hallmark of Schindler's proposal, but it takes a different form here. Goizueta's Christocentrism is Latino/a and very often Guadalupan, which gives it a specific social and cultural

76. Goizueta, *Caminemos con Jesús*, p. 124, citing Gustavo Gutiérrez, *Las Casas: In Search of the Poor of Jesus Christ* (Maryknoll, N.Y.: Orbis, 1993), p. 51.

77. Goizueta, *Caminemos con Jesús*, p. 125.

78. Goizueta, *Caminemos con Jesús*, pp. 18-76.

location. In other words, like *La Virgen de Guadalupe,* this starting point for the encounter with Christ easily admits of more universal applications but still has to be read out of its enfleshment in the lived, everyday experience of the Hispanic community. Goizueta focuses on Christ as "our Companion."[79] Through its particular situatedness in a specific community, the presence of Christ becomes visibly catholic, Catholic, and universal all at once. There are novel features to his Christology that can only be mentioned here. By highlighting the theological aesthetics of Christ's companionship, he is simultaneously able to demonstrate how it is that "crossing borders belongs to the essence of the beautiful."[80] Moreover, he emphasizes in a scripturally and liturgically significant manner that the wounds suffered by Christ remain even in his resurrected body to show that the process of social reconciliation in all of its urgency nonetheless has as its terminus point a form of justice and coincidence of opposites that only the God of Jesus Christ can enact. Christ's companionship is thus a thoroughly non-innocent form of Christian hope, one that listens to the cry of the poor and is moved by the beauty of popular Catholicism toward a real and palpable fulfillment in the kingdom of God.

WE HAVE REVIEWED three proposals regarding the concept of the human person in public reason. All three are de-privatizing. All three are rooted in an experience of God that is decidedly "contrapuntal," to use Schreiter's phrase, with regard to existing individualizing, fragmenting, and secularizing paradigms. One could place this trilogy of concepts of the person alongside Tracy's taxonomy of public reason. On the other hand, the need for a synthesis seems rather urgent in the light of the current "unbundled" state of affairs in the church and in the world. The full development of that synthesis would require a different venue for a more comprehensive elaboration, but certain building blocks would already seem to be in place. The selfhood of public reason must be socially located, grounded in a radical, sometimes even excessive, dependency on the Triune God's gift of life, capable of unmasking the powerful distortions promoted by secular and other dominant ideologies, truly revelatory of the genuine beauty expressed in communities of faith and justice, and intercultural. Each of these three starting points offers rich resources for addressing these concerns.

79. Goizueta, *Christ Our Companion,* pp. 1-24.
80. Goizueta, *Christ Our Companion,* p. 119.

5. Conclusion

In spite of this breakthrough, the question of how intercultural personhood will advance and prosper within the directionality that links together the variety of post-secularities mentioned at the outset of this essay remains difficult to answer. Secular hegemony was obviously not neutral with regard to the overt religious nature of the North-South dialogue we have been discussing; however, the post-secular family of narratives will not necessarily provide the wide berth needed to foster this dialogue. The new attention being paid to forces of globalization and the situatedness of public theology in distinct localities bodes well for welcoming intercultural dialogue as such into the mix. On the other hand, the post-secular problematic is decidedly ambiguous with regard to metaphysical claims regarding ultimate reality mentioned above since so many of the new adherents to post-secularism still remain more comfortable with standpoints that reflect the anti-metaphysical theses of Martin Heidegger and his many followers in the realm of philosophy and theology, revamped pragmatism (including the transcendental pragmatics of Karl-Otto Apel), a sociology of re-enchantment, and the like.

One reason proponents of a North-South dialogue must remain hesitant regarding post-secularity has to do with challenges inherent to the North-South dialogue itself. The social forces that invite the reappraisal of the dialogue include the politically charged presence of 11 million undocumented Hispanic immigrants in the United States. At the same time student exchange programs on the Mexican-U.S. border are subject to frequent cancellation because of rightful concerns about the safety of students in the light of new reports of violence at the border. The dialogue is unsteady because the reality that it seeks to uncover makes people on both sides of the border very nervous. It is far easier to broach the seemingly safe discourse of post-secularity rather than to bring in the constantly shifting and potentially dangerous realities of rapidly changing demographics in church and society. Samuel Huntington's awful screed against the Mexican immigrant[81] is actually quite useful for bringing to the fore, with a supposed appeal to public reason, an account of why the border and a dialogue about the border require that more attention be paid to Homeland Security. Huntington speaks publicly against the voiceless in such a way

81. Samuel P. Huntington, *Who Are We? The Challenges to America's National Identity* (New York: Simon & Schuster, 2005).

83

ePETER CASARELLA

that others on both sides of the debate are led to remain silent, for fear
either of losing a public argument or, alternatively, of publicly joining a
position that may actually gain hegemonic ground more quickly through
continued silence.

The Spanish philosopher Miguel de Unamuno wrote in 1931 about *La
Agonía del Cristianismo* and for his noble efforts his book was placed on the
Index of Prohibited Books.[82] He was not reinforcing a stereotypical image
of Hispanic Catholicism as an otherworldly retreat to self-mortification.
Nor was he advocating an elitist distancing from the true beauty of popular
piety. He was using the term *agonía* in the etymological sense of a struggle.
There is a new version of the same existential predicament that pertains
here. Within the post-secular problematic there is a new opening in which
Catholics — and not just Catholics! — in North and South America can
work together to make a broader contribution to ecclesial discourse and
to social progress. But such collaboration will be, as I have attempted to
show, a real struggle.

82. Miguel de Unamuno, *La Agonía del Cristianismo* (Madrid: Renacimiento, 1931).

3. Catholicity, Globalization, and Post-Secularity

ROBERT SCHREITER

1. Introduction

Globalization is not a major theme in Charles Taylor's *A Secular Age,* but it has, I believe, played a significant role in shifting the gravity of the secularization hypothesis that dominated most of the twentieth century. Vincent Miller's essay in this volume delineates a number of the forces that have attenuated secularization's dominance in European and North American societies. The significant rise in migration has brought religion back into the social equation in Europe, and the effects of the resurgence of religion in many parts of the world since 1990 have raised questions about secularity's narrative of the privatization and eventual disappearance of religion from the public sphere. To be sure, secularization is not about to disappear. But Taylor's re-narration of its development and progress points to a realignment that is still taking shape. Like much of the rest of social change in the West, it does not yet quite have a name; hence, the prefix "post"-secular. This moniker covers a contested area, as William Barbieri has mapped it out in the "Introduction." What does seem to be emerging, however, is that Europe's narrative of secularization as proposed by Max Weber is no longer seen to be paradigmatic as it was during much of the twentieth century; it reads now more like a *Sonderfall* — an exceptional case. At the same time, one has to account for a variety of alignments between the secular and the religious in the differing construals of modernity itself. If one must now speak of modernities — in the plural — the relations between the secular and the religious will likely yield a similar range of possibilities.

85

One of the challenges of the re-entry of religion through the matrix of globalization is finding the most useful way to talk about it in a post-secular way. Much of the writing on religion in international relations — say, in the area of peace-building, nationalism, and politics — is still dominated by the standard secular narrative.[1] William Cavanaugh has done some significant work in shifting the ground of the beginning of that narrative, usually set in the so-called Wars of Religion, or Thirty Years' War, in the seventeenth century. In this prevailing narrative, religion and the violence it incites had to be tamed, domesticated, and privatized for the sake of peace in Europe and the emergence of the modern nation-state.[2] Cavanaugh's reconstruction shows that the origins and playing out of the "problematic" were far more complicated and considerably more ambiguous than this. In light of this reconstruction, the unfolding of the secular narrative vis-à-vis religion has to be rethought. As Cavanaugh contends, the narrative is really more about the consolidation of power in the emerging nation-state than about religion.

Second, in contemporary international relations the social significance of religion is still most frequently read through Marxist or Durkheimian lenses, viewing it as an epiphenomenon of social forces. This overlooks the fact that religion is much more than an epiphenomenal experience for most of the world's population. Consequently, religion needs to be reintroduced into the equations of international relations in more varied ways if the analysis of social forces at play is to be useful.

One of the significant results of Taylor's study is seeing religion within its social contexts, but at the same time allowing religion its own agency. A narrative shaped entirely from within "the immanent frame" cannot capture the full range of meanings of religion in play, inasmuch as religion extends beyond the "buffered self" of the secular paradigm. Taylor's work in *A Secular Age,* and also in some of his shorter writings,[3] adds a distinctive voice that can be contrapuntal to those who want to reduce religion to something else.

This essay looks at such a voice (or as it turns out, a set of voices)

---

1. For a re-examination of this, see Timothy Samuel Shah, Alfred Stepan, and Monica Duffy Toft, eds., *Rethinking Religion in International Affairs* (New York: Oxford University Press, 2012).

2. William T. Cavanaugh, *The Myth of Religious Violence: Secular Ideology and the Roots of Modern Conflict* (New York: Oxford University Press, 2009).

3. Charles Taylor, *Dilemmas and Connections* (Cambridge, Mass.: Harvard University Press, 2011).

within Roman Catholicism today. Roman Catholicism is the oldest and largest transnational institution in the world. In Taylor's work it plays a major role, especially in the medieval, formative period and then again in the nineteenth century. As the largest transnational institution in its extensiveness, it comprises about 18 percent of the world's population (and roughly half of all Christians) and is the most culturally extended of all religious traditions. This is not said in some triumphalistic tone; it is only to note that given its extension, it has to deal with considerable cultural variety as well as the international dimensions of globalization in a wide range of social formations around the world.

The theological category of "catholicity" is now beginning to be seen as a key way of understanding how the Church is a global reality within a globalized world. The concept of catholicity is an ancient one in the Christian tradition; it has often taken on special valence at certain moments throughout the Church's history when the identity or meaning of the Church itself has been a concern. Both catholicity and globalization seem to encompass, each in their own sphere, the paradoxes of interconnectedness and distinctiveness that mark the world as we experience it today. Hence, to examine some dimensions of their interaction can be useful for situating religion in post-secular societies as they are now developing.

In this chapter, I explore how concepts of catholicity are shaping the Roman Catholic Church's self-understanding in a globalized world. The shaping that is going on is not an entirely reflexive one; by that I mean, the language of "catholicity" is not always in the forefront, giving shape to the discussion or debate. But certainly issues of identity are there, and I suggest that the concept of catholicity gives coherence to, and a certain perspective on, what is occurring. This is not a novel idea, invoking the concept of catholicity here. As I have already indicated, the concept tends to come to the fore at distinct moments in the Church's history when the Church has had to adjust its self-perceptions as the world changed around it. I am suggesting here that how catholicity is at work in the Church's self-understanding today can give us an insight into how a major religious player on the current world stage is seeing itself, and what of its internal resources it is calling forth to meet and engage that world. That, I believe, gives us a picture of religion as agent in the post-secular world, both in how it sees itself and in how it reads the world around it. This in turn will, I hope, contribute to a series of templates that may chart how religion acts in a post-secular setting. I use the plural "templates" here advisedly. "Religion" is a Western concept that does not adequately describe many of the phenomena attributed to it. It is, to some extent, a one-size-fits-all category created by the standard secular narrative. By looking at a single, though significant, instance of religion, I hope to reconfigure our construals of it.

In order to do this, I begin with a brief historical look at how the concept of catholicity has developed over the course of two millennia within Christian theology. This sketch is necessary since contemporary understandings of catholicity hearken back to earlier discussions. That provides the backdrop for the second part, which looks at two ways configurations of catholicity are at work within Roman Catholicism today — each with the intent of engaging a globalized world. Each of these two ways invokes a traditional understanding of catholicity as the one most able to meet the contemporary challenges that the Church faces. By invoking catholicity, we will see, the Church is reaffirming its identity and authenticity, and thereby is trying to put its stamp on this particular way and the actions and practices that flow from it. I will also adumbrate that another dimension of catholicity has been emerging out of the experience of globalization that could be added to the historic two.

In the third section, I reflect first on how these two ways will help or hinder the Church acting in a post-secular society, and then suggest what elements from this investigation contribute to developing templates for various forms of religion in a post-secular society.

2. Catholicity: A Brief History

"Catholicity" in its general sense means something that is comprehensive, all-encompassing, or universal.[4] It finds its theological origins in the early second century. It has received renewed attention within Catholic theology in recent years for two reasons. First, there is a growing awareness that, for the first time in its history, the Roman Catholic Church really is a worldwide church, as a result of the missionary efforts of the nineteenth and twentieth centuries. How to grasp that reality has given the concept new salience. Second, catholicity seems to provide a possible framework

---

4. For historical overviews of the concept of catholicity, see Yves Congar, "Die Katholizität der Kirche," in *Mysterium Salutis,* ed. Johannes Feiner and Magnus Lohrer (Einsiedeln: Benziger, 1965-72), IV/2, pp. 478-502; Peter Steinacher, "Katholizität," *Theologische Realenzyklopädie* 18:72-80.

for dealing with another all-encompassing phenomenon — globalization.[5] In order to use this concept to engage both the phenomenon of being a worldwide Church and that of globalization, it is important to trace some of the significant lines in the history of the concept.

In the Nicene-Constantinopolitan Creed promulgated in 381, the Church is confessed as being "one, holy, catholic, and apostolic" (DS 151).[6] That it made its way into this confession of faith indicates that catholicity was already a known concept. The phrase *kath'holou* does appear once in the New Testament (Acts 4:18) but not in reference to the Church. Its theological meaning is usually traced to Ignatius of Antioch, who applies the term to the Church (ca. 110). In his *Letter to the Smyrneans* (8, 2) he writes: "Wherever Jesus Christ is, there is the Catholic Church." Scholars believe that he intended by this to emphasize how each concrete community of believers, gathered around its bishop in the celebration of the Eucharist, is a concrete instance of and also participates in the universal community of the Church. This fullness of the universal community derives from the universal salvation Christ has brought into the world. This fullness of grace and truth is as a gift of Christ to the Church. It is now mediated to the world through the Church. Universality or catholicity in this earliest sense meant, therefore, this fullness of salvation and the fullness of being in Christ. As the early Church expanded, this understanding of universality came to include the geographical extension of the Church in the communion of communities of faith throughout the world.

By the end of the third century, especially in North Africa, catholicity acquired an additional meaning, as evidenced already in the *Martyrdom of Polycarp* (ca. 156) and the polemics of Tertullian and others. Catholicity was what distinguished the true Church from competing heretical sects. Thus, accepting the fullness of truth given by Christ to the Church meant that to be catholic was also to be accepting of all that had been revealed through Christ; it was to be orthodox. It was in this way that, in the Western Church, "catholic" came to be a designation of distinctive church bodies — local or particular churches — that were in communion with the See of Rome. Here one sees a first instance of "catholic" coming to express a distinctive identity.

---

5. I have explored the outlines of this in "Catholicity as a Model for Globalization," in *Theology in Intercultural Design: Interdisciplinary Challenges — Positions — Perspectives*, ed. Claude Ozankam and Chibueze Udeani (Amsterdam: Rodopi, 2010), pp. 173-86.

6. Henricus Denziger and Adolfus Schönmetzer, *Enchiridion symbolorum definitionum et declarationum de rebus fidei et morum* (Freiburg: Herder, 1967).

These two senses of catholicity — universality and fullness of truth — are brought together by Cyril of Jerusalem (ca. 315-386) in his *Catecheses:* "The Church is Catholic or universal because of its spread throughout the entire world, from one end of the earth to the other. Again, it is called Catholic because it teaches fully and unfailingly all the doctrines which ought to be brought to men's knowledge, whether they are concerned with visible or invisible things, with the realities of heaven or the things of the earth" (18, 23f.). Augustine, in his controversies with the Donatists, helped develop a new discourse of catholicity, wherein he introduces an additional dimension or perspective on catholicity, namely, adherence to the legitimate authority that guaranteed the universality and orthodoxy of the Church: the bishops united with the Bishop of Rome. Thus, the elements of universality, orthodoxy, and adherence to authority shaped the theological discourse of catholicity (at least in its Western usage),[7] connected in the concrete reality of the Church by temporal continuity.

In the sixteenth-century Reformation, the polemics about the nature of the visible and the invisible Church revived interest in catholicity, and brought forth yet another element to the discourse of catholicity. The Church of Rome emphasized the history of the three elements (universality, orthodoxy, adherence to legitimate authority) as embodied in the visible Church, governed by the pope. The Reformers, on the other hand, reached back to Ignatius of Antioch to understand catholicity as the participation of each Christian community in the eschatological, invisible Church. These divergent stances continued down into the twentieth century.

The Second Vatican Council took up at several points the catholicity of the Church (for example, *Lumen gentium*, 13, 22). Without abandoning its sense of the catholicity embodied in the visible Church, it held up in a special way Ignatius's vision of catholicity, especially in its understanding of the relationship of the particular or local church to the universal Church. How the fullness of the Church is present in each particular church, yet only inasmuch as those particular churches are united to all other particular churches and the Church of Rome, is bound up with catholicity. Catholicity is not a possession of the Church, but is rather Christ's gift to the Church, and must always be cherished and honored as such.[8]

---

7. The Eastern Churches would not subscribe to submission to the Church of Rome, of course. See, for example, John Meyendorff, *Catholicity and the Church* (Crestwood, N.Y.: St. Vladimir Seminary Press, 1983).

8. See especially J. M. R. Tillard, *L'Eglise locale* (Paris: Seuil, 1995).

The understanding of how this plurality and unity come together in a concept of catholicity was expressed by the concept of *communio* (communion) set forth in the Extraordinary Synod of Bishops in 1985. Intending to convey the rich meanings of the New Testament concept of *koinonia, communio* is an expression of the love that binds together and defines the relations of the Persons of the Trinity and is revealed in Christ's love for the Church. This communion is lived out by believers in the internal communion with one another and with their bishop, and in the particular (or local) churches with the universal Church and the See of Rome.

In reflecting on what such an understanding of catholicity means in an age of globalization, I have suggested elsewhere that a third dimension (or perhaps a more operational definition of what *communio* actually entails) of catholicity needs to be held up, namely, that of communication.[9] Communication that is grounded in the love and mutuality of the Persons of the Trinity, and one that is keenly aware of how communication can misfire in cross-cultural situations, seems necessary if catholicity is to be a lived reality in the contemporary world Church in all its contextual, doctrinal, and structural realities.

3. Two Discourses of Catholicity in the Church Today

It is possible to discern two discourses of catholicity today abroad within the Church.[10] Both of these forms of catholicity draw on traditional understandings of the concept — as universality, as fullness of faith, as visible communion — albeit in different ways and with different emphases. In so doing they present distinctive discourses within which the self-understanding of the Church can be articulated. What makes them significant for our investigation here is not so much direct debate over the concept itself, but rather how they envision the relationship of the Church to the world. To understand the differences between the two, one must be aware of two factors that have been shaping the debate about the Church's relationship to the world — one external and one internal.

The external factor has to do with how one views the world itself vis-

9. See Robert Schreiter, *The New Catholicity: Theology between the Global and the Local* (Maryknoll, N.Y.: Orbis, 1997).

10. I have worked this out in more detail in "Two Forms of Catholicity in a Time of Globalization," *Himig Ugnayan* 8 (2007): 1-18.

à-vis God, salvation history, and the Church's role within that. It asks questions like: Where and how is God revealed in the world today? Just how is one to judge the goodness of the world, in light of its fallenness? How are we to assess the human condition in light of these realities? How does the salvation offered by God in Jesus Christ manifest itself and effect a renewed communion with God? What is the role of the Church in all of this?

The internal factor within the Church that is shaping the debate between the forms of catholicity has to do with how to interpret the Second Vatican Council (1962-65) and its role in the longer history of the Church. As a Council of renewal, is its vision and the implementation of its vision one that is marked by a radical turn toward the world after two centuries of a self-imposed turning away from modernity? Is it therefore marked by a rupture with the immediate past, so as to achieve a more complex and holistic vision that will better engage the complexities of the contemporary world? Or is the "renewal" but a moment of adjustment within the internal life and disposition of the Church so that it might better manifest the truth of Christ to the world — be a more authentic *"sacramentum mundi,"* or sacrament of the world? This internal debate, which has been strongest in Europe, the United States, and Australia, posits not only two different views of the meaning of the Council, but also two different ways that the Church should see itself and its role in the larger world.[11]

These two factors are examples of contextual forces that call for a response and, in turn, summon forth a new reflection on the meaning of catholicity.

Let us turn now to the two discourses of catholicity that would help situate the Church in its efforts to address the contemporary world, especially the manifold dimensions of globalization.

The first approach focuses on catholicity as the extension of the Church throughout the entire world, with "extension" being seen both geographically and theologically. That geographical extension, already evident in the cultural diversity of the bishops who assembled for the Second Vatican Council, now for the first time makes the Church a genuinely "World Church." But this geographical reality has a theological significance as well. The Church, as bearer of the good news of Jesus Christ, is the agent of the *missio Dei,* the mission of the Trinitarian God in the world. That mission

---

11. Pope Benedict XVI set out this distinction (and his clear favoring of the second position) in his Christmas address to the Roman Curia in 2005. See his "Interpreting Vatican II: Address to the Roman Curia," *Origins* 35 (January 26, 2006): 534-39.

entails bringing the gospel message of healing, redemption, and reconciliation to every creature (Matt. 28:19-20). To do this, the Church focuses not so much on itself but rather — in imitation of its self-emptying Lord (Phil. 2:6-11) — on the world it is to engage. It does so by sharing deeply the world's joys and hopes, its sufferings and fears, as was stated so eloquently in the opening words of *Gaudium et spes,* the Pastoral Constitution on the Church in the Modern World, promulgated at the conclusion of the Council.[12] The Church exists for the sake of this mission of bringing all people and all things together in Christ. In order to carry out this mission, it must read the "signs of the times." This is done by seeking out the ways that the Trinitarian God is already at work in the world, planting the *semina Verbi,* or "seeds of the Word," in the goodness of creation. The world is indeed marked by sin, but more importantly is suffused with God's grace. These *semina Verbi* are to be identified and nurtured, and those things that stand in the way of their flourishing are to be resisted and overcome.

One can see how the substance and the tenor of *Gaudium et spes* set the tone for the Church's living in faithfulness to the gift of catholicity given to it by its Lord. What that means in practice is always trying to discern the signs of the times — those places where God, in going before us, has indicated the gospel needs to be presented and the reign of God needs to be realized. This is carried out concretely in *solidarity* with those who are poor and oppressed, in practices of *dialogue* (to discern those signs and to demonstrate solidarity) and of *inculturation* (to provide environments for the flourishing of the *semina Verbi*). These three practices — solidarity, dialogue, and inculturation — shape the grammar of the discourse of this approach to catholicity.

Solidarity, dialogue, inculturation: these are three key ways that catholicity is exercised in a global world. Solidarity is especially needed with those who are excluded from the benefits of globalization, or are simply left behind. This is the solidarity to which Pope John Paul II appealed in his discourses on globalization. In those instances, he noted the deep ambivalences within globalization, and called for a "globalization of solidarity" with the poor and excluded. Dialogue is catholicity as communication; it acknowledges and respects difference, but also proceeds from the assump-

12. "The joy and hope, the grief and anguish of the men of our time, especially of those who are poor or afflicted in any kind of way, are the joy and hope, the grief and anguish of the followers of Christ as well." Austin Flannery, ed., *Vatican Council II: The Conciliar and Post Conciliar Documents* (Northport, N.Y.: Costello, 1975), p. 903.

tion that our common bonds of human dignity make speaking and acting together possible. Inculturation recognizes the presence of the *semina Verbi* that we encounter, and provides the social space where those seeds can germinate and grow, be pruned as needed, and be allowed to flourish within the *pleroma,* or fullness, of God's plan for the world.

The second approach to catholicity focuses on the gift of the fullness of faith as the venue for the understanding of faith. This fullness of faith is the revelation given to us by God in Jesus Christ, a treasure entrusted to the Church by Christ, and which is protected and transmitted through the visible teaching authority of the Church. The Church is therefore the depository and guarantor of the full and living faith that Christ has imparted to it. It is this *regula fidei* to which the Church conforms itself, and from which it draws its identity and purpose. The world was created good by God, but is sinful and fallen in such a way that it can never hope to rescue itself. Indeed, it at times cannot even recognize the truth in which it was created and by which it must live. The Church engages this world by juxtaposing itself to that world, offering the world an alternative view of itself in light of the truth that Christ has entrusted to the Church. The Church is the bearer of light and truth for a sinful and fallen world (one thinks here of the image of the Church offered at the beginning of another document of the Second Vatican Council, *Lumen gentium* — light of the nations). The Church offers the world not only God's revelation, but also the revelation of the true nature of the world itself. The world's hope is to listen to the Church and so enter the realm of the divine, the graced, and the transcendent which is the Church. Here the models of the earthly and heavenly cities presented in Augustine's great work, *The City of God,* provide the framework for understanding the world's destiny. The focal impetus for Augustine's work was the sack of Rome by the Visigoths in 410. Adherents of the old Roman religion blamed Christianity for weakening the empire and the dreadful experience of Rome being conquered. Augustine responded with a polemic *(contra paganos)* by juxtaposing the earthly city (which found its source of strength in the old Roman religion) and the City of God (at whose heart lay the Catholic Church). When one approaches *The City of God* as part of a larger genre, it can be deemed a literature of crisis. Crisis, I would suggest, is a key to understanding this second discourse of catholicity.

The intent of a theological literature of crisis is to protect the integrity of the faith, and to ensure a vigorous identity by practices that enhance that identity. It is that shared identity that guarantees the unity (and thereby, the integrity) of the Church's witness to the fullness of Christ and his message. The liturgy plays a central role here as a practice that creates identity and a proper focus on God. Mission is not so much about going out into the world and befriending it as it is about inviting the world into the Church and its doxological practices. There the world will find its true meaning. Mission is best understood in the parable of the great feast, where all are invited in to be part of the feast (Luke 14:16-24). Indeed, this served as the motive for mission in the Western Church from the time of Augustine into the late sixteenth century. The practices of this mission involve manifesting to the world the beauty and truth of God's revealing and redeeming acts, concretely presented in the visible Church, and urging individual persons to turn away from the sinfulness of the world and to conform themselves in ever greater holiness to the Lord and his Church. Sinfulness and evil are so pervasive within the world that changing the world's social structures will not lead to overcoming that sinfulness. Such utopian schemes confuse our power with the power of God. Only personal conversion and growth in holiness will make the difference. This approach too reads the "signs of the times," but in a different way — perhaps more as a "between the times," evocative of the journal of that name published by Protestant theologians in Germany in the 1920s. It is also closer to what may be the original meaning of the concept in the Gospels.[13] The "signs of the times" and the "signs" elsewhere in the Synoptic Gospels were apocalyptic ones, evidence of God's breaking into the sinful world with judgment and redemption. They bespeak a theology of history that sees the consummation of the world as possible only through a radical cleansing and purgation that can lead to a redeemed world. Signs of the times on this reading, therefore, make us watchful and ready for God's breaking into our world.

If the first approach is shaped by practices of solidarity, dialogue, and inculturation to foster catholicity, the second approach might find as its key practices contemplation of beauty, dwelling in the truth, and a celebration of the liturgy that focuses, in its beauty, on the transcendence of God as the way to the fullness of catholicity.

As one might surmise, those who would identify themselves with the understanding of the Second Vatican Council as making a radical turn to

---

13. For a history of the term, see Giuseppe Ruggieri, "Zeichen der Zeit. Herkunft und Bedeutung einer christlich-hermeneutischen Chiffre der Geschichte," in *Das zweite Vatikanische Konzil und die Zeichen der Zeit heute,* ed. Peter Hünermann (Freiburg: Herder, 2006), pp. 61-70.

the world and engaging in a significant rupture with the two centuries immediately preceding the Council would favor the first approach to catholicity, that of extension of the Church and engagement with the world. Those who see greater continuity with the past in the Council's documents would find a more likely domicile in the second approach, that of juxtaposing the Church to the world. The first approach is more optimistic about the current state of the world, despite the suffering and oppression that is so manifestly evident. God is overcoming that situation through the ministry of the Church. The second approach takes a darker look, and sees the world's redemption coming about less by human effort and more by strong intervention on the part of God.

When we turn to how globalization is to be perceived, one can discern certain parallels between the extension of globalization throughout the world and the extension of the Church throughout that same world. As the oldest and still most extensive transnational institution in the world, the Roman Catholic Church enjoys an extraordinary level of horizontal (communion between local communities) and vertical (hierarchical ordering) organization, more so than any other religious tradition. From that perspective, it can be seen as all-encompassing, and as such would be the envy of any other transnational organization. But there are clear differences as well. Globalization, by most accounts, has no goal, or *telos,* other than its own self-replication: more wealth accumulation, more control over resources. The Church, on the other hand, is not a goal within itself, but looks beyond itself to its Lord. It has a clear earthly *telos* as well, as expressed in Catholic social teaching about the common good, social solidarity, the requisites of justice, and integral human development. The relationships it seeks to foster in the human community are not principally instrumentalist but aimed at human flourishing. Globalization's view of the human has often been characterized as the human being as producer and consumer of goods; beyond that, individual humans are of little account. The anthropology of Christian faith accords every human being dignity and respect, even (and perhaps especially) those who are poor, weak, and too old or too young to count in globalization's reading of the world. Rather than being exclusionary, the Church seeks a "globalization of solidarity," in the words of the late John Paul II.[14]

The second approach, inasmuch as its discourse is shaped by a sense of

14. A handy sketch of Church teaching on globalization may be found in Giampolo Crepaldi, *Globalizzazione. Una prospettiva cristiana* (Siena: Cantagalli, 2006).

crisis and the need to offer an alternative to the world, is critical of globalization in a somewhat different way. It bespeaks a fear of idolatry — that the extension of globalization and the extension of the Church throughout the world can come to be confused or even equated with each other. The contrasts it draws between globalization and the Church are thus different from that of the first approach. In the second approach, beauty, the offering of truth, and the gesturing toward transcendence create a critique by contrast with globalization as the world sees it. The homogenizing forces of globalization — both economic and sociocultural — are often taken as normative and constitutive of the truth, something this second approach to catholicity firmly opposes. The particularities that are often heightened in locales in the face of the homogenizing forces of globalization can lead to a slackening of moral judgment; or, as Pope Benedict XVI characterized it, a "dictatorship of relativism." Globalization can appear as the complete logical extension of an immanentism that ends up circling back on itself, leaving no room for the transcendent and, consequently, the transcendent destiny of human beings.

Bridging the two approaches to catholicity is a theology and spirituality of communion, a concept important to both approaches. The two approaches enter the realm of communion by different gateways, however. Those closer to the first approach begin with the plurality of cultures and the place of the particular church within them, and then move toward a sense of unity. Those closer to the second approach begin with the unity in Christ embodied in the Universal Church and then proceed to the particular church and to plurality. In taking their respective approaches one immediately sees the advantages and disadvantages of each. The first approach appears to honor difference and otherness much more clearly by beginning with plurality. But it is often not clear what unity might mean if all that diversity is preserved as integral to the discussion. In other words, criteria for normativity and truth can seem to be lacking. The second approach clearly secures unity and normativity, but it is often difficult to tell whether diversity and plurality are really being taken seriously. Dialogue does not have an intrinsic value since it is not part of the quest for truth.

4. The Two Discourses of Catholicity, Globalization, and Post-Secularity

In this third section, I turn first to how these discourses of catholicity within Roman Catholicism affect living and acting in a globalized world in general, and in post-secular societies in particular. What picture do they give us of one major religious actor in these settings? Then I conclude with a few suggestions about what these perceptions and actions can contribute to a set of possible templates for religion's interaction with secularity in a post-secular society.

If one were to ask many thoughtful Catholics about which form of catholicity helps the Church live more faithfully and effectively in a global-ized world, the answer might be that it is not a matter of choosing one form of catholicity over against the other. Both have solid theological grounding and enjoy having been part of the Church's self-understanding since very early in Christianity. The situation of a globalized world, and of seeking the best ways to bring the Christian message to bear on that form of the world, has evoked distinctive ways of configuring catholicity in both ap-proaches. The first approach, as we have seen, attends to the plurality to be found in the world and tries to meet that plurality as much as possible on its own terms. It is grounded in a vision of creation and of grace that seeks out God's presence in the world, and engages in practices that serve to discipline and focus that vision (dialogue, for example) so as to foster bonds of solidarity with all persons of good will. It is only in this way that we might achieve the unity of all creation that God intends and God will complete in the final reconciliation of all things in Christ.

The second approach is less optimistic about the world it encounters. It sees the world in a time of crisis that calls the Church to foster a strong identity for the sake of unity and a proclamation of the truth of Christ amid contending claims and ideologies. It presents the Church as an al-ternative to the world; it is in the Church that the Divine and the divine intention may be experienced. Sin so besets the world that there is little to be learned from the world in its unredeemed state. Rather, the light and truth of Christ are to be presented and proclaimed, especially through the liturgy. The world is invited to enter the Church and experience the beauty of the form that the world is given as it is recast in grace.

In reality, one finds a good number of Catholics trying to combine elements from the two. As Pope Benedict XVI has noted, Catholicism is a religion of "both-and" rather than "either-or." The role of analogy in the Catholic imaginary remains strong. Indeed, Benedict XVI himself gave evidence of this. He clearly favored the second approach to catholicity, but mixed it with trying to be, for example, the "green pope" or presenting himself as using the latest forms of communications technology. His encyc-lical *Caritas in veritate* shows many of the commitments to solidarity that are central to the first approach.[15] Where the two approaches encounter each other (in connection or conflict) will be evident in the unfolding discussion about the New Evangelization — what does it take to be truly "Catholic" today?

Catholics live in a globalized world where things have become "unbundled" (to use Sassen's phrase).[16] There is a great deal of division and polarization marking many societies, especially those most in the picture in Taylor's book. The unbundling makes people forget the connections between things. Post-modern picking and choosing will be much in evidence.

We are likely to see such unbundling with other religious actors as well. This cautions us against generalizations about the role of religion in a post-secular society. It is yet another caution against an unreflective reductionism of the role of religion in the public sphere and the treating of it as an epiphenomenon.

Are there elements of the Roman Catholic Church's approach here that might contribute to developing some templates for expressing religion's place in a post-secular society? I would like to conclude by suggesting three.

First, religion questions the ultimate adequacy of the immanent frame. The immanent frame has been secured as much as possible by an optimistic anthropology from the French Enlightenment, with the limits of reason being transcended by Romanticism and the nineteenth-century ideologies. The danger of those ideologies — and their twentieth- and twenty-first-century offspring in communism and fascism — indicates that immanentist utopias can quickly turn dystopic.[17] Christianity (and a good deal of other religious traditions, for that matter) makes a case for an exo-centric view of humanity; in our finitude, we cannot be our own explanation. The "porous self" keeps reasserting itself. Religions are important ways of channeling those experiences (although they, too, sometimes get it wrong). This is not to discount the achievements of immanentist thinking; only to say that, in a post-secular world, they should be honored, but also seen as but one option.

---

15. See Mary Doak's discussion of Benedict's thought in chapter 9 in this volume.

16. Saskia Sassen used it first in speaking of sovereignty, but it has come to be applied in regard to other phenomena as well. See her *Globalization and Its Discontents: Essays on the New Mobility of People and Money* (New York: New Press, 1998).

17. See in this regard Richard Wolin, *The Seduction of Unreason: The Intellectual Romance with Fascism from Nietzsche to Postmodernism* (Princeton, N.J.: Princeton University Press, 2004).

What templates do the two approaches to catholicity present to the post-secular society, wherein religion takes its place alongside secular formations? In the first approach, religion engages secularity as the natural outgrowth of the reforming impulses that have marked Christianity from the beginning — a point central to Taylor's hypothesis about the genealogy of the secular. Religion cast in the mode of solidarity with the excluded, dialogue, and a commitment to inculturation develops a sympathetic yet critical posture toward secularity. It recognizes what it would consider legitimate trajectories within secularity (such as human rights discourse), yet at the same time points toward secularity's shortcomings or shortsightedness (as regards the transcendent).

The second approach gestures more pointedly toward the shortcomings of secularity, concerned as its catholicity is with beauty, truth, and transcendence. It challenges utilitarian or instrumentalist tendencies within secularity that threaten to flatten out humanity. While this second approach may appear to be inherently hostile to secularity, and less willing to engage it in dialogue (as would the first approach), its presenting itself as an alternative vision raises questions necessarily about the vision of secularity itself. The more pessimistic vision of humanity it presents also has at least the indirect advantage of calling to mind what can happen when the darker side of the Enlightenment vision can manifest itself again in totalitarian, anti-humanist alternatives to the sunniness of secular anthropology.

Second, with all the talk about a polycentric world, most of the thinking inspired by secularity still works with the center-periphery thinking that post-colonial writing has been working so hard to unveil. One aspect of thinking about catholicity that the Second Vatican Council tried to recover is what we find in Ignatius of Antioch. The Church is in its fullness in each particular or local church, but that fullness is completely expressed only in communion with other churches. One can make a case that, in practice, Roman Catholicism works with a strong center-periphery mentality, but the theology is there to imagine it differently. The inculturation debate is a concrete place within Catholicism to encounter that. There the fullness of Christ may be found in a local church.

This concern with center and periphery manifests itself in another way in secular society as it grapples with the ambivalences of democracy. Advanced information technologies make a kind of direct democracy possible, as has been seen in popular uprisings in different parts of the world since the late 1980s. At the same time, we have experienced weakness, if not deadlock, in central democratic governments in recent years as economic crises have had to be faced. Do the focuses on communion and communication in the two approaches to catholicity as described above give any hint of how we might work through the current challenges? The theological foundation of communion in the communion of the Persons of the Trinity might indicate a need to keep a heavily human- and person-oriented focus on solutions to social participation in government and in civil society, rather than too quickly seeking instrumentalist solutions.

The third contribution comes from the second approach to catholicity explored above. The optimistic anthropology that characterizes the immanent frame does not deal well with crisis and fear. The sense that we live in a "risk society," as Ulrich Beck has termed it,[18] requires ways of coming to terms with the incursion of threat and catastrophe into our lives. The liberal model of international relations deals well with the concept of power, but less well with what Dominique Moisi has called the "geopolitics of emotion."[19] Christianity and Islam, for example, have strong narratives of forgiveness that may be one of the few remedies against humiliation, a not uncommon phenomenon in the world of politics. Bringing this to bear on international relations will be an important dimension of a post-secular society.

Indeed, the long-time reflections on morality in religious traditions (and not simply within Christianity) may help us see how cognitive and emotional dimensions of action might be better construed in post-secular society. The European Enlightenment exalted reason, only to find itself overwhelmed by emotions — first in the Romanticism of the nineteenth century and then in the totalitarian regimes of the twentieth century. Efforts are now underway to come to a deeper understanding of how emotions shape moral judgment.[20] Here, religious traditions may have a contribution to make. In terms of understandings of catholicity, the first approach addresses especially well the experience of suffering, oppression, and exclusion. The second approach is especially concerned with moral formation and the practices that sustain morality.

18. Ulrich Beck, *World at Risk* (Malden, Mass.: Polity, 2009).

19. Dominique Moisi, *The Geopolitics of Emotion: How Cultures of Fear, Humiliation and Hope Are Reshaping the World* (New York: Anchor, 2010).

20. Jonathan Haidt, *The Righteous Mind: Why Good People Are Divided by Religion and Politics* (New York: Basic, 2012).

5. Conclusion

This chapter has attempted to look at how Roman Catholicism, an extensive social formation within the contemporary globalized world, is viewing its own relationship to that world through understandings of catholicity. The two approaches to catholicity map out, as it were, differing views of that globalized world, and suggest very different strategies for engaging that world. Because of the size and impact of Roman Catholicism, those views and strategies indicate ways in which religion might take its place alongside secularity in a post-secular society. To be sure, these two approaches are given only in sketches and generalities here; but it is hoped that they will stimulate our thinking about how, concretely, religion might engage post-secular society in the twenty-first century.

PART II

Post-Secularity? Critical Reflections

4. The Invention of the Religious-Secular Distinction

WILLIAM T. CAVANAUGH

There are different ways of understanding what it means to say that we live in a secular age. One is to understand religion as a feature of human societies across space and time. A secular age would then be an age in which religion was relatively more absent or had been relatively more marginalized from public life. In this understanding, the religious-secular distinction has always applied; secularization indicates the waning of the religious and the waxing of the secular. In this chapter I argue that there are good reasons to think that this first understanding is distorting because religion is not a transcultural and transhistorical feature of human societies. A more accurate way of understanding what it means to live in a secular age is to say that we live in an age in which the religious-secular distinction has been invented. That is, the religious and the secular were not separated in the modern West; they were created in the course of a contingent set of events that marked the transition from the medieval to the modern. This means that the distinction as we know it is not simply a fact about the world; it articulates and makes possible a contingent set of social arrangements that are not inevitable.

At the same time, part of what it means to live in a secular age is that the fact that the religion-secular distinction was invented is systematically denied or obscured. To claim that religion and non-religion are standard features of all societies at a certain stage of their development allows for the kind of secularist narrative that presents their separation as the proper sorting out of two essentially distinct aspects of reality that have been, at an earlier stage of development, mixed. To obscure the way that the religious-secular divide is a modern Western invention also allows this divide to be seen not as a parochial and contingent phenomenon with limited applicability, but rather as the universal fate of every society that reaches the same advanced stage of development as Western civilization.

This misrepresentation of the religious-secular divide as transhistorical and transcultural is a problem not only for those versions of a globalized "secularization thesis" that now find themselves on the defensive, but also for those voices that tout the global "resurgence of religion." The idea that religion was a universal phenomenon that once waned before secularizing forces but now waxes anew in many parts of the globe tends to apply an uncritical and Westernized view of religion to places and times where it confuses rather than clarifies the facts on the ground. Those who believe that religion as such waxes share with those who believe it wanes the idea that there is something readily identifiable as "religion" out there that forms a binary with readily identifiable "secular" phenomena. To speak of a "resurgence of Islam" as an instance of the "resurgence of religion" distorts because many scholars and practitioners of Islam do not consider it to be a religion, precisely because it does not make the kind of distinction between "religion" and "secular" phenomena like "politics" that is integral to the Western concept of "religion."

In this chapter I give reasons why this transhistorical and transcultural conception of religion and the secular is problematic and why it matters. I first consider the problems of defining the boundary between religion and the secular. Then I provide a brief genealogy of religion to show that is not a transhistorical or transcultural phenomenon. Finally, I suggest some of the ways that the religious-secular distinction distorts our understanding of the world we inhabit.

1. The Secular Is the Opposite of What?

The secular as it is most commonly thought is a remainder concept; it is defined over against religion, as the opposite of that which is religious. Defining the secular therefore depends on defining the religious. Defining religion, however, is a notoriously fraught enterprise. Nevertheless, much of the discussion around secularization consists of chatter about religion and the secular as if we all agreed on what we were talking about.

But we do not. We are not even close. There are at least three different schools of thought on the definition of religion — substantivism, functionalism, and constructivism — and they differ quite widely. The first school is commonly called "substantivism" because it defines religion based on the substance of the beliefs and practices of a particular community. Religion is defined based on beliefs in God or gods or supernatural beings or the transcendent or on some other form of belief. Because substantivists see religion as a universal phenomenon, the simple idea of religion as belief in God or gods is generally seen as not sufficiently inclusive. Substantivist views of religion generally identify religion with one or another of the lists of "world religions" that began to be developed by European scholars in the nineteenth century, lists that include things like Buddhism that do not always involve belief in God or gods. In order to include Theravada Buddhism, Taoism, Jainism, or Confucianism, a more inclusive term such as "transcendence" must be applied. To speak of religion, then, is to speak of a universal genus whose species include Christianity, Judaism, Islam, Buddhism, Hinduism, and a few other "world religions," and may include some other catch-all categories like "animism" or "Native American religions." The secular then includes political, economic, and social ideologies and practices that do not involve such beliefs in "the transcendent" or some such.

All of this seems to make perfect sense in a modern Western context in which many people go to churches and synagogues and mosques on weekends to express belief in God, then leave explicit reference to such beliefs behind when they go to their jobs on Monday. There might be some borderline cases — is Confucianism a religion or a philosophy? — but substantivists see the center of the concept as sufficiently stable to permit ready identification in most cases of what is religious and what is secular. The center tends to be a Western center, based on the idea of a transcendent God; other beliefs that are like belief in God are also included. What are religious are those things that are similar to the "Abrahamic traditions," especially Christianity.

When we step out of a Western context and begin to inquire into the so-called borderline cases, however, things begin to get interesting. Can we really include atheistic practices like many forms of Buddhism in the category of "religion"? Martin Southwold says this:

> We have shown that practical Buddhism does not manifest a central concern with godlike beings. Hence *either* the theistic definitions and conception of religion are wrong *or* Buddhism is not a religion. But the latter proposition is not a viable option. In virtually every other aspect Buddhism markedly resembles religions, and especially the religion prototypical for our conception, i.e. Christianity. If we declare that

Buddhism is not a religion, we take on the daunting task of explaining how a non-religion can come so uncannily to resemble religions.[1]

That Christianity is the prototypical religion says something instructive about the Western bias of the approach. It might not be coincidental that the taxonomy of world religions was first developed by European Christian scholars in the West. Southwold, nevertheless, is determined to include Buddhism in his category of "religion." He expands the definition of religion to include any phenomenon that has *at least one* from a list of twelve attributes, a list that includes "ritual practices," "a mythology," and "association with an ethnic or similar group." Southwold goes on to say that more attributes could be added to his list in order to include other things we consider to be religion.[2]

The problem with such an inclusive approach is that once one has expanded the criteria for what counts as a religion to include Buddhism, it is hard to exclude other kinds of ideologies and practices that substantivists consider to be "secular." Organized sports and their attendant "fans" (from the word "fanatics" derived from the Latin *fanum,* or temple) are centered around ritual practices. More gravely, nationalism appeals to the transcendent qualities of the "imagined community" of the nation, to use Benedict Anderson's phrase.[3] The term "civil religion" is commonly used to describe the devotions and rites that inspire the willingness to kill and die for one's country and one's flag. If godless Buddhism is a religion, is not also godless Marxism, with its various forms of rites and eschatology? If Confucianism is a religion, why not Platonism, which has a much greater claim than Confucianism to the notion of transcendence? The main problem substantivists confront is the difficulty of finding a convincing way of including what they want to include and excluding what they want to exclude from the category of religion without appearing arbitrary.

There is another type of approach, usually labeled "functionalism," that responds to these problems in substantivism by openly expanding the category of religion to include many things that substantivists would consider "secular." Functionalism is indebted to the work of Émile Durkheim,

1. Martin Southwold, "Buddhism and the Definition of Religion," quoted in S. N. Balagangadhara, *"The Heathen in His Blindness . . .": Asia, the West, and the Dynamic of Religion* (Leiden: Brill, 1994), p. 286.

2. Southwold, "Buddhism and the Definition of Religion," pp. 284-85.

3. Benedict Anderson, *Imagined Communities: Reflections on the Origin and Spread of Nationalism,* rev. ed. (London: Verso, 1991).

who thought that religion is a matter of social function, not mere belief. Religion is the way that a social group represents itself to itself. According to Durkheim, "Religious force is the feeling the collectivity inspires in its members, but projected outside and objectified by the minds that feel it. It becomes objectified by being anchored in an object which then becomes sacred, but any object can play this role."[4] The content of this object is unimportant. For Durkheim it does not matter, for example, if no one consciously believes that the national flag is a god. What matters is whether or not the flag serves to organize people in such a way that ritual boundaries between the sacred and the profane are reinforced. The empirical fact that people will, in certain times and places, kill and die for the flag is what makes nationalism a religion; it does not matter at all that the same people believe that the flag is an inanimate piece of cloth without "supernatural" powers.

For functionalists, if it walks like a duck and quacks like a duck, it is a duck; if people say "Capitalism is my religion," they are likely not just speaking metaphorically. There is an extensive scholarly literature on Marxism as a religion, from both friends and foes. Antonio Gramsci called Marxism "the religion that has to kill off Christianity. It is a religion in the sense that it is also a faith with its own mysteries and practices, and because in our consciences it has replaced the transcendental God of Catholicism with faith in Man and his best energies as the only spiritual reality."[5] The literature on civil religion and nationalism as religion is equally extensive. According to Carolyn Marvin and David Ingle, "nationalism is the most powerful religion in the United States, and perhaps in many other countries."[6] Others treat capitalist economics as a religion. Robert H. Nelson's book *Economics as Religion* argues that market economics has largely replaced Christianity in the West as the purveyor of eschatology, providence, priesthood, and a plan of salvation.[7]

I could continue to give examples almost ad infinitum, but the point should be clear enough: there is nothing like consensus on what constitutes the boundary between religious and secular. Seeing the incoherence of

4. Émile Durkheim, *The Elementary Forms of Religious Life,* trans. Carol Cosman (Oxford: Oxford University Press, 2001), p. 174.

5. Antonio Gramsci, quoted in Emilio Gentile, *Politics as Religion,* trans. George Staunton (Princeton, N.J.: Princeton University Press, 2006), p. 31.

6. Carolyn Marvin and David W. Ingle, "Blood Sacrifice and the Nation: Revisiting Civil Religion," *Journal of the American Academy of Religion* 44, no. 4 (Winter 1996): 768.

7. Robert H. Nelson, *Economics as Religion: From Samuelson to Chicago and Beyond* (University Park: Pennsylvania State University Press, 2001).

substantivist attempts to include some belief systems and exclude others, functionalists pay attention to the way that ideologies and practices actually function and come up with lists that radically redraw the boundaries of religious and secular. France is commonly considered to be the very model of a secular social order because of the way that it polices the public sphere to exclude "religion," by which is meant primarily Christianity and Islam. But if French nationalism and capitalism are in fact religions, then public space in France has not been secularized at all; Catholicism has simply been replaced with other religions.

The functionalist approach should come as no surprise to Jews and Christians who read the Bible. The first commandment is what it is in recognition of the fact that people are spontaneously worshiping creatures whose devotion is apt to fall on all sorts of false gods. As in Durkheim, the object itself matters little, nor is it necessary that the worshiper consciously think that his or her object of devotion is a deity. Jesus treats God and wealth as rivals for people's service (Matt. 6:24), and Paul remarks that some people's gods are their own bellies (Phil. 3:19). Though the Bible teaches faith in one true God who really exists (a claim Durkheim would likely reject), functionalism shares the biblical insight that the line between religion and non-religion is not so bright, and it is, in any case, not merely a matter of what people claim to believe, but how they actually behave.

2. The History and Politics of the Religious-Secular Divide

There are reasons, however, why a functionalist approach is not completely satisfactory either. One problem with functionalist approaches is that they cast the term "religion" so broadly as to render the term useless. If religion is practically anything that people take seriously, then the secular is the merely trivial. But this is clearly not how people use the terms. This brings us to the other problem with functionalism. Like substantivism, it is essentialist insofar as it makes claims about what really is a religion and what really is not. Religion is just as transcultural and transhistorical in functionalism as it is in substantivism. Insufficient attention is paid to the way that people actually use the terms "religious" and "secular." A more fruitful approach — constructivism — does not try to decide once and for all if Confucianism or Marxism or consumerism is really a religion. The real question is one of the historical and contextual uses of the terms. Why are some things labeled religions under certain circumstances and others are not? Why did Western scholars at the 1893 World's Parliament of Religions in Chicago regard Confucianism as a religion, while Peng Guanyu stood before them insisting that Confucianism is not a religion but rather a law of proper human relations?[8] Why did Christopher Hitchens insist that atheist Stalinism is a religion, but American nationalism is not?[9] Constructivism takes a historical approach and sees religious and secular as invented categories; they exist as constructions. The really interesting question is always why some things are labeled religious and others are not. What types of power are being exercised in the use of these categories?

To grasp the point of this approach, it is necessary to attend to some of the histories of the ideas of religious and secular that are now being done. Wilfred Cantwell Smith's classic 1962 book *The Meaning and End of Religion* demonstrated that there is no equivalent concept to the modern idea of "religion" in the pre-modern West or in any culture that has not come in contact with the modern West. As we understand it, religion is something distinct from secular endeavors such as politics and economics and culture. No such distinctions are found in ancient Greece, India, Egypt, China, or Japan.[10] "Religion" comes from the Latin term *religio,* which included cultic observances, some of which were directed toward gods, but also included civic oaths and family rituals, which modern Westerners would label "secular." As Augustine notes,

> "religion" [*religio*] is something which is displayed in human relationships, in the family (in the narrower and the wider sense) and between friends; and so the use of the word does not avoid ambiguity when the worship of God is in question. We have no right to affirm with confidence that "religion" [*religio*] is confined to the worship of God, since it seems that this word has been detached from its normal meaning, in which it refers to an attitude of respect in relations between a man and his neighbor.[11]

8. Charles Taylor, "Western Secularity," in *Rethinking Secularism,* ed. Craig Calhoun, Mark Juergensmeyer, and Jonathan VanAntwerpen (New York: Oxford University Press, 2011), p. 51.

9. Christopher Hitchens, *God Is Not Great: How Religion Poisons Everything* (New York: Twelve, 2007), pp. 242-49.

10. Wilfred Cantwell Smith, *The Meaning and End of Religion* (New York: Macmillan, 1962), pp. 18-19, 54-55.

11. Augustine, *City of God,* trans. Henry Bettenson (Harmondsworth: Penguin, 1972), X.1 (p. 373).

In pagan Rome there was furthermore no religion-politics distinction; how could there be, when Caesar was considered a god? After Constantine's conversion to Christianity, there is a distinction between civil and ecclesiastical authorities but not a distinction between religion and politics; Constantine considered himself to be something like a universal bishop whose duties respected no religion-politics distinction. If we fast-forward to the thirteenth century, we find still in the work of Thomas Aquinas no such distinction. For Aquinas, *religio* was a type of virtue that directed the person toward the worship of God, and it was not an activity separate from other "secular" concerns. "Every deed, in so far as it is done in God's honor, belongs to religion *(religio),*"[12] says Aquinas, and this includes the acts of human government, which is directed to the same end as *religio* and cannot succeed without *religio*.[13]

There does develop a type of religious-secular distinction in medieval Europe, but it bears very little resemblance to the modern use of the terms. The *saeculum* for the Romans referred to the maximum lifespan of a person, about a century. The secular in this sense came to refer in Christian Europe to the temporal order, as opposed to God's eternity, though it was used in phrases like *in saecula saeculorum* to refer to eternity, "from ages to ages" or "forever and ever." The primary use of the religious-secular distinction in medieval Christendom was to distinguish between two different types of clergy, those who belonged to orders such as the Dominicans, Franciscans, and Benedictines, and those who belonged to a diocese.[14] The latter, "secular clergy," were seen to be more directly engaged with temporal affairs. It is an overstatement, however, to say, as José Casanova does, that secular "became one of the terms of a dyad, religious-secular, that served to structure the entire spatial and temporal reality of medieval Christendom into a binary system of classification separating two worlds, the religious-spiritual-sacred world of salvation and the secular-temporal-profane world."[15] In the first place, *religio* was a very minor term in the Middle Ages, not half of reality. As Wilfred Cantwell Smith says, "throughout the whole Middle Ages, no one, so far as I have been able to

12. Thomas Aquinas, *Summa Theologiae* II-II.81.4 ad 2.

13. Thomas Aquinas, *On Kingship to the King of Cyprus,* trans. Gerald B. Phelan (Toronto: Pontifical Institute of Medieval Studies, 1949), p. 60 (Bk. II, ch. 3).

14. John Bossy, "Some Elementary Forms of Durkheim," *Past and Present* 95 (May 1982): 4.

15. José Casanova, "The Secular, Secularizations, and Secularisms," in *Rethinking Secularism,* ed. Calhoun et al., p. 56.

ascertain, ever wrote a book specifically on 'religion.' And on the whole this concept would seem to have received little attention."[16] In the second place, the temporal, as the word indicates, was not a space but a time, the time between the first and second comings of Jesus Christ. There was no spatial separation between a "world of salvation" and a world of ordinary mundane things that were removed from the spiritual life. The Eucharists celebrated by secular priests were not somehow less "religious-spiritual-sacred" than those celebrated by priests belonging to religious orders. The civil-ecclesiastical distinction was not a politics-religion distinction. The offices of king and bishop were seen Christologically as corresponding to the two natures of Christ, human and divine. There was no sense in which the temporal authority was found spatially outside of the Church.

The Investiture Controversy in the eleventh century did drive a wedge between civil and ecclesiastical authorities, but the result was something like the very opposite of what we now refer to as "secularization." Rather than kings shunning the spiritual life to concentrate on the merely mundane, kingship became increasingly sacralized. As the work of Ernst Kantorowicz documents, after Pope Gregory VII more or less successfully stripped civil rulers of their liturgical functions and direct involvement in ecclesiastical affairs, kings began to assert their own sacred authority direct from God, unmediated by the Church.[17] Civil rulers mined ecclesiastical symbolism to appropriate divine authority. By the fifteenth century, monarchies were expropriating the symbolism of Corpus Christi feasts; Charles VIII of France was given the titles "Lamb of God, saviour, head of the mystical body of France, guardian of the book with seven seals, fountain of life-giving grace to a dry people, and deified bringer of peace."[18] In England, Elizabeth I likewise substituted herself for the Host in Corpus Christi processions. In short, early modern monarchies were absolutized and took on many of the trappings of the sacred as their power over the churches increased. The first appearance of "secularization" as a noun was in sixteenth-century France, where it *(sécularisation)* meant the transfer of goods from the possession of the Church to the possession of "worldly" authority.[19] Just as the emerging sovereign state

16. Smith, *Meaning and End*, p. 32.

17. Ernst Kantorowicz, *The King's Two Bodies: A Study in Medieval Political Theology* (Princeton, N.J.: Princeton University Press, 1957).

18. John Bossy, *Christianity in the West, 1400-1700* (Oxford: Oxford University Press, 1985), pp. 154-55.

19. Jan N. Bremmer, "Secularization: Notes Toward a Genealogy," in *Religion: Beyond a Concept*, ed. Hent de Vries (New York: Fordham University Press, 2008), p. 433.

appropriated property from the Church in the early modern period, so it also appropriated power, as it took control of ecclesiastical appointments and revenues and shut down ecclesiastical courts. More intangibly but no less real, the state also appropriated a sense of the sacred unto itself. In the rise of the modern state, we do not see anything like the process of secularization as the fading away of a public sense of the sacred. What we see instead is the "secularization" of the sacred, that is, the transfer of the holy from the church to the state.

This sacralization of the state nevertheless does contribute to the invention of the secular in the modern sense, for the rise of the state's power is predicated on the absorption of power from the church, and the consequent diminishment of the public power of ecclesiastical authority, which is one of the modern meanings of "secularization." From the late fifteenth to the late seventeenth centuries, "religion" develops in a way that breaks decisively with the medieval concept of *religio*. Beginning with Renaissance Platonists like Nicholas of Cusa and Marsilio Ficino, religion comes to be a transhistorical and transcultural human impulse implanted in the human heart that takes on different external forms.[20] Under Calvinist influence in the later sixteenth century, religion comes to be identified with sets of beliefs, and true religion is seen as something essentially interior, a matter of faith and not primarily of external rites and actions. Only in the later seventeenth century do the religion-politics and religious-secular distinctions begin to be employed in something like their modern senses.

Timothy Fitzgerald's careful work on the concept of religion in English usage has shown that in the sixteenth and seventeenth centuries "religion" in England primarily referred to revealed Christian truth, especially Protestant truth, whose opposite was not politics or the secular but superstition and falsity. There was no realm of "politics" yet, only the adjective "politic," as in the expression "the politic body" which, as Fitzgerald writes, "is not 'politics' in the modern sense of a distinct domain, secular or nonreligious, but in the sense of policy formed wisely for human salvation, godly living, and the solution of conflicts, especially between governments."[21] Fitzgerald traces the earliest recognizably modern uses of the religion-politics

20. See my genealogy of the development of religion in my book *The Myth of Religious Violence: Secular Ideology and the Roots of Modern Conflict* (New York: Oxford University Press, 2009), pp. 60-85.

21. Timothy Fitzgerald, *Discourse on Civility and Barbarity: A Critical History of Religion and Related Categories* (New York: Oxford University Press, 2007), p. 177.

distinction in English to William Penn and John Locke. In his *The Great Question to Be Considered by the King,* published in 1680, Penn writes:

> Religion and Policy, or Christianity and Magistracy, are two distinct things, have two different ends, and may be fully prosecuted without respect one to the other; the one is for purifying, and cleaning the soul, and fitting it for a future state; the other is for Maintenance and Preserving of Civil Society, in order to the outward conveniency and accommodation of men in the World. A Magistrate is a true and real Magistrate, though not a Christian; as well as a man is a true and real Christian, without being a Magistrate.[22]

Here, though the term "politics" is not yet in use, we find the modern dichotomies of religion and government policymaking, which follows soul-body, inward-outward, and otherworldly/this-worldly dichotomies. Locke likewise constructs religion as inward and otherworldly, in opposition to the business of the civil government, which takes care of external, worldly goods: "All the life and power of true religion consist in the inward and full persuasion of the mind."[23] As opposed to medieval understandings, here the interior of the person is essentially distinct from the external disciplines that form the virtues, including faith. In Locke, too, we find an early version of the modern religion-secular distinction: "In the variety and contradiction of opinions in religion, wherein the princes of the world are as much divided as in their secular interests, the narrow way would be much straitened."[24] Another crucial move is the identification of the church with religion, while the government's business is the promotion of "civil interests," which Locke defines as "life, liberty, health, and indolency of the body; and the possession of outward things, such as money, lands, houses, furniture, and the like."[25] The redefinition of the church as a "religious society" removes it spatially from worldly jurisdiction:

> The end of a religious society . . . is the public worship of God and, by means thereof, the acquisition of eternal life. All discipline ought

22. William Penn, *The Great Question to Be Considered by the King,* quoted in Fitzgerald, *Discourse on Civility,* pp. 272-73.

23. John Locke, *A Letter Concerning Toleration* (Indianapolis: Bobbs-Merrill, 1955), p. 18.

24. Locke, *A Letter,* p. 19.

25. Locke, *A Letter,* p. 17.

therefore to tend to that end, and all ecclesiastical laws to be thereunto confined. Nothing ought nor can be transacted in this society relating to the possession of civil and worldly goods. No force is here to be made use of upon any occasion whatsoever. For force belongs wholly to the civil magistrate, and the possession of all outward goods is subject to his jurisdiction.[26]

The church here is essentially concerned with preparing souls for the afterlife. At the same time that "religion" and the church take on wholly new meanings, the civil authority is also being redefined from a power within the church and within the larger structure of Christian truth that has charge, through the providence of God, of temporal judgment and punishment, to a power that stands outside of the church and religion, and has charge of worldly goods that now are seen as autonomous and not of essential concern to Christianity.

To call this process the "privatization of religion," as is commonly done, is to see religion as something transhistorical and essentially distinct from politics. Religion, we often like to say, was "mixed" with politics in the medieval era, and in modernity the two were sorted out. This is a crucial part of the process of "secularization" in most conceptions of the term. To speak in this way, however, is to regard the end result of this process as if it were already embedded in the nature of things before the process began. Religion and politics were not separated; they were inventions of the modern era. The way that Penn and Locke described these terms was prescriptive, not simply descriptive. They were both deeply involved in the creation of a new type of order, one which, not coincidentally, stood to favor their own interests. Both were associated with dissenting Christians, and both had significant business investments in the American colonies. Penn's holdings in the New World made him the largest private landowner in the world, and Locke was a major investor in the English slave trade to the Americas, as well as an overseer of the Carolina plantations. To divide the church from the realm of worldly commerce and governance meant that members of the dissenting churches could carry on business without the interference of clerics or theological ideas. To recognize this is not necessarily to reject liberal social order or to question the wisdom of the U.S. Constitution's arrangements regarding church and state, to which both Penn and Locke contributed. It is to recognize, however, that the

26. Locke, *A Letter*, pp. 22-23.

construction of religion and politics in the early modern period was itself a political process and not simply the sorting out of two essentially distinct human endeavors.

The creation of religion and its opposite — the secular realm in which all worldly pursuits such as politics, business, and the like were included — was inseparable from the rise of the modern state. It was not a coincidence that they arose at the same moment. Charles Taylor has traced the way that a new emphasis on the interior life in late medieval Europe and especially in the Reformation paved the way for the new secular age. According to Taylor, the emphasis on interior faith commitment tended to de-emphasize communal rituals that were the glue of medieval society, while simultaneously disenchanting the external world of magic and spirits. This process began in late medieval devotional practices and movements like the Devotio Moderna and the Brethren of the Common Life, and greatly accelerated in the Reformation's emphasis on *sola fide*. The Catholic Reformation also emphasized personal commitment, and rulers marshaled both Protestant and Catholic practices to create a disciplined populace through the process of "confessionalization."[27] Taylor's analysis in this regard is interesting and fairly convincing, but I do not think he takes sufficient account of the role of the rise of the modern state in the creation of the religious-secular divide. The rise of the modern state was made possible by the centralization of civil authority over against the many forms of local association that made up medieval Christendom, including ecclesiastical associations. In the fifteenth and sixteenth centuries, ecclesiastical courts were abolished, monastic foundations were dissolved, and ecclesiastical appointments and revenues fell under civil control. This was in many ways the final act of a long contest for supremacy between civil and ecclesiastical authorities dating back to the time of Constantine. When the mechanism of the modern state allowed civil rulers to consolidate their power, "religion" — defined as essentially otherworldly — became the province of ecclesiastical authorities. This account does not contradict Taylor's, but it also is not simply another, separate factor to take into account. The creation of inward religion and the emphasis on personal commitment were inseparable from the rise of the modern state. Indeed, the process of "confessionalization," which has been integral to many historians' account of the rise of the modern state,

27. Charles Taylor, *A Secular Age* (Cambridge, Mass.: Harvard University Press, 2007), pp. 90-158.

is inseparable from the process of interiorization that Taylor describes. As historian Luther Peterson summarizes it:

> The confessionalization thesis is a fruitful instrument in explaining the transformation of medieval feudal monarchies into modern states, in particular how the new states changed their inhabitants into disciplined, obedient and united subjects. According to the thesis, a key factor in that change is the establishment of religious uniformity in the state: the populace was taught a religious identity — Catholic, Lutheran, or Calvinist — through doctrinal statements (confessions and catechisms) and liturgical practices. This distinguished "us" as a religious and political community from "other," often neighboring, religious-political societies. The ruler was sacralized as the defender and — in Protestant lands — leader of the church, rightfully overseeing the church of his land. These state-led churches also aided state development by imposing moral discipline on the communities.[28]

To accept this thesis is not at all to say that the process of individualization and interiorization of Christian faith that Taylor describes was a cynical state-sponsored conspiracy to augment state control. It is to say rather that the gradual movement from traditional collective and ritualistic forms of Christianity to more individual and ethically demanding forms was inseparable from the establishment of state dominance over the church in both Protestant and Catholic territories in the early modern period. In other words, the emphasis on lay piety that Taylor documents is one with the triumph of lay over clerical authority in the early modern state.

The broader point I am trying to make is that "religion" as it appears in religious-secular, religion-politics, and other similar binaries, is not a universal feature of all human societies across time and space but is rather a contingent invention that arose from the very particular circumstances of early modern Christian Europe. "Religious" and "secular" are not neutral descriptors but help to create a different kind of world in which power is arranged in a manner quite distinct from the way it was arranged in the medieval period or in non-European contexts. Taking a brief look at some

28. Luther D. Peterson, "Johann Pfeffinger's Treatises of 1550 in Defense of Adiaphora: 'High Church' Lutheranism and Confessionalization in Albertine Saxony," in *Confessionalization in Europe, 1555-1700: Essays in Honor of Bodo Nischan*, ed. John M. Headley, Hans J. Hillerbrand, and Anthony J. Papalas (Aldershot: Ashgate, 2004), pp. 104-5.

of those latter contexts can help to make this point clearer. Looking for the concept of "religion" in non-Western contexts, Wilfred Cantwell Smith writes, "One is tempted, indeed, to ask whether there is a closely equivalent concept in any culture that has not been influenced by the modern West." His answer is "no."[29] Since Smith, a host of other scholars have produced detailed histories of the formation of the concept of "religion" in concert with the colonization of the world by European powers. In their initial encounters with local peoples, European explorers consistently reported back home that the natives had no religion at all.[30] When the local peoples were colonized, however, diverse cultural practices and rituals came to be constructed as species of the universal genus "religion," despite the awkward fit of some practices, as in the example of atheistic forms of Buddhism referred to above. The concept of religion and the religious-secular divide proved useful for colonizers because it allowed the categorization of local cultures as essentially religious and therefore essentially private. The British in India, for example, could preside over the putatively neutral and secular sphere of commerce and government without interfering with Hindu religion. When Hinduism — which encompasses much of what Westerners divide into culture, politics, religion, economics, and art — was made a religion, it cleared a public space for the British to operate.

The dividing of the world between religious and nonreligious activities, however, has seldom been uncontested. Confucian scholars at the end of the nineteenth century insisted that Confucianism was not a religion, and Liang Chichao said that "there is no religion among the indigenous products of China."[31] Chinese scholars thought that religion was inherently individualistic and therefore inimical to Chinese national unity. In the same period, and for similar reasons, the Japanese government made a strict distinction between shrine Shinto and religion, only to find Shinto defined as a religion and privatized by the U.S.-imposed constitution at the conclusion of World War II. As Sarah Thal writes, "After years of denying the religiosity of Shinto, priests and apologists found themselves suddenly

29. Smith, *Meaning and End*, pp. 18-19.

30. See the examples I give in Cavanaugh, *The Myth of Religious Violence*, p. 86. What follows is a drastically abbreviated summary of the invention of religion outside the West in my book, pp. 85-101.

31. Peter Beyer, "Defining Religion in Cross-National Perspective: Identity and Difference in Official Conceptions," in *Defining Religion: Investigating the Boundaries Between the Sacred and the Secular,* ed. Arthur L. Greil and David G. Bromley (Oxford: JAI, 2003), pp. 174-75.

defined as religious, limited by the very principle of freedom of religious belief which they had once overcome by defining themselves against religion."[32] Nor are these contests over "religion" now settled. Many advocates of Hindu nationalism reject the idea that Hinduism is a religion, precisely because their vision of Hinduism is much broader than a set of individualized beliefs about gods. They want to encourage and institutionalize an India in which Hinduism is embraced in all its fullness as culture, politics, economics, and so on. This becomes possible within the confines of an officially "secular" state if Hinduism is not a "religion."[33]

The above is just the briefest sampling of the histories being done of the concepts of religion and the secular in colonial and post-colonial contexts. The titles of the books — for example, Tomoko Masuzawa's *The Invention of World Religions,*[34] Daniel Dubuisson's *The Western Construction of Religion,*[35] Derek Peterson and Darren Walhof's *The Invention of Religion* — tell the story of religion as a constructed and contested category, not a timeless and universal human phenomenon. The global importance or "rise" of religion is a fact in the precise sense that "religion" *as a discursive category* — along with its twin, the secular — has moved out from its European roots to become a category used throughout the world. It is used in very different ways, however, and the meaning needs to be examined within each particular context.[36] Religion and its secular twin are furthermore Western categories that spread to the rest of the world through the process of Western colonialism and continued Western power in the rest of the world. As the examples above indicate, the distribution of power was involved in each case. "Religious" and "secular" as they have been constructed originally in Europe and subsequently in the rest of the world are not neutral descriptive terms, but are rather prescriptive. They help create the worlds they purport to describe. They are, as Fitzgerald says, "collective affirmations about what kind of world we want

32. Sarah Thal, "A Religion That Was Not a Religion," in *The Invention of Religion: Rethinking Belief in Politics and History,* ed. Derek Peterson and Darren Walhof (New Brunswick, N.J.: Rutgers University Press, 2002), p. 111.

33. Richard S. Cohen, "Why Study Indian Buddhism?" in *Invention of Religion,* ed. Peterson and Walhof, pp. 26-27.

34. Tomoko Masuzawa, *The Invention of World Religions; or, How European Universalism Was Preserved in the Language of Pluralism* (Chicago: University of Chicago Press, 2005).

35. Daniel Dubuisson, *The Western Construction of Religion: Myths, Knowledge, and Ideology,* trans. William Sayers (Baltimore: Johns Hopkins University Press, 2003).

36. See Casanova's comments to this effect in Casanova, "The Secular," pp. 62-63.

to experience."[37] Once this point is grasped, then we can stop taking for granted that Hinduism is a religion when significant Hindu voices insist that it is not. The real question is not whether or not Hinduism is really a religion, but what kinds of power are being deployed by either affirming or denying the "religious" nature of Hinduism. Likewise, there is little point to debating how religious and how secular any given society is when the boundaries between religious and secular are so contingent and fluid. To say that we live in a secular age is really to acknowledge that we live in an age where the religious-secular distinction has been invented and continues to be deployed to buttress certain kinds of social arrangements. A truly analytical and critical study of the secular will not treat religion and the secular as categories that are embedded in the nature of things because all the evidence points to the contingency and fluidity of the concepts. A truly critical investigation will examine how, and for what purposes, these categories are employed.

3. Disenchantment?

One way the categories are employed is to separate a realm of enchanted, otherworldly, non-rational belief and behavior from a realm of disenchanted, mundane reason. That which is labeled "religious" can be valued or not, but it is seen as essentially distinct from the public, "secular" realm of reason. One common Western trope is the idea that "religion" is essentially more prone to violence than "secular" ideologies and institutions. Violence done in the name of "religion" is considered irrational and always reprehensible, whereas violence done in the name of "secular" interests — the nation, freedom, oil, and so on — is sometimes necessary and even praiseworthy. The religious-secular divide is one way of delegitimating certain kinds of violence and legitimating others.[38]

Charles Taylor's analysis of the secular age does not identify the religious-secular divide with unreason-reason or violence-peaceableness, and he conveys a clear sense that something important has been lost in the disenchantment of the modern world.[39] Nevertheless, he does identify

---

37. Fitzgerald, *Discourse on Civility*, p. 24.

38. This is the argument I make at length in *The Myth of Religious Violence*.

39. "The process of disenchantment, which involved a change in us, can be seen as the loss of a certain sensibility, which is really an impoverishment (as opposed to the simple shedding of irrational feelings)" (Taylor, "Western Secularity," p. 39).

the religious-secular distinction with enchantment-disenchantment, and I remain unconvinced that the two distinctions track each other as closely as Taylor seems to indicate. For Taylor, the development of more interior forms of piety in the late medieval and early modern periods led to a disenchantment of the external world, a repression of magic and superstition. With the Protestant Reformation's emphasis on faith and de-emphasis on ritual came the evacuation of spirits from the external world; for example, the powers inherent in relics and places of pilgrimage faded in importance. Taylor makes clear that this is not yet the fading of religion, as in Max Weber's use of the term "disenchantment," but is closer to the root of Weber's German term *Entzauberung,* the diminishment of *Zauber,* or magic. In Taylor's sense, disenchantment is not yet the loss of religion, but paves the way for its eventual removal from public and the secularization of the world.

According to Taylor, "Everyone can agree that one of the big differences between us and our ancestors of 500 years ago is that they lived in an 'enchanted' world and we do not."[40] Taylor describes this difference as a difference in "sensibility" or "existential condition." Our ancestors lived with "porous selves," in which the boundaries between the self and the other, the inner and the outer, were much more fluid. The porous self was vulnerable to spirits, demons, and other cosmic forces not under the self's control. This was not a matter of belief; such forces existed as facts in the world. Such forces were not always spirits with wills; "black bile," for example, was associated with melancholy. Here, Taylor stresses, black bile is not the cause of melancholy, it simply *is* melancholy. There can be no distancing of one's emotional condition from one's body. For the modern, "buffered" self, by way of contrast, knowing that some chemical is the physical cause of depression helps to distance the emotional state from the physical state. "Modern Westerners have a clear and firm boundary between mind and world, even mind and body."[41] The buffered self can put distance between the self and what lies outside the self. We make up our minds about what lies beyond the self. Things outside the self do not grip us in the same way they did our pre-modern ancestors. We eagerly embrace horror movies about ghosts and vampires and zombies because we want the pleasurable frisson from things that no longer really terrorize us.[42]

---

40. Taylor, "Western Secularity," p. 38.
41. Taylor, "Western Secularity," p. 40.
42. Taylor, "Western Secularity," pp. 41-42.

There is no question that things have changed in the last five hundred years. I am not sure, however, that describing the change is as simple as describing the way people experience the world. We need to take full account not only of the way people experience the world but of the categories that people use to describe the way they experience the world. It may be that we live in Descartes's world, not in the sense that the Cartesian mind-body dualism better describes our world, but in the sense that the way we describe our experience of the world has been shaped by Cartesian categories. We may have learned that the experience of shopping is a "secular" experience, one having nothing to do with demons or gods or supernatural powers. An empirical observation of the behavior of U.S. shoppers on Black Friday, however, may indicate that the boundaries between the self and the world of material goods is not as buffered as Taylor describes it. There is a sense in which, as I have argued elsewhere, consumerism detaches the modern, affluent, Western self from production of the goods we consume and the people who manufacture them; there is even a sense in which consumers are detached from the products they consume because their desires constantly move from one product to another. But to describe this process as "disenchantment" is to miss the "magic" that is associated with products in a world made of marketing, and to miss the fantasy construction of the self as one that transcends and consumes the material world. The very construction of the self as transcendent — and, in this sense, "buffered" — in other words, can be itself a kind of enchantment.

It is certainly not the case that everyone can agree that we live in a disenchanted world. Eugene McCarraher's 2005 article "The Enchantments of Mammon" argues — persuasively, in my view — that "Far from being an unambiguous agent of disenchanted secularity, capitalism might be best understood as a perverse regime of the sacred, an order of things bearing powerful and unmistakable traces of enchantment."[43] McCarraher presents an alternative history of capitalism beginning with Marxist analyses of commodity fetishism, the way that in capitalism material objects are invested with mystical powers. Such analyses of the transfiguration of commodities are found not only in Marx himself, but in Lukacs, Jameson, Bataille, and Benjamin, and, in more explicitly theological form, in the recent work of Slavoj Zizek. McCarraher also traces this alternative history through psychoanalysis, especially Norman O. Brown's analysis

43. Eugene McCarraher, "The Enchantments of Mammon: Notes Toward a Theological History of Capitalism," *Modern Theology* 21, no. 3 (July 2005): 430.

of the "money complex," which Brown calls "the heir to and substitute for the religious complex, an attempt to find God in things," adding that "secularization is only a metamorphosis of the sacred."[44] From a Christian point of view, McCarraher agrees with these diagnoses of enchantment in modernity, but responds with a Christian theology of sacraments, a true account of finding God in things. For McCarraher, enchantment is just sacramentality gone bad. But modernity is not properly characterized as simply lacking a sense that higher powers inhere in the external world of material objects.

Economy is not the only place where we might look for enchantment in the modern world. As I have already indicated, analyses of "civil religion" and "the religion of nationalism" commonly note how patriotic ritual turns objects like the flag into sacred totems. Taylor recognizes the continuation of such rituals in the secular world, but thinks that they are essentially distinct from religious rituals as experienced in pre-modern societies. "Of course, we go on having rituals — we salute the flag, we sing the national anthem, we solemnly rededicate ourselves to the cause — but the efficacy here is inner; we are, in the best case, 'transformed' psychologically; we come out feeling more dedicated. . . . The 'symbol' now invokes in the sense that it awakens the thought of the meaning in us. We are no longer dealing with a real presence. We can now speak of an act as 'only symbolic.'"[45] I think Taylor is right that we certainly do speak this way. But I do not think Taylor is sufficiently attentive to why we speak this way now. It may not be that we are simply using new categories to describe a new kind of experience; it may be that the categories themselves help to shape the description, and therefore the experience itself. In other words, the description of patriotic ritual as "only symbolic" might not be merely descriptive, but prescriptive; it might be doing some political work. To recognize patriotic ritual as "religious," as more than only symbolic, puts it on the same level as "traditional religions" such as Christianity and Judaism, and thereby sets up a confrontation between church and state over idolatry. To deny that patriotic ritual is religious, to call it "only symbolic," is to preserve Western political arrangements from challenge.

44. Norman O. Brown, quoted in McCarraher, "The Enchantments of Mammon," p. 443. An excellent recent account of money as occupying in modern society the place that God occupied in pre-modern society is Philip Goodchild's book *Theology of Money* (Durham, N.C.: Duke University Press, 2009).

45. Taylor, "Western Secularity," p. 51.

Taylor's account of enchantment and disenchantment relies too heavily on people's descriptions of their own beliefs, and not on their empirically observable behaviors. People may fully recognize that the nation is not a god, that the flag is just a piece of cloth, that the cause to which they are dedicating themselves is a temporal one, but what really matters is what they do with their bodies. If they are willing to kill and die for something they would describe as "only symbolic," then their dedication to the cause is manifestly *not* something whose "efficacy here is inner," as Taylor puts it. It is not only that Taylor's account of internalization is itself too internalized. It is that the modern trope of internalization is itself an effect of external, political arrangements of power. To say that my ritual patriotic actions are "only symbolic" allows me to be a good Christian and a good American soldier at the same time.

Consider Taylor's account of ritual sacrifice among the Dinka, an example he offers of "enchantment":

> The major agents of the sacrifice, the "masters of the fishing spear," were in a sense "functionaries," acting for the whole society; while on the other, the whole community became involved, repeating the invocations of the masters until everyone's attention was focused and concentrated on the single ritual action. It was at the climax that those attending the ceremony were "most palpably members of a single undifferentiated body." This participation often took the form of possession by the divinity being invoked.[46]

Compare this to Mark Twain's account of his fellow citizens' behavior during wartime:

> The loud little handful — as usual — will shout for the war. The pulpit will — warily and cautiously — object . . . at first. The great, big, dull bulk of the nation will rub its sleepy eyes and try to make out why there should be a war, and will say, earnestly and indignantly, "It is unjust and dishonorable, and there is no necessity for it."
>
> Then the handful will shout louder. A few fair men on the other side will argue and reason against the war with speech and pen, and at first will have a hearing and be applauded, but it will not last long; those

---

46. Taylor, "Western Secularity," p. 43. The internal quotation is from Godfrey Lienhardt.

others will outshout them, and presently the antiwar audiences will thin out and lose popularity.

Before long, you will see this curious thing: the speakers stoned from the platform, and free speech strangled by hordes of furious men. . . .

Next the statesmen will invent cheap lies, putting the blame upon the nation that is attacked, and every man will be glad of those conscience-soothing falsities, and will diligently study them, and refuse to examine any refutations of them; and thus he will by and by convince himself that the war is just, and will thank God for the better sleep he enjoys after this process of grotesque self-deception.[47]

Do we not here too see the whole community repeating the invocations of the masters, becoming possessed by a kind of divine force, and acting as a single body to prosecute the blood sacrifice? What Twain describes is not the action of "buffered selves," and the enchanted-disenchanted or religious-secular dichotomies applied to these two examples would only obscure rather than illuminate what is going on. And that is precisely why they are used.

If we can see that what is commonly marked out as "secular" can also exhibit the traits of "enchantment," then we can see that religion is not a stable category but is defined in different ways in different places based on the kinds of power that are in play. The secular is in fact often regarded as sacred. Another way to put this is to say that the sacred-profane distinction does not track the religious-secular distinction. As Casanova puts it,

> the modern secular is by no means synonymous with the "profane," nor is the "religious" synonymous with the modern "sacred." . . . In this respect, modern secularization entails a certain profanation of religion through its privatization and individualization and a certain sacralization of the secular spheres of politics (sacred nation, sacred citizenship, sacred constitution), science (temples of knowledge), and economics (through commodity fetishism). But the truly modern sacralization, which constitutes the global civil religion in Durkheim's terms, is the cult of the individual and the sacralization of humanity through the globalization of human rights.[48]

47. Mark Twain, *The Mysterious Stranger* (1910), http://www.commondreams.org/viewso2/0920-01.htm, accessed on July 3, 2012.

48. Casanova, "The Secular," p. 65. For similar reasons, Fitzgerald suggests that sacred-

Casanova's final point about the cult of the individual indicates that the new modern subject that Taylor describes might not be adequately characterized as occupying a space that is the opposite of the sacred. This relates to Taylor's treatment of "optionality." Taylor has pointed to the idea of the optionality of religion as a genuinely new phenomenon in the world, one that sets the secular age off dramatically from all previous ages. What makes our age genuinely new is the situation in which Christianity, for example, must be chosen and internalized by the individual and could be discarded, in ways that would have been impossible for a medieval European to consider. An ambiguity in Taylor's account, however, results from the fact that, as Hent de Vries puts it, "optionality in the 'secular age' is hardly an option itself."[49] Taylor presents optionality as simply the condition of our age, and he seems to admit that this new contingent construction of reality is passed off as a simple discovery, as in Locke, such that its own provisional and optional character is obscured. But if this is the case, can we opt out of optionality? Could optionality lose its appeal, and be revealed to have been merely optional? If not, then isn't secular optionality the very kind of "naivete" that Taylor thinks we have outgrown or lost? Secular optionality may be the overarching mythos of the secular age, the transcendent and sovereignly choosing self replacing the transcendent God, liberalism as a kind of "religion" that is capable of producing the same kinds of idolatry and violence that other so-called religions have produced. If liberalism is itself a type of "religion," then the holy has not been outgrown or lost or rendered optional, but has simply migrated from the church to the state and the market. And if this is the case, then modernity and the "secular age" is not as complete a rupture with the past as Taylor habitually portrays it. The secular age — in addition to its many blessings, not least the removal of the coercive power from

---

profane is a much less misleading distinction than religious-secular. The secular is defined over against religion as neutral or hostile to religion. There was no such space in the medieval era. There was, however, a relevant distinction between sacred and profane, which was one of relative gradations, not contrasts. The blacksmith's work was relatively more profane than the work of the priest, but by no means did the blacksmith's labor occupy a space indifferent to God or Christianity. The blacksmiths' guilds participated in saints' feasts and other processions of the liturgical calendar that marked their work as an integral, if lower, part of the hierarchy that included both heaven and earth. See Fitzgerald, *Discourse on Civility,* pp. 71-108.

49. Hent de Vries, "The Deep Conditions of Secularity," *Modern Theology* 26, no. 3 (July 2010): 391.

the church — presents us with new forms of the age-old sin of idolatry to compete for our allegiances.

4. Conclusion

Dealing with the phenomenon of secularization is not a matter of determining what society ought to do with religion, as if religion were simply a basic human activity found "out there" in all times and places to which various attitudes can be taken. Secularization is clearly a modern Western phenomenon, but more importantly the religious-secular distinction itself is a modern Western phenomenon, one that, by presenting itself as the simple recognition of a fact about our world, makes certain contingent features of Western modernity seem natural. This way of narrating the world can in turn provide cover for certain kinds of violence, especially those that absolutize the secular nation-state or the liberal ideal of secular social order as ideals worth killing for.

What all of this implies for a Christian approach to the question of the secular is that we not be too quick to accept the terms under which the conversation is often conducted. If the boundaries between the religious and the secular are fluid, then every instantiation of such a boundary must be interrogated for the kind of power it reflects and reinforces. This does not necessarily mean that all religious-secular distinctions are to be rejected. It does mean, however, that we should question triumphalistic narratives of the secular nation-state and the depreciation of those, such as Muslims, who do not acquiesce to the supposed naturalness and inevitability of secular social orders. For Christians it should also mean being aware of migrations of the holy and the functional idolatries that often inhabit state and market.

5. The Post-Secular Problematic

WILLIAM A. BARBIERI JR.

One way of orienting ourselves in the world involves focusing on the very quality of *worldliness,* and this is what we do when we reflect on the secular and the varied roots and cognates associated with it: *saeculum,* secularity, secularism, secularization. What is this world in which we find ourselves?[1] ("Oh, what a world! What a world!" wails the Wicked Witch of the West, melting.)[2] What are its limits or horizons, and what lies beyond? What are its essential features? How do these features shape our condition, and even, to some extent, constitute us? How should we act given these features? How do they affect us over time; indeed, how do they affect time itself?

Conceptions of worldliness for reflective and self-transcendent beings: that is what accounts of secularity are. Attempts to capture the meaning of the mundane, to collect insights into immanence, and to plumb the nature of the natural all build on an edifice of perceptions mediating between us and our surroundings in time and space, a structure that locates us as living "in a secular world" or in a "secular age" — two phrases that flirt with redundancy as their common term, "secular," cycles through its endemic polysemy.[3]

There is an oddity to the career of the secular, in that a term tradi-

---

1. For two intriguing literary treatments of this theme, see Bruce Duffy's Wittgenstein novel *The World As I Found It* (New York: Ticknor and Fields, 1987), and Edward P. Jones, *The Known World* (New York: HarperCollins, 2003).

2. She has just discovered the world is not as she thought it was. Hence her (oft-forgotten) final words: "Who would have thought a good little girl like you could destroy my beautiful wickedness?"

3. See Charles Taylor, "The Polysemy of the Secular," *Social Research* 76, no. 4 (Winter 2009): 1143-66.

tionally constituted by boundaries and opposition ("secular" as referring to a *saeculum,* a specific period set apart from, and propaedeutic to, what comes after; or "secular," as opposed to belonging to a religious order; or "secular," as opposed to under the control of church authorities; or "secular" as opposed, generally, to "religious") comes, over time, to swallow up its opposition and become self-contained, all-encompassing, and self-sufficient. This, at least, is the picture provided us by Charles Taylor in his history of the emergence of the immanent frame of modernity.[4]

The frame of secularity is a powerful one. But it has also shown signs of instability of late. It has revealed itself to be vulnerable to the challenges of contending perceptions, arguments, occurrences, and stories. There are now, hard on the heels of some of the most persuasive accounts of the triumph of the secular, stresses and strains in the structure, and glimmerings and grumblings of alternative formations. From different directions, and in differing registers, a set of critiques and alternative vistas has emerged that call the secular into question, and that together raise the banner of the post-secular. The task taken up in this chapter is to catalogue these harbingers of post-secularity, to inquire into their interconnections, and to explore to what degree they might actually usher in a new formation or imaginary as opposed to simply producing filigrees on the façade of the secular edifice. The purpose of this exercise is to clear the ground for further work on the theological and ethical implications of what I call, after the European fashion, the post-secular problematic. Disentangling and attempting to make sense of the various theses about post-secularity is a necessary step on the path charted by this book toward exploring openings in the secular.

1. The "Secular" in Secular Modernity

If we are to delve into the topic of the *post*-secular it stands to reason that we should start with some conception of the *secular.* It will not do, of

4. Charles Taylor, *A Secular Age* (Cambridge, Mass.: Harvard University Press, 2007). See also Taylor's essay "What Is Secularism?" in which he sketches the progression of the secular as a series of dyads in which two dimensions of time — secular and higher time — are replaced by an opposition between a secular (self-sufficient, immanent) realm and the transcendent beyond of religion; which then mutates further into a dyad in which the secular refers to the real, and the religious to the invented or fictitious. In *Secularism, Religion, and Multicultural Citizenship,* ed. Geoffrey Brahm Levey and Tariq Modood (Cambridge: Cambridge University Press, 2009), pp. xi-xxii.

course, to refer to the secular in a monolithic sense when so many fine studies have set about making distinctions and tracing nuances attached to the term and its cognates.[5] Let me stipulate, then, for starters, that *secularization* describes a process whereby a society or people becomes progressively more secular, and that *secularism* denotes an ideology upholding the pre-eminence of secular reasoning, institutions, and authorities. What, though, does "secular" mean here? At this point we need to adopt some further distinctions, and from among the various available parsings of "secular" that are on offer, Charles Taylor's is as serviceable as any. In his *A Secular Age* he distinguishes and assigns numbers to several different ways of being secular or, as he terms them, secularities. In saying a word about each of these dimensions or types of secularity, I comment briefly, for purposes of my subsequent argument, on the degree of purposive human action or agency each involves.

In Taylor's schema, "**Secularity 1**" consists in the "emptying of religion from autonomous social spheres." He is referring to what he also calls "*public* secularity" — a designation, one notes, that invokes the public-private distinction bound up with the emergence of modern political orders. Taylor has in mind here large-scale political developments such as the promotion of a separation of church and state, or laicization; as well as sociological processes such as the privatization of religious practice or the de-confessionalization of European societies. Secularity in this sense, then, is the product of collective agency in the form of political projects or, less directly, institutional change.

"**Secularity 2**" refers to "the falling off of religious belief and practice, in people turning away from God." This form of secularity has an existential character to it, in that it can involve an individual rejection of religion, church, and God (and, in some societies, the taxes that go with religious membership). It also reflects changing habits and modes of formation, and for sociologists, it is this sense of secularity that is most clearly related to

5. For example, Rajeev Bhargava, ed., *Secularism and Its Critics* (Oxford: Oxford University Press, 1998); Marcel Gauchet, *The Disenchantment of the World: A Political History of Religion,* trans. Oscar Burge (Princeton, N.J.: Princeton University Press, 1999); Talal Asad, *Formations of the Secular: Christianity, Islam, Modernity* (Stanford, Calif.: Stanford University Press, 2003); Janet R. Jakobsen and Ann Pellegrini, eds., *Secularisms* (Durham, N.C.: Duke University Press, 2008); and Craig Calhoun, Mark Juergensmeyer, and Jonathan VanAntwerpen, eds., *Rethinking Secularism* (New York: Oxford University Press, 2011). For an overview, see Slavica Jakelić, "Secularism: A Bibliographic Essay," *The Hedgehog Review* 12, no. 3 (Fall 2010).

the famous "secularization thesis," the prediction that people persistently fall away from religion under the enlightened, rationalized conditions of secular modernity.[6]

Taylor's chief concern in *A Secular Age* is with what he calls "**Secularity 3**," which has to do with "the conditions of belief." This form of secularity consists in an epistemological state in which "belief in God ... is understood to be one option among others, and frequently not the easiest to embrace."[7] It is therefore a matter of "the whole context of understanding in which our moral, spiritual, or religious experience and search takes place." Secularity in this sense is operative at the level of those "imaginaries" that prefigure our thoughts and experience — at, as Merleau-Ponty would say, the level of perception. Secularity 3 envelops its occupants in an "immanent frame" constituting not a set of beliefs, but the "sensed context" in which we develop our beliefs, and in this frame naïve religious faith is eclipsed by the possibility of a self-sufficing, "exclusive humanism." It remains the case, however, that from the standpoint of the individual Secularity 3 can be experienced as *closed* — a state under which it is nonetheless still possible, even under conditions of immanence, to achieve a moral or spiritual experience of "fullness" — or, alternatively, as *open* to religious transcendence. Its essential features are, we might note, the problematization and optionalization of faith, or the pluralization of belief. In Taylor's view, the perduring religiosity of U.S. society in no way prevents it from being secular in this sense. How Secularity 3 arose is a very complex story that threatens to overflow the nine hundred pages of Taylor's tome, yet his narrative illumines identifiable dimensions of agency — in the propagation of the ideas by elites that come by subterranean processes to form the "modern social imaginary," in the drive to ongoing reform that fatefully opens the church up to the secular — that partially steer the process producing the secular formation that is itself constitutive of the conditions of agency for modern subjects.

Taylor adds to his catalogue, finally, a description of what he might, but does not, term **Secularity 4**: a specifically temporal conception rooted in the experience of ordinary, as opposed to higher, time. This sense of

6. Jose Casanova, in his own schema involving senses of the secular, links this type of secularity with what he calls "stadial consciousness," the idea that human history exhibits a dynamic of progress that prompts it to move from an age of religion to a more advanced stage characterized by the triumph of secular reason. See his "Are We Still Secular? Exploring the Post-Secular: Three Meanings of 'the Secular' and Their Possible Transcendence," paper presented at New York University, Institute for Public Knowledge, October 22-24, 2009.

7. Taylor, *A Secular Age,* p. 3.

secularity is derived from the original root of the term, such that "secular" means *of the saeculum,* the (worldly) age, as opposed to the realm of eternity or salvation history — the time of higher orders of existence that traditionally gathered, reordered, and punctuated profane time.[8] Modernity has marked an entrance into an era in which ordinary time can appear to be the only time there is. This shift in temporal consciousness is linked further, Taylor adds, to a sort of spatial shift in which people move from living in a cosmos to living in a universe.[9] Since Taylor bases his discussion of Secularity 4 in part on the analysis of shifts in modern apprehensions of time by Benedict Anderson in his study of nationalism, *Imagined Communities,*[10] it would be apposite to note that secular temporality and spatiality are also deeply marked by the structures of modern nation-states and print capitalism; that they bear, in short, a Westphalian inscription. If secular time and space, in this sense, emerged out of an agential nexus of social structural change and collective imagining, then one has occasion to ask in which directions Secularity 4 might now be tending. Manuel Castells's account of how contemporary information technologies and globalization are producing experiences of "timeless time" and the "space of flows" is one potentially useful continuation to the narrative.[11]

These dimensions of secularity, while distinct, are interrelated. They all have to do with what I called above "worldliness," and especially with how we position ourselves and *act* in the world. Yet it is clear that they occupy, one could say, different architectonic levels, with public secularity (Secularity 1) operative more or less on the surface of human activity, in the preserves of public policy and private religious exercise; while secularization (Secularity 2) occupies an intermediate stratum, a level of large-scale social forces, practices, and habitus; and the immanent frame (Secularity 3) and secular time (Secularity 4) function in the nether regions of consciousness. These discrete senses of the secular are all, as Taylor's approach highlights, historicized. In using the metaphor of depth in relating them to one another, I mean to point to the more and less accessible modes of

8. Taylor, *A Secular Age,* pp. 54-55.

9. In a similar vein, Charles Hirschkind, drawing on Talal Asad's work, has pursued the notion that we might speak of a "secular body," a "particular configuration of the human sensorium — of sensibilities, affects, embodied dispositions — specific to secular subjects"; see his "Is There a Secular Body?" *Cultural Anthropology* 26, no. 4 (November 2011): 633-47.

10. London: Verso, 1983.

11. *The Rise of the Network Society,* 2nd ed. (Oxford: Blackwell, 2000). For another assessment, see Vincent Miller's chapter in this volume.

human agency that are involved in the evolution of the secular. As I hope will become clear below, there are both an ethical and a theological point to casting the matter this way.

2. Faces of Post-Secularity

For at least a couple of decades there have been rumblings signaling the possibility of instability in the foundations of the secular edifice. A number of distinct discourses have arisen challenging, in varying ways, various aspects of secularity. For starters, over the last decade Jürgen Habermas has popularized the term "the post-secular society" in interventions reassessing the wisdom of secularism as a principle for the organization of modern political society (I will call this Post-Secularity 1). Over an even longer period, with Peter Berger leading the way, sociologists have largely scrapped their former article of faith, the "secularization thesis," and begun to speak of "desecularization" in the face of a global — or at least impressively large — religious revival (Post-Secularity 2). Meanwhile, some theologians — most notably those associated with the movement known as Radical Orthodoxy — have joined forces with postmodern critics of the Enlightenment to mount an attack on the epistemological foundations of the secular, demythologizing its claims to embody a religiously neutral application of human reason (Post-Secularity 3). Within philosophy, especially of the continental sort, believing and unbelieving thinkers alike have broken with the secular conventions of their discipline in a "turn to religion" in which they have re-engaged with classical theological texts and contemporary religious forms and figurations (Post-Secularity 4). Political theorists, for their part, have shown a renewed interest in exploring the bounds of the secular through an engagement with political theology — in the sense developed by Carl Schmitt — or, to use the term associated with Claude Lefort, Walter Benjamin, and before them, Spinoza, the theologico-political (Post-Secularity 5). Finally, an interdisciplinary coterie of scholars has set about critiquing the very concept of the secular, through a deconstruction of the religious-secular distinction and a succession of related dyads, including the distinction between public and private (Post-Secularity 6).

These discourses have in common, as I say, a program of calling into question key features of secularity, and intimating as a counterproposal various ways in which we might speak of post-secularity. Do we live in, or should we strive — even in liberal societies — to live in, a polity that is secular in the sense of being insulated from the influence of organized religions? Does secularized Europe represent the future of the rest of the developing world, or is it an anomaly that requires explanation amidst the seas of global religion and spirituality? Do the secular assumptions underpinning modern science and technological rationality actually embody a type of theology, and a heretical one at that? Is the secularizing tradition that recently trumpeted the death of onto-theology and metaphysics still nonetheless obliged to recognize the indispensable value of religious forms in philosophical inquiry? Do the political forms and ideologies that have emerged from the Enlightenment to shape international relations depend at their heart on a theological structure? And can the very notion of the secular be sustained any longer as a coherent and neutral descriptive term, or must it be acknowledged to be a contingent term, the meaning of which is ineradicably bound up with the interests of states, markets, and other powers? I do not presuppose that these pointed questions, these rattlings of the bars of the "iron cage" of secular modernity, are part of a single overarching movement, nor even that they are concerned with different body parts of one and the same elephant. ("After that, it is turtles all the way down.") They present, though, I want to suggest, lines of inquiry and points of contact that help illuminate limitations to the secular, as well as places where secularity continues to reign. For indeed it may be the case that reports of the demise of secularity are premature, or that as some dimensions of the secular are *aufgehoben,* or remodeled into something else, others persist or even expand. In my discussion of this constellation of post-secularities, I will keep in view connections to the senses of secularity adduced above. Following Taylor's example and for economy's sake, I number each discourse of post-secularity I have presented — noting that my catalogue by no means claims to exhaust the field.[12] I also remain at-

12. I leave out of consideration here, for example, the comparatively less-developed discourse of what might be called literary post-secularity. See Regina Schwartz, *Sacramental Poetics at the Dawn of Secularism: When God Left the World* (Stanford, Calif.: Stanford University Press, 2008); and Feisal G. Mohamed, *Milton and the Post-Secular Present: Ethics, Politics, Terrorism* (Stanford, Calif.: Stanford University Press, 2011). For useful overviews of the broad field of post-secular interventions, see James K. A. Smith, *After Modernity* (Waco, Tex.: Baylor University Press, 2008), pp. 9-13; Ola Sigurdson, "Beyond Secularism? Towards a Post-Secular Political Theology," *Modern Theology* 26, no. 2 (April 2010): 177-96; Gregor McLennan, "The Post-Secular Turn," *Theory, Culture and Society* 27, no. 4 (August 2010): 3-20; and Rosa Braidotti, "In Spite of the Times: The Postsecular Turn in Feminism," *Theory, Culture and Society* 25, no. 6 (2008): 1-24.

tentive to the dimensions of human agency they involve, and to their implications for the ongoing role of religion in public life.

Post-Secularity 1

One sense in which we might be described as moving into a post-secular era has to do with changes in the visibility and influence of religion in the public arena in those highly modernized societies of the West that have heretofore understood themselves as secular. The various balances of religion and politics, the varying degrees of separation of church and state, have become subject to renegotiation, with religious groups of various sorts in the ascendant, not only vying for greater prominence in public life but also challenging fundamental assumptions about the rationale for the separationism that has become an article of faith for liberal democracies. This mode of post-secularity, we can note right off, corresponds to what we termed above Secularity 1, public secularity. It engages, additionally, secular*ism* as an ideology. And it is bound up with the structures and policies of only certain kinds of societies — liberal, pluralistic ones.

As I mentioned, it is Habermas who has most influentially sponsored a debate about the "post-secular society," and following him we can profitably distinguish between descriptive and normative dimensions of this type of post-secularity.[13] There are, more specifically, two descriptive modes in which the self-understanding of secular societies has been challenged. The first mode has to do with the visibility and increasing relevance of religion in contemporary public life. This is apparent internationally in the rise in public concern, in the wake of 9/11, with religious extremism and the "clash of [religiously based] civilizations." In individual countries, the stock of religion has risen for more proximate causes. The United States, under successive administrations, has experienced a concerted effort to incorporate religious groups into the provision of public services through "Charitable Choice" or "Faith-Based Initiatives," and the Democratic Party, traditionally aligned with secularist forces in American politics, has made something of an effort to bolster its outreach to religious constituencies. Various European countries have been obliged to cope with a new religious diversity produced by immigration, and a series

---

13. Jürgen Habermas, "Die Dialektik der Säkularisierung," *Blätter für deutsche und internationale Politik* 4 (2008): 33-46.

of highly publicized events and debates — the Danish cartoon controversy, the Dutch assassination of Theo van Gogh, the debate over head coverings in France, the minaret controversy in Switzerland, to name a few — have served to problematize the presence and role of Islam in particular in Europe.[14] At the same time Turkey has found its own institution of political secularism, *"laiklik,"* pushed and prodded in the direction of ever greater acceptance of religious influence in recent years.[15] India, too, has continued to wrestle with how to cope with the challenge of Hindu nationalism.

A second descriptive component of the challenge to public secularity deals with historical questions regarding the role of religion in the creation and sustenance of modern states and their institutions. This is an issue that occasionally comes to light in public policy disputes, for example, in the debate over whether God and Christianity should be mentioned in the proposed European constitution. It is also, of course, grist for scholarly discussion, as for example when Habermas participated in a public exchange with Joseph Cardinal Ratzinger in 2004 over the topic of the "pre-political foundations of the democratic constitutional state." In this discussion Habermas, though refusing to give ground on the post-metaphysical foundations of his own normative account of law and politics, acknowledged crucial contributions that religion had made to secular society, in the form of practices such as the promotion of virtue and solidarity, and in concepts such as the *imago Dei*.[16] This recognition is symptomatic of a broad tendency toward recognizing the partial dependence of secular orders on religious forces, both historically and with respect to the current formation of citizens.

It is these descriptive features, for Habermas, which inform the central normative issue regarding the post-secular society: namely, how religious and secular citizens ought to engage one another. In weighing in on this question, Habermas takes on a debate that has occupied the energies of some of our most prominent thinkers — including John Rawls, Taylor, and Jeffrey Stout — and given rise to a formidable array of commentar-

14. For a useful collection of analyses, see Levey and Modood, eds., *Secularism, Religion, and Multicultural Citizenship*.

15. James W. Warhola and Egemen B. Bezci, "Religion and State in Contemporary Turkey: Recent Developments in *Laiklik," Journal of Church and State* 52, no. 3 (2010): 427-53.

16. Jürgen Habermas and Joseph Ratzinger, *The Dialectics of Secularization: On Reason and Religion* (San Francisco: Ignatius, 2005). One might say that Habermas appreciates the way in which religious texts and figures can function as "classics" in contemporary culture, in the manner described above by David Tracy in this volume as "Publicness Two."

ies.[17] The debate involves, in the broadest formulation, the appropriate role for religious views in the public sphere of liberal states. If we look at the views of Rawls, Habermas, and Taylor on this question, we can see that they help define a spectrum of positions, ranging from Rawls's initial tendency to exclude religious rationales from the realm of "public reason"; through Habermas's qualified acceptance of the airing of religious arguments in public debate — provided they be translatable into the terms of secular reason once applied to any particular legislative aims; to Taylor's more inclusive stance allowing religious reasons to play a role in legislative processes, but drawing a line when it comes to the formulation of constitutional ground rules. What is perhaps most striking about their views, however, is the evolution that each has shown over time toward a greater tolerance for, and even appreciation of, the role of religion in the public sphere. In Habermas's recent discussions of this issue, for example, he has moved beyond acknowledging that religions bear an important function as "communities of interpretation" in modern polities, insisting that religious citizens should not be thrown under an asymmetrical obligation to translate their views into secular terms, and endorsing a model of interaction whereby secular and religious citizens open themselves up to genuine change through engagement with each other's perspectives. In taking this step, Habermas goes some way toward meeting the claims of religious commentators that faith should be admitted back into the "naked public square."[18] He also emphasizes, to his credit, that believers should likewise be open to revising their views through the dialogue with secular reason.[19]

17. Prominent among them are Paul Weithman, *Religion and the Obligations of Citizenship* (Cambridge: Cambridge University Press, 2002); Robert Audi, *Religious Commitment and Secular Reason* (Cambridge: Cambridge University Press, 2000); and Christopher J. Eberle, *Religious Conviction in Liberal Politics* (Cambridge: Cambridge University Press, 2002). See also Alessandro Ferrara, "The Separation of Religion and Politics in a Post-Secular Society," *Philosophy and Social Criticism* 35, nos. 1-2 (2009): 77-91.

18. The phrase, of course, is from Richard Neuhaus, *The Naked Public Square: Religion and Democracy in America,* 2nd ed. (Grand Rapids: Eerdmans, 1986); others who have made this case include Troy Dostert, *Beyond Political Liberalism: Toward a Post-Secular Ethics of Public Life* (Notre Dame, Ind.: University of Notre Dame Press, 2006); Robert Gascoigne, *The Church and Secularity* (Washington, D.C.: Georgetown University Press, 2009); Raymond Plant, *Politics, Theology, and History* (Cambridge: Cambridge University Press, 2001); and Nigel Biggar, "Saving the Secular: The Public Vocation of Moral Theology," *Journal of Religious Ethics* 37, no. 1 (March 2009): 159-78.

19. Jürgen Habermas et al., *An Awareness of What Is Missing: Faith and Reason in a Post-Secular Age,* trans. Ciaran Cronin (Cambridge, Mass.: Polity, 2010).

Habermas is not so rosy in his outlook as to expect that beyond this fusion of horizons, secular and religious viewpoints can and will become synthesized in today's modern societies. Taylor, too, acknowledges that truly diverse democracies will not be able to ground coexistence and civility in a common civil religion, commenting that "we are condemned to live in an overlapping consensus."[20] Taylor himself is not particularly inclined to deploy the label of "post-secular" to describe a political sphere in which a vibrant presence for religion has been renegotiated since for him this circumstance does not bear directly on the more fundamental question of the secularity of the conditions of belief (Secularity 3); Habermas's use of the phrase is also premised on the notion that a post-secular role for religion emerges only against the backdrop of a broader ongoing process of secularization. All the same, their views help buttress the notion that a transition is afoot with regard both to the concrete role of religions in the life of democratic polities and to the articulation of reputable democratic theories justifying a retreat from a strict posture of public secularity.[21] It is in this sense that we can speak of a post-secular turn in public life.[22]

Post-Secularity 2

A second sense of "post-secular" is tied to the reassessment of the "secularization thesis" that has been carried out over the past few decades. If it was thought at one point not too long ago that the path of modernization led down a one-way street in the direction of the irreversible demise of religion, and that European societies were simply the leaders in a com-

20. Charles Taylor, "The Meaning of Secularism," *The Hedgehog Review* 12, no. 3 (Fall 2010). For a skeptical view of whether an overlapping consensus provides a sustainable basis for resolving deep differences, see Steven D. Smith, *The Disenchantment of Secular Discourse* (Cambridge, Mass.: Harvard University Press, 2010), pp. 15-16.

21. One evidence of this is the resuscitation in recent years of a vigorous debate about toleration. See, for example, Michael Walzer, *On Toleration* (New Haven, Conn.: Yale University Press, 1999); Rainer Forst, *Toleranz im Konflikt* (Frankfurt: Suhrkamp, 2003); and Melissa S. Williams and Jeremy Waldron, eds., *Toleration and Its Limits: NOMOS XLVIII* (New York: New York University Press, 2008). On the implications of critiques of secularism for international relations, see J. Paul Martin's chapter in this volume.

22. For a dissenting construal of "post-secular society" as a society that no longer needs to be self-consciously secular simply because religion has ceased to be at all relevant to public life, see Ingolf Dalferth, "Post-secular Society: Christianity and the Dialectics of the Secular," *Journal of the American Academy of Religion* 78, no. 2 (June 2010): 317-45.

mon global race to enlightened secularity, from our current vantage it now appears that religion is not only alive and well in many parts of the world — and indeed always was — but that it is surging forth in many places. It appears that secularization has become decoupled from the dynamo of modernization and consequently lost momentum in Western societies, and that we must in any event speak, with S. N. Eisenstadt, of multiple modernities. It also appears, arguably, that Europe is not only not the pacesetter for other societies it was thought to be, but that the degree of secularization of European societies was overestimated in the first place, and that the question of European exceptionalism has been overstated. As a result of these shifts in perspective, sociologists and other analysts of religion have begun to speak of "desecularization," or of the "resacralization" or "re-enchantment" of the world.[23] It is in light of this broad development that we can speak of a post-secular turn in the sociology of religion.

The idea that secularization — in the sense, primarily, of Taylor's Secularity 2 referring to the erosion of belief, but related as well to the rejection of religious authority in other spheres of social life — is inextricably tied to modernization processes goes back at least to Weber, and has been a deeply embedded assumption through much of the development of sociology and religious studies. What has happened to fracture this notion? We can point here, generally, to two overarching developments. On the one hand, we need to look at "facts on the ground" — at the demographics of rapidly growing populations of Muslims and (especially evangelical) Christians in many places around the world over the last few decades.[24] The perception of a global religious revival has been buttressed by the increased prominence in global affairs of religious actors — extremists with a violent potential, as well as advocates of peace.[25] Iran has been only the most prominent country to experience a regime committed to counter-secularization. Societies like the United States, for their part, have seen a

23. This development has not been uniform, of course. If Peter Berger and David Martin have been leaders in the effort to reassess and replace the classic secularization thesis, Steve Bruce has persisted in advocating a modified version of it.

24. For overviews, see Philip Jenkins, *The Next Christendom: The Coming of Global Christianity* (Oxford: Oxford University Press, 2002), and John Micklethwait and Adrian Woolridge, *God Is Back: How the Global Revival of Faith Is Shaping the World* (New York: Penguin, 2009).

25. For an analysis of the links between faith and militancy in regard to both violence and peace, see Scott Appleby, *The Ambivalence of the Sacred: Religion, Violence, and Reconciliation* (Lanham, Md.: Rowman and Littlefield, 1999).

striking expansion of new religious movements as well as forms of religious practice and "spirituality" that locate themselves outside the traditional denominational structure of American religions.

The diversification of forms and practices has contributed to a second large-scale development undermining the traditional secularization thesis, consisting in essence in a broadening of perspectives in the understanding of religious modernity. A recognition that religious dynamics include not just the beliefs and practices of traditional religious communities, but a range of orientations including the "spiritual but not religious" and the "nones" — people with no religious affiliation — has produced a picture in which secularization is in some respects replaced by a more nuanced conception of pluralization.[26] In this picture, it is also possible to acknowledge approaches to finding enchantment in modern life that explicitly adopt a non-religious orientation.[27] At the same time, sociologists have slowly moved beyond the parochial Eurocentrism of early secularization theories to recognize the limitations of the Western model and variations in the experiences of other modernizing societies[28] and religions,[29] to the point where they now acknowledge different patterns and trajectories of secularization. Some would emphasize, further, that secularization is a process that in key respects is endemic only to what might be called "ex-Christendom."[30] Most importantly, perhaps, the largely secularized Western establishment of religion scholars has overcome its myopia in time to notice that, as Peter Berger put it, the rest of the world "is as furiously religious as it ever was, and in some places more so than ever."[31]

The account that emerges from these developments is a complex one

26. On the U.S. experience in this respect, see Robert D. Putnam and David E. Campbell, *American Grace: How Religion Divides and Unites Us* (New York: Simon & Schuster, 2010).

27. See Jane Bennett, *The Enchantment of Modern Life: Attachments, Crossings, and Ethics* (Princeton, N.J.: Princeton University Press, 2001), and Theodore Ziolkowski, *Modes of Faith: Secular Surrogates for Lost Religious Belief* (Chicago: University of Chicago Press, 2007).

28. Linell E. Cady and Elizabeth Shakman Hurd, eds., *Comparative Secularisms in a Global Age* (New York: Palgrave Macmillan, 2010).

29. Hans Joas and Klaus Wiegandt, eds., *Secularization and the World Religions,* trans. Alex Skinner (Liverpool: Liverpool University Press, 2009).

30. Charles Taylor attributes this view to Marcel Gauchet in *The Disenchantment of the World.*

31. Peter Berger, ed., *The Desecularization of the World: Resurgent Religion and World Politics* (Grand Rapids: Eerdmans, 1999), p. 2.

that does not amount to a wholesale rejection of the idea of secularization, even if it denies that it is tethered in a straightforward way to modernization. It acknowledges, indeed, that in some ways and in some locales — with respect, for example, to indicators such as declining church attendance or vocations — secularization continues apace, even as it falters or is reversed in other respects. It shows, too, that a number of contemporary developments involving religion — such as religious fundamentalism — are responses to, and in that sense dependent on, the dynamics of secularization. Ultimately, the notion of Post-Secularity 2 does not assume that there is a zero-sum game involving secularization and the flourishing of religion. Rather, even as it rejects the simple claim that we live in a secularized world it entertains the notion that, as José Casanova puts it, "as the rest of the world modernizes, people . . . are becoming simultaneously both more secular and more religious."

Post-Secularity 3

If the Enlightenment ethos out of which modern secular societies emerged had its origins in part in a critique of religion, then there is, perhaps, a certain symmetry in the critique of the Enlightenment by theologians and religionists that forms the heart of Post-Secularity 3. The sense of post-secular that I have in mind here resides at root in a rejection of the notion that a model of universal, neutral, self-sufficient reason can function as the basis for a just public order or even sustain itself intellectually over the long haul.

This line of thought has taken some cues from the broad epistemological critiques of certain strands of Enlightenment thought by post-modern thinkers such as Lyotard, Foucault, and Rorty, and signed onto challenges to fixed components of secular modernity such as the autonomy of human reason, the hegemony of scientific method, and a meta-narrative of human progress. But because Post-Secularity 3 has as its organizing purpose the restoration of religious credibility, it can only partially make common cause with cultural critics who are not themselves equipped to affirm abiding values (it is due to this values gap, says Hans Joas, that "we should have the courage to speak of the "end of postmodernity").[32] As a consequence,

---

32. Joas and Wiegandt, *Secularization and the World Religions,* p. 3. Joas cites Zygmunt Bauman's *Modernity and the Holocaust* (Oxford: Polity, 1989), as having signaled the bankruptcy of the moral resources of late modernity.

theological post-secularism either soon parts ways with post-modernism, or produces its own explicitly theological post-modernism, in which the tools of continental philosophers are placed in the service of a confessional agenda.

A fairly wide array of religious theses has set about rehabilitating religion in the face of secularism, opting for a number of divergent strategies. Following the Second Vatican Council, some Catholics have argued for a Christian foundation for liberalism, religious freedom, human rights, and other aspects of modern secular societies. Other Christians have argued for a religion of secularity as the fulfillment of the internal dialectic of Christianity,[33] or for what detractors call a "Constantinian" colonization of the secular realm in line with religious truth. John Caputo has proposed the notion of "religion without religion," an echo in some ways of Bonhoeffer's "religionless Christianity." These are indeed all ways of claiming that room can be found within secular settings for Christian religion, ways that together contest the validity of the divide between faith and reason built into the superstructure of modern secularism. This contention is at the core of a further set of theological voices that have in common a denial of the neutrality of the secular and an affirmation of the importance of maintaining a clear division between the pagan cast of secular rationality and the truth of revelation and everything that flows from it. Post-liberal theology, Scriptural Reasoning, and especially Radical Orthodoxy are in this sense post-secular movements.

For Radical Orthodoxy as outlined by leading lights such as John Milbank and Graham Ward, the secular realm, in the particular sense of a neutral cultural arena devoid of its own ontological commitments or politics, simply does not exist.[34] Rather, what is represented as secular is understood in actuality to constitute an alternative theology, a heretical set of twists on original Christian categories, acceptance of which implicates one in a form of idolatry and predisposes one to respond violently to conflict. From the perspective of Radical Orthodoxy, the ideas of universal reason, of a liberal, value-neutral zone of public discourse, and even of natural theology are exposed as incoherent and in conflict with the transcendent source of true religion. The Christian revelation provides the only valid

---

33. For example, Don Cupitt, *The Meaning of the West: An Apologia for Secular Christianity* (London: SCM, 2008).

34. A helpful guide to this issue is James K. A. Smith, *Introducing Radical Orthodoxy: Mapping a Post-secular Theology* (Grand Rapids: Baker, 2004).

lens through which to understand not just religion, but aesthetics, human sociality and relationships, and all other spheres of prospective knowledge. In this sense Radical Orthodoxy provides, as Catherine Pickstock puts it, "a hermeneutic disposition and a style of metaphysical vision" that promise to open up an alternative to the social imaginary of secularity. The tools of Radical Orthodoxy and allied forms of theological post-secularism include the *ressourcement* of de Lubac and other practitioners of the *nouvelle théologie,* and as a consequence Augustine in particular becomes a major conversation partner in the project of reconstructing a perspective prior to the modern separation of nature and supernature and elaborating a post-secular ethos. Balthasar's theological aesthetics is another inspiration, and this is reflected in the unabashed commitment of Radical Orthodoxy to the recovery of metaphysics in religious theory. Radical Orthodoxy prominently features a historical narrative that identifies the missteps that produced the secular age and points to the ontological foundations of univocity and peace that must inform its replacement.[35] It also proposes a rereading of the Western traditions of social theory and philosophy designed to open them up to theocentric interpretation.[36] In articulating the constructive vision that flows from its theological corrective, Radical Orthodoxy proponents tend to sublate politics into ecclesiology, arguing for the centrality of the church as liturgical community and endorsing a praxis of participation in shaping common life. The ambitious program of Radical Orthodoxy thus exercises agency at a number of levels. Ultimately, in promoting the notion of post-secularity, the goal for theology, as Graham Ward puts it, is not just to query and probe the secular, but to produce "new modes of believing itself, new conditions for, and structures of,

---

35. Charles Taylor, in the final chapter of *A Secular Age,* largely endorses this narrative, acknowledging that it is complementary to his own (pp. 773-76). John Milbank, with a few caveats, agrees; see his "A Closer Walk on the Wild Side," in *Varieties of Secularism in a Secular Age,* ed. Michael Warner, Jonathan VanAntwerpen, and Craig J. Calhoun (Cambridge, Mass.: Harvard University Press, 2010), pp. 54-82. It is worth noting that Taylor's narrative, which locates the seeds of secular excess in the regrettable overemphasis on Reform in Christian tradition, highlights a sort of institutional agency, while the Radical Orthodoxy critique, in its focus on the emergence of nominalism and voluntarism, seems to point rather to a failure of intellectual vision.

36. Most influentially in John Milbank's cornerstone text *Theology and Social Theory: Beyond Secular Reason* (Oxford: Blackwell, 1990), and in Phillip Blond, ed., *Post-Secular Philosophy: Between Philosophy and Theology* (London: Routledge, 1998). See also Adrian Pabst, "The Shape of Post-Secularity: Representing Faith in an Age of Religious Decline and Revival," unpublished manuscript.

believing that allow objects of belief once thought obsolete to reappear."[37] Post-Secularity 3 takes into its sights, in short, Secularity 3, challenging the conditions of belief supporting the immanent frame.

Post-Secularity 4

A fourth variant of post-secularity has been enacting itself in the hitherto characteristically secular realm of professional philosophy. Particularly within that subspecies of the guild known abroad as "continental," a burgeoning concern with God, the Bible, and other things religious in recent years has been prominent enough to support claims of a "religious turn" in philosophy. For different reasons in different thinkers, prophetic religion in particular has taken on a new relevance in connection with philosophical inquiry.

This turn is not so surprising, perhaps, where it has taken place with philosophers who are themselves avowedly religious. The *Zeitgeist* has elicited major efforts from theistic philosophers such as Emmanuel Levinas and Jean-Luc Marion to bring the tools of phenomenology to bear on the human relation to the divine. Gianni Vattimo and John Caputo have together set out their individual perspectives on postmodern faith, with Caputo somewhat archly proclaiming the death of the death of God.[38] Not to be outdone, Richard Kearney has advertised his own conception of "anatheism" as a cultural space opening access to "faith beyond faith," and a return to "God after God."[39] Charles Taylor has also effected a religious turn in his work, a move that was foreshadowed in his masterwork *Sources of the Self,* became explicit beginning with his 1996 Marianist lecture on a Catholic modernity, and carries through his concern with the possibilities for transcendence within the immanent frame in *A Secular Age.*[40] For each

37. Graham Ward, *The Politics of Discipleship: Becoming Postmaterial Citizens* (Grand Rapids: Baker, 2009), p. 155, n. 87.

38. Gianni Vattimo and John D. Caputo, *After the Death of God* (New York: Columbia University Press, 2009).

39. Richard Kearney, *Anatheism: Returning to God after God* (New York: Columbia University Press, 2010). In some respects Kearney's project bears similarities to William Desmond's attempt to mediate between religion and philosophy by revivifying the metaphysical tradition; see his *God and the Between* (Oxford: Blackwell, 2008).

40. Charles Taylor, *Sources of the Self: The Making of the Modern Identity* (Cambridge, Mass.: Harvard University Press, 1989); and "A Catholic Modernity?" in *Dilemmas and Connections: Selected Essays* (Cambridge, Mass.: Harvard University Press, 2011), pp. 167-87.

of these thinkers, his status as believer authorizes a recourse to religious content as a ground or context for the exercise of philosophical reason.

What is more striking, however, is the upsurge in engagement with religion among philosophers who describe themselves as agnostics or atheists. This engagement is fairly casual in some thinkers, such as Richard Rorty and Habermas, who both see religion as important but regard it as dangerous (in the case of the former), or as embodying a mode of rationality that is sharply distinct from, and epistemologically inferior to, secular reason (in the case of the latter). Julia Kristeva has gone somewhat further, finding in a certain variant of Christianity necessary resources for the development of humanism.[41] Similarly instrumental appropriations of religion have been advanced by Slavoj Zizek, who is committed to support for organized religions in virtue of their liberative potential; Michael Hardt and Antonio Negri, who enlist various biblical themes in their treatises on globalization; and Terry Eagleton, who has drawn on his own religious background in his criticisms of the so-called New Atheists and identified the religions as havens of spiritual values that provide some resistance to the depredations of capitalism.[42] Most intriguing of all, perhaps, are those philosophers who have found important resources for their own philosophical projects not in the content of revelation but in the forms endemic to religion: one thinks here of Derrida, as well as Badiou and Agamben, both of whom have written reflections on St. Paul. For such thinkers, religious sources retain a function as classics, in the sense of David Tracy's Publicness Two.[43] But the appeal of religion goes beyond that: it resides in the inherent limits built into modes of philosophizing within secular modernity. The aim of these thinkers has thus been to chart an alternative to what they take to be the moribund path of onto-theology, and to found a direct, non-theological connection to religious insight.[44]

What is the significance of the religious turn in philosophy, for secularity in general and for the public sphere in particular? Philosophical postsecularity merges in certain respects with the epistemological critique of

41. Julia Kristeva, *This Incredible Need to Believe,* trans. Beverley Bie Brahic (New York: Columbia University Press, 2009). On the question of the relation of religion to humanism, see Slavica Jakelić's chapter in this volume.

42. Terry Eagleton, *Reason, Faith, and Revolution* (New Haven, Conn.: Yale University Press, 2009).

43. See his chapter in this volume.

44. See the collection of essays in Mark A. Wrathall, ed., *Religion after Metaphysics* (Cambridge: Cambridge University Press, 2003).

post-secular theology, inasmuch as it thematizes the need to reinterpret modern assumptions about the relations between faith and reason. It does not, however, attempt to do away with the secular altogether; rather, more modestly, it aims at an opening up of secularity to the conditions of attentiveness and respect that might facilitate genuine conversation with religious forms and insights.

Post-Secularity 5

Over the past decade, another front for the post-secular has opened up as the field of political theory has experienced a surge in discussions of the theme of political theology. This development occurs against the backdrop of an ever more complex exploration of theoretical connections between the religious and the political. In this context we can mention, first of all, a series of engagements with the political realm from various theological standpoints, ranging from the postwar political theology of Metz and Moltmann, through the globalized discourse of liberation theology, to more recent forays into public theology,[45] or, alternatively — for those critical of the public-private distinction and committed to theological postsecularism — into a "theopolitics" rooted in Christian ecclesiology and sacramentality.[46] Articulations of the implications of religious belief and practice for political theory are hardly limited to Christianity, of course, and the writings of a Franz Rosenzweig or a Sayyid Qutb — despite their very different tenors — would also fit under this broad rubric.[47] We would be remiss, too, not to note the importance here as well of the sociological insight, inspired by Durkheim and Rousseau and elaborated most influentially by Robert Bellah, into the ways in which the civic cults of modern

45. See Mary Doak, *Reclaiming Narrative for Public Theology* (Albany: State University of New York Press, 2004); Charles Mathewes, *A Theology of Public Life* (Cambridge: Cambridge University Press, 2007); and Eric Gregory, *Politics and the Order of Love: An Augustinian Ethic of Democratic Citizenship* (Chicago: University of Chicago Press, 2008).

46. Seminal here are the contributions of William Cavanaugh: *Torture and Eucharist: Theology, Politics, and the Body of Christ* (Oxford: Wiley Blackwell, 1998); and *Theopolitical Imagination: Christian Practices of Space and Time* (London: T&T Clark, 2003). Many of the contributions to Creston Davis, John Milbank, and Slavoj Zizek, eds., *Theology and the Political: The New Debate* (Durham, N.C.: Duke University Press, 2005), would also fit here.

47. For an overview of the field, see Peter Scott and William T. Cavanaugh, eds., *The Blackwell Companion to Political Theology* (Oxford: Blackwell, 2004).

societies may be seen to function as civil religions. But what I am point-ing to with the moniker of Post-Secularity 5 is chiefly the turn within the traditionally more-or-less secular preserve of political theory toward the exploration of a theological dimension to politics. I refer, in short, to the sense of political theology popularized primarily by Carl Schmitt in his influential theory regarding the theological derivation and structure of the modern state.[48]

There are, as Hent de Vries notes, both genealogical and analogical dimensions to the link Schmitt developed between theology and politics,[49] and these help us identify three rough ways in which there has been a recent post-secular opening of political theory. On the genealogical side, Schmitt claimed famously that "all significant concepts of the modern the-ory of the state are secularized theological concepts," suggesting at once both the religious provenance of notions like sovereignty and law, and an accompanying process of historical derivation. Working more recently along similar lines, the democratic theorist Claude Lefort, in his examina-tion of "the theologico-political," presents a historical picture in which, although religious forms have largely been transferred into the political structures of the modern state, religion continues to maintain a subter-ranean presence in which it can at any time "return to the surface" when there are "cracks in the edifice of the state" and be "reactivated at the weak points of the social."[50] One effect of the genealogical connection developed in contemporary political theology is, by recovering older connections between religion and the political, to highlight and call into question the sharp distinction between the notions of religion and politics that is partly constitutive of secular modernity.

A second opening of political theory is provided through the work of William Connolly, who, without himself staking out any religious commit-ments, has produced an influential criticism of the secularist assumptions of contemporary democratic theory.[51] Connolly's critique dovetails in

48. In his *The Concept of the Political,* trans. George Schwab (Chicago: University of Chicago Press, 2007 [1927]), and *Political Theology: Four Chapters on the Concept of Sover-eignty,* trans. George Schwab (Chicago: University of Chicago Press, 2005 [1922]).

49. Hent de Vries, "Introduction: Before, Around, and Beyond the Theologico-Political," in *Political Theologies: Public Religions in a Post-Secular World,* ed. Hent de Vries (New York: Fordham University Press, 2006), pp. 1-89, at 47.

50. Claude Lefort, "The Permanence of the Theologico-Political?" trans. David Macey, in *Political Theologies,* ed. de Vries, pp. 148-87.

51. William Connolly, *Why I Am Not a Secularist* (Minneapolis: University of Minnesota

some respects with the epistemological critique of post-secular theology, in that he focuses on ways in which universalizing, secular reason covers up and effaces deep — especially religious — differences, and produces an ethical framework in which meaningful action can be justified only as an assertion of will. Connolly believes that secularism stands in the way of a more authentic democratic order embracing a deep pluralism marked by an agonistic respect for fundamentally different outlooks, both religious and non-religious.

Perhaps the most arresting opening of political theory in recent years has to do, finally, with contemporary developments of the analogical connection between religion and politics suggested by Schmitt's political theology. If, in Schmitt's conception of the political, central concepts such as the "state of exception" and the friend-enemy distinction could be linked to analogous theological presuppositions, subsequent thinkers have unearthed and explored numerous additional ways in which present-day political forms mirror the structures of traditional religion. One thinks, for example, of the role played by the "undeconstructible" character of justice in making law possible in Derrida's political ethics;[52] or of the parallels Ernesto Laclau identifies between what he calls "mystical fullness" and "political fullness";[53] or of Philip Goodchild's striking argument that money has taken the place of God and developed into a global successor to religion complete with its own ethics, metaphysics, and mode of transcendence.[54]

It is clear that "political theology" covers a diverse array of topics, themes, and methodologies. The cumulative effect of this revived discourse, I want to suggest, however, has been to create conditions, at least in some precincts of secular society, in which it is increasingly viewed as *salonfähig,* or kosher, to incorporate theological or religious reasoning into descriptive and normative political theory. It is this situation to which I am affixing the label of Post-Secularity 5.

Press, 1999). For a theological treatment of his themes, see Kristen Deede Johnson, *Theology, Political Theory, and Pluralism: Beyond Tolerance and Difference* (Cambridge: Cambridge University Press, 2007).

52. Jacques Derrida, "Force of Law: 'The Mystical Foundation of Authority,'" trans. Mary Quaintance, in *Deconstruction and the Possibility of Justice,* ed. Drucilla Cornell, Michel Rosenfeld, and David Gray Carlson (London: Routledge, 1992), pp. 3-67.

53. Ernesto Laclau, "On the Names of God," in *Political Theologies,* ed. de Vries, pp. 137-47.

54. Philip Goodchild, *Theology of Money* (Durham, N.C.: Duke University Press, 2009).

Post-Secularity 6

It is from an exercise of self-reflection and analysis of its own subject matter on the part of religious studies that what I am calling Post-Secularity 6 arises. The work of Talal Asad, whose "anthropology of secularism" employs genealogical techniques derived from Foucault and Nietzsche, has prompted a movement in religious studies toward a recognition of the socially constructed character of the religious-secular distinction and the way in which the idea of the secular — as well as that of religion — is bound up with powerful social forces and interests.[55] In this view, the secular as we know it is revealed to be "a function of Euro-American world making."[56] This critique culminates in a sense of the contingency and instability of the very notion of secularity, and pushes toward a reformulation of how human activities and beliefs can and should interact with the sacred and profane dimensions of life.

For Asad, "the secular" is an ontological and epistemological formation that is distinct from, and precedes, the political doctrine of "secularism" that is based on it. The secular emerges in Christian history out of a binary contrast with the religious, forming a dichotomous relationship that binds together the evolution of both systems. The development of the secular must therefore be understood in twain with the invention of "religion" as a universal category constructed mainly in terms of internal, individual belief. In the historical narrative associated with genealogical post-secularity, the emergence of modern states and associated institutions such as citizenship deeply informed collective understandings of religion as a private affair and secularity as a function of the public sphere. Indeed, this history reveals the religious-secular distinction to be an indispensable part of an epistemic paradigm that is also built on the public-private binary and an associated set of assumptions about the distinction between religion and politics. Over time and through rhetorical repetition, the idea of the secular, a realm of life that is neutral, objective, and non-religious, becomes naturalized, a part of the underpinnings of social perception. Secularity conceals its own origins and takes on a factual, commonsensical air, eventually coming to be associated with notions of authoritativeness

55. Asad, *Formations of the Secular.* See also William Cavanaugh's chapter in this volume.
56. Timothy Fitzgerald, *Discourse on Civility and Barbarity: A Critical History of Religion and Related Categories* (Oxford: Oxford University Press, 2007), p. 24.

and progress. Together with religion, the secular forms part of a configuration with reference to which moral and political questions are formed, contested, and settled.

As the genealogical critics of secularity point out, the religious-secular distinction is hardly an arbitrary way of organizing human experience and action; rather, it serves concrete political and even commercial objectives. The lineaments of notions of "religion" and the secular are products of political decisions; scholarly agendas; and the efforts of missionaries, civil servants, and lawmakers. In their shape and effects, they have served to buttress the emerging structures of modern states, global markets, and colonial relationships. Important chapters in this history have involved the creation of a discourse of "world religions" as defined primarily by Western scholars;[57] the identification of Islam as a non-secular other standing in tension with an enlightened Europe;[58] and the Orientalist interplay of religion and secularity in the transition from colonialism to modern nation-states.[59] Perhaps the most fateful effect of the modern religious-secular configuration has been its role in constructing religion in such a way that it becomes perceived as a pre-eminent source of unrestrained political violence, while, at the same time, the massive violence engaged in by secular powers is at once legitimized and rendered invisible.[60]

The post-secular critique of the religious-secular distinction is in the first place an effort to challenge uncritically held assumptions about secularity, to demystify and deconstruct the classificatory system that regulates it, and to trace the ways in which this system is driven by power relations. To this extent, Post-Secularity 6 refers to a critical stance that is deeply skeptical about the coherence of the notion of secularity to begin with, and endorses a constant scrutiny of the ideological uses and distortions attached to prevailing usages of religion and the secular. Beyond this,

---

57. See Tomoko Masuzawa, *The Invention of World Religions: Or, How European Universalism Was Preserved in the Language of Pluralism* (Chicago: University of Chicago Press, 2005).

58. On this topic, see Elizabeth Shakman Hurd, *The Politics of Secularism in International Relations* (Princeton, N.J.: Princeton University Press, 2007).

59. See Peter van der Veer, *Imperial Encounters: Religion and Modernity in India and Britain* (Princeton, N.J.: Princeton University Press, 2001).

60. For reflections on this dynamic, see Talal Asad, *On Suicide Bombing* (New York: Columbia University Press, 2007), and William T. Cavanaugh, *The Myth of Religious Violence: Secular Ideology and the Roots of Modern Conflict* (New York: Oxford University Press, 2009).

the genealogical critique also raises the question of the degree to which current constructions of religion and secularity produce or reinforce discrimination, exclusion, or marginalization; help facilitate and legitimate state-sponsored violence; or otherwise become implicated in injustices. Inasmuch as this is the case, Post-Secularity 6 also entails the question of corrective action to ameliorate or remedy such effects. By focusing on the dynamics of agency active in the promotion of secular-religious configuration, critics such as Asad, who characterizes secular modernity as a political goal, an aim, and a project;[61] Fitzgerald, who points to the processes by which various functionaries struggle to "imagine, enact, authorize, and legitimate" the religion-secular dichotomy;[62] and Hurd, who concludes that as a social construction, secularity must logically be amenable to modification,[63] all place on the agenda of Post-Secularity 6 the task of finding creative ways to reconceptualize and reshape the interpenetrations of sacred traditions and worldly concerns, and to register personal stances that might not fit neatly into the received dyadic logics of religious-secular or believer-nonbeliever.[64]

3. Post-Secular Filaments

The various accounts of post-secularity I have identified here come from different quarters, address varying types of secularity, and do so in different ways. Their juxtaposition, however, reveals some common strands or themes that it is tempting to think of as giving intimations of deeper cohesion — of what we might indeed loosely call a post-secular sensibility. This sensibility can be discerned both in characteristic attitudes of critique, and in more constructive tendencies to posit alternatives to secularity along certain characteristic lines of inquiry. I address these two dimensions in turn.

For starters, the critical orientation of the post-secular stance takes its bearings from the attacks on secularist **epistemology** that have emerged

61. Asad, *Formations of the Secular,* p. 13.
62. Fitzgerald, *Discourse on Civility and Barbarity,* p. 33.
63. Hurd, *Politics of Secularism,* p. 147.
64. I have in mind here the sort of people Taylor describes as "seekers." For a philosophical attempt (inspired by Tillich's theology of culture) to challenge the breach between religious and secular through an examination of the experience of value, see J. Heath Atchley, *Encountering the Secular: Philosophical Endeavors in Religion and Culture* (Charlottesville: University of Virginia Press, 2009).

across a broad front of human and social sciences. If the epistemic critique of the deep assumptions of secularity advanced by post-secularist theologians is the most prominent entrant in this regard, it is certainly augmented by contributions from other quarters. In its reassessment of the role of religion in the public sphere, for example, Post-Secularity 1 takes aim at the picture of secular "public reason" as universal, neutral, and qualitatively different from religious reason. Philosophical post-secularity pries open for a broader audience the question of the intrinsic relations of faith and reason, while political post-secularity exposes the ideological functions bound up with the penchant of secular reason to sublate and sublimate difference. Meanwhile, the genealogical methods of Post-Secularity 6 highlight the role of the politics of the state and the knowledge industry in reifying the distinction between secular and religious knowledge.

A closely related common feature of the post-secularities I have described is their proclivity for contesting and undermining cherished **categories** on which central features of modern life are premised. This, clearly, is the decisive feature of the discourse of genealogical post-secularity, which takes on not only the dyads of secular and religious, of public and private, and of religion and politics, but also the dichotomy of sacred and profane.[65] But public post-secularity, too, challenges the character of the public with respect to the role of religion; political theology invites questions about the difference between theology and political theory; some of the strategies of post-secular theology hark back to a past in which philosophy and theology were closely interrelated, if not unified; and philosophical post-secularity blurs the boundaries of religion, Christianity, and theism. In addition, I would suggest that taken together, the discourses of post-secularity call for a reconsideration of the modern assumptions regarding the difference between "transcendence" and "immanence."[66]

Along with the post-secular critique of modern categories and classifying logics comes, not surprisingly, a hermeneutic of suspicion regarding

---

65. It should be noted here that Timothy Fitzgerald, for one, makes a point of arguing that the religious-secular distinction is in important respects not co-terminous with the sacred-profane divide; see his *Discourse on Civility and Barbarity*, chapter 3.

66. Charles Taylor registers his cognizance of this issue in *A Secular Age* (p. 632); for some criticisms of his use of the immanent-transcendent distinction, see Stanley Hauerwas and Romand Coles, " 'Long Live the Weeds and the Wilderness Yet': Reflections on *A Secular Age*," *Modern Theology* 26, no. 3 (July 2010): 349-62, and Fred Dallmayr, "A Secular Age? Reflections on Taylor and Panikkar," *International Journal for the Philosophy of Religion* 71 (2012): 189-204.

the **power relations** that have founded, or are built into, the edifice of secularity. Again, this is of course a chief concern of Post-Secularity 6, with its Foucauldian credentials. To a greater or lesser degree, however, the other modes of post-secularity also entail awareness of the implication of secularism in the programs of modern, liberal state formation and global capitalism. Theological post-secularity, in particular, is closely attuned to the links between a secularist ontology and various forms of violence. Even post-secularity in the Habermasian sense emerges from a recognition that secularism can inhibit legitimate forms of religiously grounded political expression. On the whole, then, we can observe that a central feature of post-secular discourse is a drive to demystify and expose the very real ways in which secularity arises with and reinforces certain political and economic practices.

Not surprisingly, then, post-secular perspectives also reflect a broad concern with **globalization**. For sociologists, a primary issue is how to understand the social dynamics that have contributed to the global resiliency of religion, even as Western, secular modernity has been transplanted around the globe. Theological critiques of secular materiality and consumerism have added to the post-secular sensibility a penetrating awareness of how economic globalization abets the commodification of culture, including religion.[67] As John Milbank and Slavoj Zizek's recent collaboration shows, a critique of global capitalism is one point at which representatives of the theological turn in philosophy and of theological post-secularism can make common cause.[68]

The aspects of critique I have enumerated as part of the post-secular sensibility are matched by a set of constructive responses that flow from them. For instance, several variants of post-secularity construct and stake their claims at least in part on historical **narratives** that recast the role of religious factors in the emergence of secular modernity. One sees this in the expanded acknowledgment, in both political post-secularity and contemporary political theology, of the importance of religious sources to the moral foundations of modern states and citizenries. Sociological post-secularity, meanwhile, has developed a narrative in which secularization is in key respects unhitched from the unfolding of modernization.

67. An excellent example is Vincent Miller, *Consuming Religion: Christian Faith and Practice in a Consumer Culture* (London: Continuum, 2005). See also Ward, *Politics of Discipleship.*
68. Slavoj Zizek and John Milbank, *The Monstrosity of Christ: Paradox or Dialectic?* ed. Creston Davis (Cambridge, Mass.: MIT Press, 2009).

And theological post-secularity relies heavily on the project of recovering a history revealing the heretical Christian roots of secular reason. Part of the purpose of this post-secular tactic is simply to correct the historical record, which has in certain ways diminished or effaced the contributions of religion.[69] But it seems to me that narrative also plays a deeper role here, galvanizing a sense of identity for movements such as Radical Orthodoxy and underwriting efforts to shore up the role of religious communities in the modern world.

Although I have not highlighted it above, several of the varieties of post-secularity I have sketched engage in critiques of what I presented as Secularity 4, having to do with secular constructions of time, space, and the body.[70] Because the underlying issue here is how conceptions of the secular inform the human sensorium and basic patterns of perception of temporality and spatiality — how secularity, in short, orients us in the material world — we can characterize the concern here as with **geography**, in the expansive sense that includes human geography and critical geography.[71] The geographical dimension of post-secular discourse is evident in the renegotiations of public space associated with Post-Secularity 1, in the debates over regional patterns of secularization (including discussion of "European exceptionalism"[72]) accompanying Post-Secularity 2, in the critique of secular history and the modern differentiation of religious, political, and other spheres mounted by post-secular theologies, and, of course, in the analyses of colonialism and Orientalism proffered by genealogical critics of the secular. Taken together, these efforts contribute to a collective enterprise of remapping the terrains in which we move in such a way as to enhance our agency in a post-secular world.

69. Beyond those mentioned above, additional important sources outlining the essential role of religious ideas in the emergence of secular society include Michael Allen Gillespie, *The Theological Origins of Modernity* (Chicago: University of Chicago Press, 2008), and Louis Dupré, *Religion and the Rise of Modern Culture* (Notre Dame, Ind.: University of Notre Dame Press, 2008). See also Graeme Smith, *A Short History of Secularism* (London: I. B. Tauris, 2008), and the essays in Ira Katznelson and Gareth Stedman Jones, eds., *Religion and the Political Imagination* (Cambridge: Cambridge University Press, 2010).

70. The relationship between secularity and the body features centrally in Anthony Godzieba's chapter in this volume.

71. I have in mind here geographies of space, place, and time, as practiced by thinkers such as Yi-Fu Tuan and David Harvey. James K. A. Smith's edited volume *After Modernity?* is noteworthy for its specific inclusion of geographers in its analysis of secularity.

72. See Peter Berger et al., *Religious America, Secular Europe? A Theme and Variations* (Aldershot: Ashgate, 2008).

In a slightly different key, another shared feature across a broad front of promoters of post-secularity is an endorsement of a return to **metaphysics**. Metaphysics, for many post-secularists, was a victim of secular materialism that, once reinstated, promises to serve as a bridge or meeting place for religious sensibilities and the thought structures operative in other disciplinary modes of thought. There, theological proponents of Post-Secularity 3 can join with philosophical representatives of Post-Secularity 4 to explore the "between" of religion and philosophy that has been obstructed by the secular imaginary.[73] A restored respect for and engagement with metaphysics is also characteristic of some of the contributors to the revival of the theme of political theology.[74]

A last post-secular theme that I will mention is the idea of **re-enchantment**. Not surprisingly, the strong historical association of the notion of secularization with Weber's idea of the disenchantment *(Entzauberung)* of the world leads proponents of post-secularity to look for residues or renewals of enchantment in modern life. There are three basic modes to this concern. First, those social theorists who are tracing Post-Secularity 2 look for, and even measure, signs and evidence that experiences of enchantment — religious or otherwise — are alive and well in both modernizing and modern milieus. Second, theological post-secularists, along with some philosophers and political theorists, seek to open up to experience "enchanted" dimensions of reality that had been hidden or blocked by the workings of secularity. Third, it is the hopeful project of some post-secularists of various stripes to contribute actively to a re-sacralization of the world, or perhaps specifically of the public sphere.

Now, beyond suggesting a rough post-secular sensibility, do these similarities and shared features add up to a coherent unity — an overarching post-secular condition, or moment, or event? In response, we must concede that clearly, the modes of post-secularity charted in the discourses I have described do not add up to a monolithic paradigm that promises, in grand fashion, to replace secularity. Moreover, we need to acknowledge that individual aspects of these different modes can work at cross-purposes to one another. Thus, the wholesale attack of some theological post-

73. I draw the notion here from William Desmond's work along these lines in *God and the Between.*

74. Representative here are Goodchild, *Theology of Money,* and Giorgio Agamben, *Homo Sacer: Sovereign Power and Bare Life,* trans. Daniel Heller-Roazen (Stanford, Calif.: Stanford University Press, 1998).

secularists on the secular stands in tension with those strands of public or philosophical post-secularity that continue to value various features and types of secularity. The genealogical critique of Post-Secularity 6, meanwhile, forcefully challenges and undercuts the very conceptions of religion and secular that set the terms for Post-Secularities 1 and 2.

These caveats notwithstanding, I do want to suggest that there is a sort of directionality that links together the various post-secularities I have canvassed in a common trajectory. If individual discourses present critiques of different components of the secular — the political ideology of secularism, the sociological thesis of secularization, epistemological secularity, and temporal-spatial-corporeal secularity — together they can be thought of as constituting a corrective to secularist excesses. Where modern political orders, social developments, and systems of rationality have been too zealously emplaced and have over-reached by excluding religious and other non-secular perspectives, post-secularity represents processes and efforts aiming at effecting re-openings toward the sacred. To think of post-secularity as corrective in this way, I hasten to add, is not to overlook that in some cases, the shifts endorsed by post-secularists can themselves tend to excess (one thinks here of the utter abjuration of the secular called for by some theological post-secularists).

To put it another way: returning to my earlier metaphor of the edifice of secularity, we can think of post-secularity as a major renovation project (as opposed to the creation of a new abode). As with any renovation, much of the structure will be kept, while other parts will be restored, shored up, replaced, or built onto. The post-secular overhaul is one that entails not only creating more room (for religious voices in democratic publics, for example), but also testing and modifying foundations (through, for example, an epistemological critique resulting in a broadened conception of reason). If, down the line, many of its original features have been thus modified, will the renovated edifice retain its secular character, or become a different building, post-secular or, perhaps, worthy of a different designation entirely? Like the identity of Heraclitus's river, that is not a problem we need to resolve here.

4. Post-Secularist Strategies

To think of the constellation of post-secularities I have delineated as a *corrective* or as a *renovation project* is to highlight the idea that post-secularity is not simply a fortuitous condition or event, but (also) something that might be produced or at least influenced by purposive human action. Indeed, as I pointed out here and there in the discussion above, there are various ways in which post-secularities entail, imply, or respond to different modes of human agency. For example, Post-Secularity 1, in the sense of a retreat from a secular monopoly on governance and public culture, emerges from a combination of shifting perceptions of religion, democratic debate and activism, and public policy (including legislative acts and constitutional foundings). By contrast, Post-Secularity 2 — involving desecularization and the increased visibility of religion — hinges primarily on large-scale social processes such as religious movements and societal rationalization, although it is arguably also responsive to the frames of interpretation provided by scholars and other observers. Given the range of ways in which post-secularities can be constructed, it makes sense to take at least brief note of some of the different tools, techniques, tendencies, and tactics that might contribute to a post-secularist agenda.

One of the most important contributions of post-secularity emerges primarily from the application of genealogical methods, and takes the form of a stance of reflexivity with regard to secular assumptions and categories. Another post-secular commitment — found more or less across the board in the discourses I have traced — is a valuing of plurality and, moreover, a commitment to pluralism that works against the totalizing tendencies of secularism.[75] As a function of this commitment, perhaps, the post-secular constellation offers the creative prospect of a dialectic between what might be called religious secularism and secularist theology, an engagement that promises new insight into different ways of mediating between the sacred and the worldly, including, for example, the development of different varieties of religious humanism.[76] In exploring emergent possibilities and mining historical resources for constructive ways of rethinking, or re-envisioning, how religious impulses might contribute to public life, another valuable technique identified by some post-secular thinkers is the heterological approach of Michel de Cer-

75. For a balanced exploration of ways in which pluralism can both constrain and enrich religion, see Courtney Bender and Pamela E. Klassen, *After Pluralism: Reimagining Religious Engagement* (New York: Columbia University Press, 2010).

76. It is symptomatic of the potential of such a dialectic, I think, that several key post-secular texts have taken the form of dialogues between interlocutors — Zizek and Milbank, Habermas and Ratzinger, Rorty and Vattimo — with quite distinct attitudes toward religion.

teau.[77] A key advance in the retrofitting of secularity, as Taylor and numerous others have recognized, will be the adoption of a more expansive understanding of reason than has been the norm in secular discourse, and this is an undertaking in which some valuable inroads have already been made by Michael Polanyi, William Poteat, and other expositors of post-critical thought. Finally, as I already noted above, there remains ample room for experiments in how to contribute to the re-sacralization of modern societies.

The focus of my remarks here, it will not escape the reader, has been on the intellectual work that must make up part of a post-secularist agenda. This sort of work is not the only activity that contributes to the renovation of secularity, and the measures I have described are only small steps. Arguably, they pale in comparison to the mighty forces of economics, technology, or nationalism that shape how we engage the world in ways illuminated by Vincent Miller and William Cavanaugh in this book. Yet intellectual work remains important because, if Charles Taylor has it right, it is through this kind of endeavor that shifts to the social imaginary can be inaugurated. Taylor sketches, in his account of the genesis of the modern social imaginary, how such frames ensconce themselves: they start out in the minds of influential thinkers, and then spread to various levels of society and to the broad public, before finally acquiring a self-evident status that helps render them invisible even as they intimately shape our practices and how we make sense of them.[78] The discourses of post-secularity open up at least the possibility of breaching the invisibility of the secular imaginary ("Pay no attention to that man behind the curtain!" commands the great and powerful Oz[79]) and participating in its slow transformation or conversion. Are we witnessing the signs of an emergent post-secular social imaginary? It is too early to say, but ushering in a new mode of worldliness, with a chastened and reflexive grasp of the meaning of secularity and a capaciousness for the sacred or divine, would seem to be a worthy goal.

---

77. Graham Ward and Ola Sigurdson have been particularly attentive to the potentials in Certeau's work.

78. Charles Taylor, "Modern Social Imaginaries," *Public Culture* 14, no. 1 (Winter 2002): 91-124.

79. In the book *The Wizard of Oz,* Dorothy is shocked to discover that the uniform hue of the Emerald City is, in fact, a "humbug": "But isn't everything here green?" asked Dorothy. "No more than in any other city," replied Oz; "but when you wear green spectacles, why of course everything you see looks green to you."

5. A Post-Secular Postscript

What is the role of the religious and theological community in the enterprise of contributing to the sort of post-secular corrective I have described? That is an involved question, and I will here venture only a few suggestive comments.

For the religious, for believers, for the church,[80] there is work to be done on a number of fronts. David Tracy's discussion of "Three Forms of Publicness" identifies some of the main avenues by way of which Christian tradition can engage in the processes of public reasoning at the heart of modern democratic orders. Christians — and other religionists — should continue to participate in argument (Publicness One) over the requirements of the common good in a way that pushes the boundaries of public reason in the direction of greater tolerance for theological and other forms of religious reason. Christian (and other religious) classics (St. Paul seems to be of deep interest at the moment) should continue to be offered up for public interpretation, dialogue, and engagement (Publicness Two) with their core themes (for example, theologies of incarnation and kenosis[81]). And Christians (and others) should furthermore foster public discussion of what Tracy calls the "beyond-the-limits-of-reason realities" of their faith, including the excessive drives to mystical wisdom and prophetic ethical demands (Publicness Three). Through these sorts of interventions and encounters, the religiously concerned can help along the incremental movement toward the post-secular goal of, as Taylor puts it, "making belief believable again."

The job for Christians, of course, is by no means exhausted by these tasks. The call of post-secularity also demands a process of internal self-examination and critique, aimed in part at identifying ways in which the

---

80. I recognize that the way I have framed the issues in this chapter reflects a primary concern with the implications of secularity and post-secularity for Western Christianity, and takes little account of how these implications also extend, as Asad and others have pointed out, to other religious traditions and social settings. Its historical centrality in the dialectics of secularity and modernity provides, I think, something of a rationale for this foregrounding of Latin Christianity (as Taylor calls it); and some of my observations might be applied, *mutatis mutandis,* to other traditions. Nonetheless, it is clear that the problematic of post-secularity will be posed quite differently in different societies and religious climes around the world.

81. See David Power, *Love without Calculation: A Reflection on Divine Kenosis* (New York: Crossroad, 2005).

forces of secularity — including nation-state politics, scientism, and materialist consumer culture — have informed and distorted Christian identity and practice. This critique must then help guide the way forward for the dimensions of religious *practice* — liturgical community and sacramental witness — and *action* — solidarity with the poor and the promotion of peace — that are at the heart of the church's concerns. By being true to itself in this way, the church can perhaps serve as a mediatrix in the bringing forth of a post-secular clime carrying new paradigms for linking the worldly to the sacred.

6. Media Constructions of Space, the Disciplining of Religious Traditions, and the Hidden Threat of the Post-Secular

VINCENT J. MILLER

1. Introduction

The nature and status of secularity and the consequent question of whether it is meaningful to speak of the "post-"secular are part of the horizon of contemporary religious and theological anxiety and reflection concerning tradition. Is contemporary society a place where Christianity can engage and cooperate in shared projects, or does secularity, even in its most peaceful forms, rest on such fundamentally incompatible foundations that the church is forced into countercultural witness? The tide of theological energy over the past three decades has swept in the latter direction. Post-liberal theologies emphasize particularity and contrast over the (now forgotten "critical") correlations of the preceding age.

These projects presume — explicitly and implicitly — quite specific diagnoses of our cultural predicament. Different diagnoses of our cultural context suggest different prescriptions. This chapter argues that the implicit diagnosis of the present cultural context in such ecclesial and theological responses to secularity — despite the value of their critiques of the secular — misreads the cultural context that has been emerging over the past four decades. As a result, their prescriptions address a context that no longer exists. Worse, these prescriptions, in their very "countercultural" stance, do not stand against the tide of contemporary culture, but rather swim unwittingly with the current of some of its most pernicious dynamisms.

The contemporary cultural context emerges from the myriad dynamisms of globalization that have emerged or intensified since the early

1970s: transportation, capital and commodity flows, communication and information technologies. The low cost of media production, the vast array of options from which users can choose, and the ease of communicating over vast distances have given rise to a cultural ecology marked by fragmentation, polarization, and deterritorialization.

This essay argues that secularity is helpfully analyzed in terms of an earlier national spatial scale and media culture that tended toward the homogenization of culture and the captivity of religious traditions in a denominational frame. Our current context inclines toward heterogenization. Far from suppressing particular identities, its disciplining forces elicit them, reducing complex traditions to identity fronts and discouraging complex engagement across difference and in place. The various appearances and mobilizations of religion described under the rubric of the "post-secular" fit well within this frame.

This context poses a profound and hidden challenge to religious traditions. The widespread post-liberal turn to particularity, justified in the face of homogenizing dynamisms of previous epochs, goes terribly awry in this context. The primary threat to the church is not against the integrity of its tradition (although that threat continues). The catholicity of the church is profoundly threatened as believers presume communities must be internally homogeneous and become obsessed with identity and boundary distinctions from other groups. In addition, as culture becomes deterritorialized — floating free from geographical community and local place — religious traditions lose the casuist and jurisprudential traditions that connect their fundamental doctrines and principles to a collective form of life. Religious traditions become increasingly abstract collections of beliefs whose function is reduced to identity markers, having little impact on the lives of believers and the world in which they live. This is, in short, a cultural ecology in which sectarianism is the default form. Religious communities face a daunting double challenge: preserving their traditions in a context of cultural amnesia in a manner that does not succumb to a cultural ecology that reduces broad, living traditions to narrow, voluntaristic identity fronts.

2. The Problem of the Post-Secular

Speaking of religion in a post-secular age faces two conceptual hurdles. The first lies in the sociology of religion. The once widely shared assumption that secularization is an inevitable component of modernization has long been called into question. This happened first as attempts were made to account for the American exception as a thoroughly modernized society with a persistently high rate of religious belief and practice; then to account for the European exception, as late modernity unfolded around the world and European-style secularization did not result. Contemporary accounts distinguish between numerous religious outcomes in modernity that are decidedly path-dependent. Thus, "post-" depends quite a lot on the secularity it succeeds.

Second, as Taylor's work shows, secularization is deeply imbricated in a modern immanent frame that shows no signs of fading, whatever the strength of religion. He does offer a set of sketches of religious figures creatively responding to the religious "cross pressures" of secular modernity. Chronologically, however, Taylor's account more or less ends with the postwar period, and thus, does not directly engage the so-called resurgence of religion in the late twentieth century.

Something new has certainly taken place in the interim. José Casanova's early study of the deprivatization of religion remains seminal, but even that text could not predict the sustained political impact of fundamentalist religion, one that has resisted the disciplining of the public sphere. (This essay argues that it is nevertheless deeply disciplined by other dynamisms.) Casanova's analysis of the emergence and *decline* of the Religious Right by the end of Ronald Reagan's second term reads in retrospect like the ending of the first *Friday the 13th* film.[1] Countless sequels have so long obscured the original that it is now hard to imagine a time when it seemed but a single episode.

Casanova's more recent consideration of the secular argues that it is best understood in terms of Taylor's description of the Enlightenment "stadial" narrative, which portrays secularization as the hard-fought work of humanity come of age, " 'having overcome' the irrationality of belief."[2] Historically, "post-secular" designates the decline of this stadial narrative as Europeans come to terms with the fact that rather than a rule, the confluence of modernity and secularity in their society seems to be the

1. José Casanova, *Public Religions in the Modern World* (Chicago: University of Chicago Press, 1994), p. 147.

2. Charles Taylor, *A Secular Age* (Cambridge, Mass.: Harvard University Press, 2007), p. 269, cited in José Casanova, "The Secular, Secularizations, Secularisms," in *Rethinking Secularism,* ed. Craig Calhoun, Mark Juergensmeyer, and Jonathan VanAntwerpen (Oxford: Oxford University Press, 2011), p. 59.

exception. Thus, in this account, "post-secular" designates the need for analytic frames that do not presume that modernity and secularity essentially coincide.

Rather than reducing "post-secular" to a special question of European exceptionalism, Casanova's analysis highlights the importance of particular religious histories and formations of civil society in the relationship between religion and modernity in all societies. Casanova argues that the stadial narrative derives its power from the varied struggles for deconfessionalization that followed on the Westphalian articulation of religion and nationalism. The fate of religion in various societies is intertwined with the particular characteristics of their civil societies. Casanova finds a solidaristic echo of the homogeneity of *cuius regio eius religio* in the robust discursive legitimation of European social welfare states, and a legacy of pluralistic disestablishment in the difficulty facing solidaristic social welfare programs in the United States.[3]

This turn to civil society is helpful for clarifying the current state of religious belief and practice vis-à-vis various accounts of secularization. Casanova's argument helps refine what, if anything, "post-secular" means. If what we might call the "classical" forms of national civil society are relatively stable historical legacies that change only on the time scale of centuries, these particular characteristics of national civil societies are imbricated in the ever-increasing pace of the revolutions of communications technology that have formed the backdrop of the modern era.

Consider the year 1978-79 — a striking *Annus mirabilis* or *horribilis* depending on one's perspective. Pope John Paul II, the Ayatollah Khomeini, and the American Religious Right emerged contemporaneously as geopolitically significant forces. They each arose from particular histories marked by secularism of varying degrees of virulence: John Paul's formation in the battle with a communist state in the footsteps of Cardinal Wyszyński; Khomeini's background in the clerisy of Qom and struggle against the Shah's (CIA-backed) White Revolution; the Religious Right's emergence from fundamentalist, Pentecostal, and evangelical churches that were culturally marginalized amidst the hegemony of mainline Protestantism and its concord with midcentury American liberalism.

The emergence of each into the public was facilitated significantly by

3. José Casanova, "Are We Still Secular? Exploring the Post-Secular: Three Meanings of 'the Secular' and Their Possible Transcendence," paper presented at New York University, Institute for Public Knowledge, October 22-24, 2009, p. 15.

communications technology. John Paul's dramatic gifts enabled him to use the modern media in a way that no other pope ever had. His use of media augmented (and perhaps replaced) the authority of Church-specific communication channels with more direct appeals to believers through the media. Whatever his rhetorical gifts, the exiled Khomeini had little access to mass media. He was, nonetheless, able to function as the spiritual leader of a revolution through cassette tapes of his sermons, which could be easily and surreptitiously reproduced and distributed.[4] A CBS evening news report on the 1972 Nixon re-election campaign featuring a youthful Karl Rove provides an early glimpse into the technological underpinnings of the Religious Right. Computerized databases were employed to target issue-specific direct mail appeals to specific interest groups.[5]

The role of media technology in these revolutionary post-secular moments suggests that it is worthwhile to consider how the technological underpinnings of civil society influence the fate of religious traditions and their impact on society. We thus turn to two accounts that explore the technological underpinnings of modernity's construction of the public realm: Jürgen Habermas and Benedict Anderson.

3. The Technological Underpinnings of the Public Sphere

Habermas's early writing portrayed the public sphere as an imaginative reality whose emergence was grounded on a range of economic, organizational, and technological factors.[6] Its imagination and practices — a community and space comprising free, equal individuals, possessed of reason, able and entitled to deliberate on matters relevant to their shared social and private lives — arose from the coalescence of a variety of material factors. The printing press alone did not produce these, but provided an essential technological capability for the wide dissemination of culture in

4. Annabelle Sreberny-Mohammadi and Ali Mohammadi, *Small Media, Big Revolution: Communication, Culture and the Iranian Revolution* (Minneapolis: University of Minnesota Press, 1994), pp. 186-88; as cited in John B. Thompson, *Media and Modernity* (Stanford, Calif.: Stanford University Press, 1995), p. 174.

5. CBS Evening News, January 19, 1972. At http://www.youtube.com/watch?v=9HPnW4EBed4, accessed 24 November 2010. See Lisa McGirr, *Suburban Warriors: The Origins of the New American Right* (Princeton, N.J.: Princeton University Press, 2001).

6. Jürgen Habermas, *The Structural Transformation of the Public Sphere: An Inquiry into a Category of Bourgeois Society* (Cambridge, Mass.: MIT Press, 1991).

writing. Other structures — regular trade routes, postal services — helped this capability blossom into "the news" and journals of opinion. Concrete new spaces — shifts from the great hall architecture to the salon and private rooms, the rise of the cafés and of paid admission performance venues — provided the location for public discourse that would replace the staged performance of representation in courtly life and the arcanum of religious rituals and knowledges.

Both "public" and "sphere" are imagined realities, projected out of and sustained by particular communities, spaces, and discourses. Changes in these structures (for example, the series of shifts from newsletters, to literary journals of opinion, to mass media) change the nature of civil society. Habermas's account ends with the undoing of the political nature of the public sphere and its degeneration into the marketing discourse of mass society. While Habermas's subsequent work greatly refined his portrayal of public reason, its material and technological underpinnings ceased to be a major concern.

Benedict Anderson's account of the emergence of nationalism complements Habermas's early account by following subsequent changes in communications technology through the twentieth century. Anderson's analysis attends to the complex interplay of cultural formations, technology, and various types of agents (capitalists, colonial state administrations, colonized peoples). His account calls attention to the often-overlooked hyphen in the term "nation-state." The "nation" did not arise automatically from the territorial state that had been developing through power struggles, ideological programs, and theoretical legitimation in the early modern period. Indeed, the modern state was developed in the bureaucracies of decidedly multinational empires, such as the Austro-Hungarian Empire that endured well into the twentieth century. The nation, despite its historical novelty and near universal acceptance, did not emerge from an intentional ideological program. "Unlike most other isms, nationalism has never produced its own grand thinkers: no Hobbeses, Tocquevilles, Marxes, or Webers."[7]

In Anderson's account, nationalism emerged from the unplanned spatial transformations that print capitalism worked on the pre-existing cultural foundations of clerisy and monarchy. This interplay of technology, capitalism, and historical context is simultaneously random and

7. Benedict Anderson, *Imagined Communities: Reflections on the Origins and Spread of Nationalism,* rev. ed. (London: Verso, 2006), p. 5.

fortuitous.[8] The burgeoning productive capacity of the print industry needed large markets. While the Latinate cosmopolitan culture provided the most ready large-scale market for early publishers, it was not one likely to experience significant growth. The vernacular languages represented a potentially vast market, but they were deeply fragmented. These would have "dissipated print capitalism into 'petty proportions.'" The path forward was found in coalescing these myriad dialects into print languages that allowed speakers who could not communicate verbally to read one another. These "monoglot mass reading publics" created "unified fields of exchange and communication below Latin and above spoken vernaculars."[9]

Elizabeth Eisenstein evokes the power of print language and the refiguration of communal space and belonging in the Reformation. "Printed materials encouraged silent adherence to causes who could not be located in any one parish and who addressed an invisible public from afar."[10] This monoglot linguistic space, with its possibility of shared public discourse, is the incipient space of the nation. "These fellow-readers, to whom they were connected through print, formed in their secular, particular, visible invisibility, the embryo of the nationally imagined community." Even as the governance structures of the modern state had long been in place, "these languages bore none but the most fortuitous relationship to existing political boundaries."[11]

Print languages had two important temporal effects as well: they created a sense of shared contemporaneous time and they facilitated shared

8. Anderson's account refuses to reduce the emergence of nationalism to an ideological program. As he acknowledges, though, once it emerged it became an ideological tool in the repertoire of politicians and groups seeking power. The "standardized vernacular" becomes the "official language of a propagandizing state." See Benedict Anderson, *The Spectre of Comparisons: Nationalism, Southeast Asia and the World* (London: Verso, 1998), pp. 64-65.

9. Anderson, *Imagined Communities,* pp. 43-44. Various "administrative vernacular" languages had existed prior to this. But these remained "state" languages; they were not the language of the populace (p. 40).

10. Elizabeth L. Eisenstein, "Some Conjectures about the Impact of Printing on Western Society and Thought," *Journal of Modern History* 40, no. 1 (March 1968): 42. Cited in Anderson, *Imagined Communities,* p. 35 n. 62. Eisenstein's later magnum opus conveys well the fortuitous cultural impacts of technology that cannot be reduced to any single coherent ideological effect or program. See her *The Printing Press as an Agent of Change: Communications and Cultural Transformations in Early-Modern Europe* (Cambridge: Cambridge University Press, 1979). See also Thompson, *Media and Modernity,* pp. 52-63.

11. Anderson, *Imagined Communities,* pp. 44, 46.

national memory. Taylor engages the first of these in *A Secular Age*.[12] Anderson explains how what Walter Benjamin described as "homogeneous empty time" replaced sacred experiences of time in which everyday experience was suffused with touch points to the eternal.[13] Modern "transverse" simultaneity was born of the novel and the newspaper. The modern novel takes place in a "meanwhile" in which various elements of the plot unwind, the actors unaware of one another until the plotlines they inhabit intersect. The newspaper enshrines this temporality in a more quotidian rhythm. Newspapers are novels written in the same temporal frame, whose authors have "abandoned any thought of a coherent plot."[14] The date, "the single most important emblem" on the paper, conveys the "steady onward clocking of homogenous empty time" in which the entire world simultaneously "ambles steadily ahead."[15] Hegel's insight concerning the newspaper as a substitute for morning prayers brings the institutional handing off from religious to secular structures of time into the fore. A new "ceremony . . . repeated at daily or half-daily intervals throughout the calendar" is a "vivid figure for the secular, historically clocked, imagined community."[16] These transformations provided the temporal frame within which people could imagine themselves as members of a larger community comprising a vast number of members with whom they had no direct relationship.

In addition to this shallow temporal simultaneity, print capitalism also deepened intergenerational memory. The creation of print vernaculars slowed linguistic change. Readers could now easily read printed vernacular texts from the previous century, in a way that had not been possible with the level of linguistic dynamism that preceded the printing press. This enabled the linguistic community constituted in print language to develop a sense of temporal continuity, which would contribute much to the fictive sense of antiquity that is such a universal aspect of nationalism.[17]

Anderson describes other formations of space more easily linked to intentional projects of colonization and control: longitude, Mercatorian

12. Taylor, *A Secular Age*, pp. 55, 195.

13. Anderson, *Imagined Communities*, pp. 24ff.

14. Anderson, *Imagined Communities*, p. 33 n. 54.

15. Anderson, *Imagined Communities*, p. 33; Anderson, *The Spectre of Comparison*, pp. 32-34.

16. Anderson, *Imagined Communities*, p. 35.

17. Anderson, *Imagined Communities*, p. 44.

mapping, and censuses. These were unwieldy tools for governance. Censuses rendered the politically marginal visible as minorities, or in colonial context, made clear in stark numbers the minority of the colonial power holders. Maps created more than territory for control: as logos, they symbolized the shape of the nation and focused questions of indigenous versus colonial sovereignty. These may have created the spaces of state-administered "interiors" and *staatliche "Statistiken,"* but these remained empty spaces and "phantom communities" until they were filled by the imagined community of the nation.[18]

This new space replaced the "complex" space of multiple alliances and hierarchical relations that preceded it. The modern state wished to fill it with individual citizens, simpler versions of the medieval subject shorn of the unruly, complex, overlapping allegiances.[19] Unplanned nationalism, however, produced a different outcome: a populace who imagine themselves as sharing a common heritage and destiny with the myriad others who inhabit that space, for whom they feel a "natural" solidarity. Such enthusiasms both legitimated and placed undesired, even revolutionary, demands on state power.

Thus, we see that print capitalism and print vernaculars give rise to a national-scale construction of space. Linguistic homogeneity fosters a national-scale imagination of culture as a common heritage and shared symbolic universe mapped to a population contiguous with political territory. Here lie the foundations of the spatial construction of culture presumed in Herder, Durkheim, and Geertz. The national scale presumes cultural homogeneity and a spatially contiguous community.

The coincidental nature of the relationship at the heart of the nation-state, between state administrative structures and the imagined community of the nation, is important. In Anderson's account the hyphen that joins these two profoundly powerful ideological structures of late modernity signifies both their fortuitous relationship and the possibility of their separation. As we will see, further technological developments have facilitated their separation.

18. Anderson, *Imagined Communities,* pp. 65, 163-87. See also the essay entitled "Nationalism, Identity, and the Logic of Seriality," in Anderson, *The Spectre of Comparisons,* pp. 29-45.

19. John Milbank, "On Complex Space," in *The Word Made Strange: Theology, Language, Culture* (Oxford: Blackwell, 1997), pp. 268-92; William Cavanaugh, *Theopolitical Imagination: Discovering the Liturgy as a Political Act in an Age of Global Consumerism* (London: T&T Clark, 2002), pp. 43, 99-102.

4. Religion in the National Scale and the Age of Mobilization

Anderson's analysis shows that the nation-state is a form of organization whose emergence took place on a spatial scale constructed by particular technologies as much as an ideological belief. Surely myriad cultural factors were at play. But the revolutions in communication technologies created the space within which nations emerged. This analysis allows us to see how the church can conform to this order without embracing the ideological assumptions of the modern nation-state. Peter Raedts argues that the Catholic Church underwent a thoroughgoing modernization in "form" even if this was accompanied by claims of preserving traditional "content." "The transformation of the Catholic Church" can be described "in the same terms as the transformation of states into nations: rationalisation and centralisation of the administration, mobilisation of all the people, and the creation of a low-brow, homogeneous, common culture."[20] This ecclesial reform program, conforming to the national spatial order, corresponds roughly to Taylor's "Age of Mobilization."

The Catholic Restoration in France provides a literal example of ecclesial deployment in national space. The struggle with Republican France required a massive program of building, institutional organization, and lay formation. Parishes were built in every town. The pastor was deployed to counter the representative of the Republic, the schoolmaster. Taylor argues that even the most reactionary desire for a divinely sanctioned, organic, hierarchical social order had to contend with the fact that it no longer existed. Thus restoration could not be realized through alliances with the now-powerless heirs of deposed monarchs; it demanded a constructive mass movement.[21]

This marked a shift in Ultramontane Catholicism, from reactionary alliances with *ancien régimes* to a strategy that aimed, as in the motto of Pope Pius X, *"Instaurare omnia in Christo."* This shift is particularly evident in the emergence of papal social teaching. The Church possessed a long history of works of mercy and social action inspired by myriad saints and sustained by diverse spiritualities of religious orders.[22] *Rerum novarum*

---

20. Peter Raedts, "The Church as Nation State: A New Look at Ultramontane Catholicism (1850-1900)," *Dutch Review of Church History* 84 (2004): 494.

21. Taylor, *A Secular Age*, pp. 444-45.

22. Michael Schuck, "Early Modern Roman Catholic Social Thought, 1740-1890," in *Modern Catholic Social Teaching: Commentaries & Interpretation*, ed. Kenneth Himes, O.F.M. (Washington, D.C.: Georgetown University Press, 2005), pp. 99-126. In this light, *Re-*

rendered these into formal, abstract principles and inaugurated a central-ized, institutional program of social reform. One need not go as far as Mil-bank's labeling of Catholic social teaching as "incipiently fascistic" to see its formal similarity to other major ideological movements of the time.[23]

In addition to the changes to time and space, Anderson describes changes to language. Print vernaculars supplanted the sacred languages that grounded the power of clerisies and courts. Language, like time, was flattened out. Concepts were assumed to be readily translatable from one language to another. Events taking place in the shared calendar time could be understood and appreciated everywhere in translation.[24] The establish-ment of the Vatican polyglot press in 1908 fits perfectly with this analysis. While Latin would remain a sacred (and legal) language for two-thirds of a century, the polyglot press fully embraced the new linguistic order. The linguistic shift accompanied the mobilization of the entire Church in what Staf Hellemans has termed "Ultramontane mass Catholicism." Clergy were trained to educate and to form the laity in the doctrine of the Church, who would, in turn, carry out its social teaching in the world in what became Catholic Action.[25]

Media were essential to this transformation. Advances in media tech-nology have a dialectical effect. They delocalize traditions from settled scales and relocate them within new ones. Reterritorialization accom-panies delocalization.[26] Papal teaching was translated and distributed through an ecclesial network that spanned the globe and reached into the interior of nation-states. This dialectic is evident in Taylor's portrayal of mobilization as a permutation of the reform agenda, in which the Church adapts the political forms of the nation-state. Rather then repressing the

rum novarum should be read with Leo XIII's other programmatic encyclical, *Aeterni patris,* which retrieved Thomistic scholasticism as the fundamental thought-form for the Church.

23. Milbank, "On Complex Space," p. 274.

24. Anderson, *The Spectre of Comparisons,* pp. 32ff.

25. Staf Hellemans, "Is There a Future for Catholic Social Teaching after the Waning of Ultramontane Mass Catholicism?" in *Catholic Social Thought: Twilight or Renaissance?* Bibliotheca Ephemeridum Theologicarum Lovaniensium, CLVII, ed. Jonathan S. Boswell, Frank P. McHugh, and Johan Verstraeten (Leuven: Leuven University Press, 2000), pp. 14, 19. "The Catholic Church in the nineteenth century went through a process of bureaucrati-sation, mass mobilisation and cultural homogenisation that was very similar to the formation of nation states" (Raedts, "The Church as Nation State," p. 484).

26. Thompson, *Media and Modernity,* p. 187. Thompson's insight is a valuable supple-ment to analyses that stress the usurpation and eclipse of the local by larger-scale political entities such as the state, empire, or market.

lived *religion du terroir* ("religion of the soil"), clerics turned it toward trans-local national (pilgrimage sites La Salette, Lourdes) and transnational church devotions and celebrations (for example, the Rosary, Sacred Heart, Christ the King).[27] In their spatial dynamics, these transformations closely resemble nationalist moves to create civil religions and invent traditions.

The transnational character of this program and the fact that the Catholic Church gradually abandoned its commitment to a contiguous and exclusive relationship to geographic and political territory during this very time period run counter to the spatial logic of the national order. Nonetheless, its construction of the socially comprehensive milieu of the so-called ghetto reproduced the logic of the national scale in a demographic subculture. This spatial logic was even more apparent in the related, but more intensive system of the lowlands structure of *verzuiling*, or "columnization." In this system, multiple social groups (the Reformed churches, the Roman Catholic Church, and the Socialist Party) maintained their distinct identities in the midst of a pluralistic culture through separate, national-scale educational, social, and media institutions.

The church had no choice but to mobilize in its conflict with national political movements. It was enormously successful in its response: constructing buildings, institutions, organizations, and formation systems necessary to counter competing ideologies and constructions of space. The peak of the age of mobilization (1800-1960) corresponds to what is certainly the most highly organized, institutionalized, settled, and fully participated epoch in the history of Christianity. In Taylor's account, this victory was at the same time a Trojan horse. To compete in the form of mobilization was to accept the modern moral order that presumed human agency working in secular time, the "direct-access" construction of the person as an individual citizen, the construction of church as a denomination, and a neo-Durkheimian "political" construction of identity.[28]

The age of mobilization displays many of the characteristics we attribute to secularity: large-scale, homogeneous cultures, with robust, often

---

27. Taylor, *A Secular Age,* pp. 468-69. Leo XIII published eleven encyclicals on the Rosary.

28. Taylor, *A Secular Age,* pp. 460, 458. "But these tightly organized churches, often suspicious of outsiders, with their strongly puritanical codes, their inherent links, of whatever sort, to political identities, and their claims to ground civilizational order, were perfectly set up for a precipitate fall in the next age that was beginning to dawn at mid-century" (p. 472).

state-sanctioned understandings of the proper range and limits of religious participation in the public sphere. Religious groups in this period are likewise large and relatively homogeneous. This was the era of substantial theological reflection on and ecclesial engagement with secular public discourse and liberal state development programs. In this highly structured and stable context, shared norms for public discourse could function and religious traditions could arrive at negotiations with such norms on the basis of their own traditional resources. Religious communities could likewise ally themselves with various secular projects of furthering human flourishing through scientific discovery, technological innovation, and economic development, even if they held to more ultimate and transcendent ends for humankind. This was the era of mid-twentieth-century liberal theology and secularization theologies.

Although mobilization was centrally administered, its creation of myriad organizations and channels of communication resulted in new forms of lay religious authority. All of these factors have contributed to the deregulation, polarization, and politicization that mark the contemporary church. To understand those, we must now turn to the technological and economic changes that led to the unwinding of the national scale, which provides the historical context for the contemporary church.

5. The Unraveling of the National Scale

Anderson's account foregrounds the dynamic character of cultural-political formations. New technologies disrupt previous equilibria and support the emergence of new spatial and cultural formations. The national formation is no less susceptible to technologically catalyzed change than the formations it supplanted. The twentieth century saw growth in transportation, communication, and organizational technologies with effects as revolutionary as those of the printing press four centuries earlier. "Ironically . . . just as this classical nation-state project was coming fully into its own with the formation of the League of Nations in 1919, advancing capitalism was beginning to sap its foundations."[29] Here Anderson's account of the fortuitous, but non-essential, relationship between the state and the nation provides a framework to understand the epoch in which we currently live, when the nation-state has been "pried open" by the centrifugal effects of

29. Anderson, *The Spectre of Comparisons,* p. 66.

ever-developing technology. The result is not the disappearance of the nation-state, but its profound transformation.[30]

Anderson catalogues numerous technological developments in the twentieth century that transgress or erode the national scale (radio, television, air travel, personal computers).[31] If these technologies bore within them the seeds of the undoing of the national scale, for much of the century they were nonetheless still deployed within an economy that created national-scale mass markets. The so-called Fordist era of capitalism was driven by the massive, vertically integrated national corporation that mass-produced goods for sale through nationwide distribution chains. The high costs of design, production tooling, and distribution networks required high-volume sales for profitability. For similar reasons, communications and media (telephone, radio, music, film, television) were oriented toward the same national scales. Thus, the massifying effects and national scale of earlier print capitalism lingered through much of the twentieth century even as communication technologies developed the capability of disrupting it.

This economic formation underwent sustained crisis in the 1970s. By the end of the 1960s domestic consumer markets had begun to approach near saturation. Thus, quantitative market expansion could no longer sustain the growth that Fordist production required. The so-called post-Fordist forms of capitalism that have emerged since then are marked by increased "flexibility" in production by vertical disintegration of corporations, globalization of production chains, and the disempowering of organized labor. Information technologies revolutionized design, production, and marketing, enabling the massive productive capacity of industrial capitalism and the culture industries to focus on ever smaller niche markets.[32] This is particularly evident in the culture industries, where

30. Saskia Sassen, *Territory, Authority, Rights: From Medieval to Global Assemblages,* updated ed. (Princeton, N.J.: Princeton University Press, 2008), p. 423. Nationalism does not cease to be a political force. Indeed, it may in fact increase in frantic psychological compensation for the "decaying fetish" of the nation-state that ceases to provide for and to protect its citizens. See Ulrich Beck, *Cosmopolitan Vision* (New York: Polity, 2006); Arjun Appadurai, *Fear of Small Numbers: An Essay in the Geography of Anger* (Durham, N.C.: Duke University Press, 2006); and Zygmunt Bauman, *Globalization: The Human Consequences* (New York: Columbia University Press, 2000).

31. Anderson, *The Spectre of Comparisons,* p. 67.

32. Michael Aglietta, *A Theory of Capitalist Regulation: The U.S. Experience* (London: NLB, 1979); Martyn J. Lee, *Consumer Culture Reborn: The Cultural Politics of Consumption* (New York: Routledge, 1993); Ash Amin, ed., *Post-Fordism: A Reader* (Oxford: Blackwell,

the increased bandwidth of cable, satellite, and digital networks has dissolved the massifying effects of television, FM radio, record labels, and publishing houses.

If Fordist capitalism sustained a homogenizing foundation on which nationalism could continue to grow, these further technological and economic developments tended in the other direction: toward fragmentation and heterogeneity. Furthermore, these same technologies facilitated communication, commerce, and organization on scales that exceeded state control, creating a new global scale of agency and imagination that overruns state boundaries and penetrates into everyday life.[33]

6. Incipient Global Space

These "disaggregating" dynamisms bring about a new "centrifugal" ordering of the world. Saskia Sassen describes the emergence of a "new type of modernity" arising out of the *"partial unbundling"* of the "centripetal normative order" of the nation-state into "multiple particularized segmentations."[34] Arjun Appadurai describes these dynamics as the result of the development of "print capitalism" into global "electronic capitalism."[35] This new space can be considered in two aspects: cultural heterogenization, and a cultural geometry of disjuncture and deterritorialization.

Cultural Heterogenization

Even on a global scale, the media continue to have a linguistic massifying effect. This is evident in the audiences constituted by the emergence of Spanish, Arabic, and other transnational television networks. Univision,

---

1994). See the discussion in Vincent Miller, *Consuming Religion: Christian Faith and Practice in a Consumer Culture* (New York: Continuum, 2004).

33. Margit Mayer speaks of "perforated sovereignty" in which nations become more open to trans-sovereign contacts by subnational governments, and regional-local forces become more active in advancing their own locational policy strategies oriented directly to the world market. Margit Mayer, "Post-Fordist City Politics," in *Post-Fordism,* ed. Ash Amin (Oxford: Blackwell, 1994), pp. 316-37, at 317.

34. Sassen, *Territory, Authority, Rights,* p. 423.

35. Arjun Appadurai, *Modernity at Large* (Minneapolis: University of Minnesota Press, 1996), p. 161.

Telemundo, Al Jazeera, Al Arabiya, and other such networks foster linguistic spheres that create imagined communities on a decidedly transnational scale. Nevertheless, the explosion of bandwidth with its concurrent market segmentation has an opposing, heterogenizing effect. If the Big Three television networks constructed a shared sphere of discourse with common genres, subjects, and standards of access within which a limited range of voices and opinions could be heard, the five hundred channel offerings of digital television (let alone the uncountable options on the Internet) construct instead a vast range of options from which one can choose.

As communications costs fall, individuals are freed from the friction and inertia of geography and constrained media systems and able to choose to communicate with those who possess similar knowledge, commitments, and preferences.[36] Such freedom of choice heterogenizes culture into enclaves of the like-minded, fracturing larger-scale communities in the process. This effect is clearly illustrated by the way the Internet facilitates conspiracy theories. Rather than being buffered by the surrounding majority opinion, those with radically contrarian views can communicate with one another in Internet space to develop and reinforce their views.[37] This same dynamic applies to the range of views within various communities and traditions. Thus heterogenization is accompanied by the radicalization of views within the enclaves it constructs.[38]

If these communications revolutions undercut the large-scale homogenization of the nation-state, they preserve and intensify the expectation of homogeneity and imagined community that marked the national imagination. Fox News serves as the paradigm for this new cultural order. Its particular editorial perspective overrides any effort to seriously engage differing views on their own terms. It openly disregards any normative understanding of the public sphere. This strategy has attracted an enormous

36. See Marshall Van Alstyne and Erik Brynjolfsson, "Global Village or Cyber-Balkans? Modeling and Measuring the Integration of Electronic Communities," *Management Science* 51, no. 6 (June 2005): 851-68. Their mathematical analysis portrays the systemic effects of increased choice well, even if one does not accept their anthropology.

37. "The emergence of the Internet as a communications medium, he noted, makes it possible for once-scattered believers to find one another. 'It allows the theory to continue to exist, to continue to be available — it's not just some old dusty books on the half-price shelf.'" Mark Fenster quoted in John Schwartz, "Vocal Minority Insists It Was All Smoke and Mirrors," *The New York Times*, July 13, 2009, http://www.nytimes.com/2009/07/14/science/space/14hoax.html?_r=1, accessed Nov. 24, 2010.

38. Cass Sunstein, *Going to Extremes: How Like Minds Unite and Divide* (New York: Oxford University Press, 2009).

market share of viewers who very much imagine themselves as community. Rather than large-scale imagined communities, this technological-economic formation encourages the multiplication of smaller-scale (if still quite large), ideologically homogeneous enclaves that shear through national communities.

These changes remake the nature of culture once again. The national scale of print capitalism and the nation-state territorialized culture as a shared set of symbols, a worldview and ethos extended over a contiguous national space. Difference appeared between national cultures (and minority and regional cultures that proved the rule). In the new moment, difference no longer appears taxonomically between national cultures, but is manifest equally within and across them. Culture is transformed into "a volatile form of difference" increasingly reduced to a resource for the production of identity.[39] Identity does not emerge from broad consensus, or arise as an epiphenomenon of shared life and practices, but is rather a product of polarizing contrast. Identity in this context is best served by the deployment of symbols, concerns, and values that most pointedly set a group apart from others in a cultural market glutted with options. Thus, there is a systematic bias toward emotional symbols, powerful grievances, and polarizing distinctions, and a concomitant bias against comprehensive logics and systematic ideologies. This produces a cultural ecology of divisiveness and sectarianism.

A Cultural Geometry of Disjuncture and Deterritorialization

This centrifugal formation is manifest in more than the seemingly infinite choices within a postmodern cultural field. It is manifest, as well, in a proliferation of global-scale structural realities working between, through, and within nation-states. An illuminative metaphor for this disjunctive geometry can be found in the different backbones of global data networks. If the Internet forms the basis for whatever sort of global public sphere that will emerge, it is an evocative fact that the digital pulse of global financial exchange is carried out on separate proprietary data networks.[40]

Globalization arises from and encourages the proliferation of networks, organizations, and operations that escape and erode the national

39. Appadurai, *Modernity at Large,* p. 60.
40. Saskia Sassen, *Sociology of Globalization* (New York: W. W. Norton, 2007), pp. 90ff.

scale. Among these are what Sassen terms the proliferation of "normative orders" that function as specialized "partial systems" not subordinated to any broader normative order (for example, medieval Church or empire) or integrated into an encompassing architectural and normative order (for example, the nation-state).[41] Commonly cited examples include international governmental organizations such as the World Trade Organization (WTO) to which participant nation-states voluntarily cede significant control over their domestic economies. A more striking example can be found in the less remarked rise of privatized global normative systems, such as international commercial arbitration, which allow parties to pursue disputes without submitting to national legal regimes. These private systems of justice are largely invisible because they are not subject to local juridical and political systems, even though they can exert a profound impact on persons within them.[42]

The invisibility of these networks, the fact that they do not map coherently into any ready frame of reference or space, causes them radically to extend the fragmentation of modern systems of differentiation. These proliferating normative orders do not simply claim and apportion various domains of human existence for sphere-specific logics. They interact in chaotic and unpredictable ways that cannot be easily brought into reflection because they do not appear in a common space.

Appadurai describes this emergent global space as non-contiguous, disjunctive, and fractal. His well-known terminology of "scapes" describes the "dimensions" of global cultural flows. Ethnoscapes, technoscapes, financescapes, ideoscapes, and mediascapes are not simply contents that travel in generic channels of globalization. Although scapes may touch down in the same nodes in global space, they are material-spatial networks in themselves that interconnect and overrun localities around the world in different ways. They do not overlap with one another as much as intersect.

Ethnoscapes consist both of the bodied human currents of travel, migration, and trafficking and of the new forms of ethnic identity and politics that develop in the satellite and Internet-linked diasporas they constitute.

---

41. Sassen, *Territory, Authority, Rights,* p. 422.

42. The number of arbitration centers grew from 120 in 1991 to 9,000 in 2006 (Sassen, *Territory, Authority, Rights,* pp. 242-45). In Appadurai's words, "The emergent postnational order may not be a system of homogenous units (as with the current system of nation-states), but a system based on relations between heterogeneous units (some social movements, some interest groups, some professional bodies, some nongovernmental organizations, some armed constabularies, some judicial bodies)" (Appadurai, *Modernity at Large,* p. 23).

The paths of migrants trace various circuits from the global city-hopping business-class journeys of global mobiles who arrive at their hotels in limos, to the hidden itineraries of the global underclass and victims of trafficking. These are forced into dangerous crossings of deserts and seas. On arrival, they travel the same highways as the airport limos, invisible in unventilated cargo trailers, working both in the hotels that serve the globals and in difficult and dangerous jobs in industries far from metropolitan centers. These two ethnoscapes connect the same points in space, but do not overlap in a shared place. "We are the people you do not see."[43]

These scapes transect national space in more than personal ways. Appadurai describes the emergence of "diasporic public spheres" that serve as "the crucibles of a postnational political order."[44] New communication and information technologies allow expatriates to remain tied to their countries of origin, giving rise to new forms of "long-distance nationalism." Anderson documents the rise of transnational politicians: expatriate citizens of one state, running for office in their ancestral or ethnic state, frequently without renouncing the citizenship of their country of residence. Such individuals, whatever disproportionate resources they possess in wealth or fame (as with Wyclef Jean's presidential bid in Haiti), must, however, submit to the electoral process and legal regime in their ancestral or ethnic nation-states.[45]

Another quantitatively more significant form of long-distance nationalism faces no such constraints. Expatriates have increasing power in their ethnic nations by participating in their political processes through financial and communication technologies. They are able to follow and to provide financial support to political movements in their ethnic countries. Their politics are often driven by the quite specific identity needs arising from their life in exile. "The problem of cultural reproduction for Hindus abroad has become tied to the politics of Hindu fundamentalism at home." Such long-distance nationalism can affect electoral change and other very significant forms of political organization. Expatriate funding was crucial for the Vishwa Hindu Parishad (World Hindu Council) that carried out the intricate planning and training for the destruction of the Babri Masjid in Ayodhya.[46]

43. These are the concluding lines uttered by three migrant hotel workers — a bellhop, a housekeeper, and a prostitute in the film *Dirty Pretty Things,* directed by Stephen Frears (Miramax Films, 2002).

44. Appadurai, *Modernity at Large,* p. 22.

45. Anderson, *The Spectre of Comparisons,* p. 71.

46. Appadurai, *Modernity at Large,* pp. 38, 196.

The politics of long-distance nationalism illustrate the workings of deterritorialized social space. Serious public engagement is spread over vast, noncontiguous spaces. Despite their seriousness, these politics are at the same time "radically unaccountable." The long-distance nationalist is insulated from consequences; he will not pay taxes, or live with the regimes and policies he helps establish. "He need not fear prison, torture, death, nor need his immediate family. But, well and safely positioned in the First World, he can send money and guns, circulate propaganda, and build intercontinental computer information circuits, all of which can have incalculable consequences in the zones of their ultimate destinations."[47]

This chapter has been arguing that technological change transforms the workings of civil society. In the previous section we observed how technological developments undergird the rise of the national scale, and how religions conformed to the various national civil societies and worked within the spaces open to them in the age of mobilization. In this section we have observed how the further development of technology has contributed to the unwinding of the national scale of social space. If national space was homogeneous and contiguous, contemporary space is increasingly fissiparous and fractal. The expectations of homogeneity and imagined community remain, but are deployed on smaller scales and across a discontinuous, deterritorialized social space where cooperation and responsibility become difficult to imagine. I now turn to a consideration of how religious traditions are formed and disciplined in this space.

7. The Unraveling of the National Scale as Post-Secular Space

In her discussion of the unbundling of the order of the nation-state, Sassen observes that "normative orders such as religion reassume great importance where they had been confined to distinct specialized spheres by the secular normative order of states. This does not signal a return to a pre-modern, pre-secular cultural order, but "a systematic outcome of cutting edge developments" that heralds a new type of modernity.[48] From this perspective we can consider the "post-secular" as a dimension of the broader cultural trends of globalization. Religion is one of many cultural

---

47. Anderson, *The Spectre of Comparisons,* p. 74.
48. Sassen, *Territory, Authority, Rights,* p. 423.

and normative orders unbound by the technologically driven dissolution of the homogenizing national scale. This unbinding frees religious traditions from the secular mores of public rationality and the policing of the sacred. Thus, we can think of the unwinding of the national scale as the unwinding of many of the disciplining structures of secularity. This is not to say that secularity is undone. Many of its intellectual, cultural, and social presences and structures endure, as Taylor has documented. Nonetheless, the decline of homogenizing national-scale social and cultural structures frees religion in myriad ways that correspond with the so-called resurgence of religion. This freedom does not, however, come as pure liberation. The technological changes that liberate religion from one disciplining order transform and discipline it in new ways.

Print capitalism provided a new communicative realm that supplanted the constrained, hierarchical Latinate communications network of medieval Christianity.[49] The result was not simply the loss of the papal monopoly on doctrinal authority and the rise of competing forms of Christianity, but a fundamental transformation of the nature of tradition and religious community.[50] Likewise, the emergence of electronic capitalism has similarly challenged traditional religious authority, brought forth new forms of community, and transformed the imagination and practice of tradition. We consider the fate of religious traditions in the contemporary cultural ecology in terms of deregulation, fragmentation, and deterritorialization.

Deregulation

The widespread cultural agency made possible by the new media allows for the emergence of new collective forms of religion. These include both new religious movements and new interpretations of venerable religious traditions. Taylor spoke of the "nova effect" as elites responded to the cross pressures of modernity at a time when Christianity had lost its legitimacy, but reductionist philosophies could not speak to life's anxieties. This initial

49. Anderson, *Imagined Communities,* pp. 15-16.
50. Elizabeth Eisenstein argues that the printing press both undermined traditional authority and reified it. Print reproduction and the iterative editing it allowed combined to convey a sense of the true text, in a way that manuscript reproduction did not. The printing press thus undergirded both Protestant innovation and Tridentine standardization. See Elizabeth Eisenstein, *The Printing Revolution in Early Modern Europe* (Cambridge: Cambridge University Press, 1983), pp. 152-57.

multiplication of options among elites expands into the rest of society, forming a "spiritual super-nova."[51]

In the sociology of religion, the term "deregulation" is often associated with "supply-side" accounts of secularization that argue the importance of a vigorous open market of religious providers for sustaining a high level of religious belief and practice.[52] Our concern here is rather the concept's usefulness for analyzing transformations in religious authority.[53]

Danièle Hervieu-Léger speaks of a shift in the "repository of the truth of belief from the institution to the believer." A "metaphor-fed subjectivizing of the contents of belief" poses a fundamental challenge to religious institutions' "prime purpose of preserving and transmitting a tradition."[54] This individualized "fragmentation of memory" leads paradoxically to its homogenization with broader cultural norms.[55] New forms of religious community are biased toward voluntaristic, highly affective forms of community, without reference to a broader "institutionally regulated orthodoxy."[56] The notion of deregulation connects secularization debates with studies of mediation. The sort of settled institutional authority presumed in deregulation is a product of large-scale organization and media production.

John Thompson notes that while mediation "fixes symbolic content in a material substratum, reception 'unfixes' it for divergent uses."[57] New

51. Taylor, *A Secular Age,* pp. 300, 374.

52. For example, Roger Finke, "Religious Deregulation: Origins and Consequences," *Journal of Church and State* 32, no. 3 (1990): 609-26; Roger Finke and Rodney Stark, *The Churching Of America, 1776-2005: Winners and Losers in Our Religious Economy* (New Brunswick, N.J.: Rutgers University Press, 2005).

53. The debate concerning deregulation presumes a largely Christian, if not Catholic, understanding of the role of religious elites. For an account of similar transformations of authority in Islam, see Peter Mandaville, "Globalization and the Politics of Religious Knowledge: Pluralizing Authority in the Muslim World," *Theory, Culture & Society* 24, no. 2 (2007): 101-15; Peter Mandaville, *Global Political Islam* (New York: Routledge, 2007); and Bryan Turner, "Religious Authority and the New Media," *Theory, Culture & Society* 24, no. 2 (2007): 117-34.

54. Danièle Hervieu-Léger, *Religion as a Chain of Memory* (New Brunswick, N.J.: Rutgers University Press, 2000), p. 168.

55. Hervieu-Léger, *Religion as a Chain of Memory,* pp. 128-30; Danièle Hervieu-Léger, *La Religion en Miettes ou La Question des Sectes* (Paris: Calmann-Lévy, 2001), p. 131.

56. Hervieu-Léger, *Religion as a Chain of Memory,* p. 155.

57. Thompson, *Media and Modernity,* p. 39. See as well Michel de Certeau, "Reading as Poaching," in *The Practice of Everyday Life* (Berkeley: University of California Press, 1984), pp. 165-77.

communications structures do not simply erode traditional authority by creating new engagements with religious traditions; they also facilitate the emergence of new forms of religious authority. Early accounts of this transformation focused on the emergence of a new class of cultural intermediaries. These serve the needs of a new bourgeois class employed in new professions, such as cultural production and therapeutic and professional services, which do not fit into traditional class hierarchies.[58] This analysis describes well the emergence of various lifestyle experts (relationship, sex, childrearing) and of the generalized, generic spirituality of successful figures such as Oprah Winfrey and her many predecessors. It does not adequately explain the rise of new forms of religious authority.

James Dobson is a useful bridge figure in this regard. He gained national prominence in 1972 with the publication of *Dare to Discipline,* a conservative evangelical version of Dr. Benjamin Spock's family lifestyle manual. Whereas Spock questioned traditional childrearing and encouraged the development of individuality, Dobson wove from the proverb "Spare the rod, spoil the child" both a parenting manual and a repudiation of the moral laxity of the 1960s.[59] He rose to national prominence through continued publishing, a national radio program, the massive Focus on the Family ministry outreach, and what was one of the most successful special agenda organizations of the Christian Right: the Family Research Council. Dobson's success was undergirded by the rolling development of new media technologies: radio networks, cable television, direct mail, and the Internet.

Dobson operates in the trans-denominational space of the special purpose group and the special agenda organization. Other figures have created authority positions with much more focus on specific churches: for example, Mother Angelica's Eternal Word Television Network has become a force in the Catholic Church, with a reach into 54 million homes and a devoted following.[60] Similar new authority positions are evident

58. Pierre Bourdieu, *Distinction: A Social Critique of the Judgment of Taste,* trans. Richard Nice (Cambridge, Mass.: Harvard University Press, 1984), pp. 359-69; Mike Featherstone, *Consumer Culture and Postmodernism* (London: Sage, 1991), pp. 43-44; and Miller, *Consuming Religion,* pp. 91-103.

59. James Dobson, *Dare to Discipline* (Chicago: Gospel Light, 1972). See Robert Wuthnow, *After Heaven: Spirituality in America since the 1950s* (Berkeley: University of California Press, 1998), pp. 90-93.

60. See Richard Gaillardetz, "The New E-Magisterium," *America* 182, no. 16 (May 6, 2000): 8; Anthony Godzieba, "*Quaestio Disputata:* The Magisterium in an Age of Digital

in Islam. These range from the mainstream Islamicist teaching of Sheikh Yusuf al-Qaradawi, who reaches a global audience via satellite television, to Amr Khaled, often dubbed "the Muslim Oprah." Dispensing with the dour tone and formal Islamic scholarly discourse of the traditional 'ulama, Khaled dresses in stylish suits and presents Islam in inspirational and motivational discourse.[61]

These new channels of communication have supplanted older established religious networks of communication, such as denominational presses, periodicals, and diocesan newspapers. In these new communicative domains, traditional religious authorities compete directly with new figures, popes with pundits, bishops with media personalities, theologians with bloggers. Some traditional religious authorities are capable of competing on this level. Pope John Paul II had the media charisma and the ecclesial vision to work on the world stage of the global media. In so doing, however, he bypassed more traditional Catholic structures of communication (the hierarchical network stretching from the Vatican to parishes; the theological guild) and appealed directly to believers. This had the dual result of broadening his appeal beyond Catholicism, and eroding the capillary communal structures of the Church.[62]

In addition to empowering individual interpretations and facilitating new forms of authority, the technologically driven deregulation of religion also gives rise to new collective forms of religion. In later work, Hervieu-Léger stresses that deregulation does not mean pure individualization, but the rise of "small-scale regimes of communal validation."[63] "Mediated quasi-interaction" forms believers to expect more interpersonal forms of validation.[64] Although John Paul II was as geographically and institutionally distant from believers as previous popes, his media visage came into

---

Reproduction," in *When the Magisterium Intervenes,* ed. Richard Gaillardetz (Collegeville, Minn.: Liturgical, 2012), pp. 140-53; and Vincent Miller, "When Mediating Structures Change: The Magisterium, the Media, and the Culture Wars," in *When the Magisterium Intervenes,* pp. 154-74.

61. Mandaville, *Global Political Islam,* pp. 327-30.

62. Olivier Roy compares John Paul II's habit of bypassing "institutional and generational hierarchies" in order to appeal directly to youth to the contemporaneous strategies of Fethullah Gülen and Khomeini. See his *Globalized Islam: The Search for a New Ummah* (New York: Columbia University Press, 2004), p. 29. For a discussion of John Paul II's use of media, see Miller, *Consuming Religion,* pp. 95-103.

63. Danièle Hervieu-Léger, "Individualism and the Validation of Faith," in *The Blackwell Companion to the Sociology of Religion,* ed. Richard K. Fenn (Oxford: Blackwell, 2001), p. 173.

64. Thompson, *Media and Modernity,* pp. 84ff.

the domestic spaces of people's everyday lives. Such experiences of mediated intimacy incline believers within large-scale institutional religions to expect more communal forms of religious authority.

The symbolic resources of religious traditions are opened to "reprocessing" and "incorporation into other symbolic constructions" as well. Hervieu-Léger offers the example of Catholicism in communist Poland, where it functioned as an organizing symbol of opposition to the communist regime without engendering commitment to its particular doctrines.[65] Such reprocessing will only grow. The Internet can be a fully interactive medium that frees users to be creators as well.[66] The social networking sites that are the main use of the Internet by contemporary adolescents are almost completely composed of user-provided content. Traditional notions of authorized interpretation and authoritative discourse will appear ever more unnatural to generations formed by such media spaces.

When, in John Beckford's words, "religion comes adrift from former points of anchorage," it "is no less potentially powerful as a result."[67] This power is mobilized by religious groups in a manner akin to other social movements.[68] Robert Wuthnow and James Davison Hunter have explored recent reorganizations of religious groups in a manner that compares them to broader social movement structures. Wuthnow documented the rise of "special purpose groups" that exist independently of traditional denominations. While they are religious movements, they are not directed at the formation of local religious communities, as are sects or new denominations. They are instrumentally oriented toward specific objectives and membership is organized through mobilization to meet these objectives.[69] These groups do not compete with denominations; they work around and within them. Churches continue to gather people in traditional worship settings, but the engaged practice of faith within these communities takes place within special purpose groups focused on spirituality, such as bible

65. Hervieu-Léger, *Religion as a Chain of Memory,* pp. 158-60.

66. Turner, "Religious Authority and the New Media," p. 127.

67. James Beckford, *Religion and Advanced Industrial Society* (Boston: Unwin Hyman, 1989), p. 170.

68. Traditional religious authorities lose the ability to "control the definition and use of religious symbols." See James Beckford, "Social Movements as Free-Floating Religious Phenomena," in *The Blackwell Companion to the Sociology of Religion,* p. 232.

69. Robert Wuthnow, *The Restructuring of American Religion* (Princeton, N.J.: Princeton University Press, 1990), pp. 101-5, 317.

study or charismatic prayer groups; or on matters of public life, such as civil rights, peace and justice, or pro-life.[70]

Their effects extend beyond religious communities. Hunter's study of the culture war centers on the "special agenda organization" — "a wide variety of religiously based public affairs organizations, political lobbies, and associations" that are "concerned with promoting particular social or political agenda in the public domain."[71] These have become increasingly influential in the public sphere and within churches. They are neither burdened by the responsibility to address the full range of issues of concern to the church, nor do they need to balance the interests of a complex constituency. Their membership is composed entirely of people concerned enough about their issue to be active members. This politicization of religion by special agenda groups is one of the most powerful drivers of the sustained deprivatization of religion in recent decades. (As we will see below, this has not brought with it the expected disciplining of the public sphere.)

The most effective religious special agenda organizations over the past forty years in the United States have been in the constellation of the Religious Right. Putnam and Campbell document the effects of these special agenda organizations on the public perception of religion in the United States and among the political and policy commitments of highly religious Americans. They find strong identification of Christianity with the conservative side of culture war issues both among believers scoring high on an index of "religiosity" and among the general public. High scores on the religiosity scale correlate with conservative positions on a range of policy issues regardless of official teaching on the issue in question.[72] This study illuminates the declining power of traditional religious leaders in defining the public face of their traditions and in inculcating a traditional breadth of orthodoxy among believers.

The deregulation of religion provides an understanding of the resurgence of religion that takes account of the role of media and organizational technology. Religious symbols and sentiment can be mobilized in public life outside of the control of traditional religious authorities and free from the complexities and checks and balances of comprehensive systems of orthodoxy. The symbolic power of religious traditions remains strong, even

70. Wuthnow, *The Restructuring of American Religion,* p. 130.

71. James Davison Hunter, *Culture Wars: The Struggle to Define America* (New York: Basic, 1991), p. 90.

72. Robert Putnam and David Campbell, *American Grace: How Religion Divides and Unites Us* (New York: Simon and Schuster, 2010), p. 386.

as religious literacy declines. Although the contexts are quite different, the situation bears a troubling resemblance to Scott Appleby's analysis of the preconditions for ethno-religious violence in Northern Ireland and in the Balkans.[73] Religion provides a powerful symbolic source of identity, but is relatively weak in guiding behavior.

Michel de Certeau's observations are particularly apt for considering its theological challenge of deregulation. He observed that the links between religious signs and doctrines, practices, and forms of life are "obscure, frequently dramatic, increasingly ambivalent, and slowly uncoupling." Religious symbols are

> imperceptibly taking on a different meaning, in one case remaining an expression of faith, and in another a catchphrase for conservatism in political strategy. . . . The ecclesialogical [*sic*] constellation disintegrates as its elements move out of orbit. The centre no longer "holds" because there is no longer a firm link between the act of believing and objective signs. Each sign follows its own path, wanders off, submits the different employment, as if the words in the sentence were scattered across the page and produce different combinations of meaning.[74]

In a deregulated context, elements of religious traditions are dispersed in a discursive field of vectoral memes. "Vectoral" refers to their innate semantic power that orients them toward certain meanings and uses, but that can be relocated and redirected. In this context, the semantic aura of doctrines, symbols, and practices can be redirected to contribute to ideologies and practices counter to their proper meanings. Rather than doctrinal relationships, they are grouped into constellations of meanings.

These constellations cluster around powerful interests, symbols, narratives, and psychosocial dynamisms (for example, for narratives, nation vs. republic; for psychosocial dynamisms, scapegoating, sacred purity, sexual desire, frustration, and shame; and opportunities for political-cultural agency). At times religious memes are yoked to these frames because of their doctrinal relevance; at other times they are simply there to provide emotional charge and rhetorical energy, their dogmatic-semantic vectors

73. R. Scott Appleby, *The Ambivalence of the Sacred: Religion, Violence and Reconciliation* (Lanham, Md.: Rowman and Littlefield, 2000), p. 69.
74. Michel de Certeau and Jean-Marie Domenach, *Le Christianisme éclaté* (Paris: Éditions du Seuil, 1974), pp. 11-12. Cited in Hervieu-Léger, *Religion as a Chain of Memory*, p. 159.

subordinated to an alien logic. This dynamism is exacerbated by other dimensions of the current cultural context.

Fragmentation and Identity

If print capitalism and mass communications in the nineteenth and twentieth centuries tended toward large-scale homogenization of culture and religion, contemporary media enable smaller-scale communities to flourish. Indeed, by reducing their cost so drastically and providing a frictionless array of choice to media users, they constitute a cultural ecology of sectarianism in which culture is increasingly heterogenized as groups separate into internally homogeneous enclaves. The "lifestyle enclaves" warned of by Bellah in the 1980s, based on consumption separated from politics and religion, have grown to encompass increasingly public dimensions of community.[75]

Charles Hirschkind's provocative term "public sphericles," which describes the small-scale, but intense engagement of Egyptian Muslims with sermons on cassette tapes, evokes the technological fragmentation of the public sphere.[76] Normative or formal descriptions of the nature of public discourse become problematic in light of this mediated pluralization and fragmentation.[77] Casanova's illuminative argument that entering into the public sphere changes religion, requiring it to conform to norms of public discourse, and that the norms of the public realm will enter the church and transform it from within is thrown into question by the proliferation of media.[78] This is not an entirely new story. When fundamentalist and Pentecostal voices were excluded by local ministerial boards from the FCC-mandated airtime set aside for religious programming in the early to mid-twentieth century, they turned to the open market and bought airtime on

---

75. Robert N. Bellah et al., *Habits of the Heart: Individualism and Commitment in American Life* (New York: Harper, 1985), pp. 71-74.

76. Charles Hirschkind, "Cassette Ethics: Public Piety and Popular Media in Egypt," in *Religion, Media and the Public Sphere,* ed. Birgit Meyer and Annelies Moors (Bloomington: Indiana University Press, 2006), pp. 29-51, and Charles Hirschkind, *The Ethical Soundscape: Cassette Sermons and Islamic Counterpublics* (New York: Columbia University Press, 2006).

77. Hent de Vries, "In Media Res: Global Religions, Public Spheres, and the Task of Contemporary Comparative Religious Studies," in *Religion and Media,* ed. Hent de Vries and Samuel Weber (Stanford, Calif.: Stanford University Press, 2001), p. 19.

78. Casanova, *Public Religions,* pp. 135, 207.

independent stations. Although outside of mainstream civil society, they found their audience.[79] Unnoticed by mainstream society, they built the broadcasting networks that would facilitate their rapid public mobilization in the 1970s and 1980s. These same networks enabled them to have a public influence without conforming to mainstream public discourse. What was once a (rather large) exception to the homogeneity of the public sphere is now much closer to the norm.

Wuthnow expressed prescient concern about special purpose groups' tendency to attract homogeneous memberships. He feared that this would contribute to "the development of cultural cleavages." Such groups can sort out allegiances within denominations and congregations and thus lessen the ability of religious communities to sustain the complex unities their traditions demand. The growth of such groups brings "heightened potential for religious communities to become fractured along the lines of larger cleavages in society."[80]

Likewise, special agenda groups' appeals and media messaging often speak more to their committed members than to the broader public who presumably must be convinced to support their cause. Although their raison d'être is advocacy, their survival depends on attracting committed supporters. Thus they employ rhetoric of denunciation and outrage to move their supporters to action and donation. Indeed, the fundamental genre of communication has remained constant through changes in technology — the targeted direct mail, email, or web ad. These usually warn of some dire action about to be accomplished by enemies of the cause (whose own special agenda organizations are no doubt doing the same in their own letters). A token advocacy action is included — a survey, a postcard, or click-through email message to a legislator — along with a chance to donate to the organization (and build its mailing list) so that it may continue its noble fight for the cause.

Such groups live only if they attract a committed core of supporters. They do so by identifying symbols, issues, and values that sharply distinguish them from competing groups. As noted above, this cultural ecology is thus biased toward emotional symbols, powerful grievances, and polarizing distinctions, with a concomitant bias against comprehensive logics and systematic ideologies. This leads to a refiguring of identity. Identity

79. R. Laurence Moore, *Selling God: American Religion in the Marketplace of Culture* (New York: Oxford University Press, 1994), pp. 229-33.

80. Wuthnow, *The Restructuring of American Religion*, p. 130.

ceases to be an ascribed characteristic or a matter of belonging to a comprehensive tradition and form of life. It is rendered increasingly reflexive and contrastive, consisting of a manageable set of markers that distinguish one group from others.

This poses a profound problem for the discipline of theology. "Identity," for all the integrity evoked by its rhetorical use, is a very limited cultural practice. Far from preserving the complex orthodoxy and orthopraxis of a tradition, it shears off what does not serve its limited needs. Olivier Roy's observations about the lack of hearing received by moderate Muslim voices are hauntingly relevant in a Catholic context. Scholars "wish to propound their academic theological learning. They therefore do not appeal to born-again Muslims, who prefer gurus to teachers, consider that too much intellectualism spoils the faith, and seek a ready-made and easily accessible set of norms and values that might order their daily lives and define a practical and visible identity. Liberal thinkers do not meet the demands of the religious market."[81] Not only liberal interpretations, but any comprehensive commitment to orthodoxy is disadvantaged in such a context because it will always trouble attempts to reconcile a given tradition with cultural divides to which it cannot be easily reduced. This particular construction of identity deepens the challenge to the traditional authority of religious leaders in teaching comprehensive orthodoxy in the current context. They face profound pressures to refocus their teaching authority in a manner more consistent with a special agenda group focus.

This cultural ecology also undermines non-ideological notions of religious belonging and solidarity. Ethnic and familial connections, theological understandings of baptism, or principles such as catholicity construct church belonging in a way that cannot be reconciled with the expectation of uniformity and contrastive identity. The default sectarian social physics clashes with these non-ideological conceptions of church boundaries. This focus on identity amidst a broad range of options reconstrues excommunication from an extraordinary disciplinary medicine to confront a believer with his or her errors, to a normal part of communal sorting. Those who cannot embrace a particular ecclesial-party line are expected to go elsewhere to find another community more consistent with their views. Religious communities cease to comprise diversity in their unities. Believers lose the habits of cohabiting with people who are different from

---

81. Roy, *Globalized Islam*, p. 31.

themselves. The communication and rhetorical skills required to engage and to convince others atrophy.

This provokes crisis for tradition, in MacIntyre's sense of an extended argument carried out over time. As large-scale communions fragment and local communities become ever more internally homogeneous, the give and take of reception, debate, and reflection on tradition declines. Intergenerational memory and formation fade. The ongoing argument of a living tradition fragments into myriad shallow, dispersed monologues.

Traditions also lose their "bleeding edges" — those places where unforeseen consequences and insights of the tradition get applied in unauthorized ways; where the logic and practice of traditions transgress established boundaries; where particular religious imaginations penetrate and illuminate broader experience. Bleeding edges do not serve the task of identity. Deregulated traditions lack the robustness to transgress or to color outside the lines of their assigned role.

Deterritorialization

The deterritorialization of the contemporary cultural context further exacerbates these transformations of religious traditions. The nation-state provided a spatial domain within which the consequences and consistency of belief and behavior could be evaluated as the basis for responsibility. Aiwa Ong has argued that American higher education has long addressed students as both rationally calculative professional actors and as citizens.[82] The spatial overlap of these two roles provided an educational and anthropological synthesis that curricula or character alone could not achieve. Responsibility requires a heuristic space within which consequences of individual and collective action can appear. National space is not simply a matter of ideological commitment. The global perforation and erosion of the national scale deprive religious communities of the spatial scale within which they have spent much of the past two centuries imagining responsibility. Even if it could never be accepted as the only scale of responsibility, it was the fundamental one to which smaller and larger scales were articulated.

---

82. Aihwa Ong, *Neoliberalism as Exception: Mutations in Citizenship and Sovereignty* (Durham, N.C.: Duke University Press, 2006), p. 149. See also Vincent Miller, "Where Is the University Now? Education and Place in Global Space," *The Cresset* 74 (April 2011): 4, 28-40.

The unbundled space of the global order has no similar heuristic space within which consequences can appear and responsibility can be faced. This brings about the abstraction of religious doctrines and moral principles through a decline in systems of jurisprudence and casuistry. These forms of practical reason mediate between doctrines and practice in the complexity of life. This mediation depends on a manageable model of reality. Deterritorialization erodes shared understandings of the moral dimensions of everyday life, and thus the moral casuistry necessary to act within it. Doctrines and principles float free from the refractory difficulties of everyday life. As a result, they become increasingly abstract and essentialized, providing more fitting material for the task of identity projection than for active, transformative engagement in the world.

This moral deterritorialization exacerbates the fragmentation discussed above. We are not held together in common space to face the consequences of our beliefs and forms of life, to debate our complicity in them, or to act responsibly. Fragmentation and deterritorialization contribute to what is frequently described as the "relativism" of our epoch. This is misread if it is conceived as a principled commitment. The pluralism of culture and the lack of any shared anchoring in a heuristic space make finding a common basis for reason profoundly difficult.

Deterritorialization places religions alongside other discrete and autonomous normative orders that work within global space. This renders their practices similar to the operationalized practices of global capitalist firms. These do what they are able according to their own interests without concern for the consequences in their place of action. There is a danger that radical ecclesiologies exacerbate this problem by presenting such contexts as irredeemably flawed, and thus not capable of being constructively engaged. Such theological perspectives unwittingly reinforce the very disengagement that deterritorialization renders the cultural default.

Here we see a new way in which religion is "privatized." Its presence is rendered illegible in a world where shared public space is being replaced by deterritorialized networks that do not comprise a whole. More than 1 billion people are now on Facebook — a population that would rank as the third largest country in the world. While this may instill shared communicative habits, it does not unite them in any shared space. One billion people relating to their private friends lists do not add up to any social unity in the way that 1 billion viewers, listeners, or readers would in previous eras. Facebook is a non-nation that is nowhere — a fitting metaphor for the fragmented and deterritorialized global space.

Clearly there is a need for a new territorialization of the global. It is equally clear that this will not be forthcoming anytime soon. If the emergence of the nation-state is a historical parallel, the process will likely take a matter of centuries, and tumultuous ones at that. The turn to various forms of localism have profound appeal in theological circles. But this does not escape the global construction of space, which reaches into every locale, even into our bodies, which are themselves constituted in global commodity chains.[83]

8. Conclusion

Attending to media technology and its role in the construction of social space provides a different perspective on secularization that can distinguish the cultural changes of the past four decades. It calls attention to the non-ideological dimensions of the national and global spatial scales and to the material structures that construct and discipline religious communities' practice of their traditions.

If we read secularization primarily as an ideological system administered through homogenizing state power that is ontologically and anthropologically incompatible with Christianity, then the required response will be some form of refusal and reassertion of threatened identity. When the technologically mediated cultural ecology and construction of space are factored into our analysis, however, different problems appear and different strategies are demanded. While the ontological-anthropological challenge of secular ideology remains, alongside it we face other equally profound challenges: the deregulation at the heart of the resurgence of religion that yokes the sematic power of religious doctrines and symbols to alien political projects and to the shallow task of identity projection; the fragmentation and polarization of culture that reduces the theological complexity of the church to sectarian voluntarism with the concomitant consequence of the loss of the catholic dialogue necessary for a living tradition; a deterritorialization that shears dogmatic and moral principles from casuist engagement with the concreteness of life.

83. See Vincent Miller, "The Body Globalized: Problems for a Sacramental Imagination in an Age of Global Commodity Chains," in *Religion, Economics, and Culture in Conversation,* College Theology Society Annual Volume 56, ed. Laurie Cassidy and Maureen H. O'Connell (Maryknoll, N.Y.: Orbis, 2011), pp. 108-20.

These other challenges complicate a strategic response. A reassertion of identity and the project of dogmatic consistency and ecclesial purification appear, not as counter-cultural resistance, but as conforming to the dominant cultural logic. Certainly the task of preserving and handing on the integrity of the tradition in fullness must be a fundamental ecclesial objective in any context. The deregulation of religion makes this a particular imperative for the current context. This must, however, be done in a manner that contests the dominant cultural logic.

Against the logic of heterogenization and fragmentation, the church should emphasize the living and contested nature of tradition in its retrievals and presentation. The living tradition comprises a diverse community of subtraditions that live out its central dogmatic commitments. This diversity should be presented as an expression of the church's catholicity, a capacious unity that can hold great diversity in communion.[84] This need not be done at the expense of stressing essentials when necessary. It must, however, be a major part of our presentation of tradition.

Against the abstractions of deterritorialization, the church should retrieve and publicly practice its rich systems of casuistry and prudence. These convey a richer sense of tradition than line-drawing absolutes. The laity are capable of high levels of sophistication, and traditional practical distinctions present that tradition as confident and engaged. The authority of tradition is conveyed in engaged practice. A living, responsible tradition requires prudential judgments. Highlighting the provisional and limited nature of such judgments, far from eroding authority, displays the necessity of wading into the details of public life and the seriousness of the details of our decisions. It also highlights the greater centrality of more dogmatic teachings.

Finally, the bricolage-style character of deregulated religion and its public use places new demands on theologians. Even the most ill-fitting associations are dependent on some semantic resonance. Such constellations of meaning place new demands on us. They need to be studied in order to understand their logics, their ruptures, and the basis of their appeal. This cultural realm is a particularly complex space. This requires of theologians the familiar skills of dogmatic knowledge and ideology critique.[85] It also demands the more sympathetic skills of ethnography to attend to

---

84. Cf. Robert Schreiter's discussion of catholicity in chapter 3 in this volume.

85. See David Tracy's treatment of "Publicness One" and "Publicness Two" in chapter 1 in this volume.

the social, psychological, cultural, economic, and political context of the reception and enactment of these cultural constellations. Such knowledge is essential for a response that does more than abstractly reassert proper doctrine over its misuse. Such ethnographic sensitivity is needed to guide a tactical rhetorical engagement that redirects such ad hoc religious constellations toward a greater dogmatic coherence and consistency.

These are but sketches of the characteristics requisite to an adequate theological and ecclesial response to the context that this essay has described. If the "resurgence of religion" is a result of the unwinding of the national scale and the emergence of a still incipient global spatial scale, then it is difficult to offer a precise prescription for this new cultural moment. Indeed, given that the national scale emerged only over the course of centuries, we can expect that the global — if it emerges as coherent spatial scale — will take a similarly protracted period of time. Thus, religious responses to this new spatial order will remain necessarily provisional.

PART III

In and Beyond a Secular Age:
Theological Anthropology

7. Imagination, the Body, and the Transfiguration of Limits

ANTHONY J. GODZIEBA

It is an odd and perhaps ironic twist that Charles Taylor's *A Secular Age* makes the "social imaginary" a focal point of its narrative but nowhere addresses the particular workings of the imagination. Taylor loosely describes the social imaginary as "the ways in which [people] imagine their social existence, how they fit together with others, how things go on between them and their fellows, the expectations which are normally met, and the deeper normative notions and images which underlie these expectations."[1] This "pre-theoretical" common understanding "carried in images, stories, legends" legitimates the common construals and practices that a society holds as normative.[2] But how these legitimating social narratives are generated, what they respond to in particular, and why these frameworks might be susceptible to change are questions that Taylor leaves unanswered.

They can only begin to be answered by taking the workings of the imagination into account. So, then, there is a gap to be filled, an analysis that needs to be added to the mix. And an important advantage to a focus on the imagination is that it can aid in the search for the "moments of ascent" and conversion that Taylor sketches in the book's conclusion as ways of responding to a deeply felt contemporary restlessness "at the barriers of the human sphere."[3] If anything, the imagination is always about what is different, unprecedented, other than business-as-usual — its operations

---

1. Charles Taylor, *A Secular Age* (Cambridge, Mass.: Harvard University Press, 2007), p. 171.
2. Taylor, *A Secular Age*, p. 146 (pre-theoretical); p. 172.
3. Taylor, *A Secular Age*, p. 726 (restlessness); p. 772 (moments of ascent).

always intend new possibilities for human existence, whether micro or macro in scale.

This chapter, then, fills the gap to some degree with a philosophical and theological analysis of the imagination.[4] The first two parts of this essay focus on the imagination and on its necessary connection with the religious imagination. The remaining parts apply this analysis to one particular aspect of the broad topic of "secularity" derived from *A Secular Age,* namely, the limits imposed by "the immanent frame." The goal, ultimately, is a theological anthropology that takes Taylor's analysis of the "buffered self" seriously while contesting it with an analysis of an alternative "self," the intentional embodied self that both experiences its limits and has the capacity to exceed them. While my main focus is on the intentionality of the embodied imagination, at the same time I keep track of two other issues: a legitimate complaint regarding the abstract nature of much of the current discussion of secularity and public discourse, and the question of the "public" value of this link between the imagination and theological anthropology.

1. Three Vignettes

Let me begin by offering three vignettes: one meteorological, one sculptural, and one musical. These examples of the operations of the imagination are purposely drawn from the sixteenth, seventeenth, and eighteenth centuries — thus, early and "middle" modernity, the very period when, in Taylor's reading, exclusive humanism was coalescing into the dominant Western attitude that gave us the buffered self.[5] These vignettes will return

---

4. This chapter borrows material I have published elsewhere. See Anthony J. Godzieba, "'Stay with Us . . .' (Lk. 24:29) — 'Come, Lord Jesus' (Rev. 22:20): Incarnation, Eschatology, and Theology's Sweet Predicament," *Theological Studies* 67 (2006): 783-95; "Knowing Differently: Incarnation, Imagination, and the Body," *Louvain Studies* 32 (2007): 361-82; "The Catholic Sacramental Imagination and the Access/Excess of Grace," *New Theology Review* 21, no. 3 (August 2008): 14-26; "'Refuge of Sinners, Pray for Us': Augustine, Aquinas, and the Salvation of Modernity," in *Augustine and Postmodern Thought: A New Alliance Against Modernity?* BETL 219, ed. Lieven Boeve, Frederiek Depoortere, and Maarten Wisse (Leuven: Peeters, 2009), pp. 147-65. My analysis of the imagination is part of a larger project devoted to developing a theological anthropology for a post-postmodern context.

5. For example, Taylor mentions the year 1500 as a rough dividing line (*A Secular Age,* p. 25), and later specifies "the Reformation as Reform" — thus 1517 and beyond — as key to his narrative "of the abolition of the enchanted cosmos, and the eventual creation of a humanist alternative to faith" (*A Secular Age,* p. 77).

at the end as well, as examples of the operations of the ec-static imagination in an incarnational and sacramental context.

The first vignette. In April 1569, José de Acosta — Jesuit priest, missionary, one of the sharpest minds of sixteenth-century Europe — was on board a ship bound for Peru. He was being sent by his Jesuit superiors to Lima to teach theology at the college the Jesuits had established there the previous year. While crossing the equator, he had a shocking experience that completely contradicted the greatest of the ancient authorities whom he had closely studied.

> I will describe what happened to me when I passed to the Indies. Having read what poets and philosophers write of the Torrid Zone, I persuaded myself that when I came to the Equator, I would not be able to endure the violent heat, but it turned out otherwise. For when I passed [the Equator], which was when the sun was at its zenith there, having entered the zodiacal sign of Aries, in March, I felt so cold that I was forced to go into the sun to warm myself. What could I do then but laugh at Aristotle's *Meteorology* and his philosophy? For in that place and that season, where everything, by his rules, should have been scorched by the heat, I and my companions were cold.[6]

Acosta had experienced a lightning-flash of surprising insight, an epiphany that profoundly changed him and his views. And it happened in a tiny, almost throw-away moment: he felt cold; he moved into the sunlight. Then he laughed, and he would never be the same. The geography, the history, the studies of climate, all the ancient authorities in which he had been trained — he could no longer completely trust any of it. And with Acosta's laugh, echoing along with all those other thinkers who laughed with surprise and delight and insight throughout the sixteenth and seventeenth centuries, the heretofore carefully crafted scientific framework of Western civilization, passed on by libraries of ancient texts, crumbled. Knowledge now seemed as wonderfully varied as did the world that these thinkers were now exploring firsthand.[7]

The second vignette. One of the last works created by the brilliant ba-

6. Anthony Grafton, April Shelford, and Nancy Siraisi, *New Worlds, Ancient Texts: The Power of Tradition and the Shock of Discovery* (Cambridge, Mass.: Belknap Press of Harvard University Press, 1992), p. 1, quoting Acosta's *Historia Natural y Moral de las Indias* (Seville, 1590).

7. Grafton et al., *New Worlds*, p. 3.

roque sculptor, architect, draughtsman, and painter Gianlorenzo Bernini is his over-life-size marble sculpture of Blessed Ludovica Albertoni for the Altieri Chapel of the Roman church of S. Francesco a Ripa.[8]

Gianlorenzo Bernini, *Bl. Ludovica Albertoni,* **1671-74**
(S. Francesco a Ripa, Rome)

The Altieri family had commissioned this monument from the seventy-three-year-old Bernini during their campaign to have their most famous ancestor canonized. Widowed at thirty-three, Ludovica became a Franciscan tertiary and was famed for her devotion to a life of prayer and her care of the poor and sick in the Roman area of Trastevere. The biography written for her beatification reported that on the day before her death she experienced a mystical rapture and that she was "anxious to achieve the blessed vision of Jesus Christ."[9] At the hour of her death she clutched a crucifix, tenderly kissed the wounds of the crucified Christ, and while in fervent prayer died on January 31, 1533.

8. For discussions of the work, see Shelley Karen Perlove, *Bernini and the Idealization of Death: The "Blessed Ludovica Albertoni" and the Altieri Chapel* (University Park: Pennsylvania State University Press, 1990); Charles Scribner III, *Gianlorenzo Bernini* (New York: Abrams, 1991), pp. 45, 118-19.

9. Giovanni Paolo, *Vita della B. Ludovica Albertoni* (Rome, 1672), p. 229, quoted in Perlove, *Bernini,* p. 5.

By conflating the saintly body and the erotic body, Bernini captures with great precision the intense affective spirituality of his subject and of his time.

> Ludovica lies on her deathbed . . . and at the threshold of eternity. . . . The marble altar is wedded with the tomb sculpture in a luminous apparition at the end of the small, dark chapel. The walls converge as though wings of a huge triptych had been opened to reveal Bernini's most painterly tableau. With her head thrown back, *in extremis,* lips parted, and eyes upturned, Ludovica clutches her breast. Physical agony and metaphysical "movements of the soul" resonate through the folds of her dress. White cherubs float like snowflakes down streams of daylight from concealed side windows (the right one partially walled up); at the top of the vault the dove of the Holy Spirit hovers as the symbolic source. Behind Ludovica, Bacciccio's paradisaic painting of the Virgin and Child with St. Anne, to whom the chapel was dedicated, provides the window into Ludovica's vision.[10]

Here the baroque aim to break down the barrier between the spectator and the work through fantasy and manipulation of materiality and light is in full play. The jasper pall cascading toward the viewer unites Ludovica's intimate scene with the viewer's world. The full-blown eroticism of that intimacy — even more erotic than Bernini's *St. Teresa in Ecstasy* because it is more active, more convoluted, more private — shocks us with its agitation. However, the pomegranates and flaming hearts on the lower walls surrounding Ludovica's contorted figure, symbols of the fire of love noted in contemporary devotional manuals, leave no doubt that the physical consummation suggested here is symbolic of the mystical consummation of divine love that she experienced in the rapture before her death, a consummation that is "shared sacramentally by all who partake of the Eucharist at her altar/tomb."[11]

The third vignette. In 1727, on the feast of the Purification (February 2), Johann Sebastian Bach first performed the cantata "Ich habe genug" ("I have enough") in Leipzig's St. Thomas Church.[12] He composed it during

10. Scribner, *Gianlorenzo Bernini,* p. 118.

11. Scribner, *Gianlorenzo Bernini,* p. 118.

12. "Ich habe genug," BWV 82 (for bass soloist, oboe, strings, and basso continuo). Cf. Alfred Dürr, *The Cantatas of J. S. Bach,* rev. and trans. Richard P. Jones (Oxford: Oxford University Press, 2005), pp. 661-65; Malcolm Boyd, ed., *J. S. Bach,* Oxford Composer

the frenzied period of writing that had begun with his appointment in 1723 as the cantor of the Thomaskirche and director of music for the city of Leipzig. That early period lasted about five years, during which Bach was composing at the rate of one cantata per week.

This cantata's five movements reflect the structural pattern of baroque opera to which the Lutheran sacred cantata of the first half of the eighteenth century thoroughly conformed: the thoughts, actions, and decisions of the speaker are portrayed in the recitatives, while the arias express the speaker's resulting affective state. The cantata text makes slight reference to the feast of the day: Simeon's prophecy regarding the child Jesus is mentioned in the first recitative ("for I too see with Simeon the joy of the other life already"), and the following aria "Schlummert ein, ihr matten Augen" ("Slumber, you tired eyes") might be seen as a meditative paraphrase of Simeon's *Nunc dimittis* prayer (Luke 2:29-32). The last two movements, though, underline the cantata's main theme, a favorite of Bach: the affective journey "from world-weariness to joyful anticipation of death."[13] The texts are steeped in the Lutheran view of a "world turned upside down" that was forcefully emphasized in seventeenth- and eighteenth-century sermons and grounded in Luther's own theology of the cross, which holds that "the only place God's glory is revealed to humans is, paradoxically, hidden in Christ's suffering on the cross."[14] In these two movements, the exquisite artifice of baroque affect is on display. The recitative bids the world farewell as the speaker awaits the "beautiful" call of God to undergo death in order to pass over into heaven. In the aria, the speaker rejoices over his eventual death and his escape from the distress that binds him to the world. Here Bach gives the contradictions a surprising setting: the da capo (A-B-A′) aria is set as a dance movement, a gigue

Companions (Oxford: Oxford University Press, 1999), p. 230 (s.v. "Ich habe genung/genug" [by David Schulenberg]). The critical edition of the score is published in Johann Sebastian Bach, *Neue Ausgabe sämtlicher Werke* [Neue Bach-Ausgabe], I/28.1: *Kantaten zu Marienfesten I,* ed. Matthias Wendt and Uwe Wolf (Kassel: Bärenreiter, 1994-95). This cantata has been recorded many times; a particularly fine performance is by Stephan MacLeod, bass; Montréal Baroque; Eric Milnes, direction and organ (Atma SACD2 2402).

13. Schulenberg, "Ich habe genung/genug," *J. S. Bach,* p. 230.

14. Michael Marissen, "The Theological Character of J. S. Bach's *Musical Offering,*" in *Bach Studies 2,* ed. Daniel R. Melamed (Cambridge: Cambridge University Press, 1995), pp. 85-106, at 103. For his interpretation, Marissen relies on Paul Althaus, *The Theology of Martin Luther,* trans. Robert C. Schultz (Philadelphia: Fortress, 1966), and Alister McGrath, *Luther's Theology of the Cross: Martin Luther's Theological Breakthrough* (Oxford: Blackwell, 1985).

with exultant melismas depicting "Ich freue mich" ("I rejoice"), while the final chord transforms the prevailing key of C minor into a radiant C major.

Recitative (bass, basso continuo)[15]

Mein Gott! wenn kömmt das schöne Nun!
Da ich im Friede fahren werde
Und in dem Sande kühler Erde
Und dort bei dir im Schoße ruhn?
Der Abschied ist gemacht,
Welt, gute Nacht!

> My God! When will the beautiful "Now!" come,
> When I shall depart in peace
> And rest in the sand of the cool earth
> And there rest, with you, in your bosom?
> I have made my farewell.
> World, good night!

Aria (bass, oboe, strings, basso continuo)

Ich freue mich auf meinen Tod,
Ach! hätt' er sich schon eingefunden.
Da entkomm ich aller Not,
Die mich noch auf der Welt gebunden.

> I rejoice over my death,
> Ah! if only it had arrived already.
> When I [will] escape all the distress
> That still bound me to the world.

Three vignettes, three unexpected juxtapositions, three exercises of the kind of imagination the philosopher Richard Kearney has called "poetic": the ability to "think otherwise" than the usual, to entertain new, different, unprecedented possibilities. Acosta discovers the clash between theory and practice: the claims of the classical authorities crumble when put to the practical test. He reacts with the laugh of discovery and wel-

---

15. Translation from Dürr, *Cantatas of J. S. Bach,* 662.

comes a new view of God's wonderfully variegated creation as he sails off on his evangelical mission, keeping true to the mandate of Jesuits' founder, Ignatius of Loyola, to "see God in all things." Bernini's juxtaposition of almost orgasmic eroticism and deep mysticism, and Bach's eager, even ecstatic anticipation of God in the face of death might disturb *our* religious sensibilities, but were seen by both artists as completely within the boundaries of the Christianity they fervently espoused, in fact, as *exemplary* of Christianity. They both create a contemporary religious understanding through the transformation of the possibilities offered by "secular" materials. Such interpenetration of the sacred and the secular, the affective and the contemplative, suffering and joy — as we know from the history of spirituality and devotion from the late medieval period on into modernity — were common ways of conveying the essential *incarnational* reality of the salvation offered by God in Christ. All three personages — the Jesuit sailing for Peru, the artist polymath who attended Mass every day in the Jesuit church he designed across from Rome's Quirinale Palace, the Lutheran musician-composer who saw his craft as a divinely bestowed vocation — practiced an immersion in and indulgence of the world beyond the boundaries of the contemporary stereotype of "the religious," an imaginative engagement that occurs at the behest of Christian belief. All three illustrate the *sacramental imagination,* the conviction that the finite can mediate the infinite.

2. Imagination

How might we explain the work of the imagination as it functions in these cases? The question is important, given our epoch where imagination is Disneyfied, access to transcendence is supposedly closed down, and limits that are actively embraced by the self and society in the wake of modernity threaten to crush us with the numbing familiarity of "more of the same." My proposal is a phenomenological theory of the imagination that does justice to both the intentionality of the embodied self and the particular social and historical context in which that self is rooted.

Richard Kearney's valuable work on the imagination provides a foundation on which to build our own analysis. In recalling Emanuel Lévinas's ethical "first philosophy" and Paul Ricoeur's work on narrative and the productive hermeneutical imagination, Kearney has argued that the postmodern dismantling of the modern humanist imagination and its anthropocentric bias should not lead to a denial of the role of "the creative human subject . . . in the shaping of meaning." With commodified imagery and "pseudoevents" all around us, where "image and reality have dissolved into a play of mutual parody," a new interpretation of imagination is needed, one that views the other not as a mirror image or a commodity but as an image with a referent: the particular person who demands a response from me, "whose very *otherness* refuses to be reduced to an empty mimicry of *sameness.*"[16]

Kearney's antidote to pessimism and parody is to retrieve the power of the imagination, in two modes. Imagination is first of all *critical,* demystifying the onto-theological and humanist notions of "origin" and carefully discriminating between authentic and inauthentic aspects of the present context. Second and even more importantly, the imagination is to be *poetic* (in the sense of *poiēsis,* "inventive"), challenging the status quo of endless imitation by daring to invent new possibilities of existence that break free of any technological and ethical quagmire. Kearney's definition is pivotal: "Renouncing the pervasive sense of social paralysis, the poetic imagination would attempt to restore man's faith in history and to nourish the belief that things can be changed. The first and most effective step in this direction is to begin to *imagine* that the world as it is could be *otherwise.*"[17]

Despite some questionable points (for example, the unilateral characterization of modernity in epistemological terms,[18] the downplaying of the recuperative aspect of the critical imagination), the formal outlines of

16. Richard Kearney, "Ethics and the Postmodern Imagination," *Thought* 62 (1987): 42-43. See also Richard Kearney, *The Wake of Imagination* (Minneapolis: University of Minnesota Press, 1988), pp. 361-97.

17. "Ethics and the Postmodern Imagination," p. 44.

18. Kearney's unilateral view, like a number of other continental philosophical estimations of "modernity," no longer holds up under closer scrutiny since it hardly does justice to the complex interweavings of various *modernities* that characterize the period in question (that is, roughly from 1450 to 1950). For a "thicker" view of modernity, see not only Taylor's *A Secular Age* but also Louis Dupré, *Passage to Modernity: An Essay in the Hermeneutics of Nature and Culture* (New Haven, Conn.: Yale University Press, 1993), and *The Enlightenment and the Intellectual Foundations of Modern Culture* (New Haven, Conn.: Yale University Press, 2004); Eyal Chowers, *The Modern Self in the Labyrinth: Politics and the Entrapment Imagination* (Cambridge, Mass.: Harvard University Press, 2004); Michael P. Steinberg, *Listening to Reason: Culture, Subjectivity, and Nineteenth-Century Music* (Princeton, N.J.: Princeton University Press, 2004); Andrew Bowie, *Music, Philosophy, and Modernity,* Modern European Philosophy (Cambridge: Cambridge University Press, 2007); and Michael Allen Gillespie, *The Theological Origins of Modernity* (Chicago: University of Chicago Press, 2008). See also my essay, " 'Refuge of Sinners, Pray for Us' " (see n. 4 above).

Kearney's theory are still viable. The key is his theory of the "otherwise" and the imagination's capacity for *poiēsis*. This form of the imagination is both a realistic response to contemporary situations and a direct probing of new possibilities for existence which those situations present. "Thinking otherwise" asks "what if . . . ?" — what if the present were different, if things were changed? The poetic imagination is thus critical in its own right: it judges the status quo as inadequate, unable to fulfill our desires; indeed, it is not *humanizing* enough. Thinking otherwise than the present norm reactivates historical consciousness and allows for what is new, different, unprecedented to break into our consciousness. Historical consciousness — the recognition that the past is not the same as the present, and the present is not the same as the future — threatens the status quo by disclosing that the present is not absolute and that life is not simply repetition. The poetic imagination suggests a reconstrual or refiguration of reality that can act as a catalyst for change: to *think* otherwise (that is, entertaining new possibilities that could be made real and satisfy the human desire for happiness) can serve as a catalyst for *acting* otherwise (that is, transformative praxis, the actualization of those possibilities, changing the situation for the better). "Thinking otherwise" beyond the status quo restores a belief that the present is neither circular nor absolute, as well as a hope in newly imagined possibilities for a different and better future that can exceed our abilities and expectations.

Thinking otherwise is the catalyst for *acting* otherwise with the confidence that the transformation promised by these new possibilities can be appropriated through action. The "otherwise" is thus not "fantastic" in any trivial sense but rather practices *poiēsis* in a vitally important way. The poetic imagination is *intentional* in two senses: as a realistic evaluation and response to contemporary situations, and as a direct probing of the new possibilities for existence that those situations present.[19] This imagination is truly *aesthetic,* in that its practice of inventing alternative figurations mirrors the fundamental workings of the artist. "Invention" here refers to the classical rhetorical tool of *inventio,* defined by Cicero as "discoveries"; even more specifically it can be described as "a mechanism that triggers further elaborative thought" that explores all the possibilities of a topic, example, or figure in order to craft a work of art or musical

19. "Intentionality" is used here in its original phenomenological sense of "consciousness of . . . ," that is, the primordial orientation of incarnate conscious awareness toward what is other than the subject, the dynamism that drives subjectivity outward toward the world.

composition.[20] When this imaginative reconstrual is directly linked to our response to the other, who is neither mimetic image nor commodified object but rather a source of new possibilities, we have an "otherwise" with the power to reconfigure the present and look with hope to the future. It offers a way out of the prison-house of commodified consumer culture and a response to "that scruple of answerability to the other which cannot be dispelled in our Civilization of the Image."[21]

The weakness in Kearney's theory, though, is exposed by this question: How are we to discriminate among the new possibilities for existence — all the "otherwises" — called forth by the imagination? How might we distinguish possibilities that are productive from those that are destructive, the life-affirming from those that are life-denying? Kearney's simple appeal to alterity and the "call of the other" is too thin to provide such criteria. In this situation religion has played and continues to plays a fundamental role, for the religions have always claimed to provide standards to judge a meaningful human life, even when life is in the midst of being overwhelmed by various forces (social, cultural, economic, political, and spiritual).[22] The religions maintain that in order to be fully human, one must be aware of humanity's finitude and its rootedness in the divine.[23] As Leszek Kolakowski puts it, "a religious world perception is indeed able to teach us *how to be a failure.* And the latent assumption behind such teaching is that on earth everybody *is* a failure."[24] The religious worldview is the most realistic because it impresses on us the realization that the world and human experience have inescapable limits and achieve only degrees of perfection, never any totality or perfect fulfillment of our desires. "Religion," Kolakowski reminds us, "is man's way of accepting life as an inevitable

20. Laurence Dreyfus, *Bach and the Patterns of Invention* (Cambridge, Mass.: Harvard University Press, 1996), pp. 2-3. Dreyfus cites Cicero, *De oratore*, I, xxxi, 142-43, trans. E. W. Sutton, Loeb Classical Library, 2 vols. (Cambridge, Mass.: Harvard University Press, 1942), 1:99.

21. Richard Kearney, *Poetics of Imagining: From Husserl to Lyotard* (London: Harper-Collins Academic, 1991), p. 210.

22. See David F. Ford, *Theology: A Very Short Introduction* (Oxford: Oxford University Press, 1999), pp. 7-14, on the role of religion in the midst of "multiple overwhelmings."

23. And not only the religions. At the heart of modernity, Immanuel Kant's *Critique of Practical Judgment* makes a similar argument, as Philip Rossi demonstrates in his essay in this volume.

24. Leszek Kolakowski, *Religion, If There Is No God . . . : On God, the Devil, Sin and Other Worries of the So-Called Philosophy of Religion* (New York: Oxford University Press, 1982), p. 40.

defeat. That it is not an inevitable defeat is a claim that cannot be defended in good faith. . . . One can accept life, and accept it, at the same time, as a defeat only if one accepts that there is a sense [i.e., a meaning] beyond that which is inherent in human history — if, in other words, one accepts the order of the sacred."[25] Religion's crucial role in contemporary society is to recognize and actively disclose the "otherwise" that is the sacred, thereby revealing both the intrinsic limitations and inevitable lack of fulfillment of the profane, but also its dependence on the sacred for its own intentional thrust beyond its limitations for the fulfillment of its inherent desires. The religions, then, are prime examples of the poetic imagination.[26]

3. The Intentional Body and Particularity

The intentionality of the imagination is a constitutive aspect of the intentionality of the embodied subject and of the lived body itself. In order to see this, we must acknowledge the duality of embodied human experience; the embodied self that is visible in its incarnate actions also carries a mystery that is ineffable. In other words, we need a conceptuality and a language that will communicate this non-negotiable duality without turning it into an outmoded body-soul dualism or, worse, capitulating to what has been called the fundamentally reductive and objectifying "commonsense notion of the body."[27]

Shifting the commonsense attitude in the present context may prove harder than we think, however. Reductionism today is less a Cartesian leftover that has permeated both the modern and post-modern contexts and more so a "normal" unilateral mentality imposed by contemporary capitalism — that is, if the sociologist Bryan Turner's description of the new bio-politics is correct:

25. Leszek Kolakowski, "The Revenge of the Sacred in Secular Culture," trans. A. Kolakowska, in Leszek Kolakowski, *Modernity on Endless Trial* (Chicago: University of Chicago Press, 1990), pp. 63-74, at 73.

26. This adds yet another characterization of "religion" to those offered by David Tracy and William Cavanaugh in this volume. A preliminary comparison will reveal that while Cavanaugh speaks primarily of a modern social and political construction called "religion," Tracy, Kolakowski, and I discuss "religion" in what I would term a more phenomenological way, in the sense of bringing the fundamental structures of "being religious" to the fore.

27. Mark Johnson, *The Meaning of the Body: Aesthetics of Human Understanding* (Chicago: University of Chicago Press, 2007), pp. 274-75.

In contemporary society, the body is in one sense disappearing; it is being converted into an information system whose genetic code can be manipulated and sold as a commercial product in the new biotech economy. In global terms, the disorders and diseases of the human body have become productive in a post-industrial economy. In terms of media debate, the new reproductive technologies, cloning and genetic screening are important illustrations of public concern about the social consequences of the new genetics. Improvements in scientific understanding of genetics have already had major consequences for the circumstances under which people reproduce, and genetic surveillance and forensic genetics may also transform criminal investigation and the policing of societies. . . . The government of the body, as a consequence, remains a critical issue in the management and regulation of individuals and populations in contemporary society.[28]

The range of the "buffered self" thus shrinks even further than Charles Taylor has envisioned. I discuss this crucial aspect of our public context later in this chapter. My own attempt to resist the "commonsense reductionism" that affects even well-meaning theological anthropologies focuses on embodiment and particularity, emphasizing the intentionality and polyvalency of the body.

One way to express this intentionality and polyvalency is to craft a theological anthropology that takes a page from the medieval method for interpreting scripture. Just as the medievals asserted the fourfold sense of scripture, so too there is a *fourfold sense of the body* (literal, allegorical, moral, and anagogical-eschatological). According to the original schema, the truth of the scriptural text turns out to be a *multivalent* truth. Such a schema can be applied analogously to the body to help disclose its non-negotiable polyvalent character. The *literal* meaning of the body is its biological or material-empirical substratum. The *allegorical* aspect of the body is disclosed in the meaningfulness of bodily gestures and embodied actions. The *moral* meaning is the humanizing or dehumanizing character of those actions. Finally, the *anagogical* or eschatological meaning refers to the ultimate intentional goal of all of the body's possibilities of transformation, namely, *theōsis,* the union with God promised to us by our baptism into the dying and

28. Bryan S. Turner, "Body," *Theory, Culture & Society* 23, nos. 2-3 (2006): 222-29, at 228-29.

rising of Christ.[29] My fourfold schema thus opens up our understanding of the body beyond the literal sense and trumps the sense of closure and desiccated autonomy that results from reductionism by insisting on the body's fundamental intentional structure that is revealed in its everyday doings. It offers, in other words, a way to think "otherwise" about the body.

What this schema expresses is similar to what Maurice Merleau-Ponty insists is the dynamic intentional structure of the lived body.

> My body appears to me as an attitude directed towards a certain existing or possible task. And indeed its spatiality is not, like that of external objects or like that of "spatial sensations," a *spatiality of position,* but a *spatiality of situation.* . . . In the last analysis, if my body can be a "form" and if there can be, in front of it, important figures against indifferent backgrounds, this occurs in virtue of its being polarized by its tasks, of its *existence towards* them, of its collecting together of itself in its pursuit of its aim: the body image is finally a way of stating that my body is in-the-world.[30]

This phenomenological analysis is indeed a "thinking otherwise" that, in its inventive reconstrual of embodiment away from the merely "literal" (material-empirical) sense, reveals a truth about the body: its intentional focus on the world as its perceptual task, and its ec-static deployment toward the world in fulfillment of that task. The lived body is thus essentially ec-static intentional performance that "surges toward objects to be grasped and perceives them,"[31] embodied action with intentional meaning. "Man taken as a concrete being is not a psyche joined to an organism, but the movement to and fro of existence which at one time allows itself to take corporeal form and at others moves towards personal acts."[32]

The body is not only a series of intentional actions sedimented in time and united by consciousness (itself temporal in structure), but is conscious

29. For more on the fourfold schema, see Anthony J. Godzieba, "Bodies and Persons, Resurrected and Postmodern: Towards a Relational Eschatology," in *Theology and Conversation: Toward a Relational Theology,* ed. Jacques Haers and Peter De Mey, BETL 172 (Leuven: Peeters, 2003), pp. 211-25.

30. Maurice Merleau-Ponty, *Phenomenology of Perception,* trans. Colin Smith (1962; rev. reprint, London: Routledge & Kegan Paul, 1978), pp. 100-101.

31. Merleau-Ponty, *Phenomenology,* p. 106.

32. Merleau-Ponty, *Phenomenology,* p. 88.

of the world in a way different from and prior to logical consciousness.[33] In other words, the body knows the world before the intellect clarifies conceptually what has been grasped. Perception is an "existential" function related to "the pre-logical act by which the subject takes up his place in the world."[34] The imagination, then, has its roots in *body consciousness* and that way of revealing the structure of the world. The world is known differently, not as a container of isolated objects but as a network of meanings revealed by the body, a connected network for which the body is the necessary precondition. But we know the *body* differently as well. It is not, nor could it ever be, a *thing,* despite its materiality. Its intentionality, while grounded in its material-empirical substratum, thrusts us beyond its material-empirical limits. As Merleau-Ponty puts it, "my experience breaks forth into things and transcends itself in them, because it always comes into being within the framework of a certain setting in relation to the world which is the definition of my body."[35] The body is indeed experienced as a quasi-object, especially at those times when it outruns our rational reflections and to some degree has a life of its own. I am my body, and yet I am also not my body. The sinus headache you wake up with; the recalcitrant body you have to drag out of bed in the morning by sheer force of will; skin that can feel texture, or give comfort to those we hold, or go electric with sexual passion difficult to control: moments such as these, when the body outruns our immediate control, reveal surprising meanings and configurations of the world and disclose a depth of connection to the world and to others that outstrips any of our attempts at description. This is because "neither body *nor existence* can be regarded as the original of the human being, since they presuppose each other, and because the body is solidified or generalized existence, and existence a perpetual incarnation."[36]

The body, by the intentional and revelatory way it makes its way through the world, resists the closure of reduction. But the body's "surging" toward and intertwining with the world does not eliminate what Bryan Turner has termed "our ontological frailty and sociological precariousness."[37] He argues that the lived body has three interrelated aspects: *embodiment* ("the ensemble of corporeal practices that produces

33. Merleau-Ponty, *Phenomenology,* especially part one, chap. 1, and part two, chap. 3.
34. Merleau-Ponty, *Phenomenology,* p. 303 n. 1.
35. Merleau-Ponty, *Phenomenology,* p. 303.
36. Merleau-Ponty, *Phenomenology,* p. 166.
37. Bryan S. Turner, "The End(s) of Humanity: Vulnerability and the Metaphors of Membership," *The Hedgehog Review* 3, no. 2 (Summer 2001): 7-32, at 7.

and gives 'a body' its place in everyday life"), *emplacement* (the placing of "particular bodies within a social habitus" that occurs in a particular location), and *enselfment* (the constitution of self-identity within a specific spatial context and "a specific social nexus where the continuous self depends on successful embodiment, a social habitus, and memory").[38] The body is shadowed by physical vulnerability (our propensity for disease) and an unshakeable precariousness that permeates all life. Vulnerability is the reason we generate social institutions: they are supposed to create a protective, stable environment that makes meaningful living possible. As Turner points out, however, modernization has brought destabilizing change and deinstitutionalization that exposes our physical vulnerability even further.[39] Once-stable background institutions that we have inherited from modernity (such as those involved with healthcare, business, and politics) have been foregrounded by global pressures and exposed as relatively unstable and unable adequately to protect human beings from threats such as global disease, financial instability, and crime.

Turner argues, though, that human vulnerability can reveal something positive, namely, a human solidarity that can become "a basis, however minimalist, for some universalistic criterion of justice in relation to separate and particular social groups and communities."[40] "The ubiquity of human misery" understood across all cultures, as well as my own experience of physical pain and the desire for delivery from it, while occurring to me at what is the most particular and most individual point of the social nexus, are precisely what unite me with all other human persons. Thus the cross-cultural bond of vulnerability could function as a "minimalist" grounding for a universal theory of human rights, a "set of effective 'plausibility structures' giving the everyday world a legitimate sense of stability" and assuring "the continuity of an embodied self through time and space."[41] Here it is the vulnerability of the body that is revelatory: the *particular* — that is, *my* fear or *my* suffering in *this* particular place — can be the new *universal* since everyone suffers. The physical precariousness we endure can be revelatory of our solidarity with others — an "otherwise" we might not have expected.

38. Turner, "The End(s) of Humanity," p. 13. Turner also notes his debt to Merleau-Ponty.
39. Turner, "The End(s) of Humanity," pp. 15-16.
40. Turner, "The End(s) of Humanity," p. 21.
41. Turner, "The End(s) of Humanity," p. 29. See also Turner's *Vulnerability and Human Rights,* Essays on Human Rights (University Park: Pennsylvania State University Press, 2006).

Finally, what about the all-important "duality" of the self? The perpetual incarnation that is the vulnerable self is not an immediately transparent self. Rather, it is characterized by a lack, a non-presence: its final significance is never settled because the self is constituted over time. The truth of the human self always remains relative to the interpretation of its partial significations, the only ones in our grasp.[42] The embodied self is visible in its incarnate actions yet also ineffable. An older anthropology articulated this ineffability through the concept of "soul." Anthropology loses something essential when the notion of the "soul" is suppressed, and that is why I have argued elsewhere that in the Western philosophical and Christian traditions "soul" language has played a crucial *aesthetic* role by offering us a way to imagine everyday life "otherwise" and bring the self's ineffability to the fore, as well as helping us articulate the Christian faith-claim that human identity, by the grace of God, does not end with death. It is precisely this aesthetic function that gets to the heart of the anthropological enterprise that grounds our notion of the imagination and its intentional thrust that resists the closure symbolized by the buffered self.[43]

An insight from the Tübingen philosopher Manfred Frank helps in this retrieval. He has emphasized the importance of the individual's freedom, rooted in self-consciousness, which can never be grasped as a perceived object in reflection and exists prior to any structured systems of signs or discourse.[44] "Every human practice," he argues, "participates in two orders," structuring and application. Structure is the sphere of universal certainty and homogeneity, the formation of general conceptualizations that order experience by emphasizing what is "the same" and can be specified by prediction. Application, on the other hand, is the realm of individual experience, which can never be predicted or reduced to a rule. While

42. Manfred Frank, *What Is Neostructuralism?* trans. Sabine Wilke and Richard Gray, Theory and History of Literature, 45 (Minneapolis: University of Minnesota Press, 1989), pp. 363-64.

43. See my "Bodies and Persons, Resurrected and Postmodern: Towards a Relational Eschatology" (see n. 29 above).

44. Manfred Frank, *Stil in der Philosophie* (Stuttgart: Reclam, 1992), pp. 49-52; English translation of the complete work: "Style in Philosophy," trans. Julia Jansen and Michael K. Shin, *Metaphilosophy* 30 (1999): 145-67 and 264-310, at 264-66; English translation of part II: "Toward a Philosophy of Style," trans. Richard E. Palmer, *Common Knowledge* 1, 1 (1992): 54-77, at 54-56 (hereafter I will cite Palmer's translation). See also Frank, *What Is Neostructuralism?* pp. 362-66, as well as Andrew Bowie's summary in his introduction to Frank's *The Subject and the Text: Essays on Literary Theory and Philosophy,* trans. Helen Atkins, ed. Andrew Bowie (Cambridge: Cambridge University Press, 1997), pp. xx-xxvi, xxxi-xxxvi.

structure may be conveyed by a tradition, application by an individual within that individual's specific situation ensures "the irreducibility of the individual to the universal."[45] Frank calls the combination of structure and application "style." Its task is to highlight the irreducibly individual aspects of human activity and the individual's freedom, manifested in the self's discerning application of structure. This freedom is a basic human right that cannot be obliterated by those who argue that the self is totally determined by its social setting or by the linguisticality of experience.

> What comes forward here on a very basic level is the freedom possessed by human beings, a freedom made manifest in the *unforeseeability of interpretation*. Interpretation . . . is neither determined solely by the object nor is it simply derived from the concept through which a "community of investigators" or of "speakers/interlocutors" has somehow "codified" it into something "intersubjectively sharable."[46]

This theory offers a way to resist any reductive interpretation of the embodied self and unblinkingly acknowledge the *duality* of human experience without falling into dualism. The description of the self constituted by freedom of application parallels Merleau-Ponty's argument for the lived body's transcending intentionality. It also parallels the Christian anthropological claim for the individual self whose identity persists beyond the closure of death. But it is only a parallel, not an equivalence; demonstrating non-closure does not prove the persistence of the self after death, which remains a mystery. The Christian believes that only the revelation of human destiny through the resurrection of Christ gives us the freedom to imagine eternal life with God as a real human possibility — that is, to imagine human life otherwise than any reduction of life to its material-empirical basis.

A philosophical anthropology can offer theological anthropology a way to make the mystery of the duality of the self intelligible insofar as this is possible. Here we have a model of the self as an ensemble of events, realized possibilities, and effects constituted and played out over time. The self's identity, while incomplete, is nonetheless composed of both

45. Frank, "Toward a Philosophy," p. 54.
46. Frank, "Toward a Philosophy," p. 54 (my italics). Frank strongly argues for the individual subject's existence already before all signs and structures since these are artificial and are empowered by meaning-giving subjects whose self-consciousness is recognized prior to all differential representations and significations (pp. 55-56). See also Bowie in *The Subject and the Text,* pp. xxxv-xxxvi.

exteriority (structure) and interiority (intentional consciousness). Both qualities are temporally situated, each is the condition for the other, and neither is reducible to the other. Frank's "style" — the intersection of socially constructed code and unique application resulting in the "unforeseeability of interpretation," an irreducibly individualized constitution of real meaning that nonetheless is intersubjectively sharable — comes close in tone to the religiously imaginative use of "soul" to stand for the uniquely constituted and deeply unified "I" that is nonetheless recognizable as a human among humans. "Style" and "soul" symbolize the intersubjectively sharable incarnated depth of the self that is responsible for the intentional "surging" of our bodies toward the world and the ability to "think otherwise." They are ways of representing the unique-yet-relational "I" that exceeds the immediately perceptible, the "incarnate personal style," an unrepeatable incarnate configuration of personal experience — yet another exercise of the poetic imagination that, by knowing differently, is revelatory as well.

4. A Theological Heuristic:
True Contingency and the Limits of Illusion

The discussion of faith and secularity is, in my view, fundamentally a discussion about anthropology: which view of *the person* governs the claims made about self and society? My basic proposal should be clear at this point: any discussion of "imagination" is ultimately a discussion about *limits and their transcending*. My argument here has focused on using imagination and a phenomenology of the body — two exercises in "transcending" — as clues to human intentionality, and in turn using intentionality as a resource with which to develop a renewed (and even aesthetic) theological anthropology and natural theology that takes contingency seriously yet also makes the case for our access to transcendence. In doing so, I am picking up on a key metaphor that drives this discussion, that of "limit."

To support his thesis that "secularization" is not a process of subtraction but rather a transformation of perspective, Charles Taylor explicates how *past* conceptual transformations have constituted the present context and limited the range of the human imagination to the buffered self. Bryan Turner, for his part, focuses directly on the *present*, on the body's physical and psychological limits for coping with vulnerability, the limits of various compensating social structures, and the ontological limits that are revealed in these negotiations of embodiment — a post-modern present that in many ways differs radically from past configurations. Both authors document the limits of the human imagination and the difficult struggle to imagine alternatives to the current "distressed" situation of the buffered self in its ontological frailty.

If we focus on the limits that Taylor and Turner outline — one a set of conceptual limits, the other an ensemble of material and ontological limits — we would be right to feel stymied. The crucial question to be asked here is this: if human life is inherently constituted by both the limits of our cultural conceptions and the limits of our physical and imaginative abilities, then where do we stand in order to be able to avoid being crushed by those limits and to imagine new possibilities of existence? Being constrained by those epistemological, physical, and ontological limits and being "doomed" to instability and unfulfillment — is *that* the most likely story of human life?

There is yet another aspect of "limit" that drives secularized Western culture, one more amorphous and dispiriting: the specific mode of the commodification of experience that prevails in contemporary culture. It has had a noticeable impact on public discourse, and restricts the range of the already-truncated self.[47] To call it merely "commodification" is both old news and inadequate. The cultural critic Chris Hedges has gone further and argued that Western commodified culture has more recently morphed into celebrity culture and thus functions as a willfully chosen truncation of the range of experience.

> Celebrity culture plunges us into a moral void. No one has any worth beyond his or her appearance, usefulness, or ability to "succeed." The highest achievements in a celebrity culture are wealth, sexual conquest, and fame. It does not matter how these are obtained. [These values] are hollow. . . . They urge us toward a life of narcissistic self-absorption. They tell us that existence is to be centered on the practices and desires of the self rather than the common good. . . . The cult of self dominates our cultural landscape. This cult has within it the classic traits of psychopaths: superficial charm, grandiosity, and self-importance; a need for constant stimulation, a penchant for lying, deception, and manip-

---

47. Taylor does not discuss commodification. Turner, however, does so in his analysis of how "the body" disappears into genetic code that eventually becomes commercialized ("End(s) of Humanity," p. 13). Cf. Turner, *Vulnerability and Human Rights,* chap. 2.

ulation, and the inability to feel remorse or guilt. This is, of course, the ethic promoted by corporations. It is the ethic of unfettered capitalism. It is the misguided belief that personal style and personal advancement, mistaken for individualism, are the same as democratic equality.[48]

These values, Hedges notes, offer only the *illusion* of love, wisdom, and happiness. They are the "perverted" ethical principles that guide the denizens of reality shows like *Survivor* and *Big Brother* as well as the Wall Street bankers and brokers (or as one blogger dubbed them, "the banksters") who crashed the economy.[49]

To acknowledge the perceptual grid constructed by this specific mode of commodification alongside Taylor's "macro" narrative and Turner's "micro" analysis is to give a direct response both to the recent plea for less abstractness in the discussion of religion and secularization and the query about what is precisely "public" about such a theological anthropology. In order to discuss "faith in public life" with any hope of responding to actual forms of public life (at least in the North Atlantic communities), we must be ruthlessly phenomenological. That is, we must delve directly into the essential operations of the various forms of late capitalist, aestheticized consumer culture that construct what counts as contemporary public life.[50] It is true that past formulations and philosophical presuppositions (Taylor) and present constructions (Turner and Hedges) guide how we discriminate between what is life-affirming and what is life-denying for the *polis.* But we cannot afford to ignore the fact that our appropriation of these presuppositions and constructions is to some (arguably large) extent shaped by celebrity-driven consumer culture and the visual and media cultures that support it.[51] Many "buffered selves" actively choose to fine-tune their social, political, and aesthetic possibilities to fit into that smaller frame constructed by reality TV, *TMZ,* Twitter, and twenty-four-

48. Chris Hedges, *Empire of Illusion: The End of Literacy and the Triumph of Spectacle* (New York: Nation Books, 2009), pp. 32-33.

49. Hedges, *Empire of Illusion,* p. 34: "The heads of these corporations, like the winners on a reality television program who lied and manipulated others to succeed, walked away with hundreds of millions of dollars in bonuses and compensation." The blogger is Atrios (Duncan Black; http://www.eschatonblog.com/).

50. Mary Doak pursues this point in her discussion in chapter 9 in this volume of the practice of justice and love in a market economy.

51. See, for example, a headline on the front page of *The Philadelphia Inquirer,* Sunday, May 16, 2010: "Reality TV saturating life in the real world."

hour cable news. In order to trump the perceptual grid of illusion, we need more specificity than Taylor's "macro" narrative provides.

Both Taylor and Turner are aware that an alternative imaginative construal is needed. In Taylor's account, the re-imagining takes the form of a counter-narrative to the dominant narrative of exclusive humanism and the "immanent frame" within which it is practiced, a counter-narrative that appears primarily Catholic and sacramental.[52] He emphasizes specifically the issue of transcendence as essential to human meaning and fullness, and does not shy away from arguing for the fundamental human need for God's presence. Turner's account of embodiment-at-risk highlights the body's paradoxical quality: the radical particularity of its status and locus (which cannot be theorized away) is the condition for the possibility of its radical openness to all other bodies (beyond its localized "emplacement"). A particular self's ontological frailty and desire for release from suffering and pain become the conditions for the possibility of understanding not only the character of one's own "enselfment" but the travails of all other human persons in their own constitution of self-identity. Limits, then, can be more than barriers to the experience of transcendence; they function as the preconditions for experiencing and understanding the quality of existence that exceeds the limits.

I have argued elsewhere that a productive way of opening out the self and the social imaginary beyond these constraining limits is to *think by means of the body,* and for me this implies a Catholic theology of embodiment.[53] A theological anthropology and theological aesthetics built around the incarnational and sacramental imagination offers a *more* likely story that acknowledges limits while pointing to transcendence. "Transcendence" here has a twofold meaning, philosophical and theological: the disclosure of new possibilities for existence that exceed the accustomed and sedimented frameworks ("thinking otherwise," a transcendence that is epistemic and praxical) as well as the ontological and eschatological fullness that comes from our participation in divine life, already in the present and promised for the future. This "more likely story" has its basis not only in Merleau-Ponty's phenomenology of embodiment but especially in the recognition that the incarnation is the fundamental hermeneutical strategy

52. See Taylor's acknowledgment of this in his chapter on "Conversions" (*A Secular Age,* pp. 728-72, esp. at 765).

53. Anthony J. Godzieba, "Incarnation, Theory, and Catholic Bodies: What Should Post-Postmodern Catholic Theology Look Like?" *Louvain Studies* 28 (2003): 217-31, and "The Catholic Sacramental Imagination and the Access/Excess of Grace" (see n. 4 above).

for Christian theology.[54] I will not repeat these earlier arguments, except to highlight two crucial issues.

First, as I argued above, embodiment extends beyond its merely "literal" sense (that is, the material-empirical), thus revealing a core truth about the body: its intentional focus on the world as its perceptual task and its ec-static deployment toward the world in fulfillment of that task. The lived body is thus essentially ec-static intentional performance, embodied action with intentional meaning. Second, there are intimate connections among creation, the Incarnation, and the resurrection of Christ. The theonomous ground of creation's autonomy,[55] namely, the participation in divine life granted to creation "in the beginning" by God's initiative and to humanity made in God's "image and likeness" (Gen. 1:1, 26), is intensified at the incarnation (where God embraces human finitude and vulnerability to the fullest extent, except for sin [Heb. 4:15]) and ratified at the resurrection of Christ as the ultimate possibility of human life. The Paschal Mystery reveals clues about embodiment, its possibilities, and its role in the economy of salvation.

The grammar of resurrection is impossible without the grammar of incarnation. Indeed, the grammar of resurrection is the most intense expression of the grammar of incarnation. And the doctrine of the Incarnation, in one of its most fundamental meanings, is the recognition and celebration of the capacity of the material and the particular to mediate divine presence. The incarnation of God in Christ confirms the revelatory value of this always-vulnerable embodied mediation. In other words, it is *God's embrace of vulnerability and ontological frailty from within.* What is also revealed, moreover, is that this mortal destiny is indeed not ultimate, but penultimate: embodied life's rootedness in God, ratified at creation and made more explicit with the Incarnation, has its ultimate destiny in *theōsis*. We become holy not in spite of our lives but because of our lives, and because ontological frailty is the necessary precondition for the experience of the grace of relationship with God. The body's paradoxical status — radically particular, and yet open to universal solidarity — is both confirmed and intensified by the Incarnation. Indeed, the Incarnation reveals and performs the body's dialectical "and yet" structure: singular, *and yet* open to others;

54. See Godzieba, " 'Stay with Us . . .' (Lk. 24:29) — 'Come, Lord Jesus' (Rev. 22:20)" (see n. 4 above).

55. See Walter Kasper, "Autonomy and Theonomy: The Place of Christianity in the Modern World," *Theology and Church,* trans. M. Kohl (New York: Crossroad, 1989), pp. 32-53, esp. 34-37.

finite, *and yet* open to infinite grace; vulnerable, *and yet* redeemed *not in spite of, but because of its vulnerability.* On God's initiative, this dialectical "and yet" structure becomes a *locus theologicus* and the arena within which the economy of salvation is played out.

For Christians, the complex of Creation-Incarnation-Resurrection is the performance of God's own "otherwise," the divine poetic imagination: the revelation of the continual possibilities of materiality and human life that can fuel the human imagination. The fundamental Christian claims thus confirm that "thinking otherwise" leading to "acting otherwise" is not simply wishful thinking, but can transcend the status quo with realized possibilities that are not merely different but better. The recognition of grace-within-embodiment provides us with a way of differentiating the two treatments of limits. "Ontological frailty," as Turner emphasizes, is the fundamental constitutive factor of human life, a non-negotiable. Its limits cannot be eliminated or surpassed but only redeemed and transcended by the grace of creation and incarnation. What first appears as a physical, psychological, or moral failure of the self is transformed into the very means of solidarity with others and with God's will to save. And so the re-imagined vulnerable self remains vulnerable, but with that vulnerability now opened outward and transformed into an instance of salvation.

The buffered self, on the other hand, closes itself off from any transcendental horizon and inhabits a solely immanent frame. Taylor characterizes it this way: "So the buffered identity of the disciplined individual moves in a constructed social space, where instrumental rationality is a key value, and time is pervasively secular. All of this makes up what I want to call 'the immanent frame.' . . . This frame constitutes a 'natural' order, to be contrasted to a 'supernatural' one, an 'immanent' world, over against a possible 'transcendent' one."[56]

Can the buffered self and the narrative of the immanent frame be redeemed? No — on its own terms and claims it cannot be transformed from within. *It can only be exceeded.* As Taylor notes, the human desire for "fullness" never subsides. This signals the insatiable intentionality of the buffered self for transcendence, even when that horizon is denied. Once again, the graced intentionality of the body offers a clue as to the quality of the surpassing. The "disciplined individual" is also the embodied subject who eventually comes face to face with bodily crisis, vulnerability, but also the desire for fullness and the need for solidarity in a time of suffering. In

56. Taylor, *A Secular Age,* p. 542.

those extreme situations, the cohesion of the "drama" of the self (which is an emplotted unity, as Maurice Blondel reminds us, independent of our will) points us in the direction of the supernatural, which is "indispensable and at the same time . . . inaccessible for man."[57]

This emphasis on the nexus between the natural and the supernatural does not rule out asking whether there is a "secular body," namely, "a particular configuration of the human sensorium . . . specific to secular subjects, and thus constitutive of what we mean by 'secular society.' "[58] There is nothing surprising in the claim that the body has historically and socially constructed meanings; it is a staple of hermeneutical understanding.[59] The power of the modern "immanent frame" to reshape everyday meanings, including aspects of embodiment, is amply documented by *A Secular Age*. This claim regarding a body constructed by secularity, while appearing analytical, however, is merely descriptive. What is needed is a deeper analysis of the conditions for social construction. A phenomenology of the lived body supplies this: it identifies the essential intentional structures of incarnated subjectivity and imagination that form the more primordial necessary conditions for the various projections of meaning. In other words, by analyzing the body's dynamic operations in its everyday contexts, it discloses an essential understanding of the body that is prior to and grounds all the other historically and socially constructed interpretations. The "particular configuration" that is the secular body is already a contextualized secondary interpretive gloss on the more primordial intentional and relational structure that is incarnate subjectivity.

If we return to our three vignettes, we can view quite clearly the operation of this intentional thrust beyond the "usual." The first offers a "hori-

57. Maurice Blondel, *The Letter on Apologetics,* in *The Letter on Apologetics* and *History and Dogma,* trans. A. Dru and I. Trethowan (Grand Rapids: Eerdmans, 1994 [Fr. orig., 1896]), p. 161.

58. Charles Hirschkind, "Is There a Secular Body?" *Cultural Anthropology* 26, no. 4 (2011): 633-47, at 633.

59. A classic example is Judith Butler's *Gender Trouble: Feminism and the Subversion of Identity* (New York: Routledge, 1990). See also the continuing controversy in art history touched off roughly thirty years ago by Svetlana Alpers' *The Art of Describing: Dutch Art in the Seventeenth Century* (Chicago: University of Chicago Press, 1983), which claimed that Dutch painters *saw differently* than did Italian painters; that the different cultures shaped different practices of vision. Dutch art, she argued, is "descriptive" and cares about surface; its meaning "resides in the careful *representation* of the world" (p. 229). Italian art, rooted in a more textual culture, is a narrative art whose meaning lies behind the picture itself, to be revealed by a careful emblematic and symbolic "reading" of the painting.

zontal" example: Acosta confronts an empirical situation that defeats the classical cosmology based on Aristotle and the Bible. The "otherwise" to which he is led involves not only a new construal of the material world, but a challenge to the classical view of what knowledge is and how it is obtained. The traditional view was that knowledge lay in authoritative texts and that only professionals "could manipulate the texts and master the terms of canonical knowledge." But now "knowledge had burst the bounds of the library [and] now seemed as large and varied as the world itself."[60] As an exercise of the imagination, this epiphany is not sacramental per se, of course. While the Jesuit dictum to do all things *ad majorem Dei gloriam* ("to the greater glory of God") would be the context in which Acosta viewed this new construal of God's creation, one cannot exclude the possibility that he considered this a further insight into the divine ground of all reality.

The second and third vignettes show us the "otherwise" in a more overtly sacramental mode. Bernini's imagination leads him in two directions: how to envision solid marble not only as dynamic but as seductive, and how to envision the resulting seductive eroticism as emblematic of mystical ecstasy. The undulating columns of the baldachino of St. Peter and the smoldering sexuality of *St. Teresa in Ecstasy* give us an idea of the majestic "otherwise" that put Bernini on a level high above his artistic and architectural rivals, but neither of these prepares us for the surprising (and indeed provocative) spiritual seduction that overwhelms the viewer of *Bl. Ludovica Albertoni.* Bach's imagination also results in an act of seduction, using not only the unlikely mixture of baroque opera, courtly French dance (the gigue), and rigorous Lutheran orthodoxy (Bach was no Pietist), but also the conflicting affective states of sober preparation for death (most clearly in the recitative), criticism of the everyday world, and ecstatic joy. What we experience in performance is — literally — the world turned upside down, as Luther taught: death is beautiful, and death in Christ is joy. The aria's own harmonic structure performs a "thinking otherwise": C minor, associated in the baroque with sadness and painful longing, and in Bach especially with burial and the sleep of death,[61] is transfigured with the very last chord into a pure and radiant C major.

60. Grafton et al., *New Worlds,* p. 3.

61. Cf. Peter Williams, *The Organ Music of J. S. Bach,* 2nd ed. (Cambridge: Cambridge University Press, 2003), p. 185; and David Ledbetter, *Bach's "Well-tempered Clavier": The 48 Preludes and Fugues* (New Haven, Conn.: Yale University Press, 2002), p. 116.

In each of the three cases the possibilities inherent to the material at hand (theory, stone, musical genre) are realized in such a way as to shatter expectations and exceed the supposed limits of the material — all true examples of "thinking otherwise." And the shattering that occurs in the latter two cases (and possibly the first as well) provides a glimpse of the divine truth revealed in creation, intensified at the incarnation, and confirmed at the resurrection: that finite materiality can mediate and be transfigured by infinite grace. This is the "otherwise" generated from the sacramental imagination, grounded on the creation-incarnation-resurrection complex that makes that "otherwise" possible.

In summary, then, the task of the embodied imagination is to wrestle with limits, diagnosing which can be embraced and which need to be surpassed. From the standpoint of the Christian imagination, what is to be embraced is what was embraced in the incarnation and ratified by the resurrection: the potential of the materiality to mediate the supernatural. What is to be surpassed are ideological commitments that "buffer" or screen out the very conditions of the possibility for the "fullness" of life. Christian life offers a way of taking limits seriously as well as discerning which limits are eventually life-affirming and which are life-denying. This is a method of discernment that can be applied to the individual self as well as to the self-in-society by starting with what is common to all selves in a vulnerable world, namely, *corporeality as ec-static intentional performance,* surging outward to encounter and know the world — the same corporeality that is embraced by God in Christ. The body thus can be the starting point for a conversation about the imagination, the immanent frame, its inadequacies, and what a more likely story about human desire and fulfillment would be: a story of excess and grace, of solidarity and hope, and — in a fragmented world — a taste of the unity and fullness we crave as God's creation.

8. Faith, Autonomy, and the Limits of Agency in a Secular Age

PHILIP J. ROSSI, S.J.

1. Introduction

The autonomy of individual human agents, particularly when construed as the capacity to govern freely one's own actions, has often served as a principal marker of the cultures of Western modernity. Whether one is, in Charles Taylor's terms, a "booster" or a "knocker" of modernity, individual autonomy looms large as a defining feature of what each recognizes as a characteristically modern account of what it means to be human. Yet, even though autonomy has taken center stage in modernity, it is useful to recall that modern thinkers were not the first to construe self-governance of one's actions as an important ingredient in the exercise of morally responsible human agency.[1] Once we attend to the fact that a capacity for self-governance is central to traditions of moral discourse and reflection that focus on virtue and character as structurally constitutive of moral agency, the emergence of autonomy as a core element in the dynamics of modernity can no longer be considered to issue primarily from an insight totally original with "modernity" about the form, operation, or capacity of human agency.[2] In this respect, the emphasis the ethics of modernity

1. See, for instance, Aristotle, *Nicomachean Ethics,* book III, chapter 5, 1113b-1115a; Thomas Aquinas, *Commentary on the Nicomachean Ethics,* book III, lectures XI-XIII; Duns Scotus, "The Will and Its Inclinations," in *Duns Scotus on the Will and Morality,* ed. and trans. Allan B. Wolter, O.F.M. (Washington, D.C.: Catholic University of America Press, 1986), pp. 188-91, 194-97, 200-203. (I thank James South for directing me to these texts of Scotus.)

2. This point may also be articulated as a construal of moral agency in terms of the *accountability* that agential self-governance entails for shaping and directing one's conduct. The

places on autonomy may not be so much a major break from previous ways of construing agency as it is a significant enhancement of a role that the moral traditions from which the ethics of modernity emerged had already given to responsible self-governance within the structure of moral agency.

Kant, whose work plays a formative role in placing responsibility for one's own self-governance at center stage of discussions of moral agency, is instructive on this point. In his seminal treatment of autonomy in the *Groundwork of the Metaphysics of Morals* he explicitly presents his account as nothing more than a precise articulation of a principle that every agent already grasps, as a matter of practical knowledge, in acting morally.[3] This principle bears on the manner in which the exercise of moral agency carries within its very form a commitment to order one's actions to unconditioned good, that is, to that good which requires, under penalty of rendering one's agency practically unintelligible, unconditional recognition by all rational agents.[4]

Why might it be significant to point out that, even as autonomy has served as a defining marker of moral agency for the cultures of modernity (and remains so in the aftermath of modernity), it has fundamental antecedents in traditions of understanding human agency that antedate the modernity that gives autonomy such prominence? In what follows, I argue that understanding autonomy within a context locating its continuity with the long stream of moral reflection that Alan Donagan designates "the common morality"[5] is significant for two reasons. First, it allows us to see

---

articulation of autonomy emerging in modernity can thus be understood as reconfiguring the scope of accountability: agents are now explicitly and reflexively accountable for the *normativity* of their moral judgments as well as for their conduct. Agential accountability for normativity, however, does not thereby render it, as one influential line of criticism has it, merely "subjective."

3. *Groundwork of the Metaphysics of Morals,* in Immanuel Kant, *Practical Philosophy,* trans. and ed. Mary J. Gregor, The Cambridge Edition of the Works of Immanuel Kant (Cambridge: Cambridge University Press, 1996), pp. 58-59. [German: in *Kants gesammelte Schriften,* herausgegeben von der königlich preussischen Akademie der Wissenschaften, Berlin 1900-, Bd. 4:403-4; hereafter KGS.] In this regard, the thrust of his argument is not principally against theoretical moral skepticism but against practical exemptions from the moral order that we are inclined to enact for our own benefit.

4. See, for instance, Stephen Engstrom, *The Form of Practical Knowledge: A Study of the Categorical Imperative* (Cambridge, Mass.: Harvard University Press, 2009), pp. 124-27, 155-59, 167-78.

5. *The Theory of Morality* (Chicago: University of Chicago Press, 1977), pp. 4-9; this classic study explores commonalities in the moral theories of Aquinas and Kant.

how it need not be the case that autonomy is inevitably packaged with the "isms" — for example, individualism, relativism, subjectivism — that the "knockers" of modernity have inveighed against, and, often enough, "boosters" of modernity have celebrated among its glories. Second, dislodging autonomy from its presumed home in the dynamics of social atomism and resituating it as embedded in a mutual recognition of agency that is expressed in practices of social respect[6] provides a basis for a different construal of its relation to faith. In accord with this proposed social reading of autonomy, I then show how faith, understood as an affirmation of an order of transcendence that makes possible the robust exercise of human moral finitude, may be construed to offer to the structure and workings of autonomous moral agency a formative social context that is particularly fitting for moral engagement with a secular age's fracturing interplay of contingency.

Making the case for the first reason is the task of the second section of this essay. This involves exploring the social dimensions of Kant's account of moral agency that, long overlooked in many standard twentieth-century readings of his ethics, have now been highlighted in a significant body of scholarship published since the mid-1980s.[7] Taking these social dimensions into account, I argue, provides a basis for re-contextualizing the role of autonomy in the dynamics of modernity in a way that brings into question that part of the influential "subtraction" narratives according to which the unfolding of modernity and secularity has inexorably required the elimination of transcendence and the end of religious faith. Such re-contextualization challenges narratives that take autonomy as a fitting and, indeed, necessary trope for human emancipation from God and from demands on moral action indexed to a transcendent order; it offers, instead, an account of autonomy in which God's transcendence renders intelligible an unreserved affirmation of the full dignity and worth of the finitude of human agency. On a reading that attends to the social embedding of human autonomy as a necessary condition for its intelligibility and exercise, au-

---

6. This way of reading autonomy cuts against the grain of certain renderings of "modernity" and "secularity" even prior to referencing it to a horizon of faith.

7. A notable precursor for this line of interpretation is Lucien Goldmann, *Immanuel Kant* (London: NLB, 1971 [French: *La communauté humaine et l'univers chez Kant* 1948; German: *Mensch, Gemeinschaft und Welt in der Philosophie Immanuel Kants,* 1945]). Other Kant commentators who have later articulated this social dimension include Sharon Anderson Gold, Allen Wood, Roger Sullivan, Robert Louden, Philip J. Rossi, Howard Williams, Holly Wilson, and, most recently, James DiCenso.

tonomy does not inevitably set humanity as a whole, nor individual human agents, in a zero-sum agential competition with one another (or, for that matter, with a transcendent God) in order for it to function as the origin and ground of the principles of moral life.[8] Indeed, it may be the case that humans can be properly autonomous only to the extent that the exercise of their autonomy carries within it an affirmation of moral normativity that is not merely immanent to human subjectivity but is referenced to an order that can be legitimately designated as "objective" as well as "transcendent."

This social re-contextualization of autonomy has consequences both for a larger recasting of the narratives of modernity and secularity and for the efforts of this volume to articulate how faith[9] can engage the socio-political order of a secular age. Such re-contextualization places in question those narratives of modernity and secularity that frame autonomy as the paradigmatic form of human moral agency that inevitably eventuates in intractable opposition to faith as a locus for principles for morally responsible conduct. In contrast, this social re-contextualization does not take it to be the case that autonomy inevitably stands in incompatible rivalry to faith as a principle for the integrity of moral agency, or that faith necessarily functions as a heteronomous principle for moral agency. While it is of major importance eventually to address this kind of "meta" question — and Taylor's work provides a range of strategies for doing so — that task is not the primary one for this essay. That task, instead, is to show how a socially robust understanding of autonomy bears on articulating possibilities for

---

8. Hobbes's image of the "state of nature" as *bellum omnium contra omnes* is an influential model for such zero-sum competition. I take Kant's account of autonomy, particularly the relational philosophical anthropology implicit in his account of an "ethical commonwealth," to contrast sharply with this image.

9. A comment on how "faith" is being construed in this discussion: I take faith in its most general sense to encompass both the personal (individual) and social dimensions of those practices (including linguistic ones) of a community through which that community expresses and articulates *both* the relationship *in which what it affirms as transcendent stands to the community* (and its members), *and* the relationship *in which all in the community stand to that transcendent.* Faith is also neither merely a personal inner attitude (though it includes that), nor radically incommunicable or ineffable (though it may be the case that no particular articulation of faith is fully adequate). Faith's links to a community's practices and traditions thus provide the primary contexts for locating the intelligibility of its affirmations and articulations. In consequence of these links, faith is thus both social and publicly communicable. Faith, moreover, has both articulated and enacted dimensions, so the intelligibility of faith is a function of the mutual correlation and interaction of these dimensions. Enacted faith serves to render intelligible what is articulated as profession of faith; profession of faith provides the grammar to render intelligible faith's enactment.

how moral agency, as reflectively formed in a community in which faith enters the formative dynamics of agency, appropriately engages pressing issues in the socio-political order. Such possibilities for engagement should thus manifest the structural capacity of an autonomous agency formed in faith to provide the sphere of public discourse with responsible analyses and critiques of these issues and constructive approaches for their resolution.

The third section of this essay thus explores these possibilities, which presuppose a reading of autonomy and faith as both embedded in a mutual recognition of agency (in Kant's terms, the relation that agents bear to one another in "a kingdom of ends" or an "ethical commonwealth") that is expressed in practices of social respect.[10] In accord with this reading of autonomy, I show how faith may be construed so that it offers to autonomous agency a formative social context that is particularly apt for responding to the moral challenges posed by the fracturing interplay of contingency that marks a secular age. This section thus articulates a construal of faith in terms of the enlarged social context it provides for the exercise of an autonomy already referenced to practices of mutual recognition. I argue that faith offers to the social respect embedded in the structure of autonomy an expansive horizon of welcoming of the other that brings social respect to a completion fully inclusive of the range of otherness before which our humanity stands.

2. The Finitude of Human Agency: The Commonwealth of Autonomous Subjects in the Space of Contingency

In many readings of the intellectual trajectory of modernity and secularity, Kant's articulation of autonomy as crucial to human moral agency plays a prominent role. Although Descartes is most often credited (and castigated) for fathering "the turn to the subject," this modern subject reaches full moral "adulthood" only as Kant makes it possible for the subject to claim reflectively its own "autonomy of the will" as "the supreme moral principle" for decision and conduct. It may be a historical and conceptual oversimplification to argue that Kant's account of autonomy transposes the

---

10. For "social respect," see Philip J. Rossi, *The Social Authority of Reason: Kant's Critique, Radical Evil, and the Destiny of Humankind* (Albany: State University of New York Press, 2005), pp. 152-62.

Cartesian "I think, therefore I am" into "I will, therefore I am," but Kant's uncompromising affirmation of the human subject's moral freedom has, nonetheless, often been read as providing moral subjectivity with a contour of self-determining agency that brings the chaos of moral relativism inevitably in its wake. Embedded in such relativism, moreover, seems to be an agential subjectivity that radically challenges any moral claim made on behalf of a transcendent authority. On this reading, Kantian autonomy begets a modern Protagorean relativism well suited to a secular age in which God has been pronounced dead: autonomy frees each of us to decree what is right and what is good with a moral authority once the prerogative of God.[11]

Iris Murdoch concluded her classic description of autonomy, read as a cipher for an absolute moral subjectivism willfully displacing God, with the devastating comment: "Kant's [autonomous] man had already received a glorious incarnation nearly a century earlier in the work of Milton: His proper name is Lucifer."[12] More recently, Susan Neiman, who does not read Kant as a relativist nor take his account of autonomy to entail relativism, characterized the robustness with which Kant affirms the autonomy of human freedom in terms that strikingly resonate with Murdoch's association of autonomy with godlike power. Commenting on the "universal law of nature" formulation of the categorical imperative, she notes: "Universal laws can be imagined by anyone; universal laws of nature are given by one Being alone. In giving us this formula, Kant gave us a chance to pretend to be God. Every time we face a moral dilemma, we are to imagine reenacting the Creation."[13]

On Neiman's reading, however, "playing God" in a Kantian manner does not require us to place human agency in rivalry with divine agency; it requires, instead, a recognition that fundamental to the integrity of our

11. This modality of relativism, at once Promethean and Protagorean, accords well with a secularity that gives moral urgency to the human project of displacing God, but does not exhaust the possibilities for an agential subjectivity in tune with other variations on secularity. Attention also needs to be paid to that form of secularity in which God is not so much displaced as rendered irrelevant, a secularity whose atheism is marked more by shrugs of indifference than by defiant fists.

12. Iris Murdoch, *The Sovereignty of Good* (New York: Schocken, 1971), p. 80. She offers a quite different account of Kant, which takes him to affirm an (objective) metaphysical primacy to the good, in her later Gifford lectures, *Metaphysics as a Guide to Morals* (London: Chatto and Windus, 1992).

13. Susan Neiman, *Evil in Modern Thought: An Alternative History of Philosophy* (Princeton, N.J.: Princeton University Press, 2002), p. 76.

PHILIP J. ROSSI, S.J.

human moral situation is the acknowledgment of both the difference and the affinity between divine and human agency. That twofold acknowledgment then bears on our capacity to envision what *human* moral agency requires of us. She sees this recognition as crucial to Kant's articulation of the limits of theoretical reason and the consequences those limits have for exercising practical reason to shape our conduct: "*Dissatisfaction* [with the limits of our knowledge] *comes from the wish to be God*. If any one claim is the message of Kant's metaphysics, this is it.[14] . . . The desire to surpass our limits is as essential to the structure of the human as the recognition that we cannot."[15] On her account, the "wish to be God" does not, in the first instance, stem from a will to exercise omnipotent power on one's own behalf; it arises from an experiential apprehension of the depth to which contingency, as it escapes both our capacity for understanding and the control of our finite agency, shapes the trajectory of our lives: "Yet the wish to determine the world can't be coherently limited, for you cannot know which event will turn out to be not just another event, but the one that will change your life.[16] . . . The wish to be God isn't simply pathological; its alternative is blind trust in the world to work as it should."[17]

Neiman's reading of the moral autonomy expressed in "the law of nature" formulation takes on added significance for articulating the place of human agency in a secular age once we note her placement of the exercise of autonomy within Kant's overall depiction of our human situation, which he sees as inextricably tied to reason's efforts to render that situation intelligible, theoretically and practically, with respect both to nature and to God. For Kant, contingency, and our recognition of human finitude with respect to that contingency, are central for the dynamics that give our human situation its moral and its religious structure. He situates the operation of human autonomy within the framework of a contingency, embedded in the workings of both the cosmos and our agency, which serves as a marker for both the limits of finite reason and the dynamism driving reason to surpass those limits. On this reading of Kant, contingency presents no puzzle for the use of our reason that, by seeking the principles at work in the operations of nature, enables us to make sense of the world theoretically: "Where it's only a matter of knowledge, the fact

14. Neiman, *Evil*, p. 62, emphasis in original.
15. Neiman, *Evil*, p. 80.
16. Neiman, *Evil*, p. 74.
17. Neiman, *Evil*, p. 75.

that what affects us is not created by us causes little problem."[18] Matters stand differently, however, for our practical use of reason that seeks to render ourselves and the world in which we must act morally intelligible: "It would be easy to acknowledge that not controlling the world is part of being human, were it not for the fact that *things go wrong*. The thought that the rift between reason and nature is neither error nor punishment but the fault line along which the universe is structured can be a source of perfect terror."[19]

Behind the "wish to be God" thus lies a desire to rid the world of the contingent, a desire that Neiman sees framing the central goal of Hegel's enterprise, even as Kant, on her reading, finds such a desire both unavoidable and deeply problematic.[20] It is problematic inasmuch as Kant takes a capacity to conceal from ourselves the recognition that we cannot surpass the limits of our human finitude to be embedded within the structure of the human just as deeply as the wish to be God: "Kant reminds us as often as possible of all that God can do and all that we cannot. Nobody in the history of philosophy was more aware of the number of ways we can forget it. He was equally conscious of the temptation to idolatry, the alternative route to confusing God with other beings."[21] Such inveterate capacity for self-concealment of our limitation in the face of human reason's unbridled ambitions is precisely why our reason needs a discipline of "critique" to train us in an intellectual humility from which we can acknowledge that *the dignity properly ours as human is inestimable precisely in virtue of, not in spite of, our finitude.* Kant recognizes that our finitude is so deeply constitutive of the moral shape of human agency that, were we to convince ourselves that we had succeeded in overcoming the moral limits of our finitude, we would not thereby have made our agency more "godly"; we would, instead, have deflated its capacity to engage the play of contingency that stands at the core of the human moral enterprise.

If Neiman's reading is correct, she has identified a contrast between Kant and Hegel that is crucial both for locating the different influences their work has had on shaping the cultures of modernity and for discerning how their work may — and may not — continue to provide useful coordinates for navigating the aftermath of modernity in which we find ourselves.

18. Neiman, *Evil,* p. 80.
19. Neiman, *Evil,* pp. 80-81.
20. Neiman, *Evil,* p. 89.
21. Neiman, *Evil,* p. 75.

Kant affirms, as Hegel does not, that the proper relation between human finitude and divine transcendence is one that, from the side of finite human reason, maintains, rather than seeks to overcome, the difference between the finite in its full contingency and the transcendent in its fully radical and non-contingent otherness. On Kant's account, it is only in virtue of recognizing the difference between the human and the divine — a recognition, moreover, that acknowledges that overcoming that difference is not within our human power — that it becomes possible for us to act in full and proper accord with our human finitude. Human agency can be exercised in a fully human manner only in function of an awareness and an affirmation — often exacted from us neither readily nor easily — that the "godly" *perspective* presented to us as a "universal law of nature" for our finite agency to "enact" as pattern for our moral maxims does not thereby enable us to act with an unfailingly omnipotent "godly" *power* of doing "whatever we might wish." That perspective enables us, rather, to exercise a properly finite *human* power to do as we ought in a world that contingency shapes.[22]

This contrast, in my judgment, renders Kant a more helpful ally than Hegel for articulating the proper contours for understanding the significance of the exercise of human agency in a secular-post-secular age that poses fundamental challenges to the possibility and intelligibility of faith as an appropriate human response to a transcendence properly construed as divine. Neiman's reading of this contrast parses Kant's account by attending to its affirmation of finitude and contingency as that which provides human agency with its fundamental moral range and depth, in contrast to Hegel's affirmation of the impetus to overcome them. This parsing helps to show how a construal of the relationship between divine freedom and human autonomy that pits them against one another as a "zero-sum" game may miss both *how* radically different they are from each other and *why* that difference is central for appropriately understanding what it is to be human. One consequence of missing such a difference is that the human freedom left as a legacy after the rival God has been declared dead turns out to be small change indeed for any who expect humanity thereby to gain moral capital sufficient to make the workings of the world more reliably

---

22. Put in more formally theological terms, this is a consequence of recognizing that "creating" is a "mode" of acting that, as properly divine, is radically different from any human finite "making." On this point, the work of David Burrell, Robert Sokolowski, and George Steiner provides important considerations for marking this difference and for engaging its bearing on the function of belief in contemporary culture.

conducive to the flourishing of all. Inasmuch as the obituary pronouncing God dead is also the news that God never was, there now is one less suspect to blame when human things go terribly amiss; that, however, hardly provides a guarantee that, in consequence of a recognition of the (longtime) absence of God, we have made our human selves better prepared, either now or for the future, to "do right" for the flourishing of our species and the environing world in which we dwell. As Neiman astutely points out in concluding her chapter on Nietzsche and Freud, the outcome of their unmasking of the God-illusion is that "the price is enormous, for all nature stands condemned. Human beings themselves become walking indictments of creation."[23]

Neiman is not the first to note that the death of God provides impetus for lines of anti-humanist thinking that consciously stand against the centrality that the main currents of modernity give to the human. The value of her analysis here lies not so much in the fact that she makes this connection, but rather in her presentation of Kant as champion of the utter centrality of human finitude to the integrity and worth of the human moral endeavor. Kant's account of autonomy provides support for lines of resistance to the anti-humanist and post-human options that, in consequence of both real and perceived failures of modernity, have become part of the landscape of the intellectual culture of the early twenty-first century.[24] Kant's account offers a basis for constructing positive alternatives to such options, alternatives that open possibilities for more adequately addressing, in theory and in practice, crucial ways in which the forms and dynamics of modernity have failed to deliver on their once bright promises to bring about human flourishing. Modernity's articulation of a reflective awareness of historicity may justly merit condemnation for making possible its self-conscious appropriation — and even approbation — of humanity's agency as prime executioner at history's slaughter-bench. This does not require, nonetheless, that the alternative human future be either of the main possibilities post-humanism puts on offer: on one hand, numb resignation to the fate of being a transient epiphenomenon of the dynamics of the cosmos; on the other, the hubris of relentlessly seeking mastery of the techniques and the technology to bend the cosmos — or at least our

23. *Evil*, p. 237. See also Charles Taylor's remarks in the last two sections of the concluding chapter of *Sources of the Self: The Making of Modern Identity* (Cambridge: Cambridge University Press, 1989), pp. 513-21.

24. See, for instance, Stephanos Geroulanos, *An Atheism That Is Not Humanist Emerges in French Thought* (Stanford, Calif.: Stanford University Press, 2010).

local part of it — to serve wherever may now be, or in the future emerge as, our dominant human goal and purpose.[25]

Central to this line of resistance, as well as to the possibilities for articulating an alternative robustly affirming the human, are an appropriation and enlargement of key elements in Kant's account of the relationship that contingency bears to the exercise of autonomy within the community of human finite agents. This relationship, as I argue below, first makes it possible to bring into full relief the extent to which impoverished understandings of both the human and the divine function within such post- and anti-humanist options. It also makes it possible to articulate alternatives that stand open to disclosure of what Taylor describes as the hope instanced (though not exclusively) in "Judeo-Christian theism and in its central promise of a divine affirmation of the human, more total than humans can ever attain unaided."[26]

On this reading, Kant situates the mutuality of our human freedom — or, alternately, the reciprocity of our autonomy — as fully engaged with the contingency of the cosmos, even as it also marks the moral locus in which we are mutually enabled to transcend it. His account manifests a deep sense that the common fragility of finite human freedom stands inextricably coordinate to the dignity that we must recognize in one another's humanity in the moral community he terms the "ethical commonwealth." These elements function within a reading of autonomy in which awareness of the reciprocal connections of freely offered respect within which one stands to all other human agents — in Kant's terms, awareness of one's membership in a "kingdom of ends" — brings with it a deep sense of the fragility of our finite freedom. This fragility, I argue, is exhibited in the exercise of a finite freedom inextricably enmeshed in the functioning of a world of contingency, and thus serves as fundamental locus for recognition of the dignity of our humanity that we are called on to accord to one another.

Briefly framed, my argument is that Kant's recognition of the inestimable dignity of the power of human freedom to effect good (that is, for bringing about "what ought to be" in a world of "what is") is equally a recognition that such power resides in agents who are themselves profoundly fragile, whose exercise of that power is correspondingly fragile, yet who

---

25. Who sets these human purposes, and what gives them value, are questions implicated in a larger discussion of the relation between the divine and the human.
26. Taylor, *Sources of the Self*, p. 521.

are capable of empowering each other's freedom in mutual respect for one another's fragility.[27] For Kant, the fragility of human freedom is inscribed in the embodied conditions of spatio-temporal finitude and contingency. The human power for bringing about good thoroughly pertains to, and is rooted in, a finite practical reason, exercised in a world of contingency that renders that power for bringing about good both fragmentary and fragile. Such a fragmentary and fragile character is not simply an outcome arising from the limited scope of the good we each have power to effect; it also arises to the extent that the endurance of much of the good that we each actually effect requires that others also do what is needed to sustain it. Kant recognizes that, insofar as we each stand alone, the exercise of our freedom provides thin and tenuous protection to our core dignity of spirit in a world in which the contingency of things gone wrong intersects with a finite agency that lacks power — and, even more significantly, the willingness — to effect all that is good.

The ultimate bulwark for our finitude is then not so much the solitary resoluteness that Murdoch eloquently describes as it is the mutual recognition and respect we accord each other for the fragile and vulnerable freedom we each embody. As embodied, moreover, our freedom is rendered fragile not simply by the inconstancy of intention that Kant terms the "inversion of our maxims," nor only by the inattention and distraction with which we thoughtlessly descend into evil's banality, nor by an intent so thoroughly malign that Kant calls it "diabolical" to mark it as beyond human (im)moral capacity. It is also rendered fragile by a vulnerability of both body and spirit to violence and violation. Such vulnerability provides a crucial locus from which to gain a perspective on the welcoming hospitality to the other that, as I propose in the following section, constitutes a fundamental social context within which faith can be constitutively formative of the agency required for responsible human engagement with the fragmented world inherited from modernity.

I finish this section by framing three major points it has proposed about the structure and exercise of human moral agency. These points follow from indexing Kant's account of autonomy not, as is done in standard narratives of modernity, to an anthropology of atomistic agency, but

---

27. I have developed this point in "Finite Freedom, Fractured and Fragile: Kant's Anthropology as Resource for a Postmodern Theology of Grace," *Philosophie et théologie: Festschrift Emilio Brito, SJ,* Bibliotheca Ephemeridum Theologicarum Lovaniensium, 206, ed. Éric Gaziaux (Leuven: Peeters Press, 2007), pp. 47-60; see especially part III, pp. 54-60.

rather to what I call a "social anthropology of human finite freedom." The first point is that Kant's account of autonomy functions within a social embedding of human agency that is conceived as a structural feature of human finitude. This point would have once been controversial among Kant scholars, but a significant body of recent scholarship has marshaled an array of interpretive and historical considerations in its favor. This point has significance beyond indicating a need for reconsidering the role Kant's work often plays in accounts of the emergence of those liberalisms formative of modern moral individualism.[28] Of wider importance than such historical revisionism is that, once the historical and conceptual legitimacy of a social construal of autonomy is established, we may then reconfigure — or even put aside — some bifurcations that the "standard" narratives of modernity and secularity associate with autonomy, particularly those placing it on the side of the radical moral subjectivity and individualism captured in Murdoch's reference to Milton's Lucifer or the warfare of the "state of nature" that Hobbes posits as the abiding baseline of human social dynamics.

The second and third points then bear on the relationship between, on the one hand, the social construal of the structure and exercise of autonomous agency and, on the other, the conceptual and moral functions that a recognition of divine transcendence plays within a human world of contingency and finitude.

The second point is that this social construal of autonomy repositions the moral import of an acknowledgment of divine transcendence: such acknowledgment, rather than undermining human agency, instead encompasses a robust sense of human social and historical responsibility. It provides a basis for affirming a fundamental moral priority for the role of *humanity, as a mutually interrelated whole,* in shaping the social and cultural history that forms the distinctively human mode of interaction with

28. This is not to deny the formative role that influential interpretations of Kant's work that discounted or ignored the social embedding of autonomy have played in shaping modern moral individualism; they clearly had a role. But if a social embedding of autonomy more accurately represents Kant's own views, accounts of Kant's heritage need to inquire how and why this was lost from view. Kant, moreover, cannot be fully absolved from blame; as Lewis White Beck, arguably the most important mid-twentieth-century English-language Kant commentator, observed, "It is regrettable that Kant was not more careful; though, had he been so, the race of Kant commentators would have been unemployed" (*A Commentary on Kant's Critique of Practical Reason* [Chicago: University of Chicago Press, 1960], p. 221).

the cosmos.[29] Acknowledging divine transcendence fully affirms human moral responsibility for shaping the direction of history and culture.

The third point is that re-contextualizing autonomy so that social relationality is fundamental to its exercise, shows it to be embedded in the contingencies of the cosmos and human culture that mark our human finitude. This embedding of autonomy in contingency provides, in the following section, a central locus for the mutual social engagement of autonomy and faith.

As with the first point, the latter points each have a dimension that bears on the value of Kant's work as a locus for constructive theological engagement, as well as a dimension that bears on questions about the role of faith in public life. To the extent that Kant can now be read as providing an account in which an acknowledgment of divine transcendence affirms human moral responsibility in the shaping of history, he no longer stands as an "adversary," who, in opposing affirmations of divine transcendence issuing from faith, is intent on thoroughly replacing religion with secular human moral practice. His work can now be engaged constructively in relation to faith in that it affirms faith as a human posture toward transcendence, one that plays a legitimate constitutive role in shaping autonomous moral agency.[30] Kant's account is thus an effort not to overcome or eliminate religion and faith but to exhibit how faith, construed as a critically formed acknowledgement of divine transcendence, is of crucial import for the proper exercise of human moral agency.[31] Such a critical acknowledgment of transcendence, shaped in awareness of "the limits of human reason," provides the context for rendering human finitude, exercised as autonomous agency in a world of contingency, morally intelligible. Kant takes the human relation to divine transcendence to be that which provides the moral space for human finite agency to be constitutive — though not solely by itself — of the trajectory and outcome of history by working to establish a world community abidingly shaped by the dynamics of the moral reciprocity of mutual respect.

---

29. One indication of this repositioning within Kant's work is that, as the critical project moves into the 1790s, his discussion of hope shifts focus from personal immortality toward the final outcome of humanity's career as a species.

30. This is not to be taken to imply that this is the *only* way to construe faith; this is a claim about faith viewed from the human side in terms of its consequences for moral agency. It should not be taken to stand in opposition to a construal of faith that focuses on its origin in divine gratuity.

31. Philip J. Rossi, "Moral Autonomy, Human Destiny, and Divine Transcendence: Kant's Doctrine of Hope as a Foundation for Christian Ethics," *The Thomist* 46 (1982): 441-58.

In addition to re-opening possibilities for Kant as a constructive theological interlocutor, these points also bear on the function of faith in the public life of cultures emergent in the aftermath of modernity. They help delimit the scope and the configuration of human responsibility for giving a morally fitting direction to the trajectory of the socially structured dynamics of public life and culture. Kant aptly characterizes these dynamics as humanity's "unsocial sociability,"[32] which provides the cultural conditions under which human finite agency is exercised for effecting good and resisting evil. In situating the exercise of human moral autonomy in the contingency of both the cosmos and the workings of human agency, Kant's account manifests a deep sense that the common fragility of our finite human freedom, which runs all the way down in our agency, stands inextricably coordinate to the dignity that we must recognize in one another's humanity in the moral community he terms the "ethical commonwealth."

A relationality deeply embedded in the contingencies of the cosmos and of our human fragility is thus a key element in a Kantian anthropology that inscribes human freedom in the embodied conditions of spatio-temporal finitude. Insofar as we each stand alone, our finitude provides thin and tenuous protection to our core dignity of spirit; under these conditions, human power for bringing about good, rooted in the fragmentary, fragile exercise of finite reason, stands on the slender and precarious footing of a social relationality embedded in cosmic contingency. Human fragility stands aware that, in this world of contingency, it cannot of itself, either individually or communally, provide enduring stability for an order of what "ought to be," the order that fully accords with the dignity and the fragility of our human embodied spirit.

This awareness, critically shaped by acknowledgment of both divine transcendence and human finitude, nonetheless brings with it a twofold hope enabling us to envision ourselves as responsible agents shaping the trajectory of history and culture. One element of this hope is that what we do autonomously (or differently inflected, what we do in enacting the dignity of our finitude) will have a genuine effect in helping to bring about an enduring order of what ought to be. The second element is that the stability of such enduring order of what "ought to be," even though it lies beyond

---

32. The human "tendency to enter into society, combined, however, with a thoroughgoing resistance that constantly threatens to sunder this society" ("Idea for a Universal History with a Cosmopolitan Intent," in *Perpetual Peace and Other Essays,* trans. Ted Humphrey [Indianapolis: Hackett, 1983], p. 32 (KGS Bd. 8:20).

human finite power to effect fully in a world of contingency, constantly stands on offer to us, in virtue of the moral efficacy of our critically formed acknowledgement of divine transcendence, as the one outcome fully worthy of all we enact autonomously from the dignity of our finitude.[33]

This interplay of contingency and hope in relation to a critical construal of human finitude and divine transcendence pervades Kant's philosophical enterprise. The role it plays, moreover, in his account of cosmopolitanism and perpetual peace as worldly enactments of the dignity of our autonomous finitude, provides a particularly apt place from which to make a transition to a discussion of the role of faith in the public life of a secular age. These accounts help delimit how a critically formed acknowledgment of divine transcendence frames a horizon of hope that is not just personally but also *socially* necessary for finite human agents to persevere in efforts to make the world of human interaction "what it ought to be," that is, a world in which human agents concretely and consistently exhibit the dynamics of shared membership in "a kingdom of ends."[34] Such hope is necessary inasmuch as human efforts to make the world into what "it ought to be" take place in and for a world in which the recalcitrance of the contingency of "what is" lies so deeply ingrained that it seems to rule out as unintelligible hopes for the attainment of a social order of enduring moral reciprocity. For Kant, the prime instance requiring such (social) perseverance lies in a commitment to establish an international order of enduring peace, even in the face of the recalcitrance of human self-preferential obduracy that seems to support Hobbes's image of ceaseless war as the baseline for human social dynamics. Kant marks the moral urgency of establishing an international order of enduring peace by identifying it as a categorical imperative that humanity must enjoin on itself *as a species*.[35] His urgency in pressing this

---

33. The second section, "Imagination," of Anthony Godzieba's essay in this volume provides a complementary account of the envisioning of possibilities with reference to a framing horizon of transcendence.

34. Philip J. Rossi, "Cosmopolitanism and the Interests of Reason: A Social Framework for Human Action in History," in *Recht und Frieden in der Philosophie Kants: Akten des X. Internationalen Kant-Kongresses,* vol. 4, ed. Valerio Rohden, Ricardo R. Terra, Guido A. de Almeida, and Margit Ruffing (Berlin: Walter de Gruyter, 2008), pp. 65-75; "Cosmopolitanism: Kant's Social Anthropology of Hope," in *Kant und die Philosophie in weltbürgerlicher Absicht, Akten des XI. Kant-Kongresses 2010,* vol. 4, ed. Stefano Bacin, Alfredo Ferrarin, Claudio La Rocca, Margit Ruffing (Berlin: Walter de Gruyter, 2013), pp. 827-37.

35. Cf. *The Metaphysics of Morals,* in Kant, *Practical Philosophy,* pp. 490-91 (KGS Bd. 6:354-55); "Toward Perpetual Peace," in Kant, *Practical Philosophy,* pp. 325-28 (KGS Bd. 8:354-57). Kant portrays peace as what we might term a "species imperative" bearing on

point suggests that sustaining efforts in pursuit of a cosmopolitan order of peace is a project within our human capacity to effect only in virtue of a hope that, embedded in the critical self-awareness of human moral finitude, brings with it an acknowledgment of transcendence.

Kant presses the case for humanity to enact a moral commitment to a cosmopolitan order of peace within an anthropological horizon shaped by an acknowledgement of transcendent otherness and human finitude. The final section of this essay thus engages the question of the role of faith in public life by placing the dynamics of the "unsocial sociability" of our human finitude, as they are enacted in the interplay between our embodied vulnerability and what Taylor has called "the draw to violence,"[36] within that horizon of transcendent otherness and human finitude. I propose that one fundamental way in which faith makes it possible for us to resist the draw to violence lies in its capacity for enabling an encompassing respect for our shared embodied vulnerability. Faith provides a locus for a human enacting of the primal grace by which the divine fully enters the fractured landscape of human contingency: a hospitality in which the welcoming of one another's otherness becomes so complete that it allows us to accompany each other in and through the brokenness that marks out the space of human contingency.

3. Enlarging of the Framework of Agency: Faith and the Welcoming of Otherness

In this concluding section I argue that faith, construed as that openness from which humans are empowered to stand in finitude and contingency before the transcendent Otherness of God, offers to the structure and workings of autonomous moral agency a formative social context that is particularly fitting for engaging a secular age marked by the fracturing dynamics of contingency. Faith, on the account offered here, provides a horizon for recognition of the full range of otherness — divine, cosmic, and

---

both the external social order of justice among nations and the inner social order among moral agents construed as an "ethical commonwealth"; see also *Religion within the Bounds of Mere Reason,* in *Religion and Rational Theology,* trans. and ed. Allen Wood and George di Giovanni, The Cambridge Edition of the Works of Immanuel Kant (Cambridge: Cambridge University Press, 1996), pp. 132-33 (KGS Bd. 6:96-98).

36. Cf. Charles Taylor, *A Secular Age* (Cambridge, Mass.: Harvard University Press, 2007), pp. 656-710.

human — within which autonomous agents are invited to enact, for a world of fracture, modes of healing unity that do not erase the fragmentation and brokenness of contingency into an undifferentiated Hegelian *Aufhebung* but, instead, render brokenness in all its particularities into graced loci for bringing about reconciliation.

This argument for faith's possibilities for empowering an enlarged social context for the exercise of autonomous agency builds on, first, a social reading of autonomy as embedded in a mutual recognition of agency and expressed in practices of social respect, and, second, the multiple horizons of otherness that have come into view from the interplay of the dynamics of fracture in the aftermath of modernity. As a counterpart to this social reading of autonomy, I articulate a construal of faith that, in its capacity for attending to the full range of otherness, provides an enlarged social context for an autonomous agency referenced to practices of mutual recognition. Faith, construed this way, offers to the social respect embedded in the structure of autonomy an enlarged horizon of welcoming the other, from which our agency is invited to bring social respect to completion in an inclusive hospitality of reconciliation that engages the full range of otherness in which our fractured and fragile humanity stands and participates. In so doing, faith opens possibilities for our agency to shape practices for resisting the draw to violence that all too often infects us in encountering one another's otherness.

The construal of faith proposed here is thus one for which hospitality — a trope aptly captured in George Steiner's remark, "I believe we must teach other human beings to be guests of each other"[37] — is the enacted form of the relationality fundamental to the bearing that faith has on agency.[38] Particularly helpful for setting the context for this construal is a counter-trope to hospitality that Neiman has elegantly proposed as a fitting characterization of the fragile and deeply fractured dynamics in which humanity seeks moral and spiritual intelligibility in a "post-modern" condition: "homeless." Neiman's trope puts in bleak terms the consequences of modernity's disenchantment of the world, which renders the workings of nature void of meaning, save in terms of an efficient causality absent of purpose, on which human instrumental rationality only arbitrarily gains purchase. We — at

---

37. Theo Hobson, "On Being a Perfect Guest: The Tablet Interview: George Steiner," *The Tablet* 259 (August 13, 2005): 15.

38. See Philip J. Rossi, "Sojourners, Guests, and Strangers: The Church as Enactment of the Hospitality of God," *Questions liturgiques — Liturgical Questions* 90 (2009): 121-31.

least to the extent that modernity remains deeply etched into our bearing toward the world — now live and act in a world of nature fully disenchanted of purposes that pay attention to humanity; even more ominously, we live and act in a world in which we have become acutely aware of how thoroughly capable we have become of disenchanting and disengaging ourselves from attention to our own humanity. "Homeless" captures a sense that we act within a landscape where not only an indifferent nature fractures human purposes, but also where something fundamental in ourselves and in the exercise of our agency has itself been deeply fractured. She remarks: "Auschwitz revealed the remoteness of humans from themselves"[39] and adds that "Auschwitz was conceptually devastating because it revealed a possibility in human nature that we hoped not to see."[40]

There is a connection that links these coordinates provided by Neiman's trope of "homeless," a construal of faith through a trope of "welcoming," and a social reading of autonomy. This connection is in the dynamics of mutuality within which each of these coordinates is embedded, particularly as mutuality functions in the multiple spaces and varied inflections of cosmic and human contingency.[41] Through this connection of mutuality functioning in the spaces of contingency, faith offers autonomous agency a capacity for entering into a wider horizon of engaging otherness, where such engagement can be enacted as a fully encompassing hospitality.[42]

Viewed from this connection in mutuality, Neiman's trope of "homeless" exhibits a moral poignancy that powerfully exposes our individual and systemic failures to exhibit to one another the basic human reciprocity of mutual welcome in hospitality. The conditions of living with one another that we have helped shape (sometimes actively, sometimes by acquiescence) in civic life, in the marketplace, in the dynamics of religion and of culture, which should be ones conducive to the flourishing of all, have all too often been ones we have misshaped (as much by inattention

39. Neiman, *Evil*, p. 240.

40. Neiman, *Evil*, p. 254.

41. See Philip J. Rossi, "Human Contingency, Divine Freedom, and the Normative Shape of Saving History," in *The Shaping of Tradition: Context and Normativity*, ed. Colby Dickinson, with Lieven Boeve and Terrence Merrigan (Leuven: Peeters, 2013), pp. 117-30, for a discussion of the interplay of two inflections of contingency, one the contingency of creation's absolute dependence, the other the intra-cosmic contingency of uncertain outcome.

42. Mary Doak's essay in this volume indicates how Pope Benedict XVI's relational account of the human, grounded in a Trinitarian theology, traces a complementary trajectory placing priority on a welcoming openness to those most in need.

as by ill-intent) to one another's detriment. At the outset of the twenty-first century, the dynamics of so many interactions within our dominant socio-cultural, political, and economic structures provide scant evidence from which to glean firm assurance that we, as a species, have yet learned how to make the space on which we dwell a fitting "home" for one another as fellow humans, let alone for other living beings with whom we share the earth. We seem to provide to one another, in the social worlds we construct to affirm "our" identity over against "theirs," little to suggest that we have mastered the skills to share, in a modicum of peace, even a small space side by side with fellow human beings who are not the "us" delimited in our parochialisms. Inscribed deep in our failures, great and small, to welcome the displaced, the uprooted, the homeless, as well as in the license we often give ourselves to drive strangers away with coldness, hostility, and even violence, is a refusal to recognize that we, too, stand "homeless" in our human condition and that, as George Steiner pointedly remarks, all of us "are guests of life on this crowded polluted planet."[43] Unsure of how welcome we truly are in the world, even when we stand in a privileged place, our welcome for others falters, lest opening the door to them bring with it contingencies that might displace us as well.

Although Neiman offers what looks like an unrelievedly bleak depiction of our human condition as "metaphysically homeless," she still affirms, in accord with a Kantian trajectory of hope, the capacity of moral reason to empower human imagination for reshaping "the world as it is" into "the world as it ought to be" and so enact, for and with one another, some human wholeness for our world. Her account also aligns with Kant's articulation of hope as the moral horizon of reason in affirming that the human project of rendering the world morally intelligible by enacting what ought to be is sustained only by an ordering to a point of reference — an encompassing "ideal" of the highest good — that functions "transcendentally." This ideal frames a trajectory of intelligibility for moral endeavor that is more encompassing than whatever can be rendered out of any mere juxtaposition of the fragments of human action from which we seek to exact moral sense.[44]

Neiman's philosophical grammar for this function, it must be noted, is robustly apophatic — as was Kant's — with respect to what modernity has perceived as an incurably onto-theological grammar of orthodoxy in Chris-

---

43. Hobson, "On Being a Perfect Guest," p. 14.
44. She specifies this function as a "regulative" one.

tian theology's affirmation of a transcendent God. Though not identical to "faith" as I construe it in terms of hospitality and welcome, Neiman's reading of "hope" does take a dynamic of human accompaniment to be central to the attainment of whatever human wholeness we have the capacity to effect for one another through our agency. In this she captures a central dimension of Kant's cosmopolitan vision pointing us toward the enlargement of mutuality — particularly in circumstances in which possibilities for mutuality seem deeply broken or even erased — as a fundamental horizon for sustaining the exercise of our agency.[45]

Neiman's construal of hope locates its moral function in the attention we pay to the mutuality of our common condition of being "homeless." Hope, as the readiness to accompany one another, particularly in the most shattering circumstances, provides a fundamental pattern for exhibiting how attention to our mutuality empowers us to open for one another a welcoming human space on which we can dwell with each other in a manner that makes that space worthy to be called "home." In following a trajectory that attends to the moral profundity of human accompaniment, Neiman's account points in a direction along which we may also plot important dimensions of a construal of faith indexed to the trope of hospitality.

Hope, in Neiman's account, is an enacted trajectory of human accompaniment — of making the world "home" for each other — that provides the fundamental horizon of moral intelligibility from which to engage our "homeless" human circumstances. It thereby provides a frame of reference for concluding my account of faith by pointing to two important points along its trajectory from which faith can be seen taking form as an "enacted hospitality" of accompaniment. In the first instance, faith is a response acknowledging the gifted character of creation as "the hospitality of God." In accord with this account, the most fundamental form of "faith" is *the hospitality of divine enactment in the radical originating that brings to be, and continues to sustain, the dwelling place that is creation itself.* This faith has its origin in God; it is a faith *God enacts* in the encompassing bringing-to-be that is creation and that makes creation a "dwelling place." Creation may itself thus be viewed as a divine "making room" in which God's welcome is given to the abundance of all that God creates.

---

45. Kant's exemplary instance of this enlargement of the horizon of mutuality for sustaining the exercise of our moral agency is his identifying (in *The Metaphysics of Morals*) the imperative "There is to be no war" as categorical, "even if there is not the slightest theoretical likelihood that it can be realized" (*Practical Philosophy,* p. 491; KGS Bd. 6:354).

This dynamic is deeply embedded in the Genesis narrative (chapters 3–4) that eventuates in what Christian theology has long seen, well before modernity, as a primal instance of the fracturing that renders us "home-less." God, the most gracious host, invites the man and the woman, fashioned in God's image, to make the garden, expressive of the abundance of God's creation, their dwelling place. Yet within that abundant hospitality, the man and the woman make themselves ungracious guests: they attempt to seize for themselves what is received rightly only if accepted in response to the Creator's graciousness. The narrative then makes manifest that acknowledgment and acceptance of creation as the radically originating offer of divine hospitality is a condition for the possibility of our human enactments of mutuality. So it is altogether fitting that the next fractures narrated fray and then break the deepest bonds of human mutuality: the man and the woman set themselves at odds with one another in passing off blame; far more ominously, Cain, perceiving no divine welcoming for himself, sunders in brutal murder his fraternal bond with Abel.

The Genesis narrative provides the negative articulation of what is most appropriately construed as the positive relation between the first, originating dimension of faith as the "enacted hospitality" of God's accompaniment of creation, and the second, received dimension of that faith to empower human agency with a capacity to enact hospitality for one another. Our recognition and affirmation of the most fundamental form of hospitality as the divine enactment by which we now stand as "guests of creation" is what makes it possible for us to enact the human hospitality by which we become "guests of one another" in acknowledgment of our mutuality.

It may well be that attention to this fundamental relation between these two dimensions of faith as "enacted hospitality" lies behind the importance that many religious traditions attach to practices in which human solidarity is enacted by welcoming the stranger at our door. In these practices we learn how our human status in the world is marked by mutual vulnerability to one another, all the more so when we meet as strangers to one another. Hospitality — at least as it has been enacted in the religiously informed practices of many cultures — is thus far more than a civil, wary politeness that allows us to maintain those barriers between "us" and "them" that are transgressed at our peril. It is, instead, the enacted risk of greeting another's vulnerability out of our own — and a reciprocal acceptance of that enacted risk by the one welcomed. Such welcoming opens up a previously unimagined common ground of mutuality that allows each of us to stand on a new space of respect issuing from a mutual recognition of vulnerability.[46]

Faith, on this construal, thus takes form as recognition of the horizon of a divine hospitality that welcomes us into the space of creation and thereby empowers us to make that space home for one another.[47] In a "secular age" in which so much public space functions as a place for a zero-sum contention of narrow interests and "take-no-prisoners" protection of what are all too often parochial and tribal identities, making room for welcoming one another in mutual vulnerability presents a compelling challenge to our capacities to exercise agency in full accord with the mutuality that gives agency its fundamental moral shape. In that context, what I have articulated in this section is an argument for the role of faith, as enacted hospitality, in giving our autonomous agency a capacity to address this challenge to the mutuality that lies at the heart of its moral exercise. In that role, faith provides a horizon of divine hospitality welcoming us to the space of creation, so that we may, by our hospitality to one another, attend to the deep fractures of our "metaphysically homeless" human condition in ways that allow creation of spaces of mutuality *in which we can enact together what is needed for the overcoming of fracture.* "Faith," on the reading I am proposing here, creates a space of possibilities for us to act with one another, even as we ourselves are fractured, to heal the fractures of the world. It provides our agency with a horizon of *possibilities for enacting, through welcoming one another in mutual vulnerability, a more encompassing wholeness to our humanity and for our world.* In a world in which "hospitality" to the movement of capital resources, armaments, and instrumentally commodified information has become more valued — and

46. These practices may also be seen as loci for the enactment of what David Tracy, in his contribution to this volume, terms a "disclosive truth" issuing from the dynamics of "Publicness Two." In addition, to the extent that the truth herein disclosed bears on the possibility of enacting a welcoming embrace of otherness, particularly in circumstances of a "homeless" post-modernity in which the other is seen first and foremost as threat, these practices may also display the interruptive "excess" at work in what he terms "Publicness Three."

47. A full theological account of the "divine hospitality" and its engagement in human vulnerability would trace its trajectory through the doctrinal loci of creation, incarnation, and resurrection: for an adumbration of this, see the fourth section of Godzieba's essay in this volume; and Rossi, "Human Contingency." There is, moreover, a dynamic in the Spiritual Exercises of St. Ignatius along this trajectory, most notably in the meditation on the incarnation at the beginning of the Second Week and in the concluding *contemplatio ad amorem.*

far easier to "enact" — than hospitality to one's brother and sister human beings in their often desperate vulnerability, encouraging a hospitality of mutual vulnerability may even seem foolish and dangerous. Yet it may very well be that only in the folly of hospitality will we be enabled to recognize and articulate the mutual vulnerability that, at least as much as anything else in our humanity, makes us worthy of respect.

9. Love and Justice: Engaging Benedict XVI on Christian Discipleship in a Secular Age

MARY DOAK

The public role of religion was largely resolved in the mid-twentieth century, particularly in the United States, by relegating to private life all but the most innocuous of religious expressions. In the early twenty-first century, however, this privatization of religion is being widely rejected, and the question of the proper role of religious beliefs in society and in politics is again a pressing concern. Indeed, religious groups are currently exerting public — and often explicitly political — influence around the globe. This is no less true of Christianity than of Islam or Hinduism, and no less true in the United States than in the Middle East. Perhaps people have become dissatisfied with the loss of transcendent meaning in society, as Charles Taylor has argued.[1] In any case, there is a growing realization that religious beliefs have implications that are inherently political. While only recently many found it reasonable to assume that Christianity (for example) is a private religious option unconcerned with the affairs of Caesar, few doubt today that Christianity joins other religions in having social, and even explicitly political, implications.

At the same time, religious diversity has not decreased. The migration of peoples and ideas now calls into question any assumption that people in a particular location or of a common ethnic background share the same religious beliefs. As Taylor further contends, the "disenchanted" worldview (widespread at least in North America and western Europe) has made

1. Charles Taylor, *A Secular Age* (Cambridge, Mass.: Harvard University Press, 2007), esp. pp. 299-321. I am deeply indebted to, and grateful for, the inspiring discussions at the Secularity Project workshops and the helpful feedback I received from my colleagues there.

lack of belief in God an increasingly real option for people today.[2] Given the current rate of migrations and conversions, along with the growing number of people who reject religion altogether, even countries with an officially established or state-supported religion may no longer be able to take for granted any social consensus on basic religious beliefs and values. We thus face the practical political problem of how people with differing values can govern themselves (or be governed). Moreover, religious people are now asking themselves whether they are denying the socio-political implications of their own religious beliefs when they make concessions to the religious diversity in their polities.

Some in the Christian tradition (the religious perspective that will be of concern here) are reviving the view that Christians should accept nothing less than an officially Christian government. In the absence of the power to institute the establishment of Christianity, the preferred alternative may be withdrawal as a witness against the validity of governing by any other than the explicit principles of Christianity — a religious establishment in exile, so to speak. At the same time, others have argued to the contrary that Christians (indeed, all religious people) should be engaged in the debates of public life, but only if they argue on the basis of general moral principles and without invoking particular religious ideas.[3] All three of these approaches — seeking religious establishment, a witness of withdrawal, or appealing only to commonly accepted moral principles

2. Taylor describes a disenchanted worldview as one without the "spirits, demons, and moral forces which our predecessors acknowledged" (*A Secular Age,* p. 29).

3. Arguments that the United States must be an explicitly Christian nation have become quite common in popular political discussion, to the point that they have generated the related debate over whether Christianity in some form provides the necessary basis for the American polity. See John Fea, *Was America Founded as a Christian Nation? A Historical Introduction* (Louisville, Ky.: Westminster John Knox, 2011). Although Stanley Hauerwas insists that he never intended to argue for withdrawal from public life, he has certainly argued strenuously for the importance of an ecclesial witness in opposition to the failings of a polity that is not explicitly Christian, as in his influential article "The Church and Liberal Democracy: The Moral Limits of a Secular Polity" in Stanley Hauerwas, *A Community of Character: Toward a Constructive Christian Social Ethic* (Notre Dame, Ind.: University of Notre Dame Press, 1981), pp. 72-86. Similar tendencies toward withdrawal in protest against religious disestablishment have been developed within the "Radical Orthodoxy" movement, as I argue in my article "The Politics of Radical Orthodoxy: A Catholic Critique," *Theological Studies* 68, no. 2 (June 2007): 368-93. See also the early but still instructive discussion of the use of explicitly religious arguments in public debate in David Hollenbach, ed., "Theology and Philosophy in Public: A Symposium on John Courtney Murray's Unfinished Agenda," *Theological Studies* 40, no. 4 (December 1979): 700-715.

— are deeply flawed, however: they are inappropriate to the demands of Christian faith and inadequate to meet the needs of public life. As Pope Benedict XVI's three encyclicals demonstrate especially well, a specifically Trinitarian and Eucharistic Christianity requires the seemingly contradictory combination of respectful engagement with a diverse world along with public witness to the transcendent, indeed explicitly religious, basis for the value of our social and political endeavors.

Pope Benedict was deeply concerned throughout his pontificate with the significance of the Christian contribution to society, especially (but not only) in European societies wherein religious belief seems to be dismissed as of little social relevance. His encyclicals provide a developed account of official Catholic teachings on the social relevance of a Christian life of active love, informed by the gift of the Eucharist and by hope for a final communion in the life of the Triune God. To be sure, few would doubt that love is central to Christian faith and practice, though love is often assumed to be more appropriate to personal and to apolitical relations than to public life and politics. In opposition to any such privatized view of Christian love, Benedict undertakes in his encyclicals the challenging task of clarifying the social and political significance of Christian love and, finally, the relation of this love to the presumably more appropriately political concept of justice (which he insists cannot replace, and must not be understood as identical to, Christian love).

This essay supports the contention, especially developed in Benedict XVI's third encyclical, that the inherent value of all human beings is affirmed in a public and integrally political discipleship of Christian love. As such, an active Christian love should be particularly helpful in resisting the increasing dominance of exchange relations that is becoming a serious global threat today.[4] To defend the importance of this Christian witness, I begin with a brief description of the state of secularity in the United States, which provides a particularly clear example of market dominance despite the prevalence of a strenuously public Christianity. I then analyze the account of Christian love and its relation to justice as this is developed in Benedict's first three encyclicals. Finally, I explore the implications of Christian love-in-justice as an alternative to the hegemony of the market and as the basis for a more just and fully human public life.

---

4. For an early yet still astute critique of the dominance of exchange relations in Western society, see Johann Baptist Metz, *Faith in History and Society: Toward a Practical Fundamental Theology,* trans. David Smith (New York: Seabury, 1980), esp. pp. 36-39.

Love and Justice

1. Religion, Secularity, and the Dominance
of the Market in the United States

Secularity has multiple meanings (as Charles Taylor and others have pointed out), not all of which apply in every case.[5] For example, the United States does not show evidence of significant decline in religious belief, one of the common definitions of secularity identified by Taylor. Nevertheless, the United States clearly shares with Canada and Europe the history of religious reform that Taylor argues caused secularity in the sense he is most interested in: secularity as a social context in which lack of religious belief is a reasonable option for people. Taylor contends that religious reform focusing on the transcendence of God eventually led to a largely instrumental approach to the world. The "immanent frame" in which things are understood without reference to any purpose beyond this world is certainly evident in the cultural life of the United States. Yet however much this immanent frame might incline toward a privatization of religion, the United States is and has been for some time awash in public religion, including not only the rather vague civil religion of the mid-twentieth century (still evident in the nearly ubiquitous invocation, "God bless America") but also the more recently aggressive insistence that the United States is a Christian nation and that the lordship of Jesus as Christ must be explicitly acknowledged as the basis for just government. While the United States differs from many European countries in prohibiting a state-established religion, the United States also differs from France (and Mexico) in refusing to prohibit explicitly religious interventions or appeals in public life.

To describe the United States as "secular" is perhaps most helpful, then, when it communicates the U.S. Constitution's rejection in principle of an established state religion, even while religious positions may be and are included in political discourse.[6] (The political debate, as Franklin Gamwell has argued, thus remains free in relevant part because it does not allow the government to end the debate over ultimate purposes by

5. In addition to the three meanings articulated by Taylor (Taylor, *A Secular Age,* pp. 1-4), see also Mary Doak, "Defining Our Dilemma: Must Secularization Privatize Religion?" *American Journal of Theology and Philosophy* 29, no. 3 (September 2008): 253-56.

6. Secularity as here applied to the United States is thus Taylor's first definition of secularity, in which the political organization of society is uncoupled from particular religious beliefs and practices, so that "the political society is seen as that of believers (of all stripes) and non-believers alike" (Taylor, *A Secular Age,* p. 1).

establishing one religious answer over others.)[7] Secularity in the United States is not then properly considered the antithesis of religion; the United States has neither banned religion from public discourse nor suffered a decline in religious belief. U.S. society is, however, thoroughly secular in the disenchantment that makes non-belief feasible and all forms of belief (and unbelief) fragile. Hence, secularity in the United States is not anti-religious or a-religious, but rather is that space or sphere open equally to people of diverse religious and (occasionally) nonreligious perspectives, a place wherein religious beliefs can be contested.[8]

Given this openness to public religion, it is not surprising that considerable attention has been paid in the United States to the question of the manner of religious argumentation that is most appropriate in public debates. With major thinkers like Richard Rorty insisting that religion is a "conversation stopper," others have been concerned to demonstrate that religious perspectives are publicly debatable and that religious views can contribute to, rather than simply curtail, political discussions.[9] Indeed, many have rightly been concerned that quantifiable evidence and instrumental rationality have so dominated (and impoverished) the public understanding of reason that not only religious but also aesthetic and ethical ways of knowing have been dismissed as irrational private options not subject to public debate.[10]

In the mid-twentieth century, this dominance of instrumental rationality was particularly evident in the cultural prestige of the natural sciences. As Langdon Gilkey observed in the 1980s, scientific knowledge had by that time become the model for all forms of valid knowledge to such an extent that other disciplines — including theology — strove to emulate the methods of the natural sciences. It was largely assumed that the only real problems were those that could be solved through science, and lucrative careers were available to those well trained in the natural sciences. In Gilkey's analysis, science had come to occupy a cultural position not unlike that of theology in the Middle Ages: science was the new "queen"

7. See especially Franklin I. Gamwell, *The Meaning of Religious Freedom: Modern Politics and the Democratic Resolution* (Albany: State University of New York Press, 1995).

8. I have further developed this argument in "Defining Our Dilemma," pp. 253-70.

9. Richard Rorty, "Religion as Conversation-Stopper," *Common Knowledge* 3, no. 1 (Spring 1994): 1-6. For his later, more nuanced, argument, see his "Religion in the Public Square: A Reconsideration," *Journal of Religious Ethics* 31, no. 1 (2003): 141-49.

10. See especially David Tracy, *The Analogical Imagination: Christian Theology and the Culture of Pluralism* (New York: Crossroad, 1981), pp. 6-14.

of the disciplines. Under these circumstances, people had difficulty presenting religious arguments in ways that the public could recognize as legitimate forms of reasoning (rather than as merely personal expressions of preference).

Gilkey further argued that science had assumed an implicit sacral dimension in that science was looked to for salvation from what was then perceived as the fundamental threat to human well-being: the uncontrolled powers of nature.[11] He maintained that a theological critique was needed, not to reject science per se, but to challenge the idolatry of science's sacral pretension to satisfy all human needs. Society needed to be reminded of the limits of science as one — but only one! — of the valid forms of knowledge: not all of the problems in society can be solved through empirical reasoning alone.

Yet it is highly doubtful that scientific forms of rationality continue to dominate American public life today. Indeed, scientific arguments themselves are often on the defensive (if not altogether ignored) in U.S. public discourse. The question may no longer be how to ensure the inclusion of religion in public reasoning, but rather how to revive public reasoning in any form. After all, much of political "speech" today is or resembles advertising, implicitly assuming that people will support the positions most successfully marketed to their social niche and will choose their political candidate or party (like any consumer product) according to which celebrity or brand embodies the lifestyle and image with which they wish to identify.[12] Marketing, not technical rationality, has become prevalent in public life today to the point that religious arguments are admitted to the public realm based on their ability to garner sufficient "market share" rather than based on their ability to provide rational warrants for their assertions. Religion itself then becomes a consumer product, as we see when church leaders speak without intentional irony of doing a better job of selling their "product," Jesus.[13]

Applying Gilkey's analysis of hegemonic discourse to the United States today, it would seem that economics has replaced the natural sciences as

11. Langdon Gilkey, *Society and the Sacred: Toward a Theology of Culture in Decline* (New York: Crossroad, 1981), pp. 77-79.

12. See, for example, the Supreme Court decision in the Citizens United case (*Citizens United v. Federal Election Commission* 588 U.S. 310 [2010]), with its extensive judicial discussion of advertising as a protected form of political speech.

13. See especially the astute analysis of Vincent Jude Miller, *Consuming Religion: Christian Faith and Practice in a Consumer Culture* (New York: Continuum, 2004).

the current queen of disciplines. The most popular majors on many of our U.S. college campuses are those in economics and business, and economic rationality is commonly invoked in ethics, psychology, and even evolutionary biology. According to Taylor's analysis of the processes of secularization in the West, this dominance of the economic sphere should not surprise us. As he has argued in detail, because Western secularization reinforces the importance of daily life along with an instrumental attitude toward the world, the economic sphere and its attention to use and exchange value has increased considerably in cultural significance.[14]

In a recent book, *What Money Can't Buy,* Michael Sandel has further analyzed the dominance of the market in contemporary American life. He observes that aspects of life are being subjected to a market mentality to the point that the market is being used "to allocate health, education, public safety, national security, criminal justice, environmental protection, recreation, procreation, and other social goods" in a way that was unknown just a few decades ago.[15] Indeed, there is little that is not for sale among consenting adults today.

While Sandel's argument privileges often bizarre but fully legal examples of the social dominance of the market (such as paying people to be tattooed with advertisements), others have noted that human beings themselves are being reduced to objects being sold in the officially illegal but scarcely hidden slave trade that has arisen around the world to supply what the market demands (in terms of sexual availability, domestic services, cheap labor, and, perhaps most horrifically, body parts).[16] Sandel is surely right in noting that "today, the logic of buying and selling no longer applies to material goods alone but increasingly governs the whole of life."[17]

I submit that public discourse too has been colonized by a market mentality to the point that political debates in the United States often assume that the only significant common purpose is to secure a well-functioning economy that maximizes the multitude of consumer options. Political discussions focus a great deal on whether much, little, or no government

14. Taylor, *A Secular Age,* esp. pp. 179-81.

15. Michael J. Sandel, *What Money Can't Buy: The Moral Limits of Markets* (New York: Farrar, Straus and Giroux, 2012), p. 8.

16. See especially Siddharth Kara, *Sex Trafficking: Inside the Business of Modern Slavery* (New York: Columbia University Press, 2009); and Nicholas D. Kristof and Sheryl WuDunn, *Half the Sky: Turning Oppression into Opportunity for Women Worldwide* (New York: Knopf, 2009).

17. Sandel, *What Money Can't Buy,* p. 6.

intervention will best secure the flourishing of the economy; considerably less attention is given to determining what other common purposes we ought to pursue beyond achieving a thriving economy. Indeed, it seems that American society is united primarily by a common allegiance to the exchange relations of the market.

This dominance of a market mentality is arguably the idol that currently undermines public life, as Jürgen Moltmann observed some years ago.[18] To the extent that free economic exchanges are venerated as a panacea for all that ails us, then the market is not only hegemonic but in fact becomes an idol set up as the sacred source of all that human beings could want or need. In short, the market itself is venerated with a religious fervor, and any who question this market dominance risk being repudiated as heretics who deny the sacred truths of salvation. To be sure, we should acknowledge that market mechanisms have their proper place and can achieve much. Nevertheless, when the market becomes a new god that is venerated as the solution to all serious problems, theological resistance to the distortions and the pretensions of economic rationality is more than warranted.

If the above diagnosis of contemporary secularity is correct, then an adequate account of Christianity's implications for social and political life today will need to specify how Christianity forms people to recognize and to resist the idols that emerge in secular society, especially the current idolatry of the marketplace. Benedict XVI contends that love in truth is the church's gift to the world; it follows, then, that any evaluation of the Christian contribution to society must consider the responsibilities of Christian love to oppose idolatry and particularly to constrain the market mentality that dominates so much of contemporary life.

2. Christian Love and Its Relation to Justice in Benedict XVI's Encyclicals

Even though his thought is deeply informed by the European context, Benedict XVI's concern is properly global and his account of the contribution of Christian beliefs and practices to secular society has much to offer the whole world, including the United States. In his encyclicals, Ben-

18. Jürgen Moltmann, *God for a Secular Society: The Public Relevance of Theology* (London: SCM, 1999), esp. p. 153.

edict reworks the tradition of Catholic social teaching with an emphasis on love, developed in a manner consistent with contemporary theological attention to the doctrine of the Trinity and the centrality of the Eucharist. The result is a social teaching rooted in specifically Christian concepts and with the decidedly non-market value of love as the focus of Christian social witness.[19]

In his first encyclical, *Deus caritas est,* Benedict provides a thoroughly Trinitarian account of love, a perspective that remains consistent throughout his encyclicals. Benedict contends that God's love for humanity is most profoundly revealed in Jesus' crucifixion, which he describes as an event of God turning against God's self for the salvation of humanity. The love of God in Jesus affirms the transcendent worth of human beings while also leading into the mystery of God as Triune: a loving relationality which, out of love, opens outward to make room for and to redeem creation.[20] The proper human response to this loving relationality of the Triune God is to create networks of loving communities on Earth, always open to others and especially to those in need, in imitation of the love of the Trinity.[21] The love Christians are commanded to bring to others is fundamentally a recognition of the transcendent value of each person as loved by and destined for union with God: "seeing [others] with the eyes of Christ, I can give them the look of love which they crave," Benedict maintains.[22]

Since the church is in essence a community united in love by the God who calls the faithful to bring that love to the whole world, love is central to the life and the mission of the church. The church is thus fundamentally Eucharistic, united in and by God's self-gift of loving communion. As Benedict reminds us, the Eucharist empowers and commissions Christians to love the whole world, and thus the Eucharist is incomplete when communion with God does not result in active care for others.[23] Therefore, Benedict contends, charity is as central to the mission of the church as are the proclamation of the Word and the celebration of the sacraments. In sum, the church proclaims the good news of God's love, celebrates the

19. For excellent discussions of Benedict's thought as a whole, see the insightful articles in Lieven Boeve and Gerard Mannion, eds., *The Ratzinger Reader: Mapping a Theological Journey* (London: T&T Clark, 2010).

20. Benedict XVI, Encyclical Letter *Deus caritas est* (December 25, 2005), §12.

21. Benedict XVI, Encyclical Letter *Caritas in veritate* (June 29, 2009), §5.

22. *Deus caritas est,* §18.

23. *Deus caritas est,* §13-14.

sacramental gift of God's love, and embodies this love by responding to others in need.[24]

Even while developing this account of love in his first encyclical, Benedict is at pains to defend the priority of love over justice. Arguing especially against the Marxist claim that justice should replace charity, Benedict counters that developing just social structures does not guarantee that justice will always be done. After all, human beings can act unjustly even within the most justly structured of social systems. Further, the achievement of just structures is never permanent, so love will always be necessary.[25] Benedict also rejects the materialistic reductionism that considers human needs to be primarily physical, and societal problems to be predominantly structural.[26] The church, motivated by love, must sponsor charitable organizations that not only provide for material needs, as would any other social welfare agency, but also strive to recognize the worth of the person and to respond to each person's need for love. Acting out of concern for each unique and irreplaceable human being, the church will then be attentive to the true and deepest needs of persons.

Benedict's concern to resist an overly political interpretation of Christianity continues in his second encyclical, *Spe salvi*. Even while acknowledging that citizens should seek more just social and political institutions, Benedict warns against confidence in human progress; as he argues, the technological power that can be used for good or for evil grows in history, while the ability of humanity to control its self-centered and evil impulses does not similarly accumulate.[27] The outcome of this unequal development of power and moral wisdom, it follows, may well be greater evil effects than previously known in history if (as is likely) we humans misuse our growing technological power.

As is suggested by his assessment of the mismatch between growth in power and growth in morality, Benedict is quite clear that one should not place too much hope in social progress. The kingdom of God, he insists, will never be established in history: the kingdom is not a human accomplishment but a gift from God and, as he reminds his audience, this gift will be given in full only at the end of history.[28]

Notwithstanding this critique of any attempt to achieve the reign of

24. *Deus caritas est*, §25.
25. *Deus caritas est*, §28.
26. *Deus caritas est*, §28.
27. Benedict XVI, Encyclical Letter *Spe salvi* (November 30, 2007), §22-24.
28. *Spe salvi*, §25, 35.

God through human efforts in history, Benedict nevertheless contends that Christian hope is not properly understood as individualistic or solely otherworldly. He maintains that Christians live in deep hope for this world precisely because the world is promised a fulfillment beyond history; it is, as Charles Taylor has similarly argued, because of our transcendent hope that we can fully affirm the value and meaning immanent in the world.[29] Further, Christians seek to build up communities now, knowing that the kingdom of God is partially present whenever we love God and each other.[30] Even though Benedict insists that human achievements of justice and relations of love do not accumulate throughout history, he nevertheless views engagement with the world as integral to Christianity precisely because Christians live in hope for the *community* of humanity that God will redeem and unite at the end of time.

Benedict is concerned here to correct what he sees as the error of secular progressivism: a tendency to focus on political efforts for a better future to the point that, in his judgment, the needs of real people now — as well as the necessity of a hope beyond history — are neglected. Benedict contends that the proper contribution of Christianity to the building up of this world is precisely its faith-centered hope in God's future, a hope that makes possible self-sacrificing attention to others in the present along with resistance to fanaticism and despair.[31]

Benedict's first two encyclicals thus maintain a clear differentiation between love and justice. Benedict describes justice as the norm of the state, a norm requiring that each person be given her due share of the community's goods, whereas love is a giving of the self in active concern for the well-being of the other, giving and forgiving *beyond* what is due.[32] Though as citizens the laity have a responsibility to seek a more just state, Benedict insists that the political achievement of justice is not the direct responsibility of the church and should not be the focus of ecclesial efforts.[33] Instead, the role of the church *qua* church is to be a community of love and hope, acknowledging the transcendent value of all people, and affirming the good of human flourishing in this world by seeking to meet the human needs that remain unmet even within the best of social structures.[34]

29. Taylor, *A Secular Age,* esp. pp. 755-72.
30. *Spe salvi,* §31.
31. *Spe salvi,* §35.
32. *Deus caritas est,* esp. §26.
33. *Deus caritas est,* §29.
34. Notwithstanding Benedict's assignment of justice to the state rather than to the

That Benedict himself came to recognize the inadequacies of this too-sharp differentiation of love and justice is evident in his reworking of their relation in his third encyclical, *Caritas in veritate* (as will be discussed below). Nevertheless, there is much that is right about Benedict's work in *Deus caritas est* and *Spe salvi* to defend the church's witness to its transcendent hope, a hope that surpasses what can be achieved by any this-worldly political program. Indeed, there are echoes here of the wisdom of Reinhold Niebuhr, perhaps one of the foremost Protestant theologians on the topic of social justice. Even while Niebuhr developed a compelling defense of Christian engagement in political struggles for justice, he insisted on the importance of an eschatological proviso — a hope that cannot be fully realized in history — to combat the dangers of Marxist utopianism and liberal progressivism in the early twentieth century. Niebuhr was convinced then, as Benedict is now, that a hope beyond history is necessary to sustain a hope able to act within history without succumbing to despair. Niebuhr also (like Benedict) warned that human finitude and sin are such that the kingdom of God cannot finally be achieved within history, though Niebuhr further insisted (as Benedict has not) that there is no limit to how close to the kingdom of God we can get in this world, except that the fullness of God's reign will not be established here.[35] The fact that Niebuhr, who devoted so much of his career to defending the centrality of social justice and political activism in Christianity, also insisted on maintaining a transcendent hope beyond history underscores the validity of Benedict's concern on this point.

It is also worth noting that Niebuhr managed to defend this transcendental hope without marginalizing a Christian commitment to justice or a concern for social and political structures. While Niebuhr acknowledged,

---

church, he acknowledges in *Deus caritas est* that the church's teachings on justice in society are a worthwhile contribution. In his view, Catholic social teaching assists society and government by clarifying what reason demands of a just state, even though these requirements of justice are in principle knowable through reason alone and without the help of revelation. See especially *Deus caritas est*, §28 and 29. Nevertheless, his rejection of a proper ecclesial mission of justice is in considerable tension with the magisterial documents that most clearly move beyond addressing the proper duties of the state for justice and proclaim justice as a part of the church's mission. See especially the World Synod of Catholic Bishops' document, *Justitia in mundo* (1971), as well as the documents of the 1968 and the 1979 conferences of the Roman Catholic Bishops of Latin America (CELAM) in Medellín, Colombia, and Puebla, Mexico.

35. Reinhold Niebuhr, *The Nature and Destiny of Man: A Christian Interpretation,* vol. 2: *Human Destiny* (New York: Scribner's Sons, 1943), pp. 244, 286.

as does Benedict, that social structures alone cannot make people just or ensure a cumulative progression toward justice, Niebuhr defended a dynamic relation between human moral growth and societal structures. Niebuhr understood and clarified, with much more emphasis than does Benedict, that societal structures can make acting justly more or less difficult. In Niebuhr's view, social structures have a formative influence on people (and vice versa), so that the transformation of hearts and the transformation of institutions are mutually informative.[36]

Perhaps most significantly for our purposes here, Niebuhr insisted on a unity between love and justice that is incompatible with Benedict's account of the priority of love in his first two encyclicals. Niebuhr's thorough rejection of the claim that "only the most personal individual and direct expressions of social obligation" are manifestations of Christian love could well be cited in criticism of Benedict's early separation of love from justice.[37] In Niebuhr's perspective, love and justice are so mutually interconnected that love in this world can never avoid the demands of justice. As he observed, "as soon as a third person is introduced into the relation, even the most perfect love requires a rational estimate of conflicting needs and interest."[38] Justice, Niebuhr further maintained, is the form love takes under the conditions of finitude, even while justice cannot be achieved without a love that goes beyond strict justice: "Without the grace of love," Niebuhr argued, "justice always degenerates into something less than justice."[39] Thus, whereas Benedict states in his first two encyclicals that justice is proper to the state while love is the norm of the church's activity, Niebuhr envisioned love and justice to be inextricably intertwined in all instances.

Intriguingly, Benedict's account of the relation of love and justice in his third encyclical, *Caritas in veritate,* presents an understanding of justice that is much closer to that of Niebuhr (and hence is in some considerable tension with the arguments of Benedict's first two encyclicals). In this third encyclical, Benedict attends more specifically and carefully to Catholic social teaching, especially as expressed in Pope Paul VI's contention that integral human development, the whole development of each and every

36. Niebuhr, *Nature and Destiny,* pp. 244-86.
37. Niebuhr, *Nature and Destiny,* p. 251.
38. Niebuhr, *Nature and Destiny,* p. 248.
39. Niebuhr, "Justice and Love," in *Love and Justice: Selections from the Shorter Writings of Reinhold Niebuhr,* ed. D. B. Robertson (Louisville, Ky.: Westminster John Knox, 1957), p. 28.

person in every aspect, is the proper concern of the church.[40] Addressing the topic of "love in truth" from the perspective of integral human development, Benedict's third encyclical insists that love is the principle of *every* type of human development — and this includes what Benedict refers to as the macro-relationships of society, politics, and economy no less than it involves the micro-relationships of familial and interpersonal relationships.[41] Thus, he describes the church's social doctrine as the law of love applied to social relationships, and not merely (as Benedict's first encyclical observes) as the articulation by a "purified reason" of the state's responsibilities to govern justly.[42]

In a statement that is surely inconsistent with his earlier assignment of love to the church and justice to the state, Benedict explicitly affirms in *Caritas in veritate* that seeking justice (even justice in the state) is a work of love. Indeed, he further declares that work for justice is no less excellent an act of love and no less desirable than direct person-to-person acts of charity.[43] Justice and concern for the common good are described in *Caritas in veritate* no longer as less than love but rather as "criteria" of practical love, with Benedict here commending work for justice and peace as a necessary witness to Christ's love and as integral to the task of evangelization.[44] It would seem to follow, then, that the threefold mission of the church — to proclaim the Word, to celebrate the sacraments, and to do charity — inherently includes seeking justice as a dimension of both proclamation-evangelization and charity, and therefore justice is in fact a proper aspect of the mission of the church. At the same time, Benedict now affirms that the state must act with love and not only with justice since he argues that the "earthly city" needs the solidarity and gratuitousness of love.[45]

Caritas in veritate thus articulates a more complex and nuanced interrelation between love and justice (and therefore between church and

40. *Caritas in veritate,* §10-20. See also Paul VI, Encyclical Letter *Populorum progressio* (March 26, 1967).

41. *Caritas in veritate,* §2.

42. *Caritas in veritate,* §5.

43. As Benedict here argues, "The more we strive to secure a common good corresponding to the real needs of our neighbours, the more effectively we love them. . . . This is the institutional path — we might also call it the political path — of charity, no less excellent and effective than the kind of charity which encounters the neighbor directly, outside the institutional mediation of the *polis*" (*Caritas in veritate,* §7).

44. *Caritas in veritate,* §15.

45. *Caritas in veritate,* §6.

state) than do his earlier encyclicals. In this third encyclical, Benedict has found a way to include justice as part of a properly Christian concern for the full development of the person, as did Niebuhr, without compromising the church's orientation toward transcendence and toward a self-gift that exceeds the requirements of strict justice. In sum, Benedict finally agrees with the position that Reinhold Niebuhr had developed earlier: seeking justice is an act of love and love is necessary to achieve justice, in the state as well as in the church.

I would further argue that the dynamic understanding of love and justice in *Caritas in veritate* is required by the relational view of the self that Benedict has sought to maintain in all of his encyclicals. Insofar as the person is necessarily a person in relation to others, part of a "we" that extends beyond the Christian community to all of humanity, then it follows that concern for the quality of relations in society (the "common good") is essential to Christian love. Because human beings are not primarily solitary individuals but rather are fundamentally social and relational beings, we cannot love our neighbors without being deeply concerned with the quality of our common life, as Benedict has come to realize.

A brief discussion of the work on love and justice of another significant twentieth-century Protestant theologian may further elucidate the wisdom (indeed, the theological necessity) of Benedict's more interrelational account of love and justice. As Paul Tillich noted in his classic text, *Love, Power, and Justice*, love seeks to unite what is currently but not essentially separate; that is, love strives to overcome the divisions that ought not to be. Justice, on the other hand, preserves what is to be reunited, ensuring that the drive to unity does not become a uniformity destroying the individuality of what it unites. Thus, love requires justice, while justice aims toward love (the final fulfillment of what justice seeks to preserve).[46] In Tillich's view, then, love is not simply an overlay, an additional *bonum* that exceeds but cannot fall below the minimal requirements of justice. Rather, justice makes the achievement of love possible and love is in fact the true goal of justice.

Tillich's account of the relationship between love and justice also assumes that love is fulfilled and justice completely realized only in the union of all in God, a perspective that is thoroughly consistent with *Caritas in veritate*. Indeed, Tillich's view suggests that an understanding of justice as

---

46. Paul Tillich, *Love, Power, and Justice: Ontological Analyses and Ethical Applications* (New York: Oxford University Press, 1954), pp. 25, 67-71.

integral to the union of all in love is more appropriate to Benedict's Trinitarian emphasis than is Benedict's earlier separation of love from justice.
The role of justice in preserving individuality reinforces the dignity of justice, then, insofar as justice is integral to the achievement of the unity-in-
diversity that is communion with God.

3. Benedict's Encyclicals and Church-State Relations

If Benedict and others are finally right that love requires Christians to seek
just governing structures consistent with the integral development of the
person-in-society, then the question of the appropriate relationship between Christian communities and secular governments remains pressing.
How can Christians most effectively witness to what Benedict has called
"the truth in love" when they live in a secular society that inclines toward
instrumentalization and renders all positions of belief and unbelief fragile
(as Charles Taylor has argued)?[47] More pointedly, do Catholics — or any
Christians — still have good reasons to resist the increasingly widespread
arguments in favor of some form of religious establishment (so that the
state rules according to explicitly Christian precepts) or sectarian withdrawal (in which Christians form alternative self-governing communities
in witness against the unbelief of the state)?[48]

In light of *Caritas in veritate,* with its admission that seeking justice
is a necessary expression of Christian love, we can reasonably conclude
that Benedict ultimately affirms that the church as a whole and as church
(and not merely the laity) is required by love to do what it can to further
justice in society. Nevertheless, Benedict may well continue to maintain,
as he should, that it is not the church's responsibility to *ensure* that justice
is achieved, since the church is not given the task of governing this world.

But why is it not the church's task to govern, or at least to mandate the
principles by which the political sphere should be governed? As we have
seen above, one reason that Benedict vehemently opposes any identification of church and state is to safeguard the church's witness to its transcendent hope, a hope that exceeds what any political program can possibly

47. See Taylor, *A Secular Age,* esp. pp. 299-321.
48. The U.S. Catholic bishops' protest against national healthcare mandates including
contraception provides a fascinating test case that is clearly relevant to the discussion here,
but a detailed exploration of this matter is beyond the scope of this essay.

provide. This witness to transcendence is itself an important contribution that, properly embodied, enriches rather than devalues our concern with just social and political structures. Further, as Benedict joins Niebuhr, Tillich, and Taylor in maintaining, the church must not lose the critical distance that enables the church to identify, and to provide fraternal correction of, the inevitable flaws in current governing policies and structures.

Benedict's position is also essentially incompatible with theocracy insofar as he agrees with recent magisterial teachings emphasizing that the church seeks to persuade but not to force people to live in accord with the truth.[49] As is noted in the Second Vatican Council's *Declaration on Religious Freedom,* since God intends for people to accept the truth in freedom, the church must not take away this freedom through governmental legislation that coerces in matters of religion. Hence, the church should strive *to persuade* all in the state to seek greater justice oriented to love, whereas *to require* that all act in accord with religiously defined principles is a violation of God's gift of freedom.[50]

If the church's methods are properly persuasive rather than coercive, sectarian withdrawal as an alternative to religious establishment gains some plausibility. Withdrawal, after all, does not seek to coerce but rather endeavors to provide a compelling ecclesial witness against the injustices and imperfections of the state. Demonstrating the fulfillment to be found in living in just communal relations oriented by a transcendent hope and informed by self-giving and forgiving love might well be the most powerful form of persuasion. Certainly the church is called to be a sign to the world, and it should be a much better sign than it currently is. One can only imagine the impact worldwide if the Catholic Church were to be a living witness of what it means for a community to govern itself according to principles of justice informed by love.

Notwithstanding the value of ecclesial witness, to withdraw from participation in the larger political community that unites Christians and non-Christians is not consistent with the Christian love modeled on the

49. *Deus caritas est,* §28. See also *Caritas in veritate,* §5-7. For a statement of the church's refusal of the means of coercion, see especially Second Vatican Council, Declaration on Religious Freedom *(Dignitatis humanae),* esp. §3 and §9.

50. Benedict is clearly opposed to French *laïcisme,* as he insists that the church must be allowed to participate in a public debate open to religious perspectives. He also has argued for requiring mention of God in the European Constitution, which might be interpreted as mandating an orientation of the law toward God. He usually defends this, however, as an effort to ensure a role for religion in public debate.

Trinity that Benedict defends throughout his encyclicals. If Christians are called to love all others, to seek mutual relations universally, then Christians cannot in principle refuse to participate with non-Christians in developing common political structures and institutions. The creative love of the Divine Trinity is best represented, not by ecclesial insularity, but rather by an openness to all of humanity, an openness that welcomes the difference of the other.

A sectarian withdrawal from secular government is also problematic insofar as it suggests the mistaken notion that a fully just society (if not in the state, then in the church) is possible in this world. Benedict has rightly been concerned to repudiate the idea of perfect temporal justice, an idea that he rejects not only as unrealistic under the conditions of finitude and sin but also as dangerous: the illusory hope of perfect justice may lead people to neglect the imperfect good that is possible now in favor of a perfect good that can never be achieved. Reinhold Niebuhr would add a further warning: overconfidence in the possibility of perfect justice in this world may cause people to neglect the need for the checks and balances that prevent the abuse of power. Rather than refusing to participate in the secular governing structures of the state, Christian concern for local communities and face-to-face relations ought to inspire efforts to ensure that the state promotes conditions for smaller communities to thrive in what Franklin Gamwell aptly describes as "a mosaic of associations fitted to maximize mutuality."[51]

A secular society such as the United States, which neither establishes nor bans religious beliefs, allows the church to engage in its task of being an instrument of unity-in-diversity, working with others (including non-theists) in cooperation for the common good and toward the mutual enrichment of all in a diverse society. This open cooperation intending to persuade rather than to coerce is, I believe, the ideal upheld by the easily misunderstood Second Vatican Council's affirmation of the proper autonomy of the political sphere: the point is not to endorse a secular*ism* that removes religion from public life, but rather to affirm a secular*ization* in which Christians and non-Christians can work together to develop societies that are governed according to principles of justice oriented to sustaining all and to increasing the common good.[52]

51. Franklin I. Gamwell, *Politics as a Christian Vocation: Faith and Democracy Today* (Cambridge: Cambridge University Press, 2005), p. 116.

52. Second Vatican Council, *Pastoral Constitution on the Church in the Modern World*

Catholic social teaching largely intends to contribute to the public conversation about the common good on the basis of moral principles from which any specifically religious content has been abstracted. There is value in this approach, as it identifies points of potential consensus between people who may never agree about religion but who can unite nevertheless in their pursuit of a more just society. Despite considerable sound and fury about protecting the distinctly Christian perspective from "being positioned" by alternative views, the reality is that if and when we reason together we often find a basis for agreement on the requirements of justice, notwithstanding our religious differences.[53]

Even while one can — and should — affirm the possibility of such a common ground approach, Benedict XVI's encyclicals have provided an invaluable contribution by addressing issues of social and political justice with the specific content of Christian doctrine. As we saw above, justice requires a commitment to a love that goes beyond strict justice, and this love achieves its full meaning and motivating force for Christians as an expression of human worth in relation to the offer of redemptive participation in the communion of the Divine Love. Taken together, Benedict's first three encyclicals clarify that the central Christian affirmation of the salvific love offered by God in Jesus and the sacramental celebration of the Eucharist form Christians to witness to the world not from the periphery of their faith but from their most central and distinct faith commitments. Further, if Charles Taylor is right about the malaise caused by a secular age limited to immanent values and this-worldly hopes, then Benedict has done well to insist that Christianity's greatest contribution to the world is its witness to a hope for everlasting communion in God as the basis for affirming the value of this finite and transitory world. We need not entirely embrace Benedict's hesitation about Christian dialogical engagement with the world to appreciate his efforts to articulate a distinctly Christian contribution to the contemporary world.

Maintaining that the human good is found in loving openness to others, Christian discipleship thus properly seeks greater unity in love while

---

(*Gaudium et spes*), esp. §76. For a helpful analysis of the distinction between secularism and secularization evident in the Second Vatican Council documents, see John Courtney Murray, S.J., "The Declaration on Religious Freedom," in *Bridging the Sacred and the Secular: Selected Writings of John Courtney Murray S.J.*, ed. J. Leon Hooper (Washington, D.C.: Georgetown University Press, 1994), pp. 187-99.

53. See John Milbank, *Theology and Social Theory: Beyond Secular Reason* (Malden, Mass.: Blackwell, 1990), p. 1.

insisting on the justice that preserves difference. Especially in societies like the United States that have come to value politics and public life predominantly as instrumental goods, a Christian estimation of public life as an opportunity for persons to develop in community with others is a countercultural perspective that is deeply needed. The alternative of protecting Christian distinctness, whether through a coercive religious establishment or a sectarian withdrawal, is unworthy of those called to model their lives on the love of the Triune God. Hope in a transcendent God who is Lord of the future ought rather to empower the church to risk encountering others in love and mutual sharing.

4. A Place for Elijah at the Eucharistic Table

Affirming the eschatological fulfillment of persons-in-community, a Christianity committed to engaging the wider society has resources with which to resist the reduction of human hopes and ideals to any single aspect of life, whether that aspect be scientific, socio-psychological, or economic. Thus Benedict XVI has rightly criticized the domination of financial institutions and, more recently, he has opposed idolizing the market as the bearer of salvation, as if material well-being could provide all that humans truly need.[54]

As Benedict contends, love is the principle of all forms of human development, so that even the economy ought to be structured justly and oriented toward love, facilitating the development of persons and communities. The logic of the market ("giving in order to acquire") is not problematic in itself, as Benedict rightly maintains, but this market logic is highly destructive and must be resisted when it leaves no room for other values and purposes to be served by economic relations.[55] As Benedict further argues, "without internal forms of solidarity and mutual trust, the market cannot completely fulfill its proper economic function."[56] If even the economy cannot function well solely on the basis of exchange relations, all the more destructive, it would seem, is the dominance of exchange relations over other aspects of public life.

---

54. See *"Lectio divina" of His Holiness Benedict XVI,* Seminary Chapel (February 15, 2012).

55. *Caritas in veritate,* §39.

56. *Caritas in veritate,* §35.

Moreover, Benedict rightly calls on Christians to do what is possible, even within flawed and unjust systems, to increase relations of mutuality and to meet the needs of the suffering. In addition to charitable acts and organizations, Benedict supports sustainable economic initiatives that aim to foster human and community development as well as to earn profits; these creative business projects function within, even while they interrupt, the exchange logic of global and local markets.[57] While systemic reform of the capitalist economic system may ultimately be necessary, there is thus no need to wait for total reform before beginning to improve the current system. (Indeed, Pope Benedict has consistently cautioned against neglecting to do the good possible today while one awaits a more just system!) Opposing the hegemony of exchange relations by engaging in economic interactions motivated by concern for the common good, for natural resources, and for the flourishing of persons inserts these concerns into public life, in resistance to the idolatry that considers profit to be the ultimate value and primary source of human well-being.

Yet the ecclesial community ought to be much more troubled than it currently is by those whose lives are being destroyed by the dominance of our consumer culture. In a market-oriented society, it is perhaps especially difficult to notice the subjectivity of people who are not merely disadvantaged consumers but whom the market has reduced to objects (rather than subjects) of consumption. The spread of slavery and the trafficking of people, especially for prostitution, represent a thorough reduction of human relations to exchange value. There is profit to be made in enslavement, and so there are more than a few people willing to take part in buying and selling human beings. This is surely one of the most egregious examples of the dominance of market values as an obstacle to mutuality in human relations. Moreover, in addition to these slaves whom we know about intellectually but seldom notice, there are countless other victims: exploited labor and destroyed habitats are also among the overlooked costs of our consumer-oriented economy.

If the church is truly seeking the widest possible networks of mutual associations, it must be attentive to those who do not appear as subjects in public life. When public life is dominated by rational discourse, then those who cannot participate as subjects of such debate should be of special concern to the church. To the extent that, as I have argued above, public life is currently governed by the logic of the market, however, then those who

57. *Caritas in veritate*, §46.

are neither buyers nor sellers but rather the objects of our consumption (slaves, exploited labor, and even the non-human world) must be at the center of ecclesial life.

Benedict's most important contribution to ecclesial praxis may well be his insistence that a love grounded in the Trinity properly remains open to the future and to others, especially to those marginalized or isolated. Insofar as the celebration of the Eucharist is the source of Christian love and of its continual renewal, we must resist inclinations to make the Eucharist the practice of an enclosed community rather than a celebration that expands our openness to others. Perhaps we need a symbolic openness that interrupts the temptation toward Eucharistic closure, along with the concomitant limitations of our concerns for love and justice. Consider, for example, the open place that Jews reserve for Elijah at the Passover Seder as a reminder of those not present and of the justice not yet achieved. One of the greatest challenges in this global age, where all are in some sense neighbors and often none are truly neighbors, is to maintain the openness that enables us to recognize and to offer love to others, especially to the other whose existence is easily overlooked. Vigilantly maintaining the church as a community concerned for the ones not yet among us requires that we attend to the consumed people currently at the margins of both church and society. The eschatological hope that Benedict has so clearly maintained throughout his encyclicals must keep the church alert for the Lord who comes with transforming power not only in glory at the end of history but also in the rejected ones within history.

5. Conclusion

As the development throughout Benedict XVI's encyclicals demonstrates, it is difficult but essential to maintain the unity-in-difference of love and justice. Proclaiming the creative and self-giving love of a Triune God, Christians have reason to value public life as a sphere in which to encounter others and to seek together the common good. Christian hope for a universal communion of persons is thus consistent neither with sectarian withdrawal nor with theocratic dominance, since both rejecting and dominating over non-Christians undermine Christian witness to the God who loves in freedom and who makes humans in the image of the divine communion. Of course, the church must also beware the temptation to capitulate to the current socio-political order. Especially given the lure of a consumer society, Christian discipleship requires creative resistance to, and even active subversion of, the hegemony of the market. Perhaps most truly disruptive of the dominance of exchange relations in society would be a church in which those whom the market treats as objects are instead subjects at the center of ecclesial life.

PART IV

Religion in a Post-Secular World

10. Multiple Belongings: The Persistence of Community amidst Societal Differentiation

MICHELE DILLON

Narratives of decline enjoy much resonance among intellectuals and the public alike. And perhaps no two social phenomena have been subject to such framing as that of community and religion. This is no coincidence. Modernization scholars[1] posited that the traditional cultural salience of local (geographical) community and the authority of religious institutions would necessarily attenuate their hold on individuals as society yielded to the pull of economic progress and increased societal rationality (for example, bureaucracy, meritocracy, young people leaving their local community in order to avail themselves of the college education necessary for economic success). We currently live in an era of transformative social change. Globalization processes and Internet technology fuel the characterization of our late modern era as one marked by the disembeddedness of time and space[2] and by mobile rather than well-settled lives;[3] geographical, occupational, and emotional mobility (for example, divorce) are overarching trends. It is therefore not surprising that there is a tendency to favor narratives that emphasize how change subtracts from, rather than complicates, the manifestation and substance of community compared to that presumed, nostalgically, to characterize an earlier, "simpler" time.

1. For example, Talcott Parsons, *The System of Modern Societies* (Englewood Cliffs, N.J.: Prentice Hall, 1971); and Neil Smelser, *Social Change in the Industrial Revolution* (Chicago: University of Chicago Press, 1959), and *Essays in Sociological Explanation* (Englewood Cliffs, N.J.: Prentice Hall, 1968).

2. Anthony Giddens, *Modernity and Self-Identity: Self and Society in the Late Modern Age* (Stanford, Calif.: Stanford University Press, 1991).

3. Anthony Elliott and John Urry, *Mobile Lives* (New York: Routledge, 2010).

I begin this chapter by reviewing the dominant strands informing the narrative of community decline largely drawing on Robert Putnam's work[4] as well as encompassing the therapeutic turn highlighted by Robert Bellah et al.[5] Then, moving to consideration of Émile Durkheim's conceptualization of community, I draw on sociological case studies and survey data to argue that the current manifestations of community are in line with, rather than a rupture in, the organic solidarity that, as Durkheim elaborated, emerges out of the social interdependence fostered and required by the differentiation in modern society. Further probing the thesis of community decline and its intertwining with a narrative of the decline of religion, I then discuss the differentiation in the contemporary religious and spiritual landscape and problematize Charles Taylor's view of the current era as post-Durkheimian.[6] Drawing on empirical sociological studies, I argue that the increased tendencies toward religious and spiritual autonomy do not subtract from communal commitments. In the chapter's final section, I turn to discuss how the multiple sources of difference that are the hallmark of modernity are also given short shrift in Jürgen Habermas's understanding of political community as envisioned in his construal of post-secular society.[7]

1. Community Contextualized

Robert Putnam used his much-cited "bowling alone" metaphor to describe the "collapse of community" based on secondary analysis of surveys and other aggregate trend studies gathered across the twentieth century. He highlights many dimensions of Americans' involvement in local community and voluntary organizational activities and documents a general pattern of decline that is especially apparent in the post-1970s era. Putnam

---

4. Robert Putnam, *Bowling Alone: The Collapse and Revival of American Community* (New York: Simon and Schuster, 2000).

5. Robert Bellah, Richard Madsen, William Sullivan, Ann Swidler, and Steven Tipton, *Habits of the Heart: Individualism and Commitment in American Life* (Berkeley: University of California Press, 1985).

6. Charles Taylor, *A Secular Age* (Cambridge, Mass.: Harvard University Press, 2007).

7. For example, in Jürgen Habermas, "Notes on a Post-Secular Society," *New Perspectives Quarterly* 25, no. 4 (2008): 17-29; and Jürgen Habermas et al., *An Awareness of What Is Missing: Faith and Reason in a Post-Secular Age,* trans. Ciaran Cronin (Cambridge: Polity, 2010).

shows, for example, a decline in membership of fraternal organizations; in participation in the PTA and various club meetings and activities; in engagement in community projects; in church attendance; in union membership; in participation in informal social activities (for example, socializing with friends); and in charitable giving. He also presents evidence of a decline in Americans' perceptions of the honesty and trustworthiness of their fellow-citizens,[8] a trend that is seen as further indication of attenuated ties to community. Putnam points to the relevance of larger social changes in attenuating individuals' ties to community. In particular, he notes the increased participation of women in the labor force, the increase in urban sprawl and in the time spent commuting to work, and the increase in television watching.[9] These forces literally reduce the amount of time that individuals have for community involvement and thus the threads in the community fabric become frayed.

Unlike Putnam, who mostly emphasizes the large-scale social forces impacting individuals' connectedness to community, other scholars emphasize the significance of the post-1960s cultural shift. In particular, Bellah et al. argue that the rise of a therapeutic, self-centered, and narcissistic individualism is displacing the socially responsible individualism that had historically characterized American society and that was successfully channeled through church and other local community structures. For many generations of Americans, as Alexis de Tocqueville first observed, individual freedom translated into a voluntary obligation to participate in church, community, and civic life. Thus earlier cohorts forged a culture and society in which individualism enriched rather than diluted community attachment. Individuals used their freedom to build community institutions rather than to prop up the self, as is alleged to be the current ethos. In this latter view, the "triumph of the therapeutic"[10] in post-1960s America and the growth of interest in both psychotherapy and new forms of individuated spiritual seeking are portrayed as reflecting a desire for immediate gratification among individuals for whom feeling good rather than doing good has become the primary goal in life.

The therapeutic shift also coincides with a decline in traditional supportive relationships such as long-term marriage, and with the emergence

---

8. Putnam, *Bowling Alone,* p. 139.

9. Putnam, *Bowling Alone,* pp. 195-200, 204-15, 222-28.

10. Bellah et al., *Habits of the Heart;* Philip Rieff, *The Triumph of the Therapeutic* (Harmondsworth: Penguin, 1966).

of what Arlie Hochschild has called "emotional outsourcing,"[11] that is, paying strangers in the market for emotional support activities (for example, life coaches, surrogate parents or friends) that in the past were expected of and performed by family members, friends, and mentors. The trend of decline in the permanency of marriage relationships is itself brought about, in part, by the post-1950s shift in individuals' expectations of intimacy and the greater priority placed on personal self-fulfillment rather than economic security or family stability in intimate relationships.[12] Yet, the lack of realization of these personal goals fuels other societal trends such as, for example, divorce, that in turn exacerbate both individual mobility and a focus on self-gratification.[13] The therapeutic expectation thus creeps into social contexts and settings, such as the workplace, which in the past were the domain of instrumental goals like "getting the job done," rather than (as appears increasingly to be the case today) making people feel good about themselves even if the job does not get done well.[14] The increased prevalence of mental health counseling on college campuses is perhaps another manifestation of the therapeutic trend. Its necessity may be a reflection of the disempowerment and fragilization of the self that coincide with, and are fueled by, changes in family structure (for example, divorce), and increased emotional outsourcing.[15] As a result of these cultural shifts, there is more pressure on modern community to deliver emotional rewards that, in the past, were more likely to be realized in the more intimate spheres of marriage, family, and friendship.

Personal emotional fulfillment, however, is not the primary purpose or function of modern community. Rather, as in traditional society, the purpose of community is to attach the individual to something other than the self,[16] that is, to other individuals, groups, society as a whole, irrespective of the emotional gratification that may and frequently does, in fact, result. If we define community as the expression of how, and the sites

11. Arlie Russell Hochschild, *The Outsourced Life: Intimate Life in Market Times* (New York: Metropolitan, 2012).

12. See Giddens, *Modernity and Self-Identity.*

13. Bellah et al., *Habits of the Heart.*

14. See, for example, James Tucker, *The Therapeutic Corporation* (New York: Oxford University Press, 1999).

15. Hochschild, *The Outsourced Life.*

16. Émile Durkheim, "The Dualism of Human Nature and Its Social Conditions," in *Émile Durkheim: On Morality and Society,* ed. Robert Bellah (Chicago: University of Chicago Press, 1973), p. 151.

and spaces in which, individuals negotiate the relation between self and society, we should expect that ongoing dynamic changes in society and in self-identity would impact the character and practical organization of community in modern society.

Émile Durkheim's Conceptualization of Community

The puzzle presented by how community evolves and adapts to societal change has long preoccupied sociologists. Most notably, Émile Durkheim, writing in France in the late nineteenth century during what was a time of societal upheaval in Western Europe and the United States, outlined an analysis of how community is achieved amidst the heterogeneity of modern, urban, industrial society.[17] He was interested in how varied societal arrangements work to constrain or to loosen individuals' integration into community and society. Durkheim emphasized that we individuals are social beings, who not only spontaneously choose to be in communion with others, but who must choose "attachment to something other ourselves" in order for society to function effectively;[18] thus "morality consists in solidarity with the group."[19] He probed the evolution from traditional to modern society, and how social structures and social relationships adapt and evolve so that social institutions and society at large continue to function effectively by binding the individual to something other than the self, that is, to other individuals, to collectivities, or to society itself.

Durkheim elaborated on how different kinds of societal conditions and different types of social structures produce different kinds of communal solidarity. Communities in traditional societies, Durkheim argued, tend to be characterized by relative homogeneity. There is a relatively undifferentiated economic and occupational structure (for example, farming, fishing) and relative homogeneity in terms of family and ethnic ancestry, religious affiliation, and political loyalties. Further, the small-scale nature of traditional communities means that there are multiple overlapping family, school, work, and church ties. This structural and cultural sameness produces a relatively automatic *mechanical solidarity* (that is, a

---

17. Émile Durkheim, *The Division of Labour in Society,* introduction by Lewis Coser, trans. W. D. Halls (New York: The Free Press, 1984).

18. Durkheim, "The Dualism of Human Nature," p. 151.

19. Durkheim, *The Division of Labour,* p. 331.

set of bonds based on replicable, interchangeable similarities across the community) that binds the community into a unified collectivity, and its strong collective conscience composed of well-settled overarching beliefs and sentiments[20] is shared by the community as a whole. This exerts a highly constraining force that leaves little room for individual deviation amidst the community's tightly bound social relations and ways of acting, thinking, and feeling. In traditional communities there is little individualism, little personal freedom and anonymity; the individual, rather, "is absorbed into the collective"[21] and constrained by its force. This may bring a strong feeling of social belonging but it also means that the individual has little freedom to stray from the norms and authority of the community. Attachment to, and participation in, community is ensured, by and large, automatically (mechanically) as a result of the structural overlap of social roles and ties that permeate everyday life. These ties are reinforced, moreover, by the paucity of opportunities for geographical, occupational, or emotional mobility out of the local community.

The Organic Solidarity of Modern Community

Modern society and the communities therein are quite different. The conditions in modern, urbanized, industrial society are almost (in ideal typical terms) the exact opposite of those in traditional societies. It is not homogeneity but diversity that characterizes social relations; the economic, occupational, political, educational, and religious institutional structures are highly differentiated and specialized. Thus in the late nineteenth century, we see the emergence of a divide between work and family; factory production was organized in ways that required different social arrangements and occupational skills than was true of agricultural communities.[22] By the same token, tasks such as religious instruction that used to be thought of as within the domain of family, got shifted to the more specialized domain of church and religious institutions, while in response to the advance of democracy, religious institutions necessarily yielded political and legal power to the state and its specialized institutions. Similarly, modern society is characterized by much diversity in

20. Durkheim, *The Division of Labour*, p. 38.
21. Durkheim, *The Division of Labour*, p. 242.
22. See, for example, Smelser, *Social Change in the Industrial Revolution*.

occupational specialization, family ancestry, ethnicity, cultural interests, religious beliefs, and political views.

Amidst such differentiation and diversity, the collective conscience is inevitably weaker and does not absorb the individual. Durkheim states:

> As society spreads out and becomes denser, it envelops the individual less tightly, and in consequence can restrain less efficiently the diverging tendencies that appear . . . in large towns the individual is much more liberated from the yoke of the collectivity . . . the pressure of opinion is felt with less force in large population centers. It is because the attention of each individual is distracted in too many different directions. Moreover we do not know one another so well. Even neighbors and members of the same family are in contact less often and less regularly, separated as they are at every moment by a host of matters and other people who come between them.[23]

The tight mechanical solidarity, therefore, that derives from shared beliefs, experiences, and sentiments is harder to find in modern societies, notwithstanding the existence of many relatively homogenized enclaves of traditional community that still exist within modern society.

Yet, community does not disappear or disintegrate in modern societies. Rather, as Durkheim argues, the functional interdependence among institutions, sectors, occupations, and individuals ensures that solidarity emerges across difference. Institutional and individual differentiation means that no one institution, group, or individual is functionally self-sufficient, and hence as individuals go about their daily lives they are tied into and constrained by a wide range of interdependent social relations. Thus the structural differentiation and the individualism required, for example, by occupational specialization in modern societies produces an organic interdependence, with each individual's, group's, and institution's specialization necessarily contributing to the functioning of the whole. Hence modern, specialized individuals and groups cannot by definition live within socially impenetrable environments, and institutions too, while independent and specialized, are necessarily interdependent (for example, the executive, legislative, and judicial branches of government). Differentiation — of specialties, of goals, of interests, of identities — is the order of the day. But, as Durkheim made abundantly clear, community does

23. Durkheim, *The Division of Labour*, pp. 238-39.

not disappear amidst diversity. Differentiation, rather, because it requires cooperation among interdependent individuals, groups, and institutions, produces an *organic solidarity* (that is, based on interdependence across differences as opposed to the replicable sameness associated with mechanical solidarity). In modern community, as with the biological organism, the effective functioning of the whole is dependent on the independent and interdependent functioning of each specialized part.

The Varied Structure and Varied Nature of Community in Contemporary Society

As we look to contemporary times, the question at issue is whether Durkheim's concept of organic solidarity is still applicable, or whether the structural and cultural shifts of the last few decades beg for a new concept of solidarity. Do we need to speak of a third type of solidarity, to envision perhaps a type of self-enclosed solidarity that will capture the self-focused, therapeutic, and atomized (bowling-alone) trends emphasized by Bellah et al. and Putnam? I would like to argue that "no," a new construal of solidarity is not necessary, because for all the changes in society and in community, community endures and is resilient. Yes, with societal change, there are inevitable losses in how community is structured and how people experience community. But there are also gains — new ways of creating and experiencing community; community defies easy packaging into a narrative of subtraction. What we have witnessed in the post-1970s era is not the decline of community. Rather, community continues to matter and to evolve, and to grow in some directions and contexts while declining in others. Given that society is not static, we should not expect the manifestation of community to remain as it once was (or is imagined to have been). Change notwithstanding, Durkheim's construal of community in modern society as one based on structural differentiation, interdependence, and organic solidarity extends and is applicable to our current era.

In contemporary society, whether or not we feel a sense of community belonging, the group structures in which we participate (for example, work, church, friendship, neighborhood, recreational and purposive groups) bind us into community and reflect and reinforce our interdependence with others within and beyond particular communities. Today, shared voluntary rather than prescribed commitments and chosen collective identities anchor individuals into community (or communities).[24] In contemporary society, there is no singular source, type, or site of community. Rather communities derive from geographical place, and/or from communally shared purposeful interests, activities, and identities; communities vary in their exclusivity, their constraints, the formality and longevity of their structure, the strength of ties and levels of commitment within, and the extent to which they absorb the individual, but in all instances they attach the individual to something beyond the self, that is, to others, to society.

The varied structured opportunities for community that emerge in and constrain everyday life provide individuals with interlinked social ties. Some of these ties will, understandably, be relatively weak — in contexts where the expected commitment to, and/or the individual's investment in, the group is quite minimal in regard to time, effort and emotion — and some may be quite strong. It depends on the group, as groups tend to be structured in ways that vary in their conduciveness to the development of weak or strong ties; and it depends on the routines and life circumstances of any given individual participant. For some individuals, participation in a book club that meets once a month can be their most salient source of community, whereas for others it may be one of many communally engaged activities in which they regularly participate. The multiple differentiated sources of community and the dynamics within and across communities render the creation of thick ties a more open-ended choice in the contemporary era.

Moreover, in contemporary society, individuals typically belong to more than one community. An individual may simultaneously belong to a place-based neighborhood community, an activity-based community (for example, of readers, bikers), an interest-based community (for example, environmental preservation), or an identity community (for example, gay Catholics), among others, and is likely to vary his/her commitment, the strength of his/her intra-communal ties, and emotional investment across these communities. In any event, weak ties should not be seen a priori as inferior to strong ties. In modern pluralistic societies, cooperation across individual and group differences can be more effectively accomplished as

24. Graham Crow, "Community," in *The Concise Encyclopedia of Sociology*, ed. George Ritzer and J. Michael Ryan (Malden, Mass.: Wiley-Blackwell, 2011), pp. 74-75; Claude Fischer, *American Calling: A Social History of the Telephone to 1940* (Berkeley: University of California Press, 1992).

a result of weak ties, whereas strongly bonded cliques inhibit such collabo-ration.[25] For example, individuals who might well want to commit to some voluntary community activity (for example, organizing a high school event for students and their families) may shy away from doing so because of the dominance of a particular clique in the community who have a monopoly on these sorts of activities. Cliques — and traditional, that is, culturally ho-mogenized communities — have thick within-group ties that may provide members with a strong sense of social belonging, but these thick structures are less useful in efforts that require networking and cooperation across a broad range of diverse individuals and groups.[26]

There can certainly be a decline in participation in traditional or, more accurately phrased, era-specific community organizations (for ex-ample, the Elks). Such patterns of decline, however, need to be framed within the larger context of how new social circumstances and new structures and structured opportunities create new social ties. With any broad-scale analysis of social change, whether of community, religion, or any other social phenomenon, caution is advised in order to avoid the simplistic imposition of a narrative of decline or of progress or of a rad-ical break to describe what are invariably complicated social forces and social processes. Measurable indicators of declines in specific activities (for example, participation in a local community organization, weekly church attendance) do not necessarily portend a decline or a transforma-tive realignment in the salience of the larger phenomenon (for example, community, religion) being studied.

Moreover, even though the establishment of new structural arrange-ments may have little to do with emotional fulfillment per se, emotional ties frequently form in varied settings whose purposes are primarily in-strumental in intent. As is true of the phenomenology of everyday life more generally, the objective structural or institutional and the subjective experiential aspects of community dynamically converge and interact in

25. Mark Granovetter, "The Strength of Weak Ties," *American Journal of Sociology* 91 (1973): 481-510.

26. It is also important to keep in mind that the thick ties associated with traditional community (mechanical solidarity) also have their downside. In fabled *Peyton Place,* some residents' experiences (for example, of malicious gossip, incest, and sexual, physical, and emotional abuse) and statuses (for example, unmarried mothers, illegitimacy) rendered community more torturous than enriching and pushed them to detach from community — and society (for example, through suicide) — an effect that inevitably frays the solidarity and functioning of community.

ways that reinforce community solidarity.[27] Ethnographic research by the sociologist Mario Small, for example, shows that mothers who use a childcare center in New York City — that most pluralistic and cosmopolitan of urban sites — not only have their immediate childcare needs met, but become embedded into emotionally supportive and functionally effective social networks as a result of the constraints and obligations imposed by the childcare center on the mothers' participation in the center's activities. Even though these mothers are not looking for community, many become embedded, nevertheless, into a community structure and a set of social relations that provide them with the kinds of social support that traditional community provides its members.[28]

These relations are undoubtedly different in many ways from those that might characterize reliance on, and socio-emotional exchange within, an extended family in a traditional and economically self-sufficient rural community. But in a socio-historical context wherein large numbers of women (including mothers, grandmothers, and great-grandmothers) are active participants in the labor force and actively participate in a host of other activities, the childcare center, a structure in and of community, is effective both strategically and emotionally for its members, and provides them, to boot, with (unanticipated) community belongingness.

When we talk about community, therefore, we need to keep in mind that the kinds of activities that produce community, and the kinds of bonds that community produces, will invariably differ as society changes. These differences do not mean that community has necessarily declined; more typically, they mean that community structures and the nature of community ties have evolved and changed. The functional effectiveness of community and the appreciation for community, however, are no less salient.

Modern Community: The Integration of Differences

In modern society, new structures (for example, childcare centers) emerge that are instrumental to meeting new needs in a changing, more differentiated society (in which, for example, the spheres of work, family, and

27. Peter Berger and Thomas Luckmann, *The Social Construction of Reality: A Treatise in the Sociology of Knowledge* (New York: Anchor, 1966).

28. Mario Small, *Unanticipated Gains: Origins of Network Inequality in Everyday Life* (New York: Oxford University Press, 2009).

childcare are relatively separate from each other) and which contribute, directly and indirectly, to the formation of new sources of community. The plurality of identities in contemporary society also means that new group structures are created that intentionally seek to knit community out of and across differences (for example, the creation of support groups for "working mothers" independent of members' marital status, race, occupation, childcare arrangements, and so on). Some of these efforts are driven by the desire to give voice to intersecting identities that do not fit easily within traditional structures that emphasize a single, overarching, and homogenized identity. A case in point is provided by Dignity, an organization of gay and lesbian Catholics that has chapters located in several cities in the United States.

Enacting Community in Dignity

Local chapters of Dignity participants intentionally assemble together for Mass and other liturgical and social activities on a regular basis. Dignity provides its participants with the structure and the practices that allow them to enact and affirm an identity as gay *and* Catholic, contrary to official church teaching, which regards these identities as contradictory. Dignity members enact community by assembling together for the weekly ritual of Sunday Mass, a Mass that resembles a typical Catholic Mass even as they creatively tamper with some elements of the Catholic tradition such as, for example, the wearing of a rainbow-colored stole by the presiding priest, who may be a valid Catholic priest, a laicized priest, or a woman. The liturgical modifications they collectively deliberate about and enact are purposefully executed with the intention of building and affirming an inclusive gay community, while at the same time maintaining the authenticity of the Catholic tradition.

The Catholic community created by Dignity participants obviously differs from the Catholic community found in a traditional 1950s Catholic parish serving Catholics who lived in the same geographical neighborhood, who shared the same ethnicity and social class, and whose children attended the same parochial schools (and who most likely would have disapproved of same-sex relationships). The traditional Catholic parish community may have had more social and theological coherence and the (mechanical) solidarity that is assured by layered overlapping ties. But its sameness would also have stifled anyone within the community who might have felt "different," as well as limiting (in clique-like or parochial fashion) the parish's willingness to participate in inter-community civic collaborations. The Dignity community may be comparatively less coherent — it is a challenge, after all, to craft and enact any identity that simultaneously negotiates multiple sources of salient meaningfulness — but its participants manage to build a community that produces an organic solidarity out of the plurality of their identities. For most of its participants, moreover, the ties produced can, in fact, be described as thick. A large majority of Dignity participants say that Dignity provides them with an emotionally supportive community and strong sense of social belonging; this view is supported by the fact that many members have been participants for several years and have strong ties with one another. Further, the thickness of the community is objectively witnessed in the collective effervescence that characterizes its weekly liturgy, as well as in the shared commitment collectively demonstrated by members in planning and enacting their liturgical as well as their communal social and civic activities.[29]

The process by which Dignity crafts community does not entail the ad hoc jettisoning of aspects of Catholicism that participants may simply dislike; nor does it lean toward "reducing complex traditions to identity fronts."[30] While the plethora of choices and mobilities[31] available in contemporary times may suggest that individuals randomly pick and choose ad hoc identities that are unmoored from any meaningful tradition or meaningful community, this assumption is contradicted by groups such as Dignity. Dignity participants seek to discern what is core to Catholicism and what encrustations are less central to the multi-stranded Catholic tradition, a tradition that is replete with "pluralistic ways"[32] and intersecting continuities and discontinuities. As David Tracy has elaborated, "There is no such thing as an unambiguous tradition."[33] When Dignity participants deliberatively come together at Mass, they enact their reconstructed sense of a core Catholicism that encompasses the prioritization of Jesus' life, death, and resurrection, the Eucharist, catholicity, hospitality,[34] and

29. See Michele Dillon, *Catholic Identity: Balancing Reason, Faith, and Power* (New York: Cambridge University Press, 1999), pp. 115-63.

30. Vincent Miller, chapter 6 in this volume.

31. Dillon, *Catholic Identity.*

32. David Tracy, *Plurality and Ambiguity: Hermeneutics, Religion, Hope* (San Francisco: Harper & Row, 1987), pp. 95-96.

33. Tracy, *Plurality and Ambiguity*, pp. 36-37.

34. Cf. Philip Rossi's discussion of "enacted hospitality" in chapter 8 in this volume.

the Church's social justice teaching, among other elements. Through this communal enactment, they collectively reaffirm their particularized personal ties to one another as gay Catholics, their ties as Catholics to other local and national Catholic communities, and their sense of unity with the (imagined) universal Catholic community. Additionally, as a community they also engage in civic initiatives aimed at translating Catholic social justice principles (of equality) into the public sphere (for example, projects feeding the homeless, pioneering legislation protecting the rights of gay teenagers in schools).

The public presence of communities of gay Catholics testifies to the fact that identity in contemporary times, whatever its sources and lived experiences, is invariably plural and overlapping; it is not monolithic and not easily subsumed by a single overarching community. This does not mean, however, that individuals retreat into a therapeutic bubble of the self.[35] Some undoubtedly do. But the empirical studies drawn on in this chapter indicate that many individuals not only value community but purposefully and meaningfully participate in a range of diverse communities. The existence of Dignity also illuminates the emancipatory promise and possibility of modernity as the space in which pluralism is affirmed and engaged in ways that do not undermine the necessary dialectic between the particular and the universal. Importantly, participation in Dignity builds communal solidarity among its members, all of whom share the particularized lived experiences of being gay and Catholic. But it also bridges and integrates the participants' ties to the larger, universal Catholic community while simultaneously enriching the dynamic vibrancy of Catholicism as a living and communal tradition within which similarities and differences can be held together as one.[36]

Other Intentional Communities

Given that modern community, unlike traditional community, is not tied solely to a specific geographical place but can encompass other shared statuses and interests, new communities also emerge around specific issues. The recent dramatic growth in environmental activist groups is a case in

35. On the therapeutic dimension of "expressive individualism" see Bellah et al., *Habits of the Heart,* pp. 99-141.
36. See Dillon, *Catholic Identity.*

point. These groups incorporate their members into leadership roles and community activities that are not unlike the community ties formed by participants in more traditional fraternal and civic organizations.[37] Further, while the Internet and mobile social media are undoubtedly changing the nature of face-to-face interaction and social relations, these new and rapidly expanding forms of communication do not necessarily spell the decline of community. Just as the introduction of the telephone had a major impact on the building of community allowing, for example, isolated individuals to talk and maintain contact with geographically distant family members and friends,[38] so too today's digitalized media can facilitate an intensification rather than an attenuation in interpersonal and group communication. Parents and grandparents, for example, can maintain frequent communication (for example, via Skype, webcams) with geographically dispersed children and grandchildren, thus bolstering extended-family communities.

New media contribute to the disembedding of time and space that is part and parcel of everyday experience in late modernity.[39] But they simultaneously provide opportunities for the creation and maintenance of identity- and issue- or activity-oriented relationships and communities that transcend geographical, cultural, economic, and political boundaries. The Internet and social media are also emerging as significant forces in the mobilization of political communities both in the United States and abroad. Importantly, while many individuals may choose to participate in virtual communities, these communities do not necessarily displace the salience of non-Internet based communities in individuals' lives.[40] In any event, the sociological relevance of community is that it brings people together and attaches them, in Durkheimian language, "to something other than themselves," whether to a geographical place community, to a cause in the case of politically mobilized communities, or to some other activity-specific or identity-specific community embedded in time and space (for example, Dignity, the childcare center) or disembedded (for example, virtual communities).

37. Andrew Savage, Jonathan Isham, and Christopher McGrory Klyza, "The Greening of Social Capital: An Examination of Land-Based Groups in Two Vermont Counties," *Rural Sociology* 70 (2005): 113-31.

38. Claude Fischer, *American Calling: A Social History of the Telephone to 1940* (Berkeley: University of California Press, 1992).

39. Giddens, *Modernity and Self-Identity*.

40. Barry Wellman and Stephen D. Berkowitz, eds., *Social Structures: A Network Approach* (New York: Cambridge University Press, 1988).

Americans' Views of Community

Going beyond the specific instances of community I have described, it is quite remarkable that amid the diversity and mobility of contemporary times, Americans in general report finding, and give high marks to, community. These findings render all the more puzzling why some scholars continue to play a dirge to the decline of community. In nationwide opinion polls, 82 percent of respondents report feeling good about their community, specifically defined as their place of residence.[41] This is all the more noteworthy bearing in mind that the vast majority of Americans today live in relatively diverse urban and suburban neighborhoods, and not in the sort of urban ethnic enclaves and rural communities that invariably shadow nostalgia-soaked laments over the decline of community. Further, Americans report a sense of belonging with their neighbors that is on a par with the fellowship they experience with co-workers and fellow parishioners.[42] Indeed, close to half of all Americans (46 percent) say that they talk to their neighbors frequently, and only 18 percent, less than one-fifth, report never talking to their neighbors.[43] Yet even if some do not talk to their neighbors, this finding alone is not indicative of the demise of community; taciturn neighbors are likely to be engaged in other types of community.

Voluntarism, moreover — that deeply engrained strand in American culture and character — not only endures but has expanded through the creation of a host of new groups such as book clubs, mutual support groups, and varied activist and philanthropic groups.[44] Americans' ties beyond the self to some larger community and communal purpose are indicated by their voluntary participation across diverse activities: more than one-third of Americans (35 percent) participate in one or more religious, sports, school, service, civic, or other type of group.[45] Further, a

41. Claude Fischer and Michael Hout, *Century of Difference: How America Changed in the Last One Hundred Years* (New York: Russell Sage Foundation, 2006), pp. 164-65.

42. Fischer and Hout, *Century of Difference,* pp. 164-65, 326.

43. National Conference on Citizenship (NCOC), *Civic Health Index, 2009* (Washington, D.C.: National Conference on Citizenship, 2009), p. 7.

44. Claude Fischer, *Made in America: A Social History of American Culture and Character* (Chicago: University of Chicago Press, 2010), pp. 155-60.

45. National Conference on Citizenship (NCOC), *Civic Life in America: Key Findings on the Civic Health of the Nation,* Issue Brief (Washington, D.C.: Corporation for National and Community Service and the National Conference on Citizenship, 2010), p. 5.

substantial proportion is actively involved in trying to help their communities. More than one-quarter (27 percent) volunteer with some type of organization, and close to one in ten attend public meetings (9 percent) or work with neighbors to fix community problems (8 percent).[46] There is also a lot of informal community involvement, exemplified by the large numbers who help out neighbors with chores, food, and money. In 2009, for example, at the height of the recession's impact, 50 percent of Americans reported that they gave food or money to a non-relative in need, and 11 percent allowed a non-relative to live in their home for a period of time because they needed a place to stay.[47] More generally, 57 percent of Americans report exchanging favors with neighbors at least occasionally.[48] These are all indicators that community matters in America.

Assessing Modern Community

In sum, although "the yoke of the collectivity"[49] no longer absorbs the individual, large numbers of Americans are interlinked through, and choose to create, communal ties to others across and amidst multiple sources of and structures for community. Our empirical review of community provides support for extending Durkheim's construal of the organic solidarity of modern community to community in contemporary times. Undoubtedly, many communities today are different compared to the fabled community of the pre-industrial and pre-urban era. But this should not be a surprise. The surprise rather is that critics choose to think of community in a time-warped manner and in their nostalgia do a disservice to the dynamics of community, and to the creativity and resiliency of human-made social structures. The interdependence of the individual and community is strong in this moment of late modernity, notwithstanding the consequences wrought on the self and social relations by the (partial) dislocation of traditional anchors. Societal change is disruptive. But change — which is ever-fermenting because institutional processes and societal life and social relations are dynamic — should not be seen simply as a narrative of decline, or for that matter as one of cumulative progress. Change in any one area of

46. NCOC, *Civic Life in America*, p. 4.
47. NCOC, *Civic Health Index, 2009*.
48. NCOC, *Civic Life in America*, p. 7.
49. Durkheim, *The Division of Labour*, p. 238.

activity is invariably accompanied by a remarkable amount of stability and adaptive realignment. Discontinuities absorb and get absorbed by continuities such that social life and community processes are simultaneously dynamic and resilient.

2. Religious and Spiritual Autonomy and the Persistence of Community

When we turn our attention from community in general to the sociological relation between religion and community, we also encounter a narrative of decline. The framing here is that while in the past, church involvement was a correlate and engine of community involvement, the (alleged) decline of religion is of a piece with the (alleged) decline of community.[50] Yet, the claim that religion has declined is itself problematic. The thesis of religion's decline is largely driven by the continuing prominence of classical secularization theory. Following Max Weber, secularization (correctly) postulates the institutional differentiation of religion from other spheres (for example the state, economy, law, education, arts, and so on), and a concomitant decline of religious institutional authority. This thesis also anticipated, though somewhat erroneously, a loss in the relevance of religiously derived values and meaning in individual lives and public culture. The secularization thesis still looms in the sociology of religion, notwithstanding its partial contestation by empirical studies that paint a more complex and nuanced picture, especially if the focus is on the United States rather than Western Europe.

In the United States, aggregate survey trends since the late 1930s show a relatively stable pattern of church attendance.[51] There is some ebb and flow; church attendance peaked in the 1950s, when it was higher than it had been in earlier decades as well as subsequently. This fact in itself challenges the narrative of linear religious decline and is in accord with several historical and community-specific studies showing that many Americans in the nineteenth and early twentieth centuries were not religious or only minimally religious. Although there had been much steadiness in post–World War II trends in religious affiliation, the proportion of Americans who report having no religious affiliation has almost tripled since 1990,

---

50. See, for example, Bellah et al., *Habits of the Heart*.
51. Fischer and Hout, *Century of Difference*, p. 204.

from 7 percent to 20 percent.[52] This trend is not interpreted as strong evidence of secularization, however, but as the outcome of the interplay between generational change and the tendency of political moderates to eschew claiming a religious affiliation given the politicization of religion by the Religious Right.[53] In any event, the decline in religious affiliation has not displaced the personal meaningfulness of religious and spiritual beliefs and practices, and large majorities of Americans as well as Europeans continue to anchor their identity, at least partially, in a religious or spiritual tradition.[54] In sum, the data on religious affiliation and religious/ spiritual engagement and beliefs, rather than showing a pattern of decline, present a Janus-faced reality (especially in the United States), and suggest that religion, just as community, is a dynamic and differentiated social phenomenon that defies any simple narrative framing.

Charles Taylor: The Post-Durkheimian Loss of Community

Notwithstanding the differentiation of the religious landscape, some scholars see the increase in non-church spirituality as indicative of the decline of religion and of the decline of community. This view is intimated by Charles Taylor in *A Secular Age*. Calling ours the "Age of Authenticity," he argues that it was ushered in by the destabilizing "current cultural revolution"[55] propelled by the post-1960s emphasis on individual autonomy,

52. Michael Hout and Claude S. Fischer, "Why More Americans Have No Religious Preference: Politics and Generations," *American Sociological Review* 67, no. 2 (April 2002): 165-90; see also the General Social Survey 2012.

53. Hout and Fischer, "Why More Americans Have No Religious Preference," p. 181.

54. See, for example, Wade Clark Roof, *Spiritual Marketplace: Baby Boomers and the Remaking of American Religion* (Princeton, N.J.: Princeton University Press, 1999); William D'Antonio, Michele Dillon, and Mary Gautier, *American Catholics: Persisting and Changing* (Lanham, Md.: Rowman and Littlefield, 2013); and Dick Houtman and Stef Aupers, "The Spiritual Turn and the Decline of Tradition: The Spread of Post-Christian Spirituality in 14 Western Countries, 1981-2000," *Journal for the Scientific Study of Religion* 46 (2007): 305-20. Not only the religiously affiliated but large proportions of religiously unaffiliated Americans believe in God or a universal spirit (92 percent/70 percent), life after death (48 percent), heaven (74 percent/41 percent), that miracles still occur today as in ancient times (79 percent/55 percent), and that angels and demons are active in the world (68 percent/40 percent), and engage in regular prayer (75 percent/44 percent) or meditation (39 percent/26 percent) (Pew Forum on Religion and Public Life, *The U.S. Religious Landscape Survey: Religious Beliefs* [Washington, D.C.: Pew Research Center, 2008], pp. 11, 13, 35).

55. Taylor, *A Secular Age*, p. 505.

expressivity, and the therapeutic turn. Taylor acknowledges the positive consequences of this cultural turn. In particular, he highlights its impact in breaking down barriers between religious groups, and he also points out that "much of today's spiritual/religious life" occupies a middle ground between the extremes of "peremptory authority" (for example, papal infallibility, biblical literalism), and utter "self-sufficiency" or "self-trust."[56]

Nevertheless, Taylor also invokes a narrative of "decline." This is exemplified for him by the rising numbers of atheists, agnostics, and religiously disaffiliated individuals, and by the increase in the personal autonomy of those who are religiously and spiritually involved. In Taylor's narrative, these trends are "the *consequence* of expressivist culture."[57] This claim represents a historical and sociological stretch given that, as is well documented, Romanticism and its American variants (as epitomized by, for example, by Walt Whitman)[58] long preceded the 1960s. And while we can acknowledge that the 1960s marked an "expressive revolution" in religion,[59] the autonomy of the self is foundational in American culture and across its diverse institutional spheres (for example, economy, law, politics, religion). Narratives of personal religious autonomy have been highly salient in American everyday Protestantism since at least the American Revolution,[60] and permeate the religious biographies of Americans who came of age before the 1960s generational transformation.[61]

In any case, Taylor argues that contemporary currents of religious and spiritual autonomy reflect a "post-Durkheimian world."[62] In his historical discussion of the emergence of the secular age, Taylor distinguishes between Durkheimian social formations (wherein church and society are equivalent); paleo-Durkheimian (for example, baroque Catholicism; "ontic dependence of the state on God"); neo-Durkheimian (for example, the link between religion and the state is largely ceremonial but nonetheless central to social order and identity); and the post-Durkheimian

56. Taylor, *A Secular Age,* pp. 513, 512.

57. Taylor, *A Secular Age,* p. 513; emphasis mine.

58. Cf. Bellah et al., *Habits of the Heart,* pp. 33-37.

59. Talcott Parsons, "Religion in Post-Industrial America: The Problem of Secularization," *Social Research* 41 (1974): 193-225.

60. Nathan Hatch, *The Democratization of American Christianity* (New Haven, Conn.: Yale University Press, 1989).

61. See, for example, Michele Dillon and Paul Wink, *In the Course of a Lifetime: Tracing Religious Belief, Practice, and Change* (Berkeley: University of California Press, 2007).

62. Taylor, *A Secular Age,* p. 487.

world wherein "the spiritual dimension of existence is quite unhooked from the political."[63] Invoking the post-Durkheimian label, he elaborates that today "our relation to the spiritual is being more and more unhooked from our relation to our political societies. But that by itself doesn't say anything about whether or how our relation to the sacred will be mediated by collective connections. A thoroughly post-Durkheimian society would be one in which our religious belonging would be unconnected to our national identity."[64]

Taylor's interest is in the historical emergence of secularism, and the changing relation between religion and the social order and its institutional expression in church and state relations. Thus it may make sense for him to splice Durkheim into these varied categorizations. From a broader sociological perspective, however, there are tensions in these categorizations. Taylor's schema might be taken as implying that the most legitimate form of community is "political community," and that the more legitimate form of religion is institutional religion. Such a framing renders other forms of religious/spiritual engagement as socially lacking or inferior. Indeed, Taylor states: "The a priori principle, that a valid answer to the religious quest must meet either the paleo- or neo-Durkheimian conditions (a church, or a 'church' and/or society) has been abandoned in the new (religious/spiritual) dispensation. The spiritual as such is no longer intrinsically related to society."[65]

Durkheim, however, did not equate society or the social with national boundaries, nor did he privilege the national community or political assemblies as superior sites of religious or societal regeneration. Rather, Durkheim emphasized the plurality of communal sources and sites of religious and societal regeneration.[66] "Collective connections" — whether or not they mediate the sacred — are variously formed independent of, beyond, and in partial coexistence with political community (derived from and bounded by the nation-state). Second, historically and contemporaneously within a single nation-state, discrete religious communities coexist; for instance, the Church of England may be coterminous with British national identity, but English Catholics belong to the British nation and to the (trans-national) Catholic Church community rather than to the Church

63. Taylor, *A Secular Age,* pp. 442, 454, 455.
64. Taylor, *A Secular Age,* p. 516.
65. Taylor, *A Secular Age,* p. 490.
66. Émile Durkheim, *The Elementary Forms of Religious Life,* trans. Carol Cosman (Oxford: Oxford University Press, 2001), p. 322.

of England community. In the United States, notwithstanding the separation of church and state and notwithstanding the insightful notion of civil
religion,[67] Catholics were burdened historically with demonstrating that
coterminous belonging to the American nation and to the Catholic Church
were not incompatible. These sorts of multiple belongings have always
posed a challenge (however tacit) to social order and to the pluralistic
depth of civil religion. At the same time, they complicate the relations between religion and ostensibly neutral, legal, and political structures (for example, the state). Third, amidst the pluralism of modernity and especially
perhaps in the current era of globalizing processes whose consequences
include the institutionalization of post-national constellations and transnational identities,[68] it seems parochial to single out the relation between
(an essentialized) national identity and religious belonging when we are
encouraged, following Kant, to consider the enactment of cosmopolitan
community.[69]

Spirituality and Community

Although Taylor is careful not to use the category "non-Durkheimian," the
term "post-Durkheimian" suggests nonetheless that contemporary society
lacks organic solidarity and that communal ties are displaced by a fractured
culture of excessive individualism:

> My hypothesis is that the post-war slide in our social imaginary more
> and more into a post-Durkheimian age has destabilized and undermined
> the various Durkheimian dispensations. This has had the effect of either
> gradually releasing people to be recruited into the fractured culture,
> or in the case where the new consumer culture has quite dislocated
> the earlier outlook, of explosively expelling people into this fractured
> world. For, while remaining aware of the attractions of the new culture,

---

67. Robert Bellah, "Civil Religion in America," *Daedalus* 96 (1967): 1-21.

68. Anthony Giddens, *Runaway World: How Globalization Is Reshaping Our Lives* (New
York: Routledge, 2003); Jürgen Habermas, *The Postnational Constellation* (Cambridge,
Mass.: MIT Press, 2001).

69. See, for example, Ulrich Beck and Edgar Grande, "Varieties of Second Modernity:
The Cosmopolitan Turn in Social and Political Theory and Research," *British Journal of
Sociology* 61 (2010): 409-43; and Gerard Delanty, "The Cosmopolitan Imagination: Critical
Cosmopolitanism and Social Theory," *British Journal of Sociology* 57 (2006): 25-47.

we must never underestimate the ways in which one can also be forced into it: the village community disintegrates, the local factory closes, jobs disappear in "downsizing," the immense weight of social approval and opprobrium begins to tell on the side of the new individualism.[70]

Such generalized claims are at odds with what I have argued is the persistence of organic solidarity in contemporary community, notwithstanding structural and cultural change. Although it is true that contemporary forms of religious and spiritual engagement are relatively autonomous of and largely unhooked from the authority of religious institutions, it is important to clarify that this does not mean that they are no longer mediated by communal connections. Research indicates that many spiritual individuals are highly disciplined rather than ad hoc or flimsy about their spirituality; and while they characteristically show a strong interest in individual self-growth and authenticity, this is a project of the self that is not in contradiction with commitment to community.[71] In an in-depth, longitudinal study, for example, the highly spiritual but less church-oriented individuals scored as high as their more church-oriented, highly religious peers on various dimensions of altruism and concern for others. Spiritual individuals and religious individuals were equally likely to be active in helping the homeless, for example, and while religious individuals were more actively involved in local community issues such as neighborhood crime watch, spiritual seekers were engaged more broadly with, for example, environmental causes and AIDS activism.[72]

Moreover, "openness to experience" is an overarching personality characteristic that tends to differentiate spiritual from church-oriented religious individuals, and spiritual individuals in general tend to be more pluralistic and tolerant of social diversity.[73] This suggests that such individuals may be especially well poised to play a key role in making communal connections beyond their immediate circles. Such openness is a valuable asset in forging connections and respect across the multiple sources of intersecting differences that characterize contemporary local, national, and global communities. I draw attention to the similarities and differences

70. Taylor, *A Secular Age,* pp. 491-92.

71. See Dillon and Wink, *In the Course of a Lifetime;* Roof, *Spiritual Marketplace;* and Robert Wuthnow, *After Heaven: Spirituality in America since the 1950s* (Berkeley: University of California Press, 1998).

72. Dillon and Wink, *In the Course of a Lifetime,* pp. 167-68.

73. Dillon and Wink, *In the Course of a Lifetime,* pp. 147-48.

among religious and spiritual individuals not to accentuate the relatively artificial dichotomy that is frequently postulated between church-centered religion and a more institutionally autonomous, individualized spirituality, but to make the point that the various concerns expressed about the implications of contemporary forms of spirituality for depleting community involvement are to a large extent problematic and empirically unfounded. Further, as Courtney Bender documents, spiritual seeking is not a project of isolated individuals who are disconnected from other spiritual individuals. She finds, rather, that many participate in community-situated spiritual networks, and network members frequently overlap across specific groups and shared activities, thus constituting veritable spiritual communities.[74] In short, sociological research indicates that the unhooking of religion and spirituality from church authority does not spell the decline of community or the attenuation of collective connections.

3. Post-Secular Community: The Foreclosure of Difference

Thus far I have argued that Durkheim's concept of organic solidarity continues to be applicable to the nature of community in contemporary times. The relation of the self to society and the communal attachments individuals form necessarily evolve in response to changed social conditions (for example, industrialization, urbanization, mobility, cultural diversity, Internet technology). But as Durkheim emphasized, the solidarity that is crafted in modern community is grounded in the social interdependence organically fostered by structural and cultural differentiation (in contrast to the mechanical solidarity that derives from structurally overlapping ties in homogenized, traditional societies). Notwithstanding the fact that differentiation — including differences in beliefs and worldviews — is the hallmark of modern society,[75] recent theorizing rethinking the place of religion in the public sphere gives short shrift to some contemporary forms of religious and spiritual identity.

Most notably, the German social theorist Jürgen Habermas, who for many decades maintained that religion's inherently limited communicative

74. Courtney Bender, *The New Metaphysicals: Spirituality and the American Religious Imagination* (Chicago: University of Chicago Press, 2010).

75. Chantal Mouffe, "Democracy, Power, and the 'Political,'" in *Democracy and Difference: Contesting the Boundaries of the Political,* ed. Seyla Benhabib (Princeton, N.J.: Princeton University Press, 1996), pp. 245-56.

rationality excluded its use as a resource in the deliberatively rational public sphere,[76] has reframed his understanding. In a highly touted conversation in 2004 with Cardinal Ratzinger (now emeritus Pope Benedict XVI), Habermas conceded that the Enlightenment project of modernization had gone somewhat awry. In particular, he noted that globalizing economic markets defy the control of consensual rational judgments, and he lamented not only the extent of global socio-economic inequality, but the mass political indifference toward it.[77] This indifference is part of a longer depoliticization process resulting from modernization and increased affluence and consumerism, highlighted by Habermas decades earlier.[78] For Habermas, the threat posed by current globalizing forces to potentially "degrade the capacity for democratic self-steering" both within and across nations, makes the need for public communicative reasoning all the more necessary.[79] He thus looks to discover new, that is, underappreciated, political cultural resources toward democratic revitalization. Hence for Habermas, "a contrite modernity," one characterized by several social pathologies that need fixing, may benefit, he now argues, from religious-derived norms and ethical intuitions. He concedes that these religious resources can help human society deal with "a miscarried life, social pathologies, the failures of individual life projects, and the deformation of misarranged existential relationships."[80]

Habermas's evolving regard for religion, articulated across several venues since 2001, leads him to embrace the term *post-secular* to demarcate the current moment. For Habermas, the label can be applied to *secularized* societies where "religion maintains a public influence and relevance, while the secularistic certainty that religion will disappear worldwide in the course of modernization is losing ground."[81] Post-secular society thus "has to adjust itself to the continued existence of religious communities in an increasingly secularized environment."[82] Notwithstanding some ambiguities and limits in Habermas's use of the term, it makes sense for Habermas — as Habermas,

---

76. Jürgen Habermas, *Theory of Communicative Action*, vols. 1 and 2 (Boston: Beacon, 1984, 1987).

77. Quoted in Virgil Nemoianu, "The Church and the Secular Establishment: A Philosophical Dialog between Joseph Ratzinger and Jürgen Habermas," *Logos* 9, no. 2 (2006): 25.

78. Jürgen Habermas, *Legitimation Crisis* (Boston: Beacon, 1975).

79. Habermas, *Postnational Constellation*, p. 67.

80. Quoted in Nemoianu, "The Church and the Secular Establishment," p. 26.

81. Habermas, "Notes on a Post-Secular Society," p. 4.

82. Habermas, "Notes on a Post-Secular Society," p. 3.

and with his Habermasian worldview — to construe a post-secular age. The post-secular denotes that the secular, like the Enlightenment, fell short of its originally intended destination, and thus Habermas wonders whether "an altered perspective on the genealogy of reason [can] rescue postmeta-physical thinking" from the dilemmas attendant on the Enlightenment's unenlightened and blinkered treatment of religion.[83]

Habermas's discussion of how religion might be accommodated in post-secular public discourse suggests, however, that despite his gesture toward religion there are lingering continuities between his current un-derstanding and the polarized framing of religion and rationality in his earlier theorizing of communicative rationality. His revised position, indifferent to the empirical social realities of religion(s), still construes religion in very narrow, highly cognitivist, artificially demarcated, and undifferentiated terms.[84] Given this chapter's focus, I concentrate here on the assumptions of community that underlie and are refracted through Habermas's construal of the post-secular. Habermas's commitment to the project of a revitalized deliberative democracy is inextricably intertwined with his admiration for and commitment to modernity and its values, as opposed to post-modernity and its affirmation of chaos and disorder.[85] Yet, his conceptualization of community falls short of the affirming recognition of differences that is the conceptual hallmark of modernity. As modern communities, we have to not only tolerate but actively engage with differ-ence. As the political philosopher Chantal Mouffe argues, "Acceptance of pluralism is part of the conceptual definition of modern democracy and not simply a function of its size."[86]

The Hierarchical Ordering and Compartmentalization of Difference

In Habermas's post-secular society, however, community is characterized by the partial foreclosure of differences. This foreclosing is most clearly

83. Habermas et al., *Awareness of What Is Missing*, pp. 18-19.

84. See Michele Dillon, "Jürgen Habermas and the Post-Secular Appropriation of Re-ligion: A Sociological Critique," in *The Post-Secular in Question: Religion in Contemporary Society,* ed. Philip Gorski, David Kim, John Torpey, and Jonathan Van Antwerpen (New York: New York University Press/Social Science Research Council, 2012), pp. 249-78.

85. Thomas McCarthy, *Ideals and Illusions: On Reconstruction and Deconstruction in Contemporary Critical Theory* (Cambridge, Mass.: MIT Press, 1991).

86. Mouffe, "Democracy, Power, and the 'Political,'" p. 246.

seen in his allocation of "religious citizens," as he calls them, to what appears as an inferior status requiring the silencing of the specifically religious idiom of their religious beliefs. Habermas's post-secular society imposes highly constraining obligations on religious individuals. It requires them to be reflexively self-conscious of their own beliefs such that when "religious citizens" participate in public debate they must necessarily do so by translating their religious norms into a secular idiom.[87] He is conciliatory in acknowledging that "the persons who are neither willing nor able to divide their moral convictions and their vocabulary into profane and religious strands must be permitted to take part in political will formation even if they use religious language."[88] This gesture, nonetheless, seems more patronizing than equalizing. The core expectation is that religious individuals should discard the specifically religious vocabulary that penetrates their experiences, worldviews, and everyday language. Accordingly, the community that is construed for post-secular society is one in which a certain homogenization is required: the homogenization of language and, by extension, the approximate homogenization of experiences. The phenomenological realities that defy translation into a secular vocabulary present as differences that are suspect. Differences have to be rendered *sotte voce,* rather than explicitly acknowledged, affirmed, and negotiated in ways that challenge and reciprocally and mutually engage the vocabularies and experiences of "secular citizens."

Although Habermas emphasizes that "secular citizens in civil society . . . must be able to meet their fellow religious citizens as equals,"[89] the former are not marked as different and are less burdened by civic identity challenges. Secular citizens are required only to acknowledge the persistence of religion; to respect the rights of religious citizens to hold religiously informed, but secularly translated, views; and not to discount religious utterances a priori.[90] They are under no obligation to seek proactively to know or to try to understand the worldviews that religious citizens might have developed as a result of their participation in a religious or spiritual community, nor are they required to adopt the same reflexive attitude toward their secular views that religious citizens are expected to adopt toward their beliefs. It would seem that Habermas's secular citizens

87. Quoted in Nemoianu, "The Church and the Secular Establishment," p. 27.
88. Habermas, "Notes on a Post-Secular Society," p. 11.
89. Habermas, "Notes on a Post-Secular Society," p. 11.
90. Habermas, "Notes on a Post-Secular Society," p. 12.

are, by definition, reflexive and, by extension, cognitively more competent and complex than, and superior to, religious citizens. The differentiation in post-secular community is not one of cultural or dialogical interdependence, or of mutual learning with a view toward the communicative achievement of action outcomes that might alleviate the problems of the newly contrite modernity. Rather, it is a remarkably hierarchical community wherein one class of citizens must defer to the pre-eminent secular vocabulary, even though that vocabulary has thus far, as Habermas intimates, not prevented modernity from anticipating and dealing with its miscarriages. In sum, post-secular community's differentiation of secular and religious citizens accomplishes the compartmentalization, rather than the ongoing dialogical bridging and integration, of differences.

By starkly differentiating secular citizens and religious citizens, Habermas forecloses recognition of community as emergent from and across, and maintained by, plural identities. Although individuals for the most part are well able to differentiate their religious and their non-religious habits and vocabularies, they do not necessarily think of themselves either as *secular* citizens or as *religious* citizens. Yet Habermas uses these terms as if they in fact comprise separate, clear-cut, bounded identities in contemporary society.[91] Habermas's dichotomization of religious and secular citizens suggests that individuals who have religious affiliations and beliefs are nothing else, essentially, but religious believers, rather than modern citizens who, while simultaneously holding religious beliefs and highly rational beliefs, fully participate in secular society's variegated secular and religious communities. But this melding is readily observable in the United States among mainstream religious adherents (for example, mainline Protestants, Catholics, liberal Jews) for whom being religious and secular are, for the most part, mutually reinforcing identities and orientations. Moreover, the salience of one or another identity is not fixed, but varies depending on life-course obligations and socio-cultural contexts. Modern community encompasses differentiation, and precisely because of the mutuality between, rather than the compartmentalization of, religious and secular identities, community evolves in highly dynamic and open-ended ways. In the context of the United States, it is hard to imagine a purely secular or a purely religious "community." Even institutionalized religious communities such as the Catholic Church are characterized by the dynamic interaction between religious and secular ideas and traditions,

91. Habermas, "Notes on a Post-Secular Society," pp. 11-12.

and by the participants who as the carriers of particular intersecting, and frequently fluid, religious and secular identities regenerate the Church as a living tradition and as a living (universal) community of local Catholic church communities and groups.

The exclusivity of Habermas's post-secular community is further underscored by the fact that it excludes fundamentalists and New Age believers. Habermas is indisposed toward what he refers to as New Age syncretic movements and excludes them along with fundamentalist traditions (for example, Islam and Pentecostalism) from post-secular dialogical community.[92] Yet, it would seem that if society is to move forward in efforts to build political communities that embody and integrate differences, then these groups precisely need to be accommodated within the folds of sincere attempts to forge dialogue across difference. It may well be that, as Pope Benedict stated, "In theological terms, a true dialogue is not possible without putting one's faith in parentheses."[93] Nevertheless, if we are to forge the kinds of culturally inclusive communities required of our late modern condition, then we need somehow to find the common strands derived from faith and culture that open up the possibility of creating ties, however fragile, across difference.

4. Conclusion

Our contemporary era is characterized by a remarkable amount of fast-paced change, propelled by technological and globalizing forces that accentuate the disembeddedness of time and space and the mobility of everyday life. Yet, the resiliency of community, the forging of connections beyond the self, remains remarkably strong. Although nostalgia for traditional forms of homogenized community is frequently expressed, the diverse and differentiated structures of contemporary society continue to provide plentiful and relatively stable opportunities for connecting with others in ways that nurture the organic solidarity associated with modern community. The shift from rural to urban and suburban society has not diminished the salience and attractiveness of local community. Geographical community still matters, and while there is a decline in the

---

92. Habermas, "Notes on a Post-Secular Society," pp. 2-3.

93. Rachel Donadio, "In Letter, Pope Puts Focus on the Limits of Interfaith Dialogue," *New York Times,* November 24, 2008, p. A7.

vibrancy of some traditional community associations, this is offset by the emergence of a broad array of other sources of community, some intentionally formed through collective agency anchored by a particular, intersecting social identity, activity, or issue, and others the by-products of new structures (for example, childcare centers, Internet-based communities) that are part and parcel of a changing society. The role of institutionalized religion in anchoring individuals in a church community has diminished. Nonetheless, individuated spiritual paths do not emerge in isolation from other individuals. Moreover, spiritual engagement does not preclude but frequently occurs in tandem with simultaneous participation in traditional church communities; in new spiritual groups, centers, and networks; and in the forging of communal connections across an array of diverse and unexpected places.

Despite much social progress, there is consensus among scholars and others that late modernity is a contrite modernity impoverished by increasing levels of economic inequality, depoliticization, and existential emptiness. Further, the secular arc of modernity is forestalled by evidence that both institutionalized religion and deinstitutionalized spiritual beliefs and practices continue to persist and to matter in public culture and in individual lives. New awareness of the limits of the promise of Enlightenment has motivated scholars such as Habermas who previously dismissed the place of religion in public discourse to look to religion as a cultural resource in moving society forward from its current pathologies. Given that religious and other cultural differences are the hallmark of modernity, we are under an obligation to look for ways to create dialogue across differences and with a view to creating institutional and communal practices that incorporate rather than silence differences. These are not easy tasks. Habermas's construal of the post-secular is an important step in this endeavor. The criteria he outlines, however, ones still deeply wedded to the cognitivist-rationalist perspective that has long permeated his theoretical stance, tend toward the construal of a post-secular community in which differences are foreclosed. In particular, Habermas's hierarchical differentiation of secular argumentation over religious vocabulary, his polarized construal of secular citizens and religious citizens, and his exclusion of non-mainstream religious and spiritual traditions converge in producing a model of community in which the plurality and intersectionality of identities are marginalized rather than affirmed and incorporated into building community out of diversity.

11. Engaging Religious and Secular Humanisms

Slavica Jakelić

*Man is a creature who makes pictures of himself and then
comes to resemble the picture.*

Iris Murdoch[1]

Charles Taylor uses the term "exclusive humanism" as interchangeable
with the notions of "modern humanism," "anti-transcendent humanism,"
and "secular humanism." These humanisms, according to Taylor, are characterized by the exclusive orientation toward flourishing here and now, but
they do not exist in isolation. The immanent frame — defined by increasing
rationality, secular understanding of time, and awareness about the constructed nature of social order — is shared by nonbelievers and believers
alike, even as they differ in their interpretations of that frame. All of us,
Taylor writes, "are brothers under the skin [and] emerge from the same
long process,"[2] the drive to Reform, which originally intended to draw

1. Iris Murdoch, "Metaphysics and Ethics," in *Iris Murdoch and the Search for Human
Goodness,* ed. Maria Antonaccio and William Schweiker (Chicago: University of Chicago
Press, 1996), p. 252.
2. Charles Taylor, *A Secular Age* (Cambridge, Mass.: Harvard University Press, 2007),
p. 675.

This chapter was written with the generous support of the Notre Dame Institute for Advanced Study (NDIAS). While writing this essay, I benefited from conversations with the
2011-12 NDIAS fellows as well as from the insights of the NDIAS directors Vittorio Hösle
and Donald Stelutto. I am especially grateful for the critical and constructive reading of this
chapter by William Barbieri, J. Paul Martin, and Jason Varsoke.

the laity closer to the life of religious elites but also inaugurated a vision of human agency as able to construct and reconstruct societies.

In its "rage for order," the drive to Reform established confidence in the human capacity to order the world, but it also brought about the interventionist, uniformizing, homogenizing, and rationalizing impulses driven by a desire to abolish exception and difference. At first moving toward transcendence and toward the excellence and prosperity of humankind, the drive to Reform ultimately resulted in the idea that flourishing "involves no relation to anything higher."[3] This process of disenchantment and the turning away from transcendence, however, is only one layer of Taylor's genealogy of the secular. Its other layer uncovers the complicated relationship between religious and secular humanisms, which has been forged through conflict as well as through deep moral connections. As Taylor explains, secularism was able to counter the immense force that religion had in human life for so long only by "using a modality of the most powerful ethical ideas [that] this religion itself had helped to entrench."[4] The same moral drive, in other words, stands at the roots of both modern Western Christianity and modern Western secularity: this is the impulse to reform individuals so that they might apply themselves to creating a better world.[5]

Taylor's focus is on the emergence of secular humanisms, but in a scholarly context in which the dominant discourse about the religious-secular encounter is the one of conflict, it is Taylor's gesture toward the shared moral origins and moral spaces of religious and secular humanisms that calls for more attention. The concern for the shared spaces of religious and secular humanisms is not meant to minimize but to affirm the differences between them, particularly in the understanding of the source of ultimate authority. At the same time, one of the central objectives of this chapter is to highlight the *practice* of humanisms as a possible and productive site of encounter between believers and nonbelievers.

The essay is organized with two central questions.

First, what are we to make of contemporary religious humanisms and secular humanisms that attempt to overcome the negative sides of the Enlightenment (or "exclusive") humanistic orientations? The contemporary humanisms are pertinent to our discussion because they are critical of the

3. Taylor, *A Secular Age,* p. 151.
4. Taylor, *A Secular Age,* p. 267.
5. Taylor, *A Secular Age,* pp. 61, 222-23, 259, 269.

"imprudent ignoring of limits"[6] of our ordering of the world while also affirming a restrained yet hopeful humanistic stance, which calls for an active (rather than a detached) presence in this world.[7]

Second, what is the potential of the encounter between religious and secular humanisms? Taylor writes that ours is a pluralist world in which different "forms of belief and unbelief jostle, and hence *fragilize* each other."[8] But does the relationship between religious and secular humanisms have to be one of fragilization, or could it not also be one of mutual enrichment? This essay proposes that precisely when fully engaging each other's differences, religious and secular humanists can work toward the conditions of human flourishing while also chastening each other's ontological absoluteness. I therefore support William Connolly's argument that the tensions that result from the critical engagement of different perspectives are valuable for democratic politics.[9] Religio-secular pluralism may be a problem but it is also a value — to be nurtured and to be explored. I approach these questions and themes in two steps. In the first part, I explore William Schweiker's "theological humanism" and Edward Said's "secular humanism" as two examples of contemporary humanistic thinking — two projects that acknowledge the problems of Enlightenment humanisms but move the humanistic endeavor forward with a deep understanding of its constraints. Schweiker's and Said's ideas of humanisms, then, carry an awareness of the problems of universal or overly optimistic and radical humanistic claims. These two humanisms, however, remain particularistic in nature: they are assured in the ability of self-critique and do not probe the religious-secular encounters as a contribution to the contemporary humanistic project(s).

The potential of such encounters, I suggest in the second part of this essay, is evident in the context of social movements in which believers and nonbelievers collaborate to address concrete and pressing historical challenges. In a snapshot of the Polish Solidarity movement, and with a particular focus on two influential representatives of secular and religious humanisms in communist Poland — Adam Michnik and Father Józef Tischner — I want to illustrate how religious and secular activists gave the

---

6. See Taylor, *A Secular Age*, p. 125.

7. This is not the same as arguing that the "later-arising forms of unbelief" and "attempts to redefine and recover belief . . . define themselves in relation to this first pathbreaking humanism of freedom, discipline and order" (Taylor, *A Secular Age*, p. 269).

8. Taylor, *A Secular Age*, p. 531; italics are mine.

9. William Connolly, *Why I Am Not a Secularist* (Minneapolis: University of Minnesota Press, 1999).

ideals of human flourishing very concrete meanings — socio-economic fairness, freedom of religion, democratic pluralism. Solidarity, I propose, is a rich referent for understanding the democratic potential of the *practice* of religious and secular humanisms: in the realm of practice, humanisms can become both a normative and a critical stance, serving to disclose rather than to legitimize power,[10] and affirming the pluralism of ontological positions while chastening their exclusivistic claims.

1. Religious and Secular Humanisms

Contrary to a common assumption among some secular thinkers, and against the skepticism of some religious thinkers, "humanism" is neither inherently secular nor necessarily a secularizing ideal.[11] To be sure, humanism is an ideal that is articulated within, and serves as the foundation of, many secular philosophies. But humanism is also constitutive of many religious traditions — the range of humanistic concerns can be found in Buddhism and Confucianism, as well as in all three Abrahamic traditions. Contemporary scholars of Judaism, Christianity, and Islam, for example, suggest that it is possible to trace the meanings of religious humanism in the idea of "humanity before God," and particularly in the discussions of what constitutes the inalienable worth of human life — the sanctity of human life "understood in the religious and moral context of the human-Divine relationship" and the notion of moral responsibility toward other creatures of God.[12]

---

10. Frits de Lange as quoted in John W. de Gruchy, "Christian Humanism: Reclaiming a Tradition; Affirming an Identity," *CTI Reflections* 8, April 19, 2009 (http://dir.groups.yahoo.com/group/friends-in-conversation/message/2776?var=1).

11. As David Klemm and William Schweiker write, humanistic values of "freedom, reasonableness, tolerance, and human dignity" came to be "judged to be vacuous, mere remnants of the failed modern project, or worse, the veiled rhetoric of secular cultural imperialism." See Klemm and Schweiker, *Religion and the Human Future: An Essay on Theological Humanism* (Malden, Mass.: Blackwell, 2008), p. 3. For the differences in the North American and continental European perspectives on the religious vs. secular character of "humanism," see Kate Soper, *Humanism and Anti-Humanism* (La Salle, Ill.: Open Court, 1986).

12. See William Schweiker, Kevin Jung, and Michael A. Johnson, eds., *Humanity Before God: Contemporary Faces of Jewish, Christian, and Islamic Ethics* (Minneapolis: Augsburg Fortress, 2006), p. 11. For an account of the rich history of Christian humanism — from its biblical foundation to contemporary theological developments such as liberation theology — see Timothy G. McCarthy, *Christianity and Humanism: From Their Biblical Foundations into the Third Millennium* (Chicago: Loyola, 1996).

Any study of "humanism" is complex and requires the recognition of histories of a range of ideas: from ancient Greek philosophy and a variety of Renaissance humanisms, to the Christian, Buddhist, Enlightenment, and liberal humanisms, to communist and socialist humanisms. Considering "humanism" is additionally complicated by the fact that it was powerfully contested in the course of the twentieth century. In the context of modern French philosophy, as Kate Soper suggests, the anti-humanist critiques see "every form of humanist thinking . . . as no less obfuscatory and mythological than the theology and superstition which the 'humanist' movement has traditionally congratulated itself upon rejecting."[13] Within the larger evaluation and critique of Western modernity, and depending on the definition of the term, "humanism" has been critiqued or rejected for its obsession with agency and power and the concomitant inability to rid itself of its metaphysical origins; for its universality and rationality, which affirmed the particularistic notion of the "human" and resulted in the denial of difference; for its confidence in its ability to bring progress while, in fact, it has given rise to more suffering and the endangerment of non-human life. Critiques of humanism include a range of philosophical orientations — from Alexandre Kojève's atheist, negative anthropology and Jean-Paul Sartre's (anti-humanist) "existentalist humanism" to Theodor W. Adorno's "negative dialectics," Michel Foucault's anti-humanism, Emmanuel Levinas's posthumanism, and Tzvetan Todorov's "critical humanism."[14]

The contested nature of "humanism" is part of the history of this idea and ideal, and it is pertinent to both its past and its contemporary articulations. Even more, as the contemporary humanisms of Edward Said and William Schweiker suggest, the critical history of "humanism" is also a constitutive element of its revivals. In this essay, I consider the notion and practice of "humanism" as developed in the works of the religious ethicist William Schweiker and the literary critic Edward Said. These two thinkers are pertinent to our discussion because they both acknowledge the relevance of the anti-humanist critiques and understand the problematic historical implications of radical humanisms. But while acknowledging

---

13. Soper, *Humanism and Anti-Humanism,* p. 11.

14. On critiques of humanism and for affirmations of critical humanisms, see, among others, Soper, *Humanism and Anti-Humanism;* Stefanos Geroulanos, *An Atheism That Is Not Humanist Emerges in French Thought* (Stanford, Calif.: Stanford University Press, 2010); Tzvetan Todorov, *Imperfect Garden: The Legacy of Humanism* (Princeton, N.J.: Princeton University Press, 2002); Jean-Paul Sartre, "Existentialism and Humanism," in *Basic Writings,* ed. Stephen Priest (New York: Routledge, 2001).

the value of the anti-humanist critiques, Schweiker and Said also counter them: they propose robust religious and secular humanistic visions that do not lose sight of the need for human restraint and self-critique in the pursuit of good societies and a more just world.

William Schweiker's Theological Humanism

In keeping with the humanist traditions that have always understood human freedom "as historically, socially, and culturally situated,"[15] Schweiker starts his humanistic project by asking a question that he sees as defining of our moment: how are we rightly to "value and properly esteem human beings . . . against the backdrop of the massive extension of human power"?[16]

One answer to this question, Schweiker writes, was the anti-humanist critique.[17] The twentieth-century anti-humanist thinkers particularly responded to the Enlightenment conception of radical freedom and the ways in which it contributed to what Schweiker calls the "over-humanization of the world" — the reduction of all life solely to instrumental purposes and "the enfolding, enframing, and encoding of all existing within the kingdom of human power."[18] Yet, Schweiker explains, when the post-structuralists declared the "end of man" or when Peter Singer argued for the unsanctification of human life,[19] they did not just dismiss humanism as false and negate the distinctive dignity of human beings.[20] In an attempt to set "human life within a wider, non-human context,"[21] anti-humanists also showed their moral passion.

The neo-humanist thinkers accepted the anti-humanist rejection of a radical, unencumbered human freedom, but they opposed demands for the dismissal of humanism. Instead, they revisited the classical humanistic

15. William Schweiker, "Theological Ethics and the Question of Humanism," *The Journal of Religion* 83, no. 4 (October 2003): 539-61, at 547.

16. Schweiker, "Theological Ethics," p. 541.

17. On the long lineage of anti-humanist ideas — from the Stoics and Spinoza to Schopenhauer and Singer, see Klemm and Schweiker, *Religion and the Human Future,* pp. 27-29.

18. Schweiker, "Theological Ethics," p. 549.

19. Schweiker, "Theological Ethics," p. 540.

20. William Schweiker, *Dust That Breathes: Christian Faith and the New Humanisms* (Oxford: Wiley-Blackwell, 2010), p. 214.

21. Klemm and Schweiker, *Religion and the Human Future,* p. 24.

"focus on self-realization and cultivation" and moved toward "a principled concern for the other."[22] For Schweiker, neo-humanist thinkers such as Tzvetan Todorov, Emmanuel Levinas, and Paul Ricoeur made a great contribution to contemporary ethics when they proposed that the "I" is not the origin but an end to be reached in relation to others — the "I," in the words of Tony Davies, is "less a given set of intrinsic qualities than the goal of an epochal and never-to-be completed process."[23] For Todorov and Levinas, on Schweiker's reading, autonomy does remain important. But these two thinkers always emphasize the self as situated "with respect to the moral claim of the other," and their concern is with the well-being of each human being as the goal to be achieved on this Earth.[24]

Schweiker wants to develop his vision of theological humanism by learning from and by moving beyond the insights of both anti-humanisms and inner-worldly neo-humanisms. He affirms the anti-humanist idea of the over-humanization of the world, but argues that the main problem with most anti-humanist thinkers is their hope that "transhuman realities devoid of moral purpose or meaning" will somehow and nevertheless save us.[25] As Schweiker suggests, what we need today is not a criticism of humanism but "a renewed account of the unique responsibility of the human being for life on earth."[26]

Similarly, Schweiker maintains that the neo-humanist focus on the other opened the realm of value in important ways — it made this realm more extensive and intensive. But the neo-humanist perspective, Schweiker argues, is limited: a lateral transcendence emerges as inadequate for rethinking the place of freedom in the world and ultimately risks the reduction of value to intra-human purposes.[27] Responding to both anti-humanists and neo-humanists, Schweiker writes that we live in a moment when both

22. Klemm and Schweiker, *Religion and the Human Future*, p. 24.

23. Tony Davies as quoted in Schweiker, *Dust That Breathes*, p. 214.

24. This orientation of the neo-humanist thinkers, Schweiker underlines, is called lateral or inner-worldly transcendence. "There, too, there are differences among neo-humanists important for theological humanism. Levinas . . . finds a trace of the divine in the encounter with the face of the other; Todorov denies the reality of the divine and insists on intrahuman goods and these goods alone"; see Klemm and Schweiker, *Religion and the Human Future*, p. 36. For the Christian personalist account of the inherent relationality of the "I," see Jacques Maritain, *Integral Humanism, Freedom in the World, and A Letter on Independence*, rev. ed. (Notre Dame, Ind.: University of Notre Dame Press, 1996).

25. Schweiker, "Theological Ethics," p. 545.

26. Schweiker, "Theological Ethics," p. 553.

27. Schweiker, "Theological Ethics," p. 554.

human and nonhuman life are vulnerable to human power. This development has two major implications: first, it means that human responsibility is not removed but it is even increased, and second, it demands that the goal of human life includes but also "exceeds the human kingdom."[28]

In acknowledging but also moving away from the insights of anti-humanists and neo-humanists, one of Schweiker's objectives is to raise the question about the place and value of humanism *within* theology and religion. By insisting on being both "theological" and "humanist," Schweiker hopes to "change the terms of the debate . . . about freedom within religion,"[29] thus addressing what he sees as a standing problem for many contemporary religious traditions. Many world religions, he suggests, are guilty of "hyper-theism" — the idea that one community can alone know and "speak of the mystery, power, and truth of the divine."[30] The outcome of this process is often a denial of human freedom and even the introduction of types of authoritarianism.

Schweiker rejects the extremes of over-humanization and hyper-theism alike; both are, to him, forms of overreach. He underlines that the project of over-humanization "has brought advances in knowledge, the lessening of disease and want, and the formation of a freer world," but notes that over-humanization has also "led to the profaning of life through wars, ecological endangerment, and cultural banality."[31] If over-humanization is the inner distortion of humanism (to claim and want to go beyond human power), hyper-theization is the inner distortion of religions (to claim to know the will and mystery of God).

Theological humanism, then, has several points of departure. Moving away from hyper-theism, it emphasizes the human freedom and responsibility within religions. In doing this, theological humanism is deeply religious in its orientation yet is not the same as religious humanisms. Unlike the religious humanisms we find in Judaism, Christianity, Islam, Buddhism, and Confucianism, Schweiker's theological humanism is not developed within the confines of only one specific religious tradition. Everyone's initial humanistic theological orientations and sensibilities, Schweiker is aware, are shaped by a certain religious community.

28. Schweiker, *Dust That Breathes*, p. 203.
29. Schweiker, "of course, also endorse[s] the freedom of religion — the idea that everyone should have the right to practice openly and without coercion her or his religion"; see Klemm and Schweiker, *Religion and the Human Future*, p. 3.
30. Klemm and Schweiker, *Religion and the Human Future*, p. 15.
31. Klemm and Schweiker, *Religion and the Human Future*, p. 14.

Schweiker's own humanistic impulse comes from within Christianity: he engages and builds on the ideas of Christian humanists — among others, John de Gruchy.[32] But for Schweiker, Christian and other religious humanists who think within the constraints of organized religions tend to overvalue their own tradition and undervalue others. The theological humanist, on the other hand, even when fully embedded and living "through a religious tradition,"[33] wants to value important efforts outside that tradition and work to maintain the ability to be critical of her own community, its beliefs and commitments. In the context of Schweiker's larger view of Christian ethics, the emphasis on the critical element of theological humanism is not surprising. Christian ethics, for Schweiker, is not just a constructive endeavor, it is also a "critical . . . reflection on moral existence,"[34] and one's own religious community is part of that existence.

Schweiker's theological humanism, then, is both a contemporary articulation of religious humanism and a critical response to religious humanisms. One of the main goals of a theological humanist is to reconcile an understanding that "almost everyone has religious longings" that need to be interpreted with the idea that "radical transcendence does not and cannot detract from the pressing inner-worldly challenges people . . . face."[35] Every theological humanist is immersed in a hermeneutical act: she needs to interpret the ways in which transcendence has "the positive, substantive, and normative meaning" in people's lives "within historical existence."[36] The norm and ideal to do this work of interpretation is the imperative of responsibility at the center of theological humanistic enterprise — the idea that, "in all actions and relations," one is to "respect and enhance the integrity of life before God."[37]

For Schweiker, the ordering of these values and actions is the key element of theological humanism. To *respect* means to acknowledge "the worth and dignity of others" (thus to reject over-humanization and affirm the insights of anti-humanisms and neo-humanisms); to *enhance* is to "build up the lives of others" and "work to end suffering and injus-

---

32. See Schweiker, *Dust That Breathes,* pp. 207-21.

33. Klemm and Schweiker, *Religion and the Human Future,* p. 20.

34. William Schweiker, *Responsibility and Christian Ethics* (Cambridge: Cambridge University Press, 1999), p. 5.

35. Schweiker, *Responsibility,* p. 37.

36. Schweiker, *Responsibility,* p. 40; Klemm and Schweiker, *Religion and the Human Future,* p. 40.

37. Klemm and Schweiker, *Religion and the Human Future,* p. 82.

tice"[38] (thus to move beyond the problems of hyper-theism); to respect and enhance *the integrity of life* means to affirm the wholeness of life — "the proper integration . . . of the basic, social, natural, and reflective goods of life."[39] The imperative of responsibility — the drive to respect and enhance the integrity of life *before God* — attempts to situate the idea of human flourishing within the larger, more extensive moral vision of life than is the case with any other type of humanism.

In his writings on theological humanism, Schweiker asks: can we "learn to inhabit religious and non-religious visions of life in ways that sustain a humane future"?[40] Schweiker's work is a giant step in that direction: it refuses to posit religion-theology and humanism as mutually exclusive or irreconcilable, and it affirms the life orientation as a sign of true freedom in religion. Schweiker also recognizes that one of the greatest challenges of this world is not only what is happening between *and* inside religions and theologies but also what is happening between religious and secular worldviews and institutions. He is one of the few scholars to point out that most religious and secular humanisms agree on important values — among others, the idea that "human beings possess intrinsic worth" and that every individual life possesses dignity, regardless of religion, race, or creed.[41] Yet, while appreciating the insights of lateral humanists, Schweiker does not think secular humanisms are able to provide the moral resources needed for our time. He tells us that some secular humanists are anti-religious, scientistic, or naturalistic in orientation;[42] he also suggests that the lateral transcendence characterizing neo-humanism is limited in its moral possibilities. There is much to admire in secular humanisms, Schweiker writes, from the commitment to solving "human problems in practical ways, to moral principles, to constitutional democracy . . . and to the maximization of human potential."[43] But the horizon of lateral transcendence for secular humanists remains immanent, which makes its moral potential vulnerable to succumbing to the dictates of solely human needs.

Schweiker is clear that, in the pursuit of flourishing in this world, his theological humanism also has to wrestle with "human foibles."[44] Yet al-

---

38. Klemm and Schweiker, *Religion and the Human Future,* p. 83.
39. Klemm and Schweiker, *Religion and the Human Future,* p. 88.
40. Klemm and Schweiker, *Religion and the Human Future,* p. 2.
41. Schweiker, *Dust That Breathes,* p. 214.
42. Klemm and Schweiker, *Religion and the Human Future,* p. 2.
43. Klemm and Schweiker, *Religion and the Human Future,* p. 157.
44. Schweiker, *Dust That Breathes,* p. 10.

though he is aware of the constraints of the human condition and of other humanists' shortcomings in trying to overcome the traps of the range of traditional humanisms, Schweiker appears rather confident that his theological humanism can sustain the tension between hopefulness and restraint — on its own. He wants to convince us that the difficult act of balancing a humanistic vision, intentions, and powers is possible on the basis of two features of his theological humanism. The first, as described above, is its imperative of responsibility. The second is its double orientation: its theological drive points human life "to conform to the will of God(s)"[45] and articulates "the claim of transcendence on human beings that reduces it neither to undecidability nor to 'my' community,"[46] while its humanistic impetus gives positive meaning to transcendence in historical existence and leads human beings to use "the creative exercises of power to shape [their] existence and seek flourishing."[47]

Edward Said's Secular Humanism

Said's affirmation of humanism may seem unusual.[48] His work draws greatly on the ideas of Michel Foucault, which reject Western humanism's "essentializing and totalizing modes" and (in Said's own words) bring about "a severe if not crippling defeat of what was considered traditional humanism."[49] But while the post-modern critique of humanism has always been vital for Said's thinking, his view of humanism was and remained dialectical, as he did not accept the ideological aspects of structuralist and post-structuralist anti-humanism.[50] Said is interested in discrediting "some of humanism's practitioners" but not in dismissing humanism;[51] he offers a

45. Klemm and Schweiker, *Religion and the Human Future*, p. 12.

46. Klemm and Schweiker, *Religion and the Human Future*, p. 40.

47. Klemm and Schweiker, *Religion and the Human Future*, p. 13.

48. In his review of Said's book *History and Theory*, and in his 1988 book *The Predicament of Culture*, James Clifford (Said reports) "laments 'the relapse into the essentializing modes it [Orientalism] attacks,' and . . . complains that [Said's] book is 'ambivalently enmeshed in the totalizing habits of Western humanism'" (Edward Said, *Humanism and Democratic Criticism* [New York: Columbia University Press, 2004], pp. 8-9).

49. Said, *Humanism and Democratic Criticism*, p. 9.

50. This anti-humanist thinking went against the very core of humanistic thought — the sovereignty of the subject — and saw individuals as having no power over systems, "only the choice either to use or be used by them" (Said, *Humanism and Democratic Criticism*, pp. 9-10).

51. Said, *Humanism and Democratic Criticism*, p. 13.

critique of humanism while identifying himself as a humanist.[52] In his view, the same humanistic ideals that can be and are abused are also the ones able to "supply most disadvantaged people with the energy to resist unjust war and military occupation [and] to try to overturn despotism and tyranny."[53]

Humanism and Democratic Criticism, Said's last book, carries the same conviction as his earlier work: it is possible to be critical of humanism in the name of humanism. Said argues that humanism is able to stay critical of itself if it is conceived in a very particular way — as embedded in the humanities *and* as constitutive of democratic practice. This means that, while born out of the humanities, humanism is neither a privileged work of the intellectual elites[54] nor a study of a fixed canon of texts. It is "open to all classes and backgrounds,"[55] it stands as an *ongoing practice* inseparable from democratic criticism[56] and participatory citizenship, and most importantly, it is constituted by three, mutually dependent, features: openendedness, secularity, and critique.

The open-endedness of humanism is a result of its historicity. At the very heart of humanism, Said writes, are the historical world made by men and women and historical knowledge created in an agential manner, not "passively, reactively, and dully."[57] Since the humanities and humanism are themselves part of history, they are (like history) "in need of revision, rethinking and revitalization," as a way to avoid becoming "instruments of veneration and repression."[58] For Said, then, the main characteristic of humanism is its historical location: humanism reflects that location as well as serves as a tool to critique it.

---

52. According to W. J. T. Mitchell, "Humanism for Said was always a dialectical concept, generating oppositions it could neither absorb nor avoid. The very word used to cause in him mixed feelings of reverence and revulsion: an admiration for the great monuments of civilization that constitute the archive of humanism and a disgust at humanism's underside of suffering and oppression that, as Benjamin insisted, made them monuments of barbarism as well" (quoted in Yumna Siddiqi, "Edward Said, Humanism, and Secular Criticism," *Alif: Journal of Comparative Poetics* 25 [2005]: 69).

53. Said, *Humanism and Democratic Criticism,* p. 10.

54. Said, *Humanism and Democratic Criticism,* p. 16.

55. Said, *Humanism and Democratic Criticism,* p. 21.

56. Said, *Humanism and Democratic Criticism,* pp. 19, 22.

57. Said, *Humanism and Democratic Criticism,* p. 11.

58. Said, *Humanism and Democratic Criticism,* p. 32. Said is opposed to "reductive and didactic humanism," which, he says, we find in the work typified by Allan Bloom, or the so-called New Humanists of the 1920s and 1930s, who develop the cult of "an almost sacralized past . . . and their prescriptions for a smaller elite not only of readers but of writers" (pp. 17, 19).

The historicity of humanism also shapes the core of its secular character. As "the achievement of form by human will," humanism comes into existence through the humanities and language.[59] This historicity, to Said, signifies the exclusion of religious imaginaries: we "can only know," he writes following Vico, "what we have made."[60] The task of the humanities is to be attentive to "the products of human labor" and "the human capacity for articulate expression"; the purpose of the humanities is to study human beings who exist *in* history.[61]

What is more, the secular character of humanism is inseparable from its character as critique — as "a continuous practice of questioning and of accumulating knowledge that is open to . . . the constituent historical realities."[62] Humanism is moreover at the same time a self-critique because it is "always restlessly self-clarifying in search of freedom, enlightenment, [and] more agency."[63] This, however, does not imply that the humanist's secular, open-ended, and democratic (self-) critique is an act of deconstruction.[64] As Yumna Siddiqi explains, Said thinks that "the aim of an analysis of power is not only to lay bare the pernicious implications of imperialist knowledge practices, but to imagine or, at least, gesture to the possibility of alternative discourses and practices."[65] The goal of secular humanism, Said says, is "a worldly practice"[66] that aims to

> excavate the silences, the world of memory, of itinerant, barely surviving groups, the places of exclusion and invisibility, the kind of testimony that doesn't make it onto the reports but which more and more is about whether an overexploited environment, sustainable small economies and small nations, and marginalized peoples outside as well as inside the maw of the metropolitan center can survive the grinding down and flattening out and displacement that are such prominent features of globalization.[67]

---

59. Said, *Humanism and Democratic Criticism,* p. 15. See also pp. 49 and 58 on the inseparability of history from the rise of the humanities as a science of reading.

60. Said, *Humanism and Democratic Criticism,* p. 90.

61. Said, *Humanism and Democratic Criticism,* p. 15.

62. Said, *Humanism and Democratic Criticism,* p. 47.

63. Said, *Humanism and Democratic Criticism,* p. 73.

64. Said, *Humanism and Democratic Criticism,* p. 70.

65. Siddiqi, "Edward Said," p. 76.

66. Said, *Humanism and Democratic Criticism,* p. 75.

67. Said, *Humanism and Democratic Criticism,* pp. 81-82.

Said's humanism is dedicated to people and things usually not mentioned and easily marginalized, and to fulfill its task such humanism brings together critique *and* secularity. For Said, the secularity of critique and, by extension, of humanism secures the commitment "to non-coercive knowledge [and] freedom"[68] and the insistence that emancipation is possible even as one remains skeptical about all such claims. Said posits secular criticism at the heart of humanism because he thinks that precisely by being secular criticism enables humanism to avoid self-sacralization: because it is "*of* the world and *in* the world," humanism can continuously seek to retrieve the voices of the minority.[69]

Said's vision of the necessity and viability of humanism in the world created by women and men is an affirmation of a hopeful democratic critique and action, but nonetheless a vision that carries a strongly tragic component. Humanism for Said is an ideal that needs always to stay open in order to keep its potentiality, yet precisely this openness gestures to the reasons why humanism must fail to meet its own ideals. Said draws his tragic sensibility from the humanistic truth revealed by Walter Benjamin — the notion "that every document of civilization is also a document of barbarism."[70] But Said's recognition of the tragic character built into the very foundations of the humanistic project also comes from his appreciation for Giambattista Vico. It is Vico, Said underlines for his readers, who never loses sight of the tragic shortcomings of human knowledge — the reality that this knowledge is "permanently undermined by the 'indefinite nature of the human mind,'" and the awareness that "there is always something radically incomplete, insufficient, provisional, disputable, and arguable about" that knowledge.[71]

Hopefulness and tragedy, then, define Said's vision of humanism. He knows that, just like history, our (humanistic) interpretation of it moves not only forward but backward as well.[72] Like Schweiker, Said is aware of the problems of Western humanistic traditions that are shaped not only by ideals of universalism but also by unrestrained optimism and rationality. At the same time, Said's humanism is not a chastened type of humanism. Said knows that human history is filled with suffering. He deconstructs the colonial character and impossibility of progress, recognizes the in-

68. Siddiqi, "Edward Said," p. 73.
69. Siddiqi, "Edward Said," p. 74; italics are mine.
70. Said, *Humanism and Democratic Criticism,* p. 23.
71. Said, *Humanism and Democratic Criticism,* p. 12.
72. Said, *Humanism and Democratic Criticism,* p. 102.

completeness of our (humanistic) knowledge, and registers the provisional nature of every given critique and self-critique. But Said also believes that the tragic aspect of human knowledge and human history is a flaw that can be remedied and mitigated. Quite simply, he believes in "the power of the human mind of investigating the human mind."[73] He is assured that the humanities provide a remedy for the tragic flaw of human knowledge through "disciplines of philological learning and philosophic understanding."[74]

As a result of this trust in the capacities of human mind, Said remains confident about the ability of human beings to expose, explain, and criticize "shameful secret injustice[s]," or "manifestly imperial plan[s] for domination."[75] Said's vision of humanism — of a democratic critique as an ongoing practice of citizenship — ultimately points to an individual and solitary endeavor in which the humanist holds out against traditions of all types, including the tradition in which she stands.

This romanticization of the humanistic project as an act of heroic individualism is directly linked to one of the most highlighted — and to us most pertinent — tropes of Said's work on humanism, and that is his assertion of humanism as an exclusively secular notion and practice. One of the most dangerous threats to the humanistic enterprise, Said tells us, comes from religious enthusiasm, which is "patently anti-secular and antidemocratic in nature" and, "in its monotheistic forms as a kind of politics," is "about as intolerantly inhuman and downright unarguable as can be."[76]

Although Said addresses a very specific expression of religion as an obstacle for humanistic endeavor — religious enthusiasm — his secular humanism is in fact situated in an opposition to religions in general. Humanism, he says, is not only secular due to its historicity; humanism is secular because it is about a critique, and critique must always be secular. Said, in other words, restricts his humanistic vision exclusively to the realm of the secular. In so doing, he dismisses not only the fact that theology and religious ethics are, to quote Schweiker, both constructive and critical endeavors; Said also neglects a long history of critique that comes from within religious traditions. As Robert Bellah (among others) argues, in most religious traditions we find classes of religious elites who offer powerful criticisms of their own communities and traditions — from the

---

73. Leo Spitzer, quoted in Said, *Humanism and Democratic Criticism*, p. 26.
74. Said, *Humanism and Democratic Criticism*, p. 12.
75. Said, *Humanism and Democratic Criticism*, p. 22.
76. Said, *Humanism and Democratic Criticism*, p. 51.

Brahmin class in late Vedic India, to Hebrew prophets, to Buddhist monks and figures such as Mencius in ancient China, to Socrates and Plato in ancient Greece. These "renouncers," as Bellah calls them, critique the worldly powers and reject the strictly defined social roles in societies in which it is not easy to "imagine the social space for criticism" and where "scribal and priestly classes . . . were too tied in to the existing power systems."[77]

Said's insistence on the secularity of critique jeopardizes the very humanistic endeavor he is after. As Saba Mahmood maintains, the answer to the question whether critique is secular should be neither "yes" nor "no" because that would "foreclose thought and . . . fail to engage a rich set of questions, answers to which remain unclear . . . because these questions require a comparative dialogue across the putative divide between 'Western' and 'non-Western' traditions of critique and practice"[78] — an endeavor to which Said himself was committed both intellectually and politically.

If, as Mahmood suggests from the perspective of critical theory, "one of the most cherished definitions of critique is the incessant subjection of all norms to unyielding critique";[79] if, furthermore, the main purpose of humanism as practice, in Said's own view, is to retrieve and keep alive *all* those who are marginalized and forgotten, how can "a major part of the humanistic vocation" be the preservation of its "fully rounded secular perspective" at the expense of religious voices?[80] Can humanism stay open to constant revisions and revitalization if its imagination and its intellectual capacity are enclosed within the confines of a secular perspective? Can the open-ended practice of humanism, to which Said calls us, be affirmed and sustained just on the basis of our awareness about the historical nature of the humanistic project and the limited character of human knowledge? Indeed, if we are to accept Said's call to think of humanism as "an unsettling adventure in difference, in alternative traditions, in texts that need a new

---

77. What characterized them all are visions or utopian ideals presenting "stark contrasts to the actual world," which "have motivated some of the noblest achievements of mankind" but also "some of the worst actions of human beings"; see Robert Bellah, "The Renouncers" (blogs.ssrc.org/tif/2008/08/11/the-renouncers/); and Bellah, *Religion in Human Evolution: From the Paleolithic to the Axial Age* (Cambridge, Mass.: Harvard University Press, 2011), p. 596.

78. Saba Mahmood, "Religious Reason and Secular Affect: An Incommensurable Divide?" in *Is Critique Secular? Blasphemy, Injury, and Free Speech,* ed. Talal Asad et al. (Berkeley: University of California Press, 2009), p. 91.

79. Saba Mahmood, "Is Critique Secular?" *The Immanent Frame,* blogs.ssrc.org/tif/2008/03/30/is-critique-secular-2/.

80. Said, *Humanism and Democratic Criticism,* p. 51.

deciphering within a much wider context than has hitherto been given them";[81] and if we are to sustain the awareness of humanism's inherently fragile character and the need to keep its open-ended perspective, then at least part of the answer is to imagine humanism as a democratic critique that, rather than limiting itself within the secular enterprise, accepts religious perspectives as equal partners in the pursuit of the humanistic project and a more just world.

2. Religious and Secular Humanisms Reconsidered

Both Schweiker and Said respond to critiques of Enlightenment (that is, exclusive) humanisms by acknowledging the problematic nature of their characteristic universalism, their radical optimism, their emphasis on instrumental reason, and the unintended consequences of their historical applications. Both Said and Schweiker, in other words, propose their humanistic visions while aware of the importance and fragility,[82] the achievements and the problems, of the drive to Reform. That awareness results in the articulation of humanistic projects that attempt to remain self-critical and, hence, self-restrained. Said proposes an understanding of secular humanism as an *ongoing practice,* as always *embedded* in *localities,* as focused on the retrieval of the voices of the marginalized and the oppressed. To be sure, his humanism remains fully immanent — it is both in and of this world. But Said's humanistic vision is not meant to order the world with a sacralized list of ideals; it is rather conceived of as a practice that never loses sight of the particularities of the human condition.

Schweiker defines theological humanism as actions and relations that emerge from the desire to *respect and enhance the integrity of life before God.* The order of its demands — respect and then enhance the fullness of life before God — is this ethicist's response to what he sees as the over-humanization and hyper-theization present in our time: the former defined by an exaggerated emphasis on human power, its purposes, and its triumphs, the latter marked either by overconfidence that one's faith is identical to the truth and mystery of the divine, or by a quiet acceptance of the status quo in the name of God's sovereignty in the world. Schweiker's humanism, by contrast, has built-in boundaries in both its ideals and its orientation.

81. Said, *Humanism and Democratic Criticism,* p. 55.
82. Taylor, *A Secular Age,* p. 28.

Said's and Schweiker's humanistic projects both critique and build on the ideals and projects of humanism that came before them. But their claims, like the humanistic claims made before them, remain particularistic — secular and religious — in nature, and assured in their own ability of self-critique. As such, they can nestle next to each other, perhaps even fragilize each other, but how are they to enrich each other?

In his response to Charles Taylor's ideas, the philosopher Richard Bernstein speaks of "robust non-exclusive humanisms."[83] The latter is a useful concept as it is placed in contrast to the idea of "exclusive humanisms." But can the emphasis on the robustness of a humanistic stance be reconciled with the imperative that contemporary humanisms, whether religious or secular, be self-restrained and chastened? For this to be possible, both religious and secular humanisms require external constraints — but not those that arise from mutual critique or conflict, or from the possibility that they might jostle or fragilize each other. The sort of external constraints I have in mind emerge from direct practical engagement between religious and secular worldviews in a manner contributing to their mutual enrichment. One case in which this happened was the Solidarity movement in communist Poland. Here, the complex but successful religious-secular humanistic alliance worked to transform the moral and political landscape of Polish society.

3. The Practice of Religious and Secular Humanisms: The Case of Solidarity

Demanding better wages, shorter working hours, and improved working conditions, Solidarity emerged in the summer of 1980 as the first independent trade union in the Soviet bloc. Within one year, Solidarity grew into a social movement of 10 million Poles of all ranks — workers, engineers, intelligentsia, clergy — who, in addition to pressing the workers' initial demands, protested food shortages, deteriorating healthcare, the privileged status of regime supporters, and violations of freedom of religion and freedom of speech.[84]

Solidarity *was* a revolution: the sixteen months of this movement

83. See Richard Bernstein, "The Uneasy Tensions of Immanence and Transcendence," *International Journal of Politics, Culture, and Society* 21 (December 2008): 11-16.

84. Timothy Garton Ash, *The Polish Revolution: Solidarity* (New Haven, Conn.: Yale University Press, 2002 [1983]), pp. 30, 37.

brought the social conflict in Polish society to its peak. But this was a revolution different from all other revolutions because it killed nobody. Challenging the very foundations of an oppressive communist regime, Solidarity insisted on peaceful and dignified resistance. It became associated not with violence but with hunger strikes; it came to be remembered for the ban on alcohol among Solidarity's members — this in a country in which, by 1980, "one million Poles were classified as alcoholics."[85] While Solidarity's nonviolent methods and pragmatic negotiating tactics were a result of political realism and a profound awareness of the prevailing power relations in the Soviet bloc, this was a revolution as political as it was moral — a civil protest against injustices of the radical secular state as well as a call for a moral transformation of the Polish nation.

It has often been emphasized that the moral aspect of Solidarity was inspired by religious faith. Solidarity was, indeed, deeply embedded in Catholic practices and symbolism: pictures of the pope were on the walls of the Solidarity halls, while the Gdańsk workers waited on their knees during lunch breaks to have their confessions heard and to receive Holy Communion.[86] But as immersed as Solidarity was in Catholic traditions, its moral implications, especially its emphasis on limits and restraint — hence the term "self-limiting revolution"[87] — cannot be understood without appreciating the revolutionary character of the secular-religious humanistic collaboration it created. This "confluence of the secular and the religious,"[88] this "tacit alliance"[89] of believing and nonbelieving Poles, was as important as it was surprising: if anything defined the history of the relations between secular and Catholic Poles, it was the lack of trust and mutual critique. It was *not* surprising that the collaborations between the religious and secular forces were not natural or easy; nonetheless, they happened, through (to paraphrase the title of one book)[90] both dialogue and quarrel — an important point to which I will turn again below.

85. Garton Ash, *Polish Revolution*, p. 124; p. 30.

86. Garton Ash, *Polish Revolution*, p. 30.

87. The notion of "self-limiting revolution" was coined by sociologist Jadwiga Staniszkis in her book *Poland's Self-Limiting Revolution* (Princeton, N.J.: Princeton University Press, 1984). On this topic, see also Garton Ash, *Polish Revolution*, pp. 93, 202.

88. David Ost, "Introduction," in Adam Michnik, *The Church and the Left* (Chicago: University of Chicago Press, 1993), p. 1.

89. Garton Ash, *Polish Revolution*, p. 27.

90. See Józef Tischner, *Marxism and Christianity: The Quarrel and the Dialogue in Poland* (Washington, D.C.: Georgetown University Press, 1987).

One impetus for the religious-secular rapprochement was certainly the drama of the Polish historical moment. The times of communist rule "did not tolerate neutral people," so that the religious-secular collaborations in the context of Solidarity did not involve experts but rather the whole nation.[91] At the same time, several developments prior to Solidarity opened the door for the possibility of religious-secular dialogue. As "one of the main centers of reflection on fundamental issues in Marxism, especially after Stalin's death in 1953," Poland was a society in which the secular Left offered some of the most serious challenges to Marxist dogmas imposed by the regime.[92] The philosopher Leszek Kolakowski is a case in point: he moved from militant atheism toward the critique of the communist regime, and ultimately toward the affirmation of Marxist humanism.[93] In 1964, Jacek Kuroń, a founder of the Workers' Defense Committee (KOR) that preceded Solidarity, co-authored with the historian Karol Modzelewski an "Open Letter to the Party" in which they attacked the communist regime and due to which they were sent to prison. Kolakowski, Kuroń, Modzelewski — they all point to secularism not just as a political ideology but as the source of a humanistic moral stance that can be used to critique and reject the official secular (Marxist) worldview, its politics, and above all its institutions.

The importance of these intellectual and political developments among the Polish secular Left cannot be overstated. Together with the existence of liberal Catholic circles, the articulation of secular leftist humanisms made it possible for the columns of the Catholic personalist Karol Wojtyla and the Marxist humanist Leszek Kolakowski to appear on the pages of the same Catholic magazine, *Tygodnik Powszechny*. Such developments were also the background for the ideas of the younger generation of the Polish secular Left, one of whom was Adam Michnik — the son of Marxist parents, a secular liberal activist, a student of both Kolakowski and Kuroń, and a political prisoner of the communist regime.

The ideas and proposals he presented in his book *The Church and the Left*, published in Paris in 1977, stemmed from Michnik's realization that the concepts and strategies used to explore the relations between the Left and the Church in Poland had to be revisited and revised.[94] Michnik

91. The dialogue in Poland was not a dialogue of experts, wrote Tischner, but "a dialogue of an entire nation" (Tischner, *Marxism and Christianity*, p. xvii).

92. Helena Czosnyka, *The Polish Challenge: Foundations for Dialogue in the Works of Adam Schaff and Józef Tischner* (Atlanta: Scholars, 1995), p. x.

93. Garton Ash, *Polish Revolution*, p. 23.

94. Ost, "Introduction," p. 4.

was convinced that the Left and the Catholic Church in Poland could win against the communist regime only if they worked together. He also argued that the Church had to be made an ally in order to bring it out of an isolation that made it appear to be opposed to modernity. Notwithstanding the pragmatic foundations of Michnik's call for dialogue, its most striking features were his critique of the Left and his praise of the Polish Catholic Church and Christianity.

Michnik condemned the anticlericalism of the Left, especially its understanding that religious beliefs and the Catholic Church are "but synonyms for reaction and dim-witted obscurantism."[95] In Michnik's view, such anticlericalism was ahistorical. Instead of a conservative, nationalistic, all-powerful institution, he wrote, the Polish Catholic Church became the only public institution that stood "stubbornly on the side of the persecuted and the oppressed,"[96] and spoke bravely on behalf of the freedom and rights of every human being. Michnik admired the moral force of Christianity, and especially its emphasis on injunctions and limits: he saw the Christian notion of limitations as "serving a noble political purpose"[97] and endorsed it when speaking about the limits of human knowledge.[98]

In the name of humanistic ideals — freedom of conscience and the dignity of each individual — Michnik thus demanded two things from the secular Left and from himself: a self-critique and a respect toward the religious others, the latter because of the Church's capability of historical transformation but also because of what Michnik identifies as an inherent dignity of religious worldviews.

Michnik, in other words, believed that the secular Left and the Catholic Church should be unified not only because they had a common foe but also because they had a common moral goal — they shared a belief in the freedom of individual conscience, the importance of human dignity for de-

---

95. Adam Michnik, "What Is Dialogue?" in *The Church and the Left,* p. 181. See also Ost, "Introduction," p. 4.

96. Michnik, "What Is Dialogue?" p. 182.

97. Ost, "Introduction," pp. 14, 25.

98. Michnik thus argued that the Left had not only to reject the obtuse, primitive, and harsh atheism of communist states; "our search," he wrote, "must go deeper. It must touch the very roots of that oh-so-haughty conviction that it is we . . . who really do know the true path of progress and reason. The truth, of course, is that we do not know this path. Neither we nor anyone else in this world knows the road along which history will travel. . . . [So] let us respect those who believe that a supernatural world has been revealed to them. Let us judge them by their deeds, not by words that are twisted and distorted by others" ("Mutual Suspicions," in *The Church and the Left,* p. 128).

mocracy, and the need for a moral renewal of Poland. Michnik's reading of the Catholic Church was correct. The language of human rights, especially the ideals of the dignity of every human person and the inherent value of work, was the language that the Poles could hear in the homilies of the Polish Cardinal Wyszyński.[99] With the election of the Polish pope, whose theology was powerfully shaped by Christian personalism, the Catholic Church as a whole increasingly spoke of the need to protect the "human rights of all Poles, believers and nonbelievers" alike.[100]

Some of the most influential considerations of humanistic ideals were those of Father Józef Tischner, a Catholic priest, a philosopher, a chaplain of Solidarity, and a good friend of Pope John Paul II.[101] Tischner's views on dignity, freedom, and solidarity — published in the pages of *Tygodnik Powszechny* and later in a volume entitled *The Ethics of Solidarity*[102] — greatly influenced conversations among Solidarity members as well as the homilies offered from the pulpits of Polish churches. A disciple of Roman Ingarden, Tischner pursued a line of thought that located him in the phenomenological personalist tradition. But while philosophically driven, Tischner's reflections on the necessity of the freedom of individuals; his defense of the human rights "to sensible work," "to assemble," and to hope;[103] and his thinking about human solidarity as a source of human dignity[104] — all these ideas also reflected his strong belief that the highest (humanistic) principles could "be saturated with a concrete content" and could gain in substance when placed within the context of the historical experience of the Polish people.[105]

Tischner's humanistic views were theologically embedded. He saw the

99. On these aspects of Polish Catholicism during the communist period, see, for example, Barbara Strassberg, "Changes in Religious Culture in Post War II Poland," *Sociological Analysis* 48, no. 4 (Winter 1988): 342-54.

100. Garton Ash, *Polish Revolution,* p. 23.

101. As one obituary states, Tischner was such a close friend of John Paul II that he was among the very few people who "could get away with telling the Pope a slightly risqué joke"; see *The Times* (London), July 4, 2000.

102. The series of these texts was initiated with Tischner's October 1980 homily at the Wawel Castle in Kraków; see "Solidarity," *Thinking in Values: The Tischner Institute Journal of Philosophy* 1 (2007): 7. Tischner's texts were then collected and published as *Etyka solidarnosci* (Kraków: Znak, 1981), and later in English as *The Spirit of Solidarity,* trans. Marek B. Zaleski and Benjamin Fiore (San Francisco: Harper & Row, 1982).

103. Tischner, *The Spirit of Solidarity,* p. 88.

104. Tischner, *The Spirit of Solidarity,* p. 43.

105. See "Solidarity," p. 8.

source of the dignity of each person in her being created in the image of God, and he intrinsically linked human action in the world to the person's relation to God. For Tischner, *caritas,* expressed as "love of our neighbors and the world," was inseparable from our "absolute love for God."[106] Nonetheless, his experience — his thinking and living of Christianity — founded the need to affirm "social love" so that we could reduce suffering in *this* world.[107] There is, in other words, a very real and irreducible difference between Tischner's Christian personalism and Michnik's secular humanism, especially in terms of the sources they employ to justify their respective approaches to human dignity and freedom. Unlike Michnik, furthermore, Tischner was clear that the ultimate authority for Christians lies beyond the here and now. Christianity, he wrote, "teaches that a human being should believe in God and . . . above all strive for eternal salvation."[108]

This movement toward the transcendent, however, did not imply a disregard for the here and now. "Let us remember," Tischner reminded the Poles, that "during prayer a human being faces not only God but also another human being."[109] Tischner's humanism shared at least three important aspects with Michnik's secular humanism. First, they were both concerned with the possibilities and conditions of human flourishing here and now. To paraphrase Tischner, both religious and secular humanists were focused on how to bring happiness to humankind. Second, their focus was not on the self and one's own rights, but on the other: Michnik emphasized the rights of believers and Tischner wrote that, in solidarity, we were called to carry the burden of another person. Last but not least, both Tischner and Michnik were preoccupied with the true meaning of dialogue. At its heart, Tischner believed, dialogue was "not . . . a question of compassion but of . . . the recognition that someone else, from his point of view, is always to some extent right."[110] Michnik thought similarly: dialogue was for him a "readiness to understand the validity of someone else's position" and "a method by which an ideologically diverse society can learn to live together."[111]

106. See Maria Bielawka, "Camus and Tischner: In Search of Absolute Love," in *Phenomenology and Existentialism in the Twentieth Century,* Book 2, *Analecta Husserliana,* col. 104, ed. Anna-Teresa Tymieniecka (New York: Springer, 2009), p. 153.

107. Bielawka, "Camus and Tischner," p. 157.

108. Tischner, *Marxism and Christianity,* p. xv.

109. Tischner, *The Spirit of Solidarity,* p. 104.

110. Tischner, *The Spirit of Solidarity,* p. 11.

111. See Ost, "Introduction," pp. 4-5; Michnik here follows Tadeusz Mazowiecki.

Under the banner of Solidarity, the humanistic ideas of thinkers such as Tischner and Michnik inspired the movement's openness to a pluralism of worldviews and became a powerful tool in the struggle against the oppression of the communist state, with its collectivistic denial of freedom of conscience and of the importance of work for the dignity of each human person. But none of this meant the religious-secular alliance was a natural and easy endeavor. If Michnik and Tischner wrote passionately about the dialogue with the other, many members of the church hierarchy and clergy continued to be suspicious of the secular Left. The reception of Michnik's ideas was particularly indicative of that suspicion. Some Catholic thinkers accused him of condescension, and did not welcome his point about the good and bad church.[112] Even Father Tischner, while clearly seeing the difference between Michnik's secular humanism and the intolerant atheism of the Polish communists, remarked upon reading Michnik's views about changes in Polish Catholicism: "What is left for me if I do not support the ideals of the Left? Nothing but 'chauvinism, national oppression, obscurantism, lawlessness' and similar atrocities."[113]

The secular Left also had its fears. After 1976, the Left "did make its leap of faith and embraced the Church. . . . Its excited pride in the Polish pope, its unswerving support for workers marching behind religious symbols in 1980, its praise for the episcopate and willingness, even eagerness, to see the Church regain a prominent public presence all testify to the intelligentsia's readiness to disown its anti-clerical past."[114] Still, the secular Left had doubts regarding how truly democratic the Catholic Church could be. Michnik himself, while affirming the rights of Catholics and praising the Catholic Church for its courage, showed his uncertainty about the future of Catholicism. In an essay entitled "Mutual Suspicions," Michnik wrote that "the Roman Catholic Church will have to decide whether, in this world, its mission is to defend the Church or to defend the human beings. Does the Church genuinely seek freedom for every human being . . . or does it only seek 'freedom for itself'?"[115]

The circumstances and reactions of the representatives of the Catholic Church and the secular Left to each other confirm how difficult it is to build bridges among those who have a history of ideological and historical

112. Ost, "Introduction," p. 10.
113. See Tischner, *Marxism and Christianity,* p. 153.
114. Ost, "Introduction," p. 18.
115. Michnik, "Mutual Suspicions," p. 127.

opposition. But the Polish case of Solidarity also suggests that humanism — hopefulness and realism about the abilities to create the conditions of human flourishing here and now — was an ethical norm and a moral platform of the movement, whether it was articulated in religious or secular terms. The case of Solidarity shows that for the practice of religious and secular humanisms to be successful in inciting social change, humanists need to be prepared not only for self-critique but also for seeing the possibility of truth in the other.

4. Religious and Secular Humanisms: Beyond Theory

The snapshot I have presented of the emergence of Solidarity — its political context and its intellectual contents — reflects a differentiated map of humanism. Father Tischner and Michnik, I argued, shared a humanistic orientation: they focused on the conditions of human flourishing while remaining attentive to the constraints of the human condition; they looked toward common ideals and hopes while never losing sight of the divergent sources of those ideals. However, while these two humanists were positioned in different ontological frameworks, each also defined humanism and questions of human flourishing and the good society through the prism of the immediate Polish context, in which the most pressing questions were the ones of socio-economic justice, religious freedom, and democracy.

The movement of Solidarity offered a particularly Aristotelian model of practice. As Richard Bernstein pointed out several decades ago, the goal of practice according to Aristotle is not a well-defined theoretical knowledge, but a distinctive type of activity whose purpose is to get closer to the full ideal of free human activity. Precisely this latter humanistic goal — the drive to embody freedom and agency — characterized the work of Solidarity. But, although guided by very concrete objectives, and although motivated in part by a call for national rebuilding, the members of Solidarity were never inspired by a singular ideal. They encompassed a plurality of views, religious and secular, which gave rise to chastened humanisms that succumbed to neither relativism nor absolutism in their common vision and pursuit of a more just society.

In order to understand the moral and political potential that the mutual engagement of religious and secular humanisms can have for our time, it is important not just to consider their intellectual content but also to explore the practice of these humanisms.[116] Solidarity stands as a rich referent for such an endeavor, but there are other social movements where religious-secular alliances also made the difference: the labor movements in the early-twentieth-century United States, the civil rights movement, and the anti-apartheid movement in South Africa, to name a few. All these cases may offer insights into the sort of concrete experiences and normative commitments needed to speak about religions and secularisms as equal and as equally needed for democratic communities. They may also provide us with the vocabulary and the tools needed to address the burgeoning plurality of religious and secular outlooks in a democratic way. The complex practices through which religious and secular humanisms interact in the contemporary landscape of social movements might help us understand how it is possible to envision and work toward good societies despite the knowledge that in our fragmented, heterogeneous world that project can never be completed, only advanced.

116. As Jeffrey Stout writes, much of the work on the problem of religious-secular encounters has been "about intellectuals [and] not about the societies on which those intellectuals were reflecting" ("The Folly of Secularism," *The Good Society* 19, no. 2 [2010]: 10-15, at 14).

12. Religions in a Globalizing World

J. PAUL MARTIN

The emerging ideas of post-secularism with respect to religion and public life in the domestic forum also call for a search for a new *tertium quid,* that is, for new "rules of the road" to govern the place of religions in international affairs. This chapter argues that this is best achieved by treating religions on the same terms as other institutions of civil society, with the state defined as neutral but engaged — rather than simply separate, as called for in a secularist model.[1] This position is based on the recognition that there are no longer cogent reasons either to provide special rights to religious beliefs and practices, or to exclude them from the public forum. Recent events have brought about major changes in the global order that now compel states to pay attention to, and to work with, religions.[2] Thus

1. This chapter examines the specifically U.S.-based traditions and practices of secularism and the separation of religion and the state. In doing so, it accepts as a premise the distinction between secularism and secularization, the former being defined as a political and legal normative construct and the latter as an account of empirically based changes associated with a diminished presence of religion in a given society. In the U.S. tradition, secularism is a political and legal normative construct that has deep constitutional roots and a rich history of jurisprudence and political debate. Moreover, as an established normative framework in the domestic affairs of a major world power, these traditions have also been influential in the formation of international jurisprudence and human rights practice across the world.

2. See Douglas Johnston and Cynthia Sampson, eds., *Religion: The Missing Dimension of Statecraft* (Oxford: Oxford University Press, 1994). The rehabilitation of religion goes back to Peter Berger, *A Rumor of Angels: Modern Society and the Rediscovery of the Supernatural* (New York: Doubleday, 1969). More recently, see Peter Berger, ed., *The Desecularization of the World* (Washington, D.C.: The Ethics and Public Policy Center, 1999); Gilles Kepel,

the question is no longer whether to pay attention to religion or not, but how best the state and religion can engage each other in the future. Linked to this perspective is the principle that all religions should enjoy the same rights, privileges, and obligations in the public arena as other civil society actors: no more, no less. This essay examines some of the issues that have led the resurgence of religion on the international agenda, arguing that secular models hinging on the separation of religion and the state are no longer adequate to guide international affairs. It concludes with a brief analysis of what this reshuffling means from a Catholic perspective. A coda will show how the growing interreligious violence in Nigeria illustrates the urgency of the need to integrate religion into the public arena as a legitimate stakeholder. As this case shows, the international community (and perhaps also Catholic thinking) appears to be as unprepared today to prevent and contain communal violence with strong religious overtones as it was at the time of Srebrenica in 1993 and Gujarat in 2002.[3]

1. Religion and the New Globalized World

The visibility of religion in world affairs has increased substantially during the last fifty years.[4] The current religion-state tensions that are potential, if not actual, causes for concern on the part of the international community are of four types: (1) those that arise from the ways in which a state imposes rules and requirements on religious persons and institutions that

---

The Revenge of God: The Resurgence of Islam, Christianity and Judaism in the Modern World (Cambridge: Polity, 2004); and Pippa Norris and Ronald Inglehart, *Sacred and Secular: Religion and Politics Worldwide* (Cambridge: Cambridge University Press, 2004). For an academic point of view on religion in international affairs, see Jack Snyder, ed., *Religion and International Relations Theory* (New York: Columbia University Press, 2011).

3. A convenient and regularly updated source of information on religious freedom can always be found in the latest annual report of the U.S. Department of State. See http://www.state.gov/j/drl/rls/irf/. Annual reports are also prepared by the semi-independent U.S. Commission on International Religious Freedom, to be found at http://www.uscirf.gov/reports-and-briefs/annual-report.html. Less frequent reports are published by Human Rights Watch, Amnesty International, and Freedom House, as well as by smaller nongovernmental organizations such as Human Rights Without Frontiers International, Open Doors, and the Barnabas Fund.

4. See Brian J. Grimm and Roger Finke, *The Price of Freedom Denied: Religious Persecution and Conflict in the Twenty-First Century* (Cambridge: Cambridge University Press, 2010).

conflict with their religious beliefs and practices, such as restrictions on Christian worship in Saudi Arabia; (2) those that arise when individual religious institutions seek to impose their beliefs, institutions, and practices on persons and institutions that do not hold or subscribe to those beliefs and practices, such as until recently the influence of Catholic doctrine in civil law in Ireland; (3) those that arise from the ways in which states or other social actors co-opt religion for political goals, such as fascism in Italy and Spain; and (4) those that arise from conflicts among religious groups, such as in the case of the communal riots in Gujarat and Nigeria.[5] While most such state-religion conflicts are primarily internal or domestic, on account of general human rights practices and the particular interests of other state actors, they are also liable to become questions of international concern, if not also of international security.

The range of current problems and human rights abuses within these four categories is extensive and the remedies are complex. The problems bear enumerating because they illustrate the many ways in which religious issues impinge on both domestic and international agendas. The current problems that fall in the first category include contested rules, policies, and practices that govern marriage, families, gender, military service, reproduction and health services, as well as other social services such as education and social welfare. The jurisdiction of religious courts, authorized or unofficial, as well as the permissibility of the imposition of some religious laws also fall into this category. Many states control religious expression, regulate the use of property owned by religious groups, and restrict the access of religious persons and institutions to public, political, and other common spaces and services.[6] Some governments also require religious groups to obtain permits simply to exist and even to hold worship services in private.[7] Education, whether it is provided by the government or a religious group, is another sensitive sector where teaching certain topics in

5. To some degree all of the above now fall within the reporting purview of the U.S. government mandated by the 1998 International Religious Freedom Act (IRFA) that is discussed below. On individual conflicts, see Ashutosh Varshney, *Ethnic Conflict and Civic Life: Hindus and Muslims in India* (New Haven, Conn.: Yale University Press, 2002), and Abimbola O. Adesoji, "Islamic Fundamentalism and the Response of the Nigerian State," *Africa Today* 57, no. 1 (Summer 2011): 99-119.

6. See Human Rights Watch, *China: State Control of Religion* (New York: Human Rights Watch, 1997).

7. The Norwegian group Forum 18 in Rodeløkka, Oslo, has collected extensive data. See http://www.forum18.org/index.php.

both the humanities and the physical sciences can conflict with religious beliefs, ethics, and practices espoused by students and their parents.[8] Government actions in all of the above sectors can result in discrimination on religious grounds and the denial of such human rights as freedom of speech, conscience, movement, and assembly. The severe restrictions faced by Baptists and Jehovah's Witnesses in Russia, and by some Christian, Muslim, and other religious groups in China, verge on persecution.[9]

Current problems that fall in the second category, encompassing impositions by religious authorities on nonmembers or on dissident members, include the religious use of common public spaces, lobbying for rules and laws that are sectarian, and certain sorts of activities designed to recruit new members. This general problem is aggravated in countries where religious laws and systems exist parallel to civil laws and where the former, rather than civil laws, govern the domestic and religious affairs of the members of their respective denominations. Also of concern are governments whose activities are controlled by individual religious groups or belief systems, especially those that generate discrimination and hostility toward groups not associated with the religion in question.[10] Laws against blasphemy and defamation of religion, especially those with draconian sentences attached, have created a special problem most recently at the UN, where certain formulations have been proposed as additions to the corpus of international law. Finally, in a world of rapidly changing norms, religiously defined and sanctioned views of gender roles and expectations have also given rise to tensions involving public authorities and individual religious traditions.[11]

No less important is the third category where, characteristically, the state or a non-state actor closely associates its agenda, its mission, and its authority with religious fidelity to the extent that noncompliance with

8. See Kent Greenawalt, *Does God Belong in Public Schools?* (Princeton, N.J.: Princeton University Press, 2004).

9. Human Rights Watch, *Creating Enemies of the State: Religious Persecution in Uzbekistan* (New York: Human Rights Watch, 2004).

10. In Russia members of the feminist punk band Pussy Riot received recently guilty verdicts for "hooliganism motivated by religious hatred." The young women were each sentenced to two years in jail for staging a nonviolent anti-Putin protest at Moscow's main cathedral. Like other countries, Russia uses laws designed to combat hate crimes — extremism, incitement, and hostility or hatred statutes — to prosecute artists, independent media, and LGBT and other civil society groups.

11. Issues range from the prohibition of women driving cars in Saudi Arabia to rape and other forms of violence in the Congo and India.

its policies on the part of citizens is construed as nonconformity to core religious beliefs. Indeed, in largely religious states most forms of social activism and state political agendas, both for and against the established authority, can be and are authenticated in religious terms and sanctioned accordingly. In practice, states often appeal to their citizens' religious traditions, loyalties, symbols, and practices to define a particular social agenda or to label those hostile to their goals as hostile to the religion. Such appeals to religious as well as to anti-religious loyalties easily lead to human rights abuses such as discrimination, hate speech, and scapegoating. In more secularized and religiously diverse societies, however, social mobilization is likely to be authenticated by appeals to more generally accepted norms such as humanitarianism, human rights, or international peace and security.

The fourth category raises a set of international security issues not addressed directly by the concept of religious freedom[12] or by the 1998 U.S. International Religious Freedom Act (IRFA), namely, contentious relations and violence among different religious groups within a single country, region, or community. These tensions are most obvious in countries where Muslims and Christians have not worked out peaceful relations, where the hostilities are also heightened by land and other economic and cultural conflicts, and where one or the other or both can appeal to other powerful domestic or international allies. In these cases the religious identity of the parties often becomes the defining feature of the conflict even if other factors such as access to water or land are also at the roots of the tension.

The United States made itself formally a major actor in the field of religion and international affairs with the passage of IRFA.[13] The act requires, for example, annual reports by the U.S. Department of State on most but not all of the above concerns in every country in the world.[14] In

12. Religious freedom is defined in article 18 of the Universal Declaration of Human Rights thus: "Everyone has the right to freedom of thought, conscience and religion; this right includes the freedom to change his religion or belief, and freedom, either alone or in community with others and in public and private, to manifest his religion or belief in teaching, practice, worship and observance."

13. Policies on international religious freedom are determined by the U.S. Department of State. Copious information on its implementation of the 1998 International Religious Freedom Act may be found at http://www.state.gov/j/drl/irf/.

14. A copy of the current report can be found at http://www.state.gov/j/drl/rls/irf/religiousfreedom/index.htm#wrapper.

fact, IRFA requires more than just reporting. When the violations reach a certain level, the State Department is required to take action and to follow a detailed series of increasingly stringent sanctions spelled out and required in the act. Even without there being a challenge to international security calling for action by the UN Security Council, religious affairs in every other country of the world are thus now a required concern in U.S. foreign affairs. This level of U.S. involvement goes far beyond the ideals of church-state separationism. No other state has enacted legislation that requires such systematic — not just crisis-related or otherwise occasional — attention to the global promotion and monitoring of religious freedom in other countries.

Since the times when current secularist models of religion-state relations were first developed during and following the Enlightenment, the de facto place of religion in the international public sphere has evolved considerably.[15] Prior to the Reformation, the power in most states in both Roman Catholic and Eastern Orthodox Europe was seen to be divided between the secular rulers and the religious authorities, following models that had evolved from the original fourth-century Constantinian model of the two powers. Religions were then the main and by far the most powerful non-state actors. The power of the religious sector in the West was significantly diluted by the religious pluralism that followed the divisions within Christianity caused by the Reformation. More recently the power has been further reduced by the growth of nonreligious civil society organizations taking up and expanding on many of the social roles once played by the churches. Migration patterns and secularization have increased pluralism and thus decreased the ability of an individual religion to challenge the state authorities. The growth of nonreligious civil society has been especially exponential over the last fifty years. Previously there had been the various trade and professional associations, labor unions, and a handful of humanitarian organizations, such as the Anti-Slavery Society and the International Red Cross. Today new domestic and international nongovernmental organizations come to life almost every day.[16] They range from large international entities such as the World Wildlife Fund, Amnesty International, and the International Rescue Committee to small rural women's and rural development groups now to be found in virtually every country in

15. Charles Taylor, *A Secular Age* (Cambridge, Mass.: Harvard University Press, 2007).
16. See Helmut K. Anheier, *Civil Society, Measurement, Evaluation, Policy* (Sterling, Va.: Earthscan, 2004).

the world. Equally illustrative of the evolution away from the bipolar world of church and state is the growth of the worldwide philanthropic sector of organizations with access to major independent sources of funding for their own humanitarian enterprises.

Assessing the varied and substantial impact of the civil society sector is beyond the scope of this chapter. It is also important to note, however, that not all such civil society organizations are benevolent, altruistic, or indeed truly nongovernmental. Some are funded and organized by governments for government purposes. Others are funded and organized by nongovernmental actors, but they seek to achieve their goals through illicit means, including through the use of terror and violence. The important impact of this expansion of civil society is the degree to which it has been an expansion into fields once dominated by religions and state organizations.[17] As a result, the historical, political, and economic power of the religious organization has been diluted in both the domestic and international arenas.

Religious organizations still play a substantial role and are still often more powerful and complex actors than many nonreligious groups within the civil society sector. The religious groups remain actors in their own right as well as major actors within certain individual sectors such as social and humanitarian services. They are also multifaceted actors that possess deep and powerful historical and cultural roots. Religions are a conglomeration of individuals and institutions whose beliefs, loyalties, and actions reflect powerful shared written and oral traditions, images, myths, histories, and alliances, all of which are also conditioned by regional and cultural idiosyncrasies. These elements combine in different ways and need to be understood in their individuality and not just as some generic homogeneous category, as if all religions functioned in the same way, with similar sets of values, and so on. Nevertheless, powerful though they are, they are now just some of many actors in modern civil society. As a result there are no remaining reasons why they should not play according to the same rules as the other actors in the non-state sector and be treated accordingly by the civil authorities. In fact, religious actors such as Catholic Relief Services and Jewish World Services already follow these rules; indeed, the support they receive from governments and intergovernmental agencies such as the United Nations High Commission for Refugees even challenges in practice conventional rhetoric about the separation of state and religion.

This recent and multifaceted growth of civil society in most countries

17. John Keane, *Global Civil Society* (Cambridge: Cambridge University Press, 2004).

in the world owes much to the simultaneous growth of the international human rights regime. The growth of the civil society sector, which for the purposes of this chapter includes religious organizations, was energized by the 1975 Helsinki Agreements between the West and the communist-dominated countries. Based on the understanding that the West would respect the boundaries and sovereignties established in Eastern Europe, provided that governments in the Eastern states respected human rights, the Agreements opened the door to the growth of organizations independent of their governments in many parts of the world outside the West. In Eastern Europe these organizations took the form of academic, professional, and worker organizations, human rights nongovernmental organizations, and groups dedicated to religious activities, both Catholic and Protestant — and, more slowly, Orthodox Christian in Russia and its satellites. Besides being a major factor in the fall of communism in Eastern Europe, this efflorescence inspired the growth of civil society in many other parts of the world.[18]

The major human rights treaties that were being developed simultaneously by the United Nations in the wake of the 1948 Universal Declaration of Human Rights were also crucial to the expansion of civil society in a number of ways.[19] The treaties and their associated institutions encouraged and protected the growth of new intergovernmental and nongovernmental international organizations.[20] Most important was the fact that the world's states were central to this process. It was the states that developed, approved, and eventually ratified the treaties, incorporating them into their national legal systems. It is now the states that are legally obligated, through often very detailed prescriptions and articles as well as monitoring systems, to promote human rights at home and abroad. These provisions protect the rights of their respective civil societies.

Nevertheless, there is no international treaty on religion or religious freedom. The body of the human rights treaties includes many individual

18. This was evident in the size and diversity of the nongovernmental organization presence at the 1993 UN Human Rights Conference in Vienna.

19. The contributions of different religious traditions are discussed in Irene Bloom et al., eds., *Religious Diversity and Human Rights* (New York: Columbia University Press, 1996), and John Witte Jr. and M. Christian Green, eds., *Religion and Human Rights: An Introduction* (New York: Oxford University Press, 2012).

20. For example, the intergovernmental Organization for Security and Cooperation in Europe (OSCE), and the various nongovernmental organization Helsinki Commissions that grew out of the 1975 Helsinki Accords.

clauses and provisions that in practice protect religious freedom and religious observances. Indeed, freedom of religion and belief is seen by the human rights regime as a basic human right that, unlike some other rights and freedoms, cannot be denied even during a state of emergency.[21] Religion is also included in the frequently repeated proscription of all forms of discrimination. The proscribed forms are listed typically as those based on race, color, sex, language, religion, political or other opinion, national or social origin, property, birth, or other status.[22] The implications and detailed application of the individual treaty articles are further developed in other documents and rulings such as the general comments of the Human Rights Committee, the statutory body responsible for the implementation of the International Covenant on Civil and Political Rights. The human rights regime has also contributed substantially to the process of globalization through its development of universal standards of social justice. Together these various provisions define legally binding norms to guide states in their dealing with the religions of their subjects. This now-extensive regime is the product of the last sixty years and creates a completely different normative and institutional context for religion in both domestic and international affairs.[23]

A new or evolving normative regime is one step. Its implementation in practice is another. One human activity that bedevils states and religions alike as well as world peace, and which is a major worldwide source of human rights abuses, is the use of violence. The reasons are complex. Access to the tools of violence is easy through the existing legal and illegal arms sales supported by big commercial sectors and governments all over the world. The control of the violence takes different forms and is an increasing problem for all of the world's states. Religions face a different problem with respect to violence. Their emphasis on social identity based on exclusive truths and loyalties is often seen to set up animosities toward other social groups that can erupt in violence. This characterization is, of course, at variance with the claims of most of the major religions themselves. Most claim that their doctrines and practices aim at quite the contrary end, namely, peace. In recent years the world has seen the leaders of extremely violent groups in Africa and the Middle East use religion to convince their

21. UN Covenant on Civil and Political Rights, #4.
22. UN Covenant on Civil and Political Rights, #2.1.
23. On this development, see Samuel Moyn, *The Last Utopia: Human Rights in History* (Cambridge, Mass.: Harvard University Press, 2011).

followers, especially the young, that if their religious motivation is powerful enough, it will protect them from the bullets they face, or they will die as martyrs with great rewards in the next life.[24] For their part, governments can and have turned to religion and other powerful motivation systems, such as nationalism and appeals to national security, in order to mobilize their citizens and justify the use of violence. The U.S. president, for example, may now use national security as grounds to authorize the arrest, incarceration, and even assassination of a U.S. citizen anywhere in the world without any process of law.[25] In other words, the causes and the use of violence are complex issues for both religion and states. Their respective abilities to rationalize or justify violence make states and religions different from most, although not all, other modern groups within civil society in that they both can appeal for and obtain the ultimate sacrifice on the part of their members, one on nationalistic grounds and the other on the grounds of the benefits to be accrued in the afterlife, as noted above. Whether one holds religions and states to be part of the problem or part of the solution with respect to violence, they are both real actors in international affairs and need to be at any table where they are de facto stakeholders. Traditional theories of secularism that prescribe a separation of religion and the state, by contrast, have persisted in ruling out the religions.

One specific context where both states and religions have a stake in reducing violence is in those states where the identities and interests of the subnational minorities coincide with religious loyalties. Such situations are aggravated when the contentious groups turn to violence to attain their goals and when logistical and other forms of support flow from, or at least through, other countries, financed by supporters who, given modern communication, can now be anywhere else in the world. One such problem that bears an impact on international security and that has already brought about substantial communal violence and major population displacements is that of relations between Christian and Muslim communities, notably in Egypt, Indonesia, Iraq, Nigeria, Pakistan, and Syria. Tensions are to be found in other countries where significant numbers of different religions

---

24. Mark Juergensmeyer, *Terror in the Mind of God* (Berkeley: University of California Press, 2003).

25. See E. D. Cain, "President Obama Signed the National Defense Authorization Act — Now What?" *Forbes,* January 2, 2012, found at http://www.hareforhouse.com/press/Forbes%20NDAA%20article.pdf, and Jordan J. Paust, "Is the President Governed by the Supreme Law of the Land? Foreign Affairs and National Security Re-Examined," *Hastings Constitutional Law Quarterly* 9 (Summer 1982): 719-72.

are in economic and political competition and where there are no effective mechanisms to mediate the conflicts. In India the conflicts are even more complex on account of the presence of segments within the dominant Hindu group that exhibit fundamentalist and imperialist approaches to the social role of Hinduism and communal identity.[26]

As the domestic forces behind the passing and implementation of IRFA illustrate in the United States, and even without such a law in other countries, religious loyalties cross borders. Communities suffering discrimination in one country, for example, expect their fellow believers in other countries to come to their aid. When Coptic Christians suffer violence and persecution in Egypt, the Coptic community in the United States ensures that it is a significant issue on the national foreign policy agenda. India's treatment of its Muslim citizens is a major preoccupation of its Muslim neighbor, Pakistan. International problems like these are one more example of why they cannot be addressed simply by excluding religion from the public sphere. On the contrary, if they wish to cultivate peaceful community relations and effective nation-building, modern states and the international community as a whole need expertise and policies that enable them to engage their respective religious constituencies and to understand the latter's particular identities, loyalties, beliefs, fears, and commitments.

The international human rights regime has as of yet few tools to address the problems that states have been facing on account of the increasing religious pluralism of their citizens. Some states, such as Spain and Kenya, for example, have developed new constitutions that include provisions that respond directly to the challenges of religious diversity and relations between religion and the state and among the religions themselves.[27] The goal of these provisions is to avoid patterns of discrimination among their citizens linked to religious affiliation. In seeking to provide for religious diversity and nondiscrimination in their constitution and laws, the two countries have sought to define a state that is neutral and to incorporate formal institutional structures to facilitate engagement with their different religious constituencies. This goal has been challenged on account of some of their citizens' prior expectations with regard to their own religion,

26. Joaquin Mantecon, *Los Acuerdos con las Confesionas Minoritarias: Diez Anos de Vigencia* (Madrid: Ministerio de la Justicia, 2003).
27. See Alberto de la Hera and Rosa Maria Martinez de Codes, eds., *Spanish Legislation on Religious Affairs* (Madrid: Ministerio de la Justicia, 1998).

as well as by social constructs of terrorists that are often associated with the implementation of recent legislation by states designed to prevent terrorism. Nevertheless, the new constitutional provisions are examples of replacing traditional provisions for the separation of state and religion with new, more nuanced institutions that enable the state to engage its religious communities and to work with them to find ways to reduce tensions among them.[28] Engagement and interaction are seen as a necessary means to avoid claims of discrimination by one or the other religion, all without privileging one religion over the other. Among the unresolved components are how to assure fair access to religions great and small, and whom to define as legitimate representatives of the religious communities.

These trends emphasizing greater state engagement with religion are reinforced by academic studies. In Europe, for example, there is a growing field of inquiry examining the spaces of post-secularist engagement in the field of social justice with an emphasis on programs in cities.[29] These studies look at the spaces where religious organizations and other civic groups work together on common social activities such as alleviating poverty or aiding undocumented migrants.[30] There appear to be two lines of approach in this scholarship: one of theory, addressing how and why such engagement takes place; and the other dealing with praxis — that is, with what is happening on the ground. This scholarship again puts into question the practical or public validity of the distinction called for in secularist ideologies between religiously motivated and other social service groups. Both groups are organized and motivated on the basis of values, goals, principles, and particular strategies. These studies raise once more the question of why religious groups, with their influence diluted and following the demise of the bipolar state-religion world, should still be treated differently from other civic groups, as proposed in most secularist theories.

These are but some of the changes taking place in both international and domestic approaches to religion and public affairs. The overall trend is toward reaching beyond the exclusionist secularist positions to provisions that enable the state to engage religion. Moreover, while religion may still

---

28. Spain is another case in point here (see previous two notes).

29. See, for example, Justin Beaumont and Candice Dias, "Faith-Based Organizations and Urban Social Justice in the Netherlands," *Tijdschrift voor economische en sociale geografie* 99 (2008): 382-92.

30. See J. Paul Martin, Shruti Patel, and Jason Chau, "Religions and International Poverty Alleviation: The Pluses and Minuses," *Journal of International Affairs* 61, no. 1 (Fall–Winter 2007): 69-92.

hit the headlines primarily as a source of international tension, there are many other roles that religions can and do play that contribute significantly to human welfare and world peace, as well as the amelioration of social problems such as domestic violence, poverty, juvenile delinquency, and so on. In fact, engagement is already taking place, but the principle of the separation of religion and the state is still part of the rhetoric. Given the continuing secularist rhetoric, religion still has to come in the back door!

2. Re-Evaluating the Secular Models of State-Religion Relations

In the face of the social changes of the last sixty years described so far, the various secularist models calling for separation between church and state are no longer an adequate paradigm to define the place of religion in international public life. Indeed, as more and more scholars admit, in practice the models have never been perfect.[31] With only the rare exception such as North Korea, states and religions have coexisted and tolerated different forms of mutual involvement. In virtually all states in the world it is possible to identify ways in which the political landscape retains marks of a religious inheritance. The realms have never been completely separate. On the other hand, unlike in the past when there were many cases of major tension when one tried to dominate the other, in the West at least, few religious groups can compete with the state for power today. Nonetheless, the language of secularism remains an expedient political strategy to enable one side or the other to claim or to seek greater independence or less interference. The following examination of the limitations of the secularist model is designed to identify elements that might lead to new rules of the road for religion in the public sphere in both domestic and international affairs.

Fights between religion and the state have been more visible in the West than in the Islamic world, one reason being the legacy of the Prophet Mohammad, whose practice and teachings emphasized cooperation and integration between religion and civil power. In the West since Constan-

---

31. For example, Timothy Samuel Shah, Alfred Stepan, and Monica Duffy Toft, eds., *Rethinking Religion in International Affairs* (New York: Oxford University Press, 2012); Monica Duffy Toft, Daniel Philpott, and Timothy Samuel Shah, *God's Century: Resurgent Religion and Global Politics* (New York: W. W. Norton and Co., 2011); and Jaime Contreras and Rosa Maria Martinez de Codes, eds., *Trends of Secularism in a Pluralistic World* (Madrid: Iberoamericana/Vervuert, 2013).

tine, the emphasis has been on defining two separate realms, implying a degree of independence and equality between the two, but leading to many debates over the centuries about whether one was subordinate to the other. As a philosophy or ideology, secularism has emphasized both the independence of the public sphere from religion and the privatization of religion. The origin of modern secularist ideologies in the West is clearly linked to periods in history when the influence of religions and religious figures in the common public sphere was protested by other social forces. This led to formulations of separation based on political and legal normative principles, the object of which was to exclude religion from crucial dimensions of public life.[32] In the United States this position took the form of the Constitution's First Amendment proscribing "the establishment" of religion and protecting its free exercise. In France *laïcité,* the French version of secularism, was motivated by the desire to exclude not so much religion itself but more specifically religious figures and institutions from the public sphere.[33] As a principle or premise such secularisms are essentially prescriptive. The grounds were perceived past abuses during periods when some religions and religious figures were indeed powerful enough to compete with the civil power. As argued above, that level of power no longer exists, at least in the West. Without empirical evidence of this or another danger, and assuming there is no particular reason to consecrate past practices as unchangeable, there appear to be no other major arguments that justify the complete exclusion of religion from the public sphere. The absence of reasons to exclude religion from the public sphere, however, does not in itself help define any particular positive model of engagement. Still, arguments on the basis of secularism could now be deemed discriminatory against religion if at the same time other ethnic, regional, ideological, and political actors as well as social groups were given full access to the public sphere, while religious actors and groups were excluded.

This leads to a third consideration, which devolves from Charles Taylor's study *A Secular Age,* namely, that secularism is a heterogeneous concept. There are many secularisms.[34] This is especially evident if we examine its use by political traditions as diverse as those of just the five members

32. Cf. William Cavanaugh's account of the creation of the religious-secular distinction in chapter 4 in this volume.

33. See T. Jeremy Gunn, "Religious Freedom and *Laïcité:* A Comparison of the United States and France," *Brigham Young University Law Review* 2004, no. 2 (2004): 419-506.

34. Taylor, *A Secular Age,* pp. 1-4; for a feminist analysis, see Janet R. Jakobsen and Ann Pellegrini, eds., *Secularisms* (Durham, N.C.: Duke University Press, 2008).

of the UN Security Council: China, France, Russia, the United States, and the United Kingdom. All subscribe to one form or other of secularism, but the common denominators with respect to goals, political premises, jurisprudence, legislative and legal histories, and especially practice are minimal. Principally the common goal has either been to keep religion out of the public sphere or, in the case of both China and Russia, to subordinate religion to, rather than simply separate it from, the state. In all five countries, the empirical process of secularization within their respective societies has also taken place very differently.

The fourth argument, again implied in the above evidence, is that the Western models retain deep imprints from their Judeo-Christian roots. For the United Kingdom, secularism has consisted in a continuing watering-down of the status of an established church without disestablishing the crown as the titular head of the Anglican Church. After espousing *laïcité* for more than two hundred years, France finds itself once more seeking to define national identity in the face of its growing Islamic population.[35] Today many French politicians are looking to traits deep in the country's history to define its national character. They find that many such features, including public holidays, dress, monuments, public occasions, and social attitudes and celebrations, possess strong Christian characteristics which, if they are to define national identity, will exclude or reduce to second-class citizenship those citizens who do not share or want to accept that heritage. Since the turn of the century, Russia has reincorporated its religious Russian Orthodox heritage into its national image and even into party politics.[36] The net result of this de facto presence of specific religious, ethnic, or other traits in a national identity profile is to exclude from the national image, and even from legal legitimacy, groups — such as the Jehovah's Witnesses and some Baptist churches — that do not share enough of those nationalist traits.

In the international sphere, diplomats and their governments accept the need to avoid the appearance of establishing rankings among nations. On paper and in law all nations are equal and sovereign. There are no second-class citizens. Most international actors, for example, are committed to laws, institutions, and practices that assure an even playing field

---

35. Steven Erlanger, "A Presidential Race Leaves French Muslims Feeling Like Outsiders," *The New York Times,* April 5, 2012, p. A5.

36. Sophia Kishkovsky, "Russians See Church and State Come Closer," *The New York Times,* November 1, 2012, p. A4.

and do not relegate any states to second-class status on account of their particular cultural, intellectual, or political traits, beliefs, or practices. On the other hand, in practice, interstate relations exhibit distinct differences in political and economic power and influence. Within this international context the influence of religious factors is more indirect, arising principally as they impinge on the policies and actions of the state parties. Viewed in a comparative perspective, the existing patterns of separation of religion and state cover a broad spectrum. At one end are most Arab states, Israel, and the Vatican, which in different ways are strongly conditioned by their respective religious institutions and traditions. At the other are states like North Korea and China that have eliminated all traces of religion in their public spheres. The role these different domestic traditions play in the international sphere is complex. Religious beliefs and practices do not function directly as a source of discrimination among states, although their individual positions in debates could be traced to religious ideas and loyalties. One consequence of this situation is a degree of neutrality in the functioning of the UN and its agencies. There one finds little evidence of a form of secularism that exhibits a bias toward Western traditions. This permits the UN to engage as a neutral actor. Even so, as yet there are no protocols or rules of engagement that would provide guidelines for UN action in specifically religiously volatile situations.

A fifth argument that also illustrates the limits of secularism and the need for a new modus operandi is that states that adopt a secularist version of separation of state and religion, as opposed to a policy endorsing a neutral, engaged state, do not then have at their disposal the professional and institutional resources necessary to grapple with tensions resulting from the religious diversity among their citizens — especially when those identities are deeply formed by essentially "otherworldly" concerns. Some such states, such as Saudi Arabia, proscribe religious diversity in favor of a single religious tradition based on a supernatural mindset or worldview. Others, such as Nigeria, seek to treat the issue as a problem of personal and communal security. Still others, such as the United States, benefit from national traditions and institutions that have enabled them to address religious tensions through diverse constitutional and legal provisions. For other states such as those in Western Europe, it is the overall process of secularization (as opposed to secularism as an ideology) that has reduced tensions among religious communities. On the other hand, as the former Yugoslavia and Rwanda have shown, nationalistic and economic forces can revive dormant religious divisions, which in turn impinge on international security. The danger of religiously defined communal violence varies from state to state. We have also learned that violence can erupt within a religious tradition as well as between one tradition and another. Thus each state has to meet its own needs for preparedness with respect to both domestic and international religious tensions. If it conduces to the lack of any systematic attention to religious factors in domestic and international affairs, secularism has little to offer in these situations. Prudent preparedness is surely more rational. Preparedness could, for example, take the form of monitoring, by including communal relations in the reporting carried out by U.S. embassies and published in the State Department's annual reports on religious freedom. Preparedness would also need to include making institutional provisions and placing professionals in position to interpret events and propose responses that included insights into the specifically religious factors at work. Such analysis would need to recognize that although they are part of civil society, religions are also more ancient, complex, and typically more international, more loyalty-demanding, and more afterlife-oriented than other institutions in civil society. These loyalties and identities are powerful social forces that need to be understood if peaceful relations among them are to be the norm. Preparedness calls for greater involvement on the part of government than is likely to be countenanced by standard secularist concepts based on the separation of state and religion.

A sixth argument that secular models defining church-state relations are no longer adequate is related to the previous arguments and concerns the need felt by the world community to adopt common standards of social justice that ensure the equal and dignified treatment of all human beings, no matter what their condition. The contemporary human rights regime is a direct response to a long list of human rights abuses, most still prevalent in our world. It seeks to set a normative and institutional framework that defines and enforces obligations common to all states, irrespective of their heritage and resources. Unlike Western secularisms, the international human rights approach provides a common and more detailed approach to religion and the state, one that has proved more acceptable and meaningful to scholars and societies associated with other major religions, including Islam. In 1990 the Organization of the Islamic Conference, for example, developed the Cairo Declaration on Human Rights in Islam. Article 1 reads "All men are equal in terms of basic human dignity and basic obligations and responsibilities, without any discrimination on grounds of race, color, language, sex, religious belief, political affiliation, social status and other considerations." Of course, as with most other human rights statements there is a big difference between a norm and the practice. Nevertheless, statements like these are a major common starting point on the road to peaceful interfaith relations. Western secularism offers no such promising mediating tool. On the other hand, there are thinkers within the Islamic community who are moving toward a different approach to religion in the public sphere. One example is the Tunisian politician Rachid Ghannouchi, who argues for a degree of rapprochement between secularism and Islam:

> Thus, the greater part of the debate taking place nowadays in our country (Tunisia) is a misunderstanding of such concepts as secularism and Islam. We demonstrated that secularism is not an atheist philosophy but merely a set of procedural arrangements designed to safeguard the freedom of belief and thought as Abd al-Wahhab al-Masiri distinguished, in his writings, between partial and total secularisms. An example of the latter would be the Jacobin model in French history. In their war on priesthood, the Jacobins raised the following slogan: "strangle the last king with the entrails of the last priest." This is a French specificity and not the absolute definition of secularism. There is also an ambiguity regarding Islam, for there are those who believe that Islam can only be victorious by confiscating people's freedom and imposing prayers, fasting, and the veil through force. This would be far from being a success, for Allah Almighty had considered hypocrisy to be the greatest crime, and the hellfire to be the eternal abode of hypocrites.[37]

In the United States, new pressures for greater state-religion engagement are coming from the interfaith religious sectors. These ideas were evident in the report of the 2010 Chicago Council Task Force on Engaging Religious Communities Abroad, subtitled *A New Imperative for U.S. Policy.*[38] The report raises the question of whether the traditional political

37. Rachid Ghannouchi, "Secularism and the Relation Between Religion and the State from the Perspective of the Nahdha Party," lecture at CSID-Tunisia on March 2, 2012, accessible at http://blog.sami-aldeeb.com/2012/03/09/full-transcript-of-rached-ghannouch is-lecture-on-secularism-march-2-2012/.

38. Chicago Council on Global Affairs, "Engaging Religious Communities Abroad: A New Imperative for U.S. Foreign Policy," found at http://www.thechicagocouncil.org/ taskforce_details.php?taskforce_id=10.

ideologies of secularism are adequate. The drafters call for a new diplomatic language and practice based on pragmatism and problem-solving. In other words, the emerging goals they propose are to engage with and to accommodate the previously ignored religious forces, to take seriously the deep and powerful political presence of religions in public life, and to focus on common interests and collaborative solutions. They call for acknowledging and welcoming the de facto influence of religion in public affairs and seeking to maximize its constructive rather than divisive forces. In the modern world, they argue, there is little place for a secularist ideology that wants to ignore religions. Missing still are agreed-upon rules of the game that assure the peaceful participation of religions in the public fora of the world's very different polities. One of the points the report makes is that the United States often lacks the capacity to understand the broad contours of religiously driven debates because it lacks staff expertise in the field. It also recommends that, in order to accommodate the legitimate aspirations of religious communities, the United States must adopt policies that integrate religious freedom, democracy promotion, and human rights. Modern pluralism and religious diversity call for attentiveness, informed knowledge, and pragmatic responses. In short, the findings of the Chicago Council buttress the argument of this chapter that in the realm of global politics, excluding religion from the public sphere is no longer a wise option.

The analysis of this section leads to a number of important conclusions. The first is that conflicts between and within religious communities are likely to continue to increase, irrespective of the degree to which they involve and are even caused by other factors. Second, this state of affairs requires the attention and engagement of public authorities with these communities, and not just in a role as referee for their conflicts. Due diligence and good governance thus require that individual states and the international community develop greater expertise and qualified personnel able to interpret and address the peculiarly religious factors in global relations, especially those associated with each community's history, loyalties, sources of identity, and moorings in powerful, unverifiable shared belief systems. On the other hand, religions also need to find and adopt modes of operation that reconcile modern religious pluralism and the processes of public debate and political compromise, on one side, with both proselytism and advocacy for their fellow religionists and others in difficult circumstances at home and overseas on the other. This issue is addressed in the last section in this chapter with respect to the Catholic Church.

Reducing domestic tensions with religious components in situations as diverse as Saudi Arabia, Nigeria, India, Iraq, and Uzbekistan will require active and sustained dialogues between the state and the religious actors, in a manner adapted to the very different circumstances of each case. For the various actors to come together in systematic and sustainable ways, however, common rules need to be established. How might these rules of the road look in practice?

3. Toward Common Rules of the Road

Modern patterns of migration mean that religious pluralism has come or is coming to neighborhoods all over the world. The problems created by the resulting mosaic of new and old tensions are always in danger of overflowing and becoming international. The international community of states has as of yet no religion-specific task force to expand on the common understandings needed to resolve tensions peacefully. It has, however, past experiences, such as the interreligious violence that took place in Srebrenica in 1993 and Gujarat in 2002, which need to be studied in order to develop some practice-based policies both to prevent and to resolve such tensions in the future. The task is not easy because religion is rarely a stand-alone factor in communal conflict. It is often associated with other dimensions of discrimination, most notably the economic and the ethnic. Studies of communal violence in India, for example, found that such violence had not occurred and was less likely to take place in cities where the middle and professional classes of the different communities were accustomed to interact across religious lines. The examples of Kenya and Spain suggest that one of the first tasks for an emerging global regime of religious engagement is to look at existing domestic rules of the road in selected countries — namely, at the way in which constitutional and legal provisions recognize and respond to the religious diversity of the citizenry. Secularist principles excluding religions from the public sphere often assure silence and a subsequent lack of communication and dialogue. Both the Kenyan and Spanish experiences underline the benefits of public debate in developing a consensus. Developing international rules of the road must cope with added levels of complexity, but as mentioned above, the UN has a half-century of successful human rights activities that provide a basis for attention to religious and communal tensions.

At the UN there have been continuing attempts to upgrade the 1981

Declaration on the Elimination of All Forms of Discrimination Based on Religion and Belief to make it a treaty, but this effort has so far not attracted the commitment of many states. Moreover, its focus deals only with the vertical, state-religion dimension. Equally important today is the horizontal dimension, concerning relations among religions living and working in the same or contiguous spaces. At the UN work in this area is currently taking the form of seeking common norms dealing with blasphemy, the denigration of religion, and hate speech. If other successful past actions in the field of human rights at the UN are to be the guide, future change will depend on concerted action by civil society to formulate a project and then to mobilize specific governments to shepherd the proposals through the UN system. Recent examples of effective broad-based cooperative action along these lines are the ban on landmines and the campaign for the Convention of the Rights of Persons with Disabilities.[39] At the UN, there now appear to be two currents, one associated with Western democracies that focus on protecting religious freedom, and another that is more concerned with protecting religions and religious institutions from defamation and hate speech. Common ground has yet to be found.

The most historically and geographically extensive problem of interreligious relations has been and still is that of tensions between Islam and Christianity, with the period of the Crusades still providing its iconic backdrop. The points of tension span the globe. One particular conflict that is coming to the center of the international stage is the tension and resulting violence between Muslim and Christian populations in Nigeria. Nigeria is a large country, the most populous in Africa. Its approximately 170 million people are divided roughly half and half between a mostly Muslim north and a mostly Christian south. A small third segment scattered throughout the country lives according to indigenous and other religious traditions (the actual figures for this contingent are hard to establish). Nigeria is also a country where the huge oil wealth extracted in the south has not reached the rural populations of either the north or the south. Fueled by popular beliefs such as that the oil was originally in the north and flowed to the south, the northern populations are especially resentful of their lack of wealth.[40] This combination of strong religious group alle-

---

39. The U.S. Congress, however, has so far refused to ratify this treaty, in spite of the very active role of U.S. experts in its formulation and its approval by the UN General Assembly.

40. Reported in Uwem Akpan, *Say You're One of Them* (New York: Little, Brown, 2008), p. 244.

giance and substantial economic grievances augurs to be a major crisis in the not-too-distant future. Assuaging the tensions requires addressing both components: the religious aspirations and loyalties as well as the economic deprivation. So far, the responses to the periodic outbreaks of violence in Nigeria by the government and private-sector actors have given no indication that they have any strategy — beyond stopgap provisions for greater physical security — likely to address, not to mention resolve, the tensions. Moreover, the two religious communities could easily become proxies for tensions between outside actors from the West and the Islamic world. Neither of the latter would easily stand aside if their co-religionists were seriously imperiled. External support and the attraction of youth to militant groups willing to use terrorism on the civilian population have aggravated the conflicts. At the same time, even within Islam[41] there are major tensions involving both religious hostilities and economic grievances, and these also bear the potential to boil over in Nigeria and attract interventions from without — as has occurred recently in Syria and Lebanon. For all of these reasons, Nigeria looms large as a litmus test for the ability of domestic governments, and the international community if necessary, to address religious conflict.

At present there is nothing to suggest that the international community of states has much to offer beyond enforcing physical security through the presence of an international military and police force. This sort of intervention might halt the violence but it will not easily diminish its underlying causes associated with religious pluralism and, in the Nigerian and other cases, with economic deprivation. Both of these factors are typically encumbered by myths and social constructions about the other group that distort both the basic beliefs and practices and the economic circumstances of both communities. To what institutions, political alliances, interfaith organizations, and other sources of assistance should the Nigerian government and the Nigerian Christian and Muslim communities turn? It is highly unlikely that the weekly Friday and Sunday sermons will offer any remedies. So far, engagement between the religious leaders in Nigeria has been formal and limited. No public structures or visions are in place, or coming into place, to counter the violence that has started and is likely to increase with every new round of conflict, injured feelings, and rights violations.

41. On tensions within Islam, see Abdullahi An-Na'im, *Islam and the Secular State, Negotiating the Future of Sharia* (Cambridge, Mass.: Harvard University Press, 2010).

4. Religious Diversity, Globalization, and the Catholic Tradition

At first sight the interfaith violence that took place in Srebrenica between Orthodox Christians and Muslims, and in Gujarat between Hindus and Muslims, has little to do with Catholic thinking. Above it was noted that "religions also need to find and adopt modes of operation that reconcile modern religious pluralism and the processes of public debate and political compromise on one side, with advocacy for their fellow religionists and others in difficult circumstances at home and overseas on the other." This final section examines thinking within the Roman Catholic Church with respect to interfaith and religion-state relations. Traditionally in the West the Church's efforts in the public sphere have focused on managing interfaith relations and on defending the civil freedoms needed to enable the Church to grow and prosper. There has been little talk of "common civic rules of the road" to enable public authorities to prevent interfaith conflict. Within the Catholic Church there have been some activities in the field of conflict management and peace-building in the work of groups such as the Community of Sant'Egidio.[42] In Mozambique, for example, the Community initiated negotiations between the government and the insurgents that eventually brought both sides to the same table, and then enabled the Italian government to take over and finalize a peace agreement. Religion, however, while a part of the motivation of the actors, was not a significant factor in this and many of the other conflicts where such Catholic and other civil society groups have played a role in peacekeeping. In situations where religion has been a major factor in communal tensions, the Church can point to groups such as the Little Brothers of Jesus who, inspired by the life of the French priest Charles de Foucauld, followed his example by letting their lifestyles in Algeria and elsewhere in the Muslim world witness to Christianity, while avoiding any trace of proselytizing.[43] Similarly, Catholic humanitarian and development organizations such as Catholic Relief Services, working as they do in many non-Christian environments, have been able to avoid debates about interfaith relations and the place of religion in the public forum. In common with other religious aid groups from the Western world, they have served their beneficiaries in

---

42. Cameron R. Hume, *Ending Mozambique's War: The Role of Mediation and Good Offices* (Washington, D.C.: United States Institute of Peace Press, 1994).

43. Dominique Casajus, "Charles de Foucauld face aux Touaregs: Rencontre et Malentendu," *Miroirs du Colonialisme: Terrain* 28 (March 1997): 29-42.

a religiously neutral fashion, following the model of the other nonreligious secular agencies. Although there have been a few accounts of friction involving, for example, conversion being seen as a condition to receive aid, in the field of development aid and humanitarian assistance common rules of the road that exclude the promotion of religion have been established and accepted by the various actors. In such cases the traditional rules of secularism and separation of religion and the state appear to be largely adequate. When religion is part of the conflict, however, the religious factors have to be addressed. For the Catholic Church as well there is a need for new common rules of the road that address the peculiarities of religion in the international public sphere.

Within the Catholic tradition there are already some major reference points that re-examine the place of religion, religious thinking, and religious institutions in a globalizing world. The watershed phase for this development came in the 1960s in the form of two documents, Pope John XXIII's 1963 encyclical *Pacem in terris* and the Second Vatican Council's *Gaudium et spes (Pastoral Constitution on the Church in the Modern World).*[44] Both documents emphasize the compatibility of religious and nonreligious discourse with respect to social justice and world order, although they do not seek directly to examine the ways in which religious groups interface with the state and with one another. Nevertheless, their content provides elements to set out a Catholic approach to relationships between the state and religion in a post-secular world where the relationship is not defined simply in terms of the varying formulations of separation of church and state tested over the centuries since the Constantinian vision.

This engagement is well set out in both *Pacem in terris* and *Gaudium et spes.* Both cover considerable ground and need more detailed elaboration than space permits here. *Pacem in terris* sets about its task by demonstrating the compatibility of international human rights and duties with Catholic teaching and attesting to the importance of the promotion of human rights for world peace. "A well-ordered human society requires that men recognize and observe their mutual rights and duties."[45] The encyclical goes on to spell out the role of the state and the space needed for religion

44. Accessible at http://www.papalencyclicals.net/index.htm and http://www.vatican.va/archive/hist_councils/ii_vatican_council/documents/vat-ii_const_19651207_gaudium-et-spes_en.html.

45. *Pacem in terris,* §31.

within a framework of rights and duties on one hand, and the common good on the other. In fact, the paramount task assigned to government officials is that of recognizing, reconciling, protecting, and promoting the rights and duties of citizens.[46] The encyclical then discusses relations between states and the protection of minorities, eventually arguing that modern states are ill-equipped to ensure the common universal good.[47] Finally, it calls for establishing "new relationships in human society, under the mastery and guidance of truth, justice, charity and freedom."[48]

Gaudium et spes offers a different analysis, developing an argument based on the interdependence of human beings and the pursuit of justice and human fulfillment for all. Its starting point is the need for the church to respond to a rapidly changing world, marked by the forces that today we call globalization, industrialization, urbanization, secularization, migration, technology, and other forms of rapid change. The answer the Council proposed was based on human dignity and an appeal to all to act in accordance with their moral consciences and in the spirit of Jesus.[49] This is followed by a discussion of the principles to guide Christians in the modern world, which emphasize recognizing the interdependence of person and society, the centrality of the common good, and the equality and dignity of all human beings. The theological emphasis is incarnational, invoking the changes brought to the world through the life, death, and resurrection of Jesus. One task of the Church is "to uncover, cherish and ennoble all that is true, good and beautiful in the human community."[50] The 2009 encyclical of Pope Benedict XVI, *Caritas in veritate,* touches directly on the topic of secularism and religion in the modern world in the context of poverty alleviation. In chapter 5 on "The Cooperation of the Human Family," he portrays the human race as a family working together for development where primacy is placed on relationships among persons. Benedict argues that religions can contribute only if God has a place in the public realm[51] and there is fraternal collaboration between believers and nonbelievers based on a shared commitment to justice and peace.[52] He also insists, however, that "religious freedom does not mean religious indiffer-

---

46. *Pacem in terris,* §77.
47. *Pacem in terris,* §132.
48. *Pacem in terris,* §163.
49. *Gaudium et spes,* §22.
50. *Gaudium et spes,* §76.
51. *Caritas in veritate,* §56.
52. *Caritas in veritate,* §57.

entism, nor does it imply that all religions are equal."[53] He then affirms that "secularism and fundamentalism exclude the possibility of fruitful dialogue and effective cooperation between reason and religious faith."[54] His use of the word "secularism" as the exclusion of religion from the public sphere further emphasizes the ambiguity associated with the word.

All three documents open the way to new thinking within the Catholic tradition with respect to religion and the state in international affairs, some of which is reflected in other chapters in this volume. The Trinitarian and incarnational theological premises that animate the encyclicals, for example, underwrite calls for improved relationships within and engagement with the human reality in all its diversity.[55] Equally relevant is thinking consequential to the belief in the faithfulness of God, according to which he does not give up on his creation or his covenants. Another theological theme that promotes a re-examination of the interaction between religion and the secular is the new intellectual cautiousness when confronted by binaries and polarities such as those between public and private, citizen and non-citizen, community and individual, religion and politics, religion and reason, continuity and change, immanence and transcendence, love and reason, truth and culture, and especially the sacred and secular. The concerns here are twofold. The first arises from the degree to which these binaries tend to privilege one pole at the expense of the other and to pre-empt the possibility of creative interaction between each pair. The second invokes the question whether the religious and the secular are actually a binary pair rather than two completely separate dimensions. Intellectual cautiousness requires that both interpretations be on the table and that both be given serious consideration. As defined and proposed in terms of religious and secular humanisms elsewhere in this volume by Slavica Jakelić, the two perspectives — theological and intellectual — emphasize and call for engagement with and among all the stakeholders, religious and otherwise, to develop common solutions to such shared social problems as the various forms and sources of violence, the alleviation of poverty, refugees and persons without citizenship national identity, and children without parents. These are but a few examples of themes in Catholic thinking and related, real-life problems that need to be revisited attentively in

53. *Caritas in veritate*, §55.
54. *Caritas in veritate*, §56.
55. On this point, see the discussions by Anthony Godzieba, Philip J. Rossi, and Mary Doak in this volume in the part on theological anthropology (part III).

order to be addressed in future debates and projects concerned with the role of religion in international affairs.

Engaging religion and public affairs in a post-secular world is not an easy task. Secularist models of church-state separation have been in effect for centuries in individual countries and have helped shaped the activities of the United Nations, although in practice secularism has rarely produced a complete separation. The Holy See, that is, the pope as supreme authority in the Catholic Church,[56] is represented in the world of international organizations by the Vatican State. Over the years, the Vatican's status as a nonmember observer state has enabled the pope to address the General Assembly and provided the opportunity for papal representatives to lobby member states of the UN. The Vatican's role at the UN as the de facto voice of the Catholic Church around the world as well as that of a small territorial state raises questions. Islam, for example, is represented by many states, but that representation is subject to the many other interests of the states. So far, the agenda of the Vatican has been narrow. Its most visible and sustained lobbying activities in the international forum have been on issues associated with women and reproductive rights as well as religious freedom.[57] One exception to this broad pattern was the decades-long campaign to undermine the communist governments of Eastern Europe. On all of these issues, the Vatican State has sought out and worked with allies whose premises and patterns of reasoning were very different from their own but with whom they were able to find agreement with respect to overarching goals. Such cooperation extended even to the measures addressing reproductive rights forged at the 1995 Cairo Conference on Population and Development.[58]

This chapter has argued that the international community is of necessity becoming more open to dialogue with the world's religions and that in this process there will be much to learn from the development over the last

56. For a definition of the Vatican and the Holy See, see http://www.holyseemission.org/about/history-of-diplomacy-of-the-holy-see.aspx. Its status at the UN is that of non-member observer state.

57. Interestingly, these two topics have been merged recently, subsuming the former under the latter. See, for example, the statement by the Vatican Mission to the UN found at http://www.holyseemission.org/statements/statement.aspx?id=401.

58. C. Allison McIntosh and Jason L. Finkle, "The Cairo Conference on Population and Development: A New Paradigm?" *Population and Development Review* 21, no. 2 (June 1995): 223-60. The article casts the main protagonists at the Conference as the women's movement, the U.S. government, and the Holy See.

sixty years of the international human rights system. It is also important to recognize that the human rights regime has built, and has built on, a broad coalition of the world's states committed to increasing the common, legally enforceable norms of social justice. These coalitions were possible only when the parties, typically state and nongovernmental organizations, were willing to define and work from and toward commonalities without insisting on incorporating their own particular truth-claims or universalist claims. It follows that in working toward and within such coalitions, the Catholic perspective needs to be articulated in ways that make a public, not just a faith-based, case for social justice goals that it would like the world community to share and adopt. So while, for example, Trinitarian or incarnational roots may inspire the prophetic energy, the quality and depth of engagement, and the moral insights animating Catholic stances in public life — as, for example, in the opening up of self to the sufferings of others addressed by Peter Casarella in this volume[59] — such interventions will need to be formulated and argued in a language that is meaningful to others in the international community. Prophetic energy is needed to set in motion the requisite process of normative and social change and to mobilize potential allies. It might also fuel calls for forgiveness and reconciliation. Either way, the challenge of the Catholic perspective is to dig deep into its own tradition to mobilize the evidence and reasoned arguments necessary to convince the other political forces in the international public sphere to mobilize the resources necessary to effect the desired change.

Obviously, the Church has been and is active in this sphere. Recent papal and Vatican pronouncements permit a necessary next step, namely, to evaluate the choice of objectives and arguments as well as the effectiveness of their strategies. The theological perspectives proposed in other essays in this volume also identify some of the social forces that militate against the values and relationships emanating from those principles. The transcendental perspective inspired by those insights often conflicts with modern ideas of nationalism and patriotism, especially when they lead to constructs of national security that routinely authorize the use of preemptive force and engage in massive violent action incurring thousands of civilian deaths, rather than committing the same amount of resources to a wider range of potential responses. Traditional Catholic theology has deferred to theories of just war which, in practice, have tended not to stop war but rather generally enabled soldiers to kill in good faith, on the

59. See chapter 2 in this volume.

grounds that their actions were basically defensive and authorized by a legitimate civilian authority. In the case of the recent wars in Iraq and Afghanistan, the prevalent just-war mentality generated virtually no opposition to launching invasions on the part of the U.S. citizenry and their elected representatives — the Catholic sector included. It remains an open question whether a deeper Trinitarian and incarnational theology might have changed that position among Catholics.

Looking more to the future, we need to subject the arguments advanced in this chapter once again to the test provided by the situation in Nigeria, where there are still few national institutional structures in place likely to be able to stem the increase of violence between its roughly 60 million Christians and its similar number of Muslims. Nigeria has the highest number of Catholic priests in Africa — indeed, in recent years it has been supplying clergy to other parts of the world, including the United States. Whether viewed from the point of view of the governments, the religious organizations, or the international community, the challenges there are immense. This is the case not only because we have not agreed on the lessons of Srebrenica and Gujarat, nor on what we have learned from the many international and domestic civil society entities that have been active in this field of engagement and conflict management with grassroots communities and interfaith groups in other places such as Israel and Palestine. It is also because Nigeria has no state or national institutions with the expertise and resources to address conflicts arising from the religious identities and loyalties of its citizens. The key dimension of the problem, in other words, is not only and no longer primarily the vertical one, involving relations between the state and the religions of its people, but the horizontal aspect of relations among the state's two main religious groups, Muslims and Christians. For this reason, neither a human rights nor a religious freedom framework can provide all the tools needed to deal with interfaith conflicts there. New "rules of the road" and institutional structures are needed to enable the state to engage with religions in ways that go beyond applications of military force and the criminal justice system.

Unlike most other sectors of civil society, religious affiliations require special attention because of the de facto power of religious identities and loyalties, and in the case of most parts of Africa, the status granted to religion and religious identity and to a person's vision of self and overall social status. The concomitant sense of solidarity becomes a powerful force at the level of the group, especially when the group is under political or economic pressure or there are reinforcing ethnic tensions. In other words, these are not situations that states can ignore on the basis of a separation of church and state. But if the power of religious forces calls for special attention, the problem in Africa is that states are only beginning to develop their capacity to respond. The danger is not, as was the case in the French rationale for the construction of *laïcité,* that the religious authorities would be more powerful than the state. The danger is that the state does not have the power and the tools necessary to mediate and resolve tensions and conflicts among its religious groups.

Returning to the search for Catholic perspectives inspired by a Trinitarian and incarnational model: If positive engagement is accepted as the central, albeit difficult challenge, what should be the immediate goals and strategies for the Catholic Church in Nigeria? From a human rights perspective one goal would be to identify and reduce the various forms and sources of discrimination between the two religious traditions. One of the sources of discrimination and prejudice is the myriad social constructs of the other that circulate within each community. Moreover, since both the Muslim and Christian communities are proselytizing groups seeking to increase their own members, as the number of Nigerians who are neither Christian nor Muslim diminishes, the tendency to seek converts from the other religion increases, creating more tension. Should and could the two religions agree not to proselytize? As in most other religiously defined communal hostilities, there are economic dimensions, especially those associated with the huge revenues coming from petroleum extraction in the south of the country, that is, from the very largely Christian region. Already the use of these revenues is perhaps the major bone of contention in the country. Revenues disappear and fail to benefit ordinary citizens in both the north and the south. Because of this factor any resolution of the communal violence will require the collaboration of both major religious groups as well as both local and national public officials.

What can the Catholic Church do especially in the north, where Christians constitute small minorities within much larger Muslim communities, and where the violence so far has involved a degree of religious cleansing as Christian inhabitants have been forced to migrate to the south? Ideally the Church needs to develop new understandings and institutional arrangements before the intensity of the physical violence and predictable retaliations increases to the point where talking is no longer an option. It also needs to draw on studies of communal violence elsewhere, such as the recent findings from India showing that the potential for outbreaks of violence drops sharply when members of the local professional and middle classes from the major religious communities interact routinely in substantial ways. This and other empirical evidence emphasizes the importance of engagement and the need to analyze the community forces at work rather than assuming an unavoidable breakdown. This perspective coincides with the insights on community developed by Michele Dillon in her contribution to this volume, in which she outlines the conditions under which plurality and the intersectionality of beliefs and identities can be affirmed and incorporated into community-building out of and amid diversity.[60] These goals reflect religious inspiration, but they also need empirically grounded strategies and the necessary resources.

Love thy neighbor as thyself is seen to be the basic message and ethical ideal of all major religions. This chapter began by examining the many ways in which religion, religious freedom, and relations among religions have been and remain of concern to both national governments and the world community. It argued that secularist models based on the separation of church and state are no longer adequate in the modern world of international relations. Thus religions need to be full, not sidelined, actors in the public sphere, accorded the same leeway and respect as other members of civil society. On the other hand, religions are still powerful and distinctive forces that need truly qualified attention on the part of both domestic and international authorities. In the quest for new rules of the road for negotiating the interface between religions and global politics in a post-secular age, the growing religious tensions in Nigeria provide a test case demonstrating the importance of more formalized and sustained engagement across religious lines, and between religions and the public authorities. This is one illustration of an emerging model that draws on both empirical information and Catholic perspectives in working toward a new regime of domestic and international institutions dedicated to cultivating the specific expertise necessary to address the problems and possibilities raised by religion in each public sphere.

60. See chapter 10 in this volume.

Contributors

William A. Barbieri Jr. is Associate Professor of Theology and Religious Studies and a Fellow of the Institute for Policy Research and Catholic Studies at the Catholic University of America. He is the co-editor of *From Just War to Modern Peace Ethics* (2012; with Heinz-Gerhard Justenhoven) and the author of *Ethics of Citizenship: Immigration and Group Rights in Germany* (1998) and a forthcoming volume entitled *Constitutive Justice.*

Peter Casarella is Associate Professor of Systematic Theology at the University of Notre Dame. He was the founding director of the Center for World Catholicism and Intercultural Theology at DePaul University. His publications include the edited volumes *A World for All? Global Civil Society in Political Theory and Trinitarian Theology* (2011; with William F. Storrar and Paul Louis Metzger), *Cusanus: The Legacy of Learned Ignorance* (2006), *Cuerpo de Cristo: The Hispanic Presence in the U.S. Catholic Church* (2003; with Raúl Gómez, S.D.S.), and *Christian Spirituality and the Culture of Modernity: The Thought of Louis Dupré* (1998; with George Schner, S.J.). He is a past president of the Academy of Catholic Hispanic Theologians in the United States and president of the American Cusanus Society. He is also a member of the editorial board of *Communio.*

William T. Cavanaugh is Professor of Catholic Studies and Senior Research Professor at the Center for World Catholicism and Intercultural Theology at DePaul University. He is the author of *Migrations of the Holy: God, State, and the Political Meaning of the Church* (2011), *The Myth of Religious Violence: Secular Ideology and the Roots of Modern Conflict* (2009), *Being Consumed: Economics and Christian Desire* (2008), *Theopolitical Imagination: Discovering the Liturgy as a Political Act in an Age of Global Consumerism* (2002), and *Torture and Eucharist: Theology, Politics, and the Body of Christ* (1998). He has also edited *The Blackwell Companion to Political Theology* (2003; with Peter Scott). He is co-editor of the journal *Modern Theology* and an associate editor of *Pro Ecclesia.*

Contributors

Michele Dillon is Professor of Sociology and Chair of the Sociology Department at the University of New Hampshire. Among her publications are *American Catholics in Transition* (2013; with William V. D'Antonio and Mary L. Gautier), *Introduction to Sociological Theory* (2010), *In the Course of a Lifetime: Tracing Religious Belief, Practice, and Change* (2007; with Paul Wink), the edited *Handbook of the Sociology of Religion* (2003), *Catholic Identity: Balancing Reason, Faith, and Power* (1999), and *Debating Divorce: Moral Conflict in Ireland* (1993). She is past president of the Society for the Scientific Study of Religion and past president of the Association for the Sociology of Religion.

Mary Doak is Associate Professor of Theology and Religious Studies at the University of San Diego. She is the author of *Reclaiming Narrative for Public Theology* (2004) and editor of *Translating Religion* (2013; with Anita Houck). Her essays have appeared in various collections and journals, including *Theological Studies* and *The American Journal of Theology and Philosophy*.

Anthony J. Godzieba is Professor of Theology and Religious Studies at Villanova University. His publications include *Christology: Memory, Inquiry, Practice* (2003; co-edited with Anne M. Clifford) and *Bernhard Welte's Fundamental Theological Approach to Christology* (1994). In addition to numerous articles in *Theological Studies, The Heythrop Journal,* and *Louvain Studies,* he contributed the chapter "The Trinitarian Mystery of God: A 'Theological Theology'" to Francis Schüssler Fiorenza and John P. Galvin's *Systematic Theology: Roman Catholic Perspectives* (2011). He is the editor of the journal *Horizons.*

Slavica Jakelić is Assistant Professor of Humanities and Social Thought at Valparaiso University's Honor College and an associate fellow at the University of Virginia's Institute for Advanced Studies in Culture, where she directs the project "Secularism in the Late Modern Age." She is the author of *Collectivistic Religions: Religion, Choice, and Identity in Late Modernity* (2010) and has co-edited *The Future of the Study of Religion* (2004; with Lori Pearson) and *Crossing Boundaries: From Syria to Slovakia* (2003; with Jason Varsoke). She is currently at work on a monograph, *The Practice of Religious and Secular Humanisms.*

J. Paul Martin is Professor and Director of Human Rights Studies at Barnard College. He was a co-founder and, for three decades, executive director of the Center for the Study of Human Rights at Columbia University. He has contributed to numerous books and journals on moral education and human rights, and his publications include *Religious Diversity and Human Rights* (1996; co-edited with Irene Bloom and Wayne Proudfoot) and three collections of human rights documents.

Vincent J. Miller is the Gudorf Professor of Catholic Theology and Culture at the University of Dayton. He is the author of *Consuming Religion: Christian Faith and Practice* *in a Consumer Culture* (2003). Recent publications of his include "When Mediating Structures Change: The Magisterium, the Media, and the Culture Wars," in *When the Magisterium Intervenes* (2012; edited by Richard Gaillardetz) and "The Body Globalized: Problems for a Sacramental Imagination in an Age of Global Commodity Chains," in *Religion, Economics and Culture in Conflict and Conversation* (2011; edited by Laurie Cassidy and Maureen H. O'Connell).

Philip J. Rossi, S.J., is Professor of Theology and past Dean of the Klingler College of Arts and Sciences at Marquette University. He is the author of *The Social Authority of Reason: Kant's Critique, Radical Evil and the Destiny of Humankind* (2005) and *Together Toward Hope: A Journey to Moral Theology* (1983), and the editor of *God, Grace, and Creation* (2010), *Mass Media and the Moral Imagination* (1994; with Paul Soukup, S.J.), and *Kant's Philosophy of Religion Reconsidered* (1992; with Michael J. Wreen). In addition, he has published more than forty journal articles and book chapters, and served as editor for *Philosophy and Theology* and on the editorial board of *Theological Studies*.

Robert J. Schreiter, C.PP.S., is the Vatican II Professor of Theology at the Catholic Theological Union. Among his numerous books are *In Water and In Blood: A Spirituality of Solidarity and Hope* (2006), *The Ministry of Reconciliation: Spirituality and Strategies* (1998), *The New Catholicity: Theology between the Global and the Local* (1997), *Reconciliation: Mission and Ministry in a Changing Social Order* (1992), and *Constructing Local Theologies* (1985). Volumes he has edited include *Peacebuilding: Catholic Theology, Ethics, and Practice* (2010; with R. Scott Appleby and Gerard F. Powers) and *Mission in the Third Millennium* (2001). He is past president of the American Society of Missiology and the Catholic Theological Society of America.

David Tracy is the Greeley Distinguished Service Professor Emeritus of Catholic Studies and Professor of Theology and the Philosophy of Religions at the Divinity School of the University of Chicago, where he is also on the Committee on Social Thought. His books include *On Naming the Present: Reflections on God, Hermeneutics, and Church* (1994), *Dialogue with the Other: The Inter-Religious Dialogue* (1990), *Plurality and Ambiguity: Hermeneutics, Religion, Hope* (1987), *A Catholic Vision* (1984; with Stephen Happel), *The Analogical Imagination: Christian Theology and the Culture of Pluralism* (1981), and *Blessed Rage for Order: The New Pluralism in Theology* (1975). He has served as an editor for *Religious Studies Review, The Journal of Religion,* and *Concilium.* He is currently writing a book on God.

Index

Acosta, José de, 201, 205, 224

Agency, 4, 10, 16, 81, 132, 134, 144, 306; and autonomy, 229, 230, 231, 239, 242; collective, 11-13, 304; cultural, 188; divine 231; and faith, 243-44, 247-48; as finite, 232-34, 237, 239, 240; and hospitality, 237, 243, 248; human, dynamics of, 152, 173; and humanism, 235, 309, 317, 329; Kant's account of, 20-21, 228, 234; and media, 182; moral, 226-27, 229; mutual recognition of, 230, 246; and post-secularities, 19, 131, 135-36, 158; of religion, 86; and self, 72; social embedding of, 238; and technology, 176

Analogy, 70; and anagogy, 69; in the Catholic imaginary, 98

Anderson, Benedict, 108, 133, 166, 167

Anthropology: of Christian faith, 96; Christocentric, 81; and the "immanent frame," 99, 101; Kantian, 240; negative, 309; philosophical, 216; secular, 100; of secularism, 150; social anthropology of human freedom, 238; and soul, 215

Appadurai, Arjun, 176, 179-80

Aquinas, Thomas, 30, 37, 112

Aristotle, 30-31, 33, 41, 201, 224, 329

Asad, Talal, 14, 150, 152

Atheism, 324, 328

Augustine, 37-38, 45-46, 48, 90, 94-95, 111, 144

Authenticity: age of, 293; and modern modes of spiritual seeking, 5; and spiritual individuals, 297

Bach, Johann Sebastian, 203-4, 206, 224

Balthasar, Hans Urs von, 42, 44-45, 68, 76, 144

Belief, 13, 30, 46, 52, 66, 73, 122, 125, 160, 293; Christian, 206, 257, 356; and community, 80, 141, 280-81, 298, 313, 337, 341, 349, 352, 361; conditions of, 2-3, 6, 15, 24-25, 132, 139, 145; defense of, 5; and definitions of religion, 107, 110, 114; and deterritorialization, 193; and discrimination, 346, 347-48, 351; and education, 333-34; erosion of, 140; fragility of, 265, 307; freedom of, 120, 339, 348; in God, 1, 2, 107, 132, 251; as identity marker, 163; ideological, 171; individual, 150; and the nation-state, 192, 332, 334; and opinion, 49; pluralization of, 132; in the public sphere, 301-2, 304; religious, 1, 53, 131, 147, 165, 183, 250-54, 267, 325, 331; and unbelief, 53, 254